China's Transition

A Study of the East Asian Institute

China's Transition

Andrew J. Nathan

with contributions by Tianjian Shi and Helena V. S. Ho

Columbia University Press

New York

Columbia University Press

Publishers Since 1893

New York   Chichester, West Sussex

Copyright (c) 1997 Columbia University Press

Library of Congress Cataloging-in-Publication Data

Nathan, Andrew J. (Andrew James)

China's transition / Andrew J. Nathan : with contributions by
Tianjian Shi and Helena V.S. Ho.

p.   cm. — (Studies of the East Asian Institute, Columbia University)

Includes bibliographical references and index.

ISBN 0-231-11022-7 (cloth)

1. China—Politics and government—1976– 2. Taiwan—Politics and
government—1988– I. Shi, Tianjian. II. Ho, Helena V.S. III. Title. IV. Series:
Studies of the East Asian Institute.

DS779.26.N383 1997

951.05—dc21   9724417

CIP

Casebound editions of Columbia University Press books are printed
on permanent and durable acid-free paper.

Printed in the United States of America

c 10 9 8 7 6 5 4 3 2 1

For Dad and Ruth

Permissions

Grateful acknowledgment is made to the following for permission to reprint previously published and copyrighted materials. The essays are published here as they originally appeared, except that minor changes were made for the sake of stylistic consistency or clarity.

The New Republic:
"A Culture of Cruelty," (July 30 and August 6, 1990), pp. 30–35.
"The Road to Tiananmen Square," (July 31, 1989), pp. 33–36.
"The Enforcer," (April 6, 1992), pp. 32–36.
"Tiananmen and the Cosmos: What Chinese Democrats Mean by Democracy," (July 29, 1991), pp. 31–36.
"Enter the Dragon," (August 22 and 29, 1994), pp. 46–49.
"Beijing Blues," (January 23, 1995), pp. 34–40.
Random House: "Foreword," in Dr. Li Zhisui with Anne F. Thurston, *The Private Life of Chairman Mao* (New York: Random House, 1994), pp. vii–xiv.
M.E. Sharpe, the East Asian Curriculum Project, the East Asian Institute, and the Trustees of Columbia University in the City of New York: "Totalitarianism, Authoritarianism, Democracy: The Case of China," in Myron L. Cohen, ed., *Columbia Project on Asia in the Core Curriculum: Case Studies in the Social Sciences, A Guide for Teaching* (Armonk, N.Y.: M.E. Sharpe, 1992), pp. 235–256 (abridged here).
The Journal of Contemporary China: "Chinese Democracy: The Lessons of Failure," Number 4 (Fall 1993), pp. 3–13.

Shao-chuan Leng and Helena V. S. Ho: "Chiang Ching-kuo's Decision for Political Reform," in Shao-chuan Leng, ed., *Chiang Ching-kuo's Leadership in the Development of the Republic of China on Taiwan* (Lanham, MD: University Press of America, 1993), pp. 31–61 (co-authored with Helena V. S. Ho).

Asian Survey and the Regents of the University of California: "The Legislative Yuan Elections in Taiwan: Consequences of the Electoral System," 33:4 (April 1993), pp. 424–438.

Journal of Asian Studies and the Association for Asian Studies, Inc.: "Is Chinese Culture Distinctive?" 52:4 (November 1993), pp. 923–936.

Daedalus, Journal of the American Academy of Arts and Sciences, and Tianjian Shi: "Cultural Requisites for Democracy in China," from the issue entitled "China in Transformation," 122:2 (Spring 1993), pp. 95–123 (co-authored with Tianjian Shi).

Johns Hopkins University Press, *World Politics*, and Tianjian Shi: "Left and Right with Chinese Characteristics: Issues and Alignments in Deng Xiaoping's China," 48:4 (July 1996), pp. 522–550 (co-authored with Tianjian Shi).

Council on East Asian Studies Publications, Harvard University: "The Place of Values in Cross-Cultural Studies," in Paul A. Cohen and Merle Goldman, eds., *Ideas Across Cultures* (Cambridge, MA.: Council on East Asian Studies, 1990), pp. 293–314.

Johns Hopkins University Press and the *Journal of Democracy*: "China's Constitutionalist Option," 7:4 (October 1996), pp. 43–57.

MIT Press and *The Washington Quarterly*: "China: Getting Human Rights Right," 20:2 (January 1997), pp. 135–151.

Studies of the East Asian Institute, Columbia University

The East Asian Institute is Columbia University's center for research, publication, and teaching on modern East Asia. The Studies of the East Asian Institute were inaugurated in 1962 to bring to a wider public the results of significant new research on modern and contemporary East Asia.

Contents

Tables and Figures

NOTE ON ROMANIZATION: I use the pinyin Romanization system when writing about mainland China and modified Wade-Giles when writing about Taiwan, because each is familiar in that context.

China's Transition

1

China Bites Back

Mao Zedong once wrote, "If you want to know the taste of a pear, you must change the pear by eating it yourself."[1] In recent years Americans have come to know China through trade, investment, travel, cultural exchange, and political contacts. These interactions have effected substantial change in China. A large Chinese middle class consumes American-brand goods; the legal system has shaped itself to the needs of international investment and trade; ideas of economic freedom and rule of law guide Chinese reform.

But influence also returns. China supplies many of the products we use and buys a good share of what we produce. Chinese students are a major presence on our campuses and Chinese movies in our theaters. Issues relating to China play a growing role in foreign-policy debates and politics. Interests in China have grown sufficiently large to generate influential lobbies in Washington. Beijing has joined other Asian countries in criticizing American values and practices, moving us occasionally to reflection and less often to change. So the pear bites back.

And sometimes one learns not just from biting but from being bitten. Such an experience began for me in February 1995, when an open letter appeared in the pages of a Chinese-language newspaper in Queens, New York, called the *Asian American Times*. The letter attacked *The Private Life of Chairman Mao*,[2] a memoir by Mao Zedong's personal physician, Li Zhisui, to which I had contributed the Foreword. Its text appears in chapter 3 of the present book so I will not summarize it here, except to say that it argued for the significance of Mao's personality as a key to understanding his dictatorship.

The thirty-odd signers were identified as Chinese scholars, writers, and activists residing in the U.S. and Taiwan. "Andrew J. Nathan's Foreword," they wrote, "is seriously anti-China text, full of the stereotypical prejudices of the American humanities and social sciences toward the Chinese race and Chinese society, and fully exposing the cultural imperialists' contempt for the Chinese people." Referring to a project I was involved in at Columbia, the writers charged, "Nathan surrounds himself with a group of so-called democracy movement elites to work on his 'constitutionalism project.' In his eyes the billion-strong Chinese people may work to build their country, but only he can pass historical judgment on their enterprise. And based on the doctor's smears, he completely negates the road the Chinese people have taken."[3]

Before long a second open letter appeared in the same newspaper and was reprinted in Chinese media elsewhere. It was signed by more than a hundred senior personalities who were close to Mao during his lifetime, including his chief of guards Wang Dongxing, bodyguards Li Yinqiao and Ye Zilong, the Russian translator Shi Zhe, the playwright Cao Yu, and ideologists He Jingzhi, Chen Yong, and Liu Shaotang. The letter writers commended the signers of the first letter for their patriotism and endorsed their attack on Dr. Li's veracity. Their language bore the earmarks of Chinese communist discourse, mixing violence and cliché in a blend at once frightening and farcical.

> Truly it is not Mao Zedong who is exposed in [Dr. Li's] book but, just as the writers of the first open letter say, "the degenerate and dirty methods of Li Zhisui and Andrew J. Nathan. . . ." How true! The publication of this book involved both those appearing on the public stage and those scheming in the background, ranging from the author, translator, and publisher through critics and persons acknowledged by name as participants and supporters. In the history of political struggles at home or abroad there have rarely been seen such sordid methods, such wicked motives and vulgarity of writing style, or such enormous forces mobilized by back-stage bosses on such a vast scale in the publishing world, the news world, and the academic world.
>
> How low the lackeys of imperialism have fallen! Afraid of theoretical dispute and devoid of factual evidence, they can only resort to base and shameless ad hominem attacks and rumor-mongering. . . . Their despicable political purpose is not merely to drag through the mud a leader of the Chinese people and of the world communist movement, or to blacken socialist new China, but gravely to insult the Chinese race! . . . The honor of our race, of our fatherland, of our people's rev-

olution, are not to be violated. We must counterattack all those treach-
erous wolves in people's skin at home or abroad who act like thieving
rats and dogs.[4]

In the fall of 1995 the pro-Beijing press in Hong Kong heralded a third
attack—a book by three of Mao's former attendants, Lin Ke, an English
secretary; Xu Tao, a doctor; and Wu Xujun, a nurse. On the basis of their
privileged access to party documents and personnel, the authors ques-
tioned whether Dr. Li had served as Mao's doctor since 1954 or only
since 1957, whether he was present at certain events that he claimed to
have witnessed, whether his readings of Mao's motives were correct,
whether Mao had had a prostate exam, whether he had venereal disease,
and so on. They did not contest that Dr. Li was Mao's physician from at
least 1957 onward, that he had been present at most of the events he
claimed to have witnessed, and that Mao said and did most of the things
Dr. Li reported him as saying and doing.

The three authors elaborated the theory of a political plot put forward in the open letters. "The Foreword," they charged, "is a summary of
the entire memoir, the eyeball on the dragon [the final touch that gives
life to an undertaking]. It says the things that Li Zhisui himself cannot
conveniently say. Put otherwise, the memoir was written according to the
intent which is revealed in the Foreword."

> There were actually 26 persons who participated in the book in dif-
> fering degrees, as shown in the English language acknowledgments.
> [Dr. Li thanked, among others, translators, a research assistant, a
> librarian, his publisher and agent, and scholars who had reviewed
> parts of the manuscript.] . . . The name list reveals the participants and
> planners of this memoir, and shows how the original draft passed
> through the hands of many persons over the course of two or three
> years before it was processed into a finished work. These persons
> believed that . . . through Li Zhisui's mouth, they could produce for
> readers who knew nothing of the truth a completely distorted and ugli-
> fied Mao Zedong, and from there achieve their planned, step by step
> goal of uglification of the Chinese Communist Party and of funda-
> mentally shaking the Chinese people's confidence in the CCP and in
> the socialist system.[5]

The attacks on Dr. Li's book were part of a reactive nationalism that I
describe in chapter 14. In 1996 three young writers published *China Can
Say No*, a breathless survey of American offenses toward China. The book
devotes a chapter to the designs of the Central Intelligence Agency, in

which the authors embroider the theme of a political plot behind Dr. Li's book.

"A man with the experience and abilities of Li Zhisui could never have written a book like this," they charged, paying a kind of back-handed tribute.

The fact is that a certain number of ghostwriters with dark backgrounds shrouded themselves in Dr. Li's identity to design, arrange, and implement the entire 'package.' . . . The ideas and style are not those of Li Zhisui; they are the product of ghost-writing by long-time anti-communists working for Taiwan's military propaganda apparatus. To pick this choice propaganda item out of its basket, the CIA had to search for the right person for nearly a decade. After they found their man, they placed some of their dispersed agents directly into the writing group that produced the book, and so played a major role in the book's publication and promotion from start to finish.[6]

In this way, the Foreword "put the eye on the dragon" of my own dossier. For some years I had been writing about Chinese democracy and human rights, helping dissident Chinese intellectuals, and assisting human rights organizations concerned with China. These activities were occasionally reported in the Chinese-language press in Hong Kong, Taiwan, and the United States, or in the mainland *neibu* (classified) press. The "constitutionalism project" referred to in the first open letter was a three-year Columbia research and teaching program to explore the idea of constitutionalism in China, further described in chapter 16. Some of the participants were pro-democracy scholars in exile; others were legal personnel from the PRC.

Every so often we glimpse ourselves through the eyes of others as a figure familiar yet strange. My modest human rights work and academic musings were now transmuted into monstrous intentions and sinister powers, leaving me both impressed and repelled by my new self. Some Chinese friends suggested that I send correspondence concerning academic exchanges over names other than mine. A scholar I visited in China asked me to use a name card without my Chinese name so his colleagues would not recognize who I was. Around this time when an American scholar proposed marriage to a Chinese woman, her father asked, "This man is not Li Anyou [my Chinese name], is he?"

Safe in America, I sustained little harm. The second open letter and the book aroused some controversy in Hong Kong, requiring me to respond to a few interviews. In the fall of 1995 I was denied a visa to participate in a dialogue delegation visiting China, the sponsors on the Chinese side citing the foreword as the chief reason. Well-meaning Chinese in the U.S. and China reminded me that the Party is always willing to welcome reprobates back to the fold: I could get the ban lifted by publishing a recantation. At home, some colleagues acted as if I was tainted by controversies over Mao and human rights, as if a more serious scholar would have stuck to safer subjects.

This was not the first time I had observed Chinese shunning and its domestic shadow at close quarters. In the late 1970s my then wife, Roxane Witke, was punished for having published a biography of Mao's wife, Jiang Qing, after Mao's death and Jiang's fall from power.[7] In China, Roxane was portrayed in wall cartoons as a vampish CIA agent with a tape recorder. In New York, she was informed by a Chinese official that she could no longer visit China because she had offended the Chinese people. Americans quietly excluded her from a number of events to avoid embarrassing Chinese guests. Similar things had happened earlier to my mentor, the late John K. Fairbank; more recently they have happened to other China scholars and writers.

Episodes like this illuminate the gap between Chinese Communist and Western liberal norms of dialogue. They encourage reflection on challenges faced daily in cross-cultural studies, and on the risks and responsibilities of the kind of scholarship that touches politics.

The most interesting issues raised by Dr. Li's critics, I felt, were not the factual ones. Every fact about a world-historical figure is important, and should be gotten straight. During the Cultural Revolution Dr. Li had burned his diaries for fear of being discovered, and he had written his book from memory. Relating a career of more than twenty years without access to documents or interviews, he may have erred in places. Since he died of a heart attack in Chicago shortly after his book was published, we will never know his answers to the critics' questions. But judging by the attacks, his mistakes were not major. After searching the archives and conducting interviews, the critics left the bulk of his story uncontradicted, countering his picture of Mao with an icon of such improbable saintliness as to leave no plausible alternative to Dr. Li's Mao.

More instructive was the form and manner of the critics' attacks. The critics condemned Dr. Li for having exposed Mao to a foreign public, and rebuked me for presuming as a foreigner to pass judgment on the leader of a people other than my own. Yet their actions showed why an honest discussion of Mao cannot yet take place in China. Dr. Li's book was banned there, even though the Chinese translation published in

Taiwan circulated widely, at some risk to booksellers who could be jailed for selling it. Even the loyalists' attacks, except for the brief reference in *China Can Say No*, had to be published in New York and Hong Kong.

The critics claimed to be responding to a political assault that I organized, giving as evidence the list of names in the acknowledgments and the book's positive reception in the West. Yet their unanimity of viewpoint, use of shared language, and access to data denied others betrayed the coordination behind their own attacks.

The critics impugned Dr. Li's honor as a physician and my integrity as a scholar for discussing a leader's sex life. Yet their injured denial that Mao's personal life was a valid subject for history demonstrated how important Mao's image was for the Deng regime's legitimacy. They claimed to be defending scholarship from the taint of bodily functions, yet failed to honor scholarly practices of debate. Mao's good students had learned the master's lessons well: labeling, isolating, and scapegoating enemies; invoking anti-foreignism; and arguing by appeal to authority.

The power to classify others as "enemies of the people" or as "a certain kind of person" has had large consequences in history. As I suggest in chapter 2, just this kind of power made possible explosions of otherwise inexplicable cruelty in Chinese history, and in the histories of other countries. Under Mao the Great Leap Forward famine killed an estimated 30 million people.[8] The Great Proletarian Cultural Revolution was a ten-year orgy of injustice that imposed great suffering on tens of millions. Even though Deng Xiaoping's regime ended mass political persecutions and raised standards of living, human rights violations remained extensive, including political repression, appalling prison conditions, forced labor, coerced abortions, and in at least one documented instance state abuse of orphans.[9] Such events in China and elsewhere yield universal lessons. As Daniel Jonah Goldhagen says in his study of the Nazi extermination of the Jews, "For people to kill another large group of people, the ethical and emotional constraints that normally inhibit them from adopting such a radical measure must be lifted."[10] And, the Chinese example suggests, not only the ethical constraints but also the institutional constraints must be lifted, which in most legal and political systems prevent people from acting on their promptings of rage.

Who lifts these constraints? Different times and places yield different answers, but those with ideological and political power always bear the major responsibility. Daniel Chirot observes, "[T]here is no indication whatsoever that it is difficult to find plenty of jailers and killers around.

. . . What stands out in the history of Hitlerism and Stalinism, as in some other cases of modern ideological tyranny, is that such behavior was organized, sanctioned, and furthered by deliberate policy on behalf of a specific ideological goal. Only when it is a matter of policy can so many be killed in this way."[11] In China, Mao Zedong did not work alone and his power was not absolute. Yet it was he who set down the theories of class nature and revolutionary struggle that turned people into enemies of the people, and who exalted the ends of revolutionary transformation over the means of human suffering. The story of China's modern tragedy has to begin in Mao's mind, his court, and—as I argued in the foreword reprinted in chapter 3—in his bed. The chapter also explores some insights gained from recent writings about how dehumanization at Mao's court started at the top.

Yet so far as we know Mao personally killed, beat, or jailed no one. He was able to extend his way of treating people from intimate relations to society at large through the institutional system he and his colleagues built. Chapter 4 explains how institutions designed for idealistic purposes, to bring order to society and to mobilize its resources for development, at the same time created scapegoat classes and deprived citizens of the right to think for themselves. This created the situation in which so many had no choice but to persecute fellow citizens. Such conditions were ameliorated under Deng Xiaoping, as the chapter also shows. But Mao's legacy survives in the repressive political apparatus and the delegitimation of dissent.

Contemplating such events raises an enduring issue of cross-cultural studies: To what extent are such events determined by culture? My reading of recent Chinese history is that culture, and the institutions that put culture into practice and in return shape culture, do not make an iron box.[12] People reflect on their circumstances; even against the wishes of their leaders they come up with new ideas. Chapter 5 describes a series of democratic experiments from the late Qing provincial assemblies of 1909 to the PRC people's congress system, asking why each failed. Many answers contribute to the explanation, but none supports the conventional conclusion that China is culturally unsuited for democracy. Rather, the analysis emphasizes how political choices, especially those made by leaders, shape culture and institutions and the uses to which they are put, as much as or more than the reverse.

China's democratic prospect reached its modern-day high and low points at once in the spring and early summer of 1989. Chapter 6 explores Chinese ideas of democracy as they stood around the time of the Tiananmen demonstrations and the June 4, 1989, Beijing massacre. In their speeches and writings the activists displayed the universal yearning for political freedom and accountable government, together with a particular Chinese romanticism about democracy. Many Chinese democratic thinkers are ex-scientists. They attribute to democracy a quality of universal rightness that its proponents in the West do not claim. Viewing democracy as a search for truth rather than a clash of interests, they paid little attention to institutional design (which is one reason why colleagues and I thought a constitutionalism project was a good use of Chinese scholars' time).

The idea that culture is not determinative and historical choice is open is supported by the experience of another culturally Chinese society, Taiwan. Since 1986 this political system has undergone a transition to democracy. In chapter 7 Helena Ho and I explore the foreign and domestic policy circumstances that made political reform an attractive risk for Taiwan's president Chiang Ching-kuo, when he started the process. Circumstances did not dictate the outcome: a commitment to democracy had to be made and honored jointly by Chiang, the opposition movement, and Taiwan's residents. Compared to mainland China, Taiwan is richer, smaller, and more Westernized, with a more educated population and more experience with liberty, so its experience cannot be mechanically emulated by the PRC. But the lesson remains that Chinese history does not bar a democratic transition when leaders and citizens decide that they want it.

Taiwan's transition moved forward in the dramatic 1992 election for seats in the Legislative Yuan (parliament), which is described in chapter 8. This was the first full-fledged competitive national-level election in Chinese history. It brought into the highest elected body opposition leaders who had been in prison or exile a few years earlier, and solidified a tacit pact of peaceful competition between the former authoritarian ruling party and the former anti-system opposition movement. After years of struggle the opposition gained legitimacy in the political system and accepted the legitimacy of the system. The process of transition continued for several years until 1996, when Chiang Ching-kuo's successor Lee Teng-hui won reelection to the presidency in the first direct election of a chief of state in Chinese history. That election marked the consolidation of Taiwan's democracy. It did not please mainland China, which greeted it with missile exercises across the Taiwan Strait designed to remind Taiwan that it should not declare independence.

Beijing saw a similar threat in developments in another Chinese society, Hong Kong, whose story is reviewed in Chapter 9. Here partial democratization came as a late and ambiguous gift from British colonial rulers on the eve of the territory's reversion to the PRC. When they opened Hong Kong's Legislative Council to popular election, the British handed Beijing a Trojan horse. China reacted by dissolving the democratically elected council and replacing it with an appointed provisional council. Even so, democracy had proved its suitability to Hong Kong's way of life.

Although culture does not determine politics or history, it has an influence. A fascination with culture is what draws many students to study China in the first place. Yet culture is hard to describe and measure, partly because it is multilayered and internally diversified. Such problems raise another issue in cross-cultural studies: How may one think about the distinctiveness of and differences among cultures? The comparative study of culture is grounded in a methodological paradox, which is explored in chapter 10. To compare cultures, one must identify attributes or variables that are capable of being assessed in all the cultures being compared. Such attributes are by definition common, not unique, or they could be measured in only one culture and not others. In this sense some degree of cultural sameness is preordained by the method of comparison. Yet cultural difference too is preordained by the method, because no two societies display the same distributions of any important cultural attribute even if their histories and social structures are similar.

It falls to the investigator to determine how much difference counts to make a culture distinctive. How one draws this line affects what one can say about how culture affects behavior and institutions. The essay ends with a challenge to students of culture to state their claims more precisely, to specify what they mean when they say that Chinese culture is distinctive so that they can also say more clearly how they think culture influences the way in which China develops—how, for example, it constrains the development of Chinese democracy, as many commentators claim that it does, and to what extent.

Part of the reason for the vagueness about culture is that we usually study it through texts, interviews, fieldwork, and the interpretive reconstruction of historical action.[13] Not until the late 1980s did it become possible to study Chinese political culture in all its disparateness and ambiguity through the modern empirical technique of survey research, which disaggregates culture into operationally defined components and assesses their distribution across the geographic and socioeconomic landscapes. If based on a proper random sample, survey research provides a measure of culture not as a general pattern but as a variant distribution of attitudes, values, and beliefs among a population. Although the method was developed in the West from the 1920s onward, China was until recently either too chaotic or too closed to apply it. Survey research in China on political science topics was pioneered by Tianjian Shi, who co-authored two of the essays in this volume. Professor Shi's Columbia Ph.D. dissertation was based on a 1988 survey of political culture and political participation in Beijing.[14] In 1990 he conducted the first nationwide random sample survey in China on political attitudes and behavior. He and I report some of the findings in chapters 11 and 12.

Although statistical findings smack of iron laws, survey research actually portrays culture as a realm of freedom rather than determination. For example, in chapter 11 we show that no Chinese subgroup (much less the entire aggregate of the Chinese people) is composed wholly of persons who are tolerant or intolerant. Despite differences in tolerance among groups with different levels of education, some of the least-educated are as tolerant as some of the most-educated and vice versa. Likewise, in chapter 12, even the most powerful variables (education, sex, age, urban and rural residence, and others) taken together explain only twenty or thirty percent of the variance in people's attitudes toward policy issues or democracy. Findings of this size are common in social research in all societies. People in each social category show great individual variation in what they think and do.

Surveys give concreteness to our impression of the interactions between attitudes and institutions. Political efficacy, for example—the belief in one's ability to influence politics—is an attitude formed not in isolation, but on the basis of information about how the political system works for people in particular situations. As we suggest in chapter 11, people are more likely to believe themselves efficacious when they are. To take another example, in chapter 12 we show that people's decisions to be concerned about certain political issues reflect the way these issues affect them, given where they are situated in the matrix of social interests.

Surveys show how Chinese political culture is both the same as and different from other cultures. For example, education affects political attitudes everywhere, but only in China, so far as we know, does increased education produce a reduced expectation of fair treatment from the government. This distinctive pattern has a practical explanation: the repression of intellectuals under Mao. To push such analyses further, in 1993

Tianjian Shi and I joined seven other scholars to conduct surveys in mainland China, Taiwan, and Hong Kong using a common core questionnaire. We hope the data will permit us to offer fuller analyses of the relations between culture and institutions, by comparing patterns of belief and behavior in three culturally similar but institutionally distinct Chinese societies.

The technique of survey research is linked to an interest in democracy. The link is partly methodological. Surveys are rarely done in authoritarian societies because researchers can rarely gain access; in this regard our China surveys were unusual. But it is also substantive: why else would one care about the values held by ordinary citizens? So the method is scientific without being in all respects value-neutral. This raises a third issue about cross-cultural studies: Can scholarship avoid value judgments, and should it do so? It is a classic question in the social sciences, but it emerges more sharply when members of one culture undertake studies of another culture. Studies of democracy are a major theme in American political science—perhaps the major theme—but that seems less problematic when the political system itself is democratic. But to raise questions about the sources and prospects of democracy in a nondemocratic country may seem biased, an imposition of one's own blueprint on another society.

Chapter 13 presents some thoughts on these questions. Values perform at least two roles in social science scholarship. They help identify what subjects are important, and help suggest what statements of belief and preference made by actors are plausible. If only for these reasons, there is no way for a social scientist to navigate without an evaluational point of view. Besides, I argue, making reasoned value judgments is as valid an undertaking in doing social science about other societies as it is in working on one's own. History and social science would be less interesting if they always stopped at the brink of important value questions. Values should not affect methods or distort findings, but they must be part of meaningful social science. Against the counsels of one kind of cultural relativism, I suggest that the only values that can guide one's scholarship are those in which one believes, not the putative values of those one is studying. And in view of the diversity of culture, I reject the notion that basic values popular in the West find no support in China, and I challenge the pessimistic argument that the differences among cultures prohibit dialogue.

Value commitments also shape the questions we ask about the future. At the end of a previous book of essays, *China's Crisis*,[15] published shortly after Tiananmen, I suggested that China might work its way out of its political, social, and economic crises by undertaking a democratic transition guided from the top down along the lines of Taiwan's experience. Instead the regime surprised me and many other observers by accelerating economic growth, reducing inflation, and repressing dissent without undertaking political reform. It has internationalized its economy while fostering nationalism; expanded economic freedoms while violating political rights; and decentralized bureaucratic power while rolling back a nascent civil society. So far the leaders have maintained a common front over what many outsiders believe is an internal power struggle.

Chapter 14 describes problems that nonetheless continue to grow— rapid social change, polarization of wealth, lack of legitimacy, stagnation of state enterprises, power divisions at the top, and the need for political consolidation after Deng. Power has gravitated into networks of elites, giving rise to what some scholars call "local corporatism," a form of rule operating by personal influence and corruption. The regime relies on personal connections and political interventions instead of a consolidated legal system to protect entrepreneurs.

The public's response to these mixed trends has been complex. Seventy percent of respondents in our 1993 survey agreed with the proposition, "The Center's decisions are generally correct." Yet 60% agreed that "Government officials don't care much about what people like me think." And 73% held, "It is now very necessary to expand democracy in our country." Even when people are dissatisfied with the officials they encounter in everyday life, many still support the regime. Economic success has enabled the regime to separate the public's evaluation of the political system from that of the bureaucracy.

China remains in transition, but its political direction no longer seems as clear as it did in 1990. As Maurice Meisner reminds us, the rise of a middle class does not necessarily lead to democracy. When the entrepreneurial class is part of the ruling network, the bourgeois revolution is as liable to result in fascism as democracy. China's bourgeoisie today is not only dependent on the state but also lacks a grounding in legally secure private property from which to grow toward an independent status in the foreseeable future. If this continues to be the case, China's modernization may turn out to be "a late-twentieth-century variant of what Barrington Moore termed 'conservative modernization'"—a new Bismarckian Germany or Meiji Japan.[16]

What is interesting about a failed but informed prediction is not so much that it was wrong, as that historical actors chose to act differently from ways that appeared probable at the time. When social science can explain only 20 to 30 percent of the variance in individual attitudes, it is no wonder that it cannot predict future events with any greater degree of accuracy.[17] Yet attempts to peer into the future remain valuable, partly because historical actors themselves continue to function with an eye to the future.

In chapter 15 I return to the task, unrepentant. This time my somewhat similar prediction is based on the seminar discussions and papers of the Columbia constitutionalism project. Discussions about constitutional reform in China center on the idea of working within China's existing constitution to enlarge the role of the National People's Congress and reduce the arbitrary power of the Chinese Communist Party. Democracy, no matter how remote, remains part of the Chinese discourse, not a foreign imposition, and a real option in China's future.

That this should be so reflects an interaction between forces of internal development and foreign influences. Many China specialists hold that it is hopeless to try to "change China."[18] My reading of the record suggests otherwise. Although economic development will not do our political work for us, there are forces in the intelligentsia, professions, and the administrative bureaucracy working for human rights and a Chinese form of democracy. Chapter 16 summarizes evidence on how Western human rights pressure has worked together with domestic forces to promote change.[19] The essay's main point, however, is to lay out the strategic interests the rest of the world has in improving human rights in China. Without rule of law founded on respect for human rights China may repeat its earlier pattern of foreign policy disruptions and developmental disasters.[20]

If there is a motif in the work represented in this book, it is admiration for the human striving for autonomy. My brush with Chinese reality enhanced my own ability to imagine the circumstances under which hundreds of millions of Chinese lived during the Mao years, and under which politically active, independently thinking Chinese live today. It led me to appreciate anew the courage of those Chinese exiles who suffer isolation, culture shock, and poverty, while putting their lives together and continuing peaceful dissent in the face of their government's mockery. And it reaffirmed my conviction that China needs human rights for its stability and smooth development.

Human rights deprivations are grounded in the dehumanization of the victims. The process often starts with the simple, even childish, act of isolating those who differ. The power of shunning, strong enough in any society including our own, is all the more formidable when organized and enforced by the state. One of the most valuable assets in our own community is the acceptance of one another's good faith as partners in debate. So this seems a good time to thank the institution where I have worked for twenty-six years—Columbia University and its East Asian Institute and Political Science Department—for sustaining an environment of freedom, and to acknowledge the support of the Henry Luce Foundation, the National Endowment for the Humanities, the National Science Foundation, the Chiang Ching-Kuo Foundation, and other foundations, publications, colleagues, and students who have encouraged my intellectual journey. In presenting this collection of explorations and arguments, I salute those in China and the West who have resisted the forces, both hostile and benign, that try to deter or discourage dialogue on hard questions.

2

A History of Cruelty

No better proof could be imagined for Nietzsche's insight that cruelty is the great festival pleasure of mankind than the torment inflicted by the Chinese people on one another for the last 400 years. Jonathan Spence's history of that period is filled with burying alive, burning alive, slicing, strangulation, stabbing, drowning, poison gas inserted into tunnels, coerced suicide, exposure of severed heads, vengeful exhumation and dismemberment of corpses, arson, rapine, torture, corruption, epidemic, famine, forced migrations, wars, riots, strikes, rebellions, and piracy.[1] The first three pages of Liu Binyan's memoir, *A Higher Kind of Loyalty*, recount an assassination by bombing, a child killed in a car accident, a murder, an execution, the death of a young brother from scarlet fever, and a daily parade of carts filled with beggars' corpses.[2] Bette Bao Lord's snapshots from the lives of Chinese friends include beatings by Red Guards, a wife denouncing a husband, a nursing infant denied breast milk, an ear torn off, a thumb broken, and a head whacked in half by the stroke of a scythe.[3]

"Why does a culture that condemns violence," asks Stevan Harrell, "that plays down the glory of military exploits, awards its highest prestige to literary, rather than martial figures, and seeks harmony over all other values, in fact display such frequency and variety of violent behavior?"[4]

It would be difficult but unnecessary to prove that China's history is sadder than that of other countries on a per capita basis. If nothing else, the scale of horror is unique in this largest of all nations. Nearly thirty years ago Richard L. Walker, in a study for the U.S. Senate Judiciary Committee, estimated that the "human cost of communism in China" after 1949 ranged from 32 million to 60 million deaths. Walker's estimates were rough, but also incomplete. He did not include the 20 million to 30 million famine deaths in 1959–61 that scholars learned about relatively recently, nor could he touch on the revival of female infanticide since the late 1970s, which has claimed what Spence estimates as 200,000 lives a year.

And such costs include only deaths. They do not include the 1 million people who Liu says were labeled "rightists" in 1957 and punished for up to twenty years (an increase over the usual estimate of 550,000); or the 20 million young people who, with another 20 million factory workers, were "sent down" to the countryside in the Mao years to get them out of the cities; or the 20 million landlords, rich peasants, and others given discriminatory class labels in the early 1950s; or the 2.9 million cadres who Deng Xiaoping said were mistreated in the Cultural Revolution, or the 100 million persons who Hu Yaobang estimated were affected in one way or another by that cataclysm.

No one has been able to estimate the population of the Chinese gulag. Superb studies by Robin Munro for Amnesty International and Asia Watch, based on reports in the Chinese press, have detailed routine torture and mistreatment of prisoners in Chinese detention centers, jails, and camps, but it is hopeless to estimate the scale of abuse when the prison population itself is unknown. Christina Gilmartin's essay in *Violence in China*,[5] together with some anecdotes from Liu's career as an investigative reporter, scratch the surface of the vast subject of sexual abuse in Chinese jails, camps, offices, farms, factories, and families, but again the data defy attempts at quantification.

Nor have the costs paid by the Chinese been limited to the period of communism. Twenty million died during the Taiping rebellion in the mid-nineteenth century, ten million in a famine in the 1870s, half a million in a famine in the 1920s. Spence reports that about 14 million men were drafted into the Chinese military during the war against Japan; a tenth of them died of disease and malnutrition before seeing combat. One of the fine features of his book is an endless series of small maps showing troop movements across the Chinese landscape from the late Ming to 1959. "Every word is blood and grief," wrote a Chinese poet in 1944.

What has been acquired in exchange for all this misery? Today the consensus of Chinese outside officialdom is: nothing. "What Confucian culture has given us over the past several thousand years is not a national spirit of enterprise, a system of laws, or a mechanism of cultural renewal, but a fearsome self-killing machine that, as it degenerated, constantly devoured its best and its brightest, its own vital elements." So wrote the authors of the television serial *River Elegy*, whose broadcast on Chinese television helped to set the scene for the outpouring of anti-regime sentiment in the spring of 1989.

The way in which Spence interprets the "search for modernity" implies that he agrees with this tragic vision. He follows recent academic practice in placing the beginning of the modern period 300 or more years farther back than the old conventional benchmark of the mid-nineteenth century. But instead of stressing the secular rise over this time of agricultural productivity, handicraft industry, commercialization, population, urbanization, literacy, and social and geographic mobility, as other recent historians have done, Spence points out that people's average levels of consumption were no higher in the Qing than in the Ming, in the 1930s than in the nineteenth century, under Mao than under Chiang Kai-shek.

He would concede (though he never says so) that China has made itself modern in the sense that it produces computers and rockets, feeds a population of a billion, educates most of its people, provides medical care sufficient to establish a life expectancy of sixty-nine years, and participates in the international economy and political system. He also gives full play to the achievements of Chinese literature and art, its statecraft, and philosophy; and his book is beautifully illustrated with examples of these achievements. But he argues that China has not been modern in at least 400 years, in the sense of being a nation "both integrated and receptive, fairly sure of its own identity yet able to join others on equal terms in the quest for new markets, new technologies, new ideas." The quest of his title is thus one in which he believes the Chinese are still engaged, unsuccessfully.

The fact that Liu and Bette Bao Lord share Spence's despair is significant, for particular reasons in each case. To Lord, China's tragedy is personal. Herself of Chinese origin, with many friends and relatives there, she went to China believing that it would be possible to reform the Party from within, and hoping to promote "one of the most critical bilateral relationships in the world." By the end of her hardworking tour of duty as the American ambassador's wife, she had come to see the Chinese system as thoroughly brutal and corrupt. Then, staying a few extra weeks in the spring of 1989 to help CBS News cover the Gorbachev-Deng Xiaoping summit, she saw the ruins of Deng's reform come crashing down around her friends. A close cousin who stayed in China when Lord emigrated with her parents in 1946 symbolizes Lord's sense of having escaped her fair share of misery by leaving. Having enjoyed more than her share of luck, she feels that she has abandoned her relatives to one of the hardest fates in this world, the fate of being Chinese.

Liu's memoir marks the nearly complete disillusionment of one of China's last hopeful men. Liu made his name as an investigative reporter exposing power abuse and corruption in the decade after his rehabilitation in 1979 from the stigma of being a "rightist." As a rightist, he lost his party membership and his job, and spent two long periods of forced labor in the countryside. After his rehabilitation, his first—and still most famous—article was "People or Monsters?" (It is available in English in a book with the same title edited by Perry Link, published by Indiana University Press in 1983.) It argued that a major corruption case in a commune in northeastern China occurred because cliquism and mutual back-scratching had eroded the vigilance of the local party committee.

Liu's trademark answer to the problem, proposed in an essay in 1985, was "A Second Kind of Loyalty." The first kind of loyalty was what had gotten China into trouble, he said. It was the loyalty of those who are "diligent and conscientious, putting up with hardship and swallowing their resentment, doing exactly what they are told, never expressing a contradictory opinion." This loyalty allowed bad people to seize power and do their will.

The second kind of loyalty, however, would save China. Liu personified it in two protagonists, Ni Yuxian and Chen Shizhong, who stood up for the true ideals of socialism for twenty years, when those ideas were being trampled by Mao and his acolytes. They wrote letters to oppose the Great Leap and the split with the Soviet Union, hung wall posters to oppose the excesses of the Cultural Revolution, and gave speeches to defend good cadres who were attacked by Red Guards. But they never engaged in intrigue or violence or tried to evade their inevitable punishments, and each of them spent years in jail. They played the classic Chinese role of remonstrators, who sacrifice their flesh and blood in order to awaken the ruler to his duty. (Ironically, each subsequently diverged from Liu's model, but in opposite ways. Ni obtained political asylum in New York and helped found an exile party dedicated to overthrowing the Chinese Communist Party. Chen went around China, giving speeches on the topic, "I Offer the Love in My Heart to the Party and the People.")

Liu identified with Ni and Chen. His memoir was also going to be called "A Second Kind of Loyalty," but the title was apparently revised to make more sense to Americans. Liu portrays himself as telling the truth despite repression because he believed that his appeals could awaken healthy forces in the Party. He was never a dissident. As a reporter for the central party paper, he was able to conduct his investigations cloaked in the authority of the Party, publish his works under the protection of the sympathetic General Secretary Hu Yaobang, and make some of his reports not in writing to the public but orally to the relevant provincial party secretaries. Even after his expulsion from the Party in 1987 for bourgeois liberalism after the fall of his protector Hu, he saw himself as a sort of political Boddhisatva who postponed his relief from suffering to help others reach salvation.

Although he doesn't use such terms, Liu inhabits a Confucian world divided between moral persons (*junzi*) and people who are only human (*xiaoren*). For him, the human problem is not to figure out what is the right thing to do, but to make up one's mind to do it. A warm, compassionate, approachable man, he has an endless appetite and memory for the details of individual lives, and a deep understanding of human motives. But in the end he discerns, in the complexity of the human comedy, only two kinds of people—those whose self-justifications are excuses for selfishness, and those who sacrifice for justice.

Liu thus embodies what the historian Thomas A. Metzger has called the "tranformative" (as opposed to the "accommodative") impulse in Chinese culture.[6] Like Confucius, Liu sees human nature as basically good and believes in changing the world through the force of example. To borrow the title of another of his essays, corruption in China occurs because "good people" are "weak." The events of 1989 brought him to the point of predicting the fall of Li Peng-Deng Xiaoping regime, which he saw as representing a small privileged stratum of conservative bureaucrats rather than the Chinese Communist Party as a whole. Although in "Tell the World" he suggests that a non-Communist democracy will emerge after an interregnum of rule by party reformists,[7] in *A Higher Kind of Loyalty* he appears still to hope that the Chinese Communist Party will rediscover its soul and return to the path of its original ideals. However ambivalently, Liu's second kind of loyalty is still loyalty.

Younger Chinese have criticized him for this all along. When he toured American campuses in 1988, a student at Columbia confronted him with the example of Fang Lizhi (the astrophysicist and human rights activist expelled from the CCP, who later left China after a year in refuge in the American Embassy in Beijing), who had declared himself opposed to communism. "Fang's stand is based on the Western scientific viewpoint," she contended, "while yours is a kind of peasant-based pro-Communist idealism which can never solve China's fundamental problems." Many in the audience applauded. About a year later the young critic Liu Xiaobo attacked Liu for believing that "someday the master [the CCP] will wake up and appreciate his absolute sincerity because his criticisms are not intended to hurt the master, but to make him more perfect." (Liu Xiaobo was later jailed, accused of being a "sinister black hand" behind the Tiananmen demonstrations.)

Liu has moved toward the harshest view of Chinese reality compatible with a shred of faith in the goodness of man. He is a Chinese Rip Van Winkle, who returned from twenty years of feeding pigs and hauling night soil to discover a world in which evil was pervasive and the few good people were viciously oppressed. In one place that he investigated, "the so-called planned economy was . . . nothing but the continuous flow of public resources into the private pockets of the power holders." In another, "the Party secretary could pick and choose any girl from destitute families to sleep with him in return for food subsidies." In a third, a petitioner for justice was repeatedly jailed and tortured: "The children became vagrants, often beaten up, with no chance to go to school; the family's ration of wheat and kindling wood was held back; their house was destroyed." A fourth location was "a kingdom of evil, . . . a cursed land where all values had been reversed." Throughout China, malefactors who had been in power since the Cultural Revolution cooperated to protect one another, and the reformists at the center, beset by forces only murkily hinted at by Liu, were too weak to penetrate the web of evil. In all, says Liu, "China seemed like a monstrous mill, continually rolling, crushing all individuality out of the Chinese character."

A somewhat formulaic optimism informs the coda to *A Higher Kind of Loyalty.* "The Chinese people have now changed," he asserts. "The people will pay a bloody price, but in the end they will shake off this monstrous thing [the ruling clique] that is draining them of their life's blood." (The language is typical of both of Liu's books, which are more like political documents than personal reflections, and which have been translated almost too faithfully from the Chinese.) Lord, too, ends with an obligatory upbeat ending, a parable of a coverlet kept immaculate through years of prison. Spence's attempt to solace his readers leads to a last sentence that is the only really ill-considered one in the book: "There would be no truly modern China until the people were given back their voices." His own narrative shows that the Chinese people never had their voices.

Like Chernobyl, China seems to get worse the more we learn about it. Of course, we need to beware of the phenomenon—Spence traces it well—by which the Western image of China oscillates between exaggerated hopes and exaggerated fears. If it was wrong to see Mao's China as a people's Shangri-La, it is also wrong to imagine that in post-Mao China most of the people spend most of their time doing anything other than going about their daily business. Lord states that "all Chinese [are] in pain"; and I believe she is right. But what does a people in pain look like? The kind of pain she is talking about does not show on people's faces as they bicycle to work, any more than it did when travelers reported that all was well in Mao's day. The truth about such a large country is hard to discern. Still, the combined testimony of observers with such cumulative and diverse authority is impressive.

Why are things so bad? "To understand China today," observes Spence, "we need to know about China in the past." But what does the past tell us? Spence devotes an informative section to Hegel's theory that China is doomed by geography to be an inward-looking peasant nation excluded from the mainstream of history. But he does not seem to endorse such grand generalizations. The pointers he gives involve more discrete historical echoes, parallels, and precedents. The book points out that problems such as bureaucracy, regionalism, peasant poverty, abuse of women, familism, and the struggle for political power persisted or recurred, but does not try to explain why. Spence is a brilliant storyteller, endlessly curious about how things really were at the top and the bottom of society, on the plains and in the borderlands, at weddings and wars, in the rice fields and the scholar's studio. While the vast tapestry contains many patterns, however, he is chary of stating what they are. If there are "cycles" of some sort at work, as he says several times, are they any more than historical resemblances and coincidences that are bound to occur as human folly grinds repeatedly through a finite number of permutations?

Spence tends to explain violence as occurring mostly when "the Chinese people . . . threw themselves against the power of the state." This is a comforting vision. Yet his narrative contains plenty of instances of the violence of the oppressed against one another. As one of his own witnesses says, "The poor squeeze each other to death." There is also a trace of romanticism in the sections on the Communist revolution and Mao's rule. Spence portrays Mao leading the country confidently in pursuit of his vision, however flawed. He doesn't convey the constant bumbling, desperate insecurity, vicious infighting, and hysterical improvisation that the Chinese Communists disguised behind the bluster of their theory of scientific socialism.

Lord's answer to the violence of Chinese life is national character. "Chinese go through life wearing masks," she says. The masks take over the wearer, robbing him of his identity and inducing paranoia toward others. Able to adapt to any circumstance, the Chinese "never bother asking themselves who they are. They wait to be told." Under Mao, the Chinese were programmed to violence. They took their turns as victims and perpetrators in a cycle that left no one blameless and no one responsible. As one of her informants tells her, "It's over now. It was not my fault. It was not his fault. Everyone suffered. It was the times. We were all casualties of history."

Lord is a sensitive observer of human attitudes. One of the most delightful sections of the book is a series of vignettes in which Chinese recount their puzzling encounters in American society. But her well-meaning account of Chinese culture boils down to an East Asian example of the "orientalism" criticized years ago by Edward W. Said. It makes the Chinese seem less our *semblables* and *frères* than mysterious others, sinister and cruel. It offers a national stereotype instead of analyzing the situations that can make people behave savagely. It labels the symptoms of living in Chinese society as characteristics that explain Chinese behavior.

It is ironic that Lord's approach replaces understanding with exoticism, because she writes out of affection, positioning herself as a member of both cultures, interpreter of each to the other. Yet the Chinese side of her credentials is open to question. She came to the United States at the age of eight and did not visit again until 1973. Returning as the wife of the American ambasssador, she let her interest in learning about Chinese lives be known. Many Chinese obliged, in person or on tape. She herself suspects that their motives were not always disinterested, although in fact she was unable to do them favors with the American government. In any case, she received scores of anecdotes, some rather stylized, all filtered to us through a pathos-filled language that replaces her interviewees' voices with her own. The result is a book that tells the reader some of what went on in Mao's China but little about why.

Liu Binyan's notion of a "double network" of political and economic relations created by the Cultural Revolution comes closer to illuminating the structures of Chinese society. He sees the Cultural Revolution as a turmoil in which opportunistic politicians scrambled to power. Once there, they stayed through all the twists and turns of the line. As "veterans of three dynasties" they had an overweening interest in keeping down all those whom they had oppressed on their way up. "To a Party leader, it is a matter of life and death always to be right." The protective network extended from the counties at the bottom of China's administrative hierarchy to the top. At each level politicians protected those below so that they could in turn be protected. The CCP turned into a giant Mafia.

One of the saddest cases of oppression that Liu describes is that of a worker named Wang Fumian, whom Liu was finally unable to help because he was expelled from the Party before his report on the case could be acted upon. In the course of investigating Wang's case, Liu discovered that Wang had been confined to a mental hospital on a diagnosis of "mania." According to the diagnostic handbook locally in use, mania was characterized by

> overconfidence, extreme willfulness, found mostly in people of advanced cultural background. They are biased and tend to distort facts, although their delusions are not wholly divorced from reality. Taken for normal at an early age, the patient gradually asserts his (her) willpower more and more forcibly, he (she) rushes about offering petitions, writing endless letters of accusation. A few are deluded into thinking they are making exceptional contributions to humanity.

It was a perfect description of Liu himself. The only mystery is how, under such circumstances, a few independent individuals like Liu and the stubborn petitioners he wrote about could continue to exist.

On the whole, Liu's analysis is convincing, except that he is unclear about many of the details. He seems to be protecting some people himself, as he refers from time to time to higher-ups who were spiking his work from behind the scenes but does not tell us who they were. (Or did he wish to spare American readers a surfeit of names filled with X's and Z's engaged in intricate political struggles?) And Liu's tendency to judge persons rather than the system diverts attention from the question of how such things could happen. Is it because evil people are stronger than good people, as he suggests? Or does it have something to do with the design of Chinese institutions?

As Norbert Elias has written, describing the descent into savagery of German troops in the Baltics in the late days of World War I:

> [The] path towards barbarity and dehumanization . . . always takes considerable time to unfold in relatively civilized societies. Terror and horror hardly appear in such societies without a long process of social disintegration. All too often the act of naked violence . . . is analyzed with

the help of short-term, static explanations. That may be meaningful if one is not seeking explanations but only attempting to establish culpability. It is easy to see barbarism and de-civilization as the expression of a free personal decision, but that kind of voluntarist explanation is shallow and unhelpful.[8]

In their approach to the problem of violence, Lipman and Harrell and their contributors move in the direction that Elias recommends by looking at the failure of the norms that are supposed to prohibit violence. The best chapter is Anne F. Thurston's account of urban violence during the Cultural Revolution (drawing from her longer study, *Enemies of the People*, which appeared in 1987).[9] She directs attention to the processes that strip away inhibitions to violence by dehumanizing the target. In Mao's China, such processes included the labeling of class enemies, glorification of the necessity of revolutionary violence, public struggle sessions that inured people to the sight of suffering, and peer pressure based on the practice of victimizing all who refused to victimize others.

The most penetrating exposition of this constellation of institutions is Lynn T. White III's, whose arguments are summarized in a paragraph by Spence. White stresses the role of three interlocking institutions, each found in fully developed form nowhere but in Mao's China: the work unit, the system of class labels, and the political campaign. The work unit locked each individual in place for life with a set of co-workers like scorpions in a jar; the class label system created what were thought to be permanent castes (they have since disappeared) with contrary interests, and with members of the despised castes seen as subhuman; political campaigns trained people to be vicious. White traces the creation of these institutions in Shanghai in the 1950s and 1960s and then their impact on the course of Shanghai's Cultural Revolution.[10]

How the personalities of young children were shaped by class labels, units, and campaigns has been brilliantly described by Anita Chan.[11] She showed that a combination of indoctrination, competition for approval, and fear of victimization forged decent young people into Manichaean bigots. Liu provides powerful testimony about how it felt to be one of the victims in this system, isolated, assaulted, and humiliated until even a person with his powerful sense of individuality felt guilty for crimes he had not committed.

Doleful as such explanations are, at least they remove the Chinese from the ghetto of the inscrutable and show how normal human beings can be reduced to marauders. Authors like Thurston, White, and Chan are able to return the Chinese to the mainstream of history from which

Hegel excluded them, even though the history China rejoins (so far) is that of Stalinism and fascism rather than the Hegelian progress to freedom. The institutions that created violence in the period of the Cultural Revolution were creations of Mao's China. They cannot explain the upheavals of the preceding hundreds of years. (In fact, no one has yet explained how and why Mao's people invented these institutions.) But studies like these point the way to deciphering the mystery of extreme violence through the analysis of social settings that rob people of human connections to their victims.

If these are the lessons from China's modern history, they are not very encouraging. One wonders whether even the mordant Lu Xun was too upbeat when he said, as quoted by Spence, "The history of mankind's battle forward through bloodshed is like the formation of coal, where a great deal of wood is needed to produce a small amount of coal." Much human wood lies under the ground of Chinese history, but how much coal?

3

Mao and His Court

No other leader in history held as much power over so many people for so long as Mao Zedong, and none inflicted such a catastrophe on his nation.[1] Mao's lust for control and fear of betrayal kept his court and his country in turmoil. His vision and his intrigues drove China through the Great Leap Forward and its terrible consequences, the great famine and the Cultural Revolution, with deaths in the tens of millions.

Nor has any other dictator been as intimately observed as Mao is in *The Private Life of Chairman Mao*, a memoir by Dr. Li Zhisui, who served as his personal physician for twenty-two years. Suetonius's *Lives of the Twelve Caesars* shows the deranging effects of absolute power in the gluttony, lechery, greed, sadism, incest, torture, and commission of multiple murders by Tiberius, Caligula, and Nero, but the author did not know his subjects personally. Procopius's *Secret History* is a scandalous attack on the Roman Emperor Justinian and his wife, Theodora, devoid of sympathy or understanding. Albert Speer knew Hitler well, but their common interests were limited to public works and war. Stalin's daughter seldom saw her father. The diaries of Napoleon's and Hitler's personal physicians are merely clinical.[2]

Personal memoirs about great democratic leaders, like Moran's *Churchill* and Herndon's *Lincoln*, tell us less about history than the biographies of dictators do, because democratic leaders have less room to impose their personalities on events.[3] As for the Chinese tradition, the "basic annals" of each reign record the rituals, portents, alliances, memorials, and enfeoffments that made up each emperor's performance of his role, but they rarely reveal the personalities beneath the robes. Even

Chinese fictionalized accounts of historical rulers, like the *Romance of the Three Kingdoms*, deal with types rather than characters. The combination of access and insight makes *The Private Life of Chairman Mao* unique.

The real Mao could hardly have been more different from the benevolent sage-king portrayed in the authorized memoirs and poster portraits that circulate in China today. To be sure, on first meeting he could be charming, sympathetic, and casual, setting his visitor at ease to talk freely. But he drew on psychological reserves of anger and contempt to control his followers, manipulating his moods with frightening effect. Relying on the Confucian unwillingness of those around him to confront their superior, he humiliated subordinates and rivals. He undertook self-criticism only to goad others to flatter him, surrounding himself with a culture of abasement.

Emulating the first Tang emperor, Mao bound men and women to him by discovering their weaknesses. Dr. Li Zhisui came from an upper class family, was trained at an American-sponsored school in Suzhou, and had an early and trivial involvement with the Guomindang. These potentially dangerous facts enslaved him to Mao. Corruption existed within Mao's entourage and Mao knew it, but he needed people who could cut corners. Fish cannot live in pure water, Mao liked to say. He enjoyed swimming in polluted water and walking through fields of night soil.

Mao's retainers remained on permanent probation, whatever their backgrounds. Old comrades were sent into internal exile, in some cases to their deaths, although Mao's role in these tragedies was indirect. In one scene we see Mao sitting on a stage behind a curtain listening, unseen, as two of his closest colleagues are attacked at a mass meeting. Mao controlled his top colleagues' medical care, denying some of them treatment for cancer, because he was convinced that cancer could not be cured and he wanted them to work for their remaining time. Having lost children, a brother, and a wife to war and revolution, he seldom seemed moved by the suffering of lovers, children, and friends any more than he flinched from imposing misery on millions of the faceless "masses" in pursuit of his economic and political schemes. He understood human suffering chiefly as a way to control people. In politics and personal life alike, he discarded those for whom he had no present use, just as coolly calling them back when he wanted them, if they were still alive.

Dr. Li usually found Mao with a book of Chinese history in his hand. He loved the traditional stories of strategy and deception. He was an expert in when to wait, feint, and withdraw, and how to attack obliquely. He liked to "lure snakes out of their holes," encouraging others to show their hands so he could turn against them. His closest colleagues could seldom sense whether he agreed with them or was waiting to pounce. Dr. Li says Mao was a marvelous actor. He could sentence a retainer to exile with a story so convincing that the victim backed out bowing in gratitude.

Imperial power allowed the ultimate luxury, simplicity. Mao spent much of his time in bed or lounging by the side of a private pool, not dressing for days at a time. He ate oily food, rinsed his mouth with tea, and slept with country girls. During a 1958 tour of Henan, Mao's party was followed everywhere by a truckload of watermelons. Mao liked cloth shoes; if he had to wear leather ones for a diplomatic function, he let someone else break them in. He did not bathe, preferring a rubdown with hot towels, although this made it hard for Dr. Li to stop the spread of venereal infections among his female companions. He slept on a specially made huge wooden bed that was carried on his private train, set up in his villas, airlifted to Moscow.

He exercised sovereignty over clock and calendar. The court worked to Mao's rhythm, and many of its activities took place after midnight. It was not unusual to be summoned to Mao's chambers at 2 or 3 in the morning. He traveled frequently, convening meetings of the nation's leaders wherever he was. He sought to triumph over death through Daoist methods of sex. He followed no schedule except on May Day and National Day and on the rare occasions when he received foreign visitors. Then he had to dress, taking barbiturates to control his anxiety.

Women were served to order like food. While puritanism was promoted in his name, Mao's sex life was a central project of his court. A special room was set aside in the Great Hall of the People for his refreshment during high-level party meetings. Party and army political departments, guardians of the nation's morality, recruited young women of sterling proletarian background and excellent physical appearance, supposedly to engage in ballroom dancing with the leader, actually for possible service in his bed. Honored by the opportunity, some of those chosen introduced their sisters.

Each province's Party Secretary built Mao a villa. He moved from place to place partly for security concerns, partly out of paranoia. "It's not good for me to stay in one place too long," he told Dr. Li. All rail traffic stopped and stations were closed as his special train went through. Security officers posing as food vendors lent the stations an air of normality for his benefit. During the Great Leap, peasants were mobilized to tend transplanted crops along miles of tracks, creating the impression of a bumper harvest when the harvest was a disaster. Mao's favorite villa was located on a small island in the Pearl River, where he enjoyed privacy in the middle of the busy city of Guangzhou. Special food grown in a labor camp near Beijing was airlifted to him and tried by tasters before he ate it. Guards cooled his room with tubs of ice.

Absolute power affected Mao's mental and physical health, his human relations, and through these, his country and the world. He spent months in bed, ill with worry. But when the political struggle was going his way, he might fill up with cheerful energy that kept him from sleeping. Dr. Li dosed him constantly with barbiturates so he could rest. Political stress sometimes made him impotent, at other times stimulated his libido. As tens of millions starved to death during the Great Leap Forward and the Chairman lost face before the Party, he temporarily gave up meat. But he needed more women. One of them told Dr. Li that the Great Helmsman was great in everything, even in bed.

Politics in a dictatorship begins in the personality of the dictator. Mao established a regime like no other, an ensemble of economic, social, and political institutions that grew from his effort to build a unique form of socialism in a country that was poor, backward, and vulnerable.

Facing the hostility of the West, Mao aligned with Moscow. But his admiration for the West was one reason he chose the American trained Dr. Li as his physician, and was a subject of many of their conversations. He told Dr. Li that America's intentions toward China had always been benign. But he held his allies the Russians in contempt. Mao aimed to surpass the primitive Russian model with Chinese-style socialism, raise his country to the level of the advanced Western world, and by this achievement join the pantheon of Marxism-Leninism. The Great Leap Forward was his effort to create a model of socialism better than that of his northern neighbors, and the Cultural Revolution was his attempt to sustain the experiment in the face of its failure.

In a vast, continental country with a huge and poor population, Mao sought economic growth through mass mobilization, trying to substitute ideological fervor for material rewards. He froze the people's standard of living at subsistence levels in order to build a massive, wasteful industrial structure. In doing so, he ignored realities that contradicted his vision. A farmer's son from rural Hunan, he allowed himself to be deluded by vast Potemkin fields at the start of the Great Leap Forward. As Dr. Li says, why should Mao have doubted that the communist paradise had arrived when he himself was living in it? He thought there was more to learn about leadership from the pages of Chinese history than from textbooks of modern engineering. While people starved he imagined that they had more than they could eat.

The ideology that bore Mao's name promoted self-denial, defined a person's value in terms of political virtue, and dehumanized the class enemy. A system of work units, class labels, household registrations, and mass movements fixed each citizen in an organizational cage, within which people exercised political terror over themselves and each other. A pervading bureaucracy governed the economy, politics, ideology, culture, the people's private lives, and even many of their private thoughts. The apparatus led the people in singing the praises of the regime that had expropriated them. Mao toppled the party machinery when it proved insufficiently responsive to his fantasies of speed but rebuilt it when he needed it to stop factional violence.

At the top, thirty to forty men made all the major decisions. Their power was personal, fluid, and dependent on their relations with Mao. Dr. Li describes the system of Central Committee organs, political and confidential secretaries, bodyguards, kitchens, car pools, and clinics that served the leaders. An underground tunnel complex allowed the leaders to move secretly from their headquarters in Zhongnanhai to buildings elsewhere in Beijing. Mao's closest retainers bugged his premises, trying to keep better records of his decisions, but found themselves cashiered for spying on him.

Set up to serve and protect the leaders, the structures of power isolated them, Mao more than the others. Mao's comrades gradually ceded to him the Forbidden City swimming pool, the dance parties, and the best Beidaihe beach. The saga of his swim in three great rivers, over the objections of his security men, symbolized his solitary struggle against the bureaucracy, his fear that the revolution might bog down, and his challenge to comrades he thought were betraying his radical aims.

At the Eighth Party Congress in 1956, Mao's colleagues attempted to rein him in, taking advantage of de-Stalinization in the Soviet Union to write his guiding thought out of the party constitution, pledge the Party against the cult of personality, and criticize Mao's attempts to force the premature birth of communism. Mao claimed falsely to Dr. Li that he had not been consulted about these decisions. Forces abroad also threatened his control. The new Soviet leader, Khrushchev, wanted an accommodation with the West. Dr. Li portrays the bitter last meeting between the two by the side of Mao's swimming pool, which marked the start of an open split with the Soviets and the onset of China's long period of isolation.

Mao held fast to three ultimate tools of power: ideology, the army, and his spider's position at the center of the Party's factional web. He summoned up the epochal Great Leap Forward with a whistle-stop farm tour that passed a message over the heads of the economic planners to the basic-level cadres. At the Lushan Plenum in 1959, when the other leaders again tried to rein Mao in, he threatened to raise a new army and take to the hills. The others surrendered.

After the famine began, Mao retreated to a secondary position of power. As the other party leaders restored the economy, he brooded that they were "zombies," and complained about their failure to consult him. He patiently ensnared them in a debate over classic operas and enmeshed them in confusion over the issue of rural corruption. When his colleagues were vulnerable enough, he launched the Cultural Revolution.

Millions of victims later, Mao stood victorious at the Ninth Party Congress of 1969, his rivals dead or in internal exile, the nation singing his praises and waving his red book before his ubiquitous poster. By his side stood the abject Lin Biao, the sole survivor from the old ruling group. Mao's dream of development had failed, but his power was absolute in the country he had ruined. Lin Biao's coup attempt two years later disappointed Mao so badly that Dr. Li traces his final decline from then. He used his final energies to engineer the opening to the West, which later made possible Deng Xiaoping's reforms.

Psychological pathologies flourished in the atmosphere of court politics. The more complete Mao's control, the greater his fear of others' attempts to control him. Their anxiety to please made them more suspect. He thought his villas were poisoned and panicked when he heard wild animals scratching inside the roof of one. Mao spied on the other leaders by managing their secretaries through his chief secretary and their guards through his chief of guards. Although he surrounded his rivals with his men, he was never sure they were not spying on him through his women.

Mao's wife, Jiang Qing, suffered from hypochondria, aversion to noise, light, cold, and heat; and compulsive quarreling. Having driven her mad with boredom, dependency, and enforced idleness, Mao at first tried to spare her the knowledge of his love affairs. But when he needed her as a political proxy, he brought her into the inner circle. Like her equally sick colleague Lin Biao, Jiang once in power flowered into robust health, making friends with Mao's favorite female companion to get better access to the source of power.

Dr. Li shows us Lin Biao in the arms of his wife, crying with pain from a kidney stone; Hua Guofeng sitting in Mao's anteroom for hours unable to see the great leader because his companion and gatekeeper, Zhang Yufeng, is napping; Zhou Enlai kneeling on the floor before Mao to trace the route of a proposed motorcade; Jiang Qing in fury as a sick Mao hands control over the whole country to Zhou, only to recover and out-live him.

Of all Mao's followers, only Zhou kept relatively aloof from the byzan-tine networks that laced the court. Because he did so, Dr. Li and the other courtiers ironically viewed him as disloyal and dangerous. For Zhou to report information to appropriate colleagues in the formal chain of command struck the others as a sign of weakness and treachery.

At the end, the most loved man in China was friendless. During his long decline, his servants' chief obsession was to avoid blame for his demise. Only his favorite, Zhang Yufeng, had the decency to treat him like a human being by quarreling with him, fearless of being accused of angering him to death. But as he weakened, she found other interests, having become indispensable because only she could decode his slurred speech.

Dr. Li Zhisui's frank, round, slightly smiling face stands out from the rows of stony-faced retainers in the group photographs of Mao's house-hold. His open expression, soft cheeks, and neat clothes betray him as the one who came back from the West. His foreign tincture made him doubly valuable, denoting both competence and dependency. For Mao was secure to the extent that Dr. Li was vulnerable. Surviving under Mao's protection, he stuck to his business, maintaining the health of the man whose acts cost the lives of millions.

Only a certain willingness to look away from evil can make a man the ideal guardian of a dictator's life. Dr. Li's limits as an observer of history were one of his qualifications for his job. But politics sometimes forced itself on him. Mao sometimes insisted on talking about events or on send-ing Dr. Li away from the court to observe and report. At court, Dr. Li had to learn who protected and who opposed him. Aside from Mao, his patron was Wang Dongxing, chief of bodyguards. Their alliance provides the book's bias, but also much of its insight into court politics.

Since he left China, Dr. Li has been all but erased from official history. Of the countless books on Mao's personal life published by Chinese presses, only one or two mention him. Apparently, there has been a cen-tral directive to treat him as a nonperson. But his image survives in unre-touched film footage and photos, and reliable sources confirm his identity. Official and semiofficial works corroborate many details in his account but differ from his in leaving out aspects of the story that would embarrass the regime, which still rules by the soft light of Mao's official image. No authorized account offers a portrait of Mao that rings as true as Dr. Li's. It is the most revealing book ever published on Mao, perhaps on any dictator in history.

In 1981, five years after Mao's death, the Chinese Communist Party Central Committee adopted an official verdict on his life, "Resolution on Certain Questions in the History of Our Party Since the Founding of the People's Republic of China." It called Mao a great revolutionary whose contributions outweighed the costs of his mistakes. This book tells a different story. It shows how excessive power drives its possessor into a shadow world, where great visions become father to great crimes.

In 1958, at about the time covered by the texts translated in *The Secret Speeches of Chairman Mao: From the Hundred Flowers to the Great Leap Forward,*[4] Mao attended a command performance in Shanghai of the *The White Snake*, a tragic Chinese opera. As Mao's captain of bodyguards tells it in a recent memoir (published in Chinese), the chairman settled into his front row sofa to the applause of the assembled cadres, allowed the bodyguard to loosen the belt over his ample stomach, lit a cigarette, and sat back to enjoy the show. (Doctors had ordered Mao to stop eating so much fatty pork, but he was too willful to listen.) Just at the point where the feudalistic Buddhist abbot Fahai starts to bury the White Maiden beneath the Thunder Peak Pagoda, Mao jumped up, shouting, "You won't let her make revolution? You won't let her rebel?" His pants dropped around his ankles.[5]

Mao is similarly undressed in some of the nineteen texts in *The Secret Speeches*, which the editors have selected from twenty-three volumes of his speeches, monologues, and letters that were circulated in classified editions in China and have recently been obtained by Harvard's Fairbank Center for East Asian Research. The first set of texts translated here dates from the Hundred Flowers movement of the spring of 1957, and includes the original transcript of Mao's February 27, 1957, speech, "On the Correct Handling of Contradictions Among the People," which laid out the rationale for allowing the intellectuals to criticize the Party in what became known as the Hundred Flowers campaign. The second set of documents dates from 1958, the first year of the Great Leap Forward. Among them is a series of five impromptu talks Mao gave to his Politburo colleagues and other top officials at the seaside resort of Beidaihe in late

August, in which he dilated feverishly on his vision of imminent communism.

The texts have never before been available outside a small circle of party specialists in China. They add to our understanding of Mao's character and thinking at a crucial turning point in contemporary Chinese history. For a regime that was constantly torn by factionalism and was normally at war with one or another major section of its society, the years 1957 and 1958 were a unique interlude of self-confidence and optimism—at least for Mao, although many of his colleagues were skeptical. Looking back, the path of decline from the regime's relatively happy days of 1957–58 to the disaster of June 1989 is surprisingly clear, considering the amount of time and tragedy in between.

The sense of security had been earned at a large cost in earlier violence, even after the Chinese Communist Party won victory in a bloody civil war. In a passage eliminated from the official published version of "On the Correct Handling of Contradictions," Mao tells his audience that in the 1950–52 campaign to wipe out counterrevolutionaries, "700,000 were killed, [and] after that time probably over 70,000 more have been killed. But less than 80,000. . . . In the past four or five years we've only killed several tens of thousands of people." These figures do not include the costs in death and suffering of land reform, the thought reform of the intellectuals, and the so-called five-anti campaign for the takeover of private businesses. There were a few mistakes, Mao goes on, but "basically there were no errors; that group of people should have been killed."

Mao tries to convince his party colleagues that 1956 marked the end of 116 years of class struggle, counted from the Opium War of 1840, and that it is time for the Party to lay down the cudgel. He assures them that what happened in 1956 in Hungary—where they "basically did not eliminate counterrevolutionaries"—could not happen in China. The negative example of Hungary has remained a nightmare for Chinese leaders. Deng Xiaoping's speeches throughout the 1980s and Li Peng's in the 1989 crisis were full of references to counterrevolution in Hungary and Poland, both in 1956 and in the 1980s.

But in 1957, Mao denied the existence of any real threat to party control. "We won," he says. "Indeed you won, that certainly counts! Being able to win always deserves credit. Since you won, what else is there to say?" The answer he proposes is that the Party now faces a new challenge, economic construction, which it does not know how to win. It needs the cooperation of the bourgeois intellectuals until it can train its own generation of proletarian intellectuals. The Party must stop repressing the intellectuals and learn to get along with them. The intellectuals will have to be allowed to criticize the Party cadres, Mao says. But this should be no more frightening for the Party than "washing its face." The Party is too securely rooted now to be blown down even by a "force-12 typhoon."

These documents dispose of the theory that the Hundred Flowers campaign was a trick to get the Party's critics to expose themselves—to "lure snakes out of their holes." Mao's purpose was to convince Party cadres, used to treating everyone who crossed them as a counterrevolutionary, to learn how to tolerate differences of opinion among those they had to work with on the tasks of economic construction. "Our strong points are no longer any use. Our strong points are class struggle, politics, and military affairs. Our weak points are our lack of culture, lack of science, and lack of technology. We must learn these things." Mao wanted to offer the intellectuals a junior partnership in the regime. The documents also remove any doubt that Mao had agreed with Liu Shaoqi and Deng Xiaoping when they declared the effective end of class struggle at the Eighth Party Congress of 1956—a fact obscured by Cultural Revolution attacks on Liu and Deng for what they said then.

To provide a Marxist theoretical basis for the new era of class harmony, and to persuade the intellectuals that their criticisms of the Party would go unpunished, Mao developed the theory of the "two kinds of contradictions" in his February 1957 speech. He argued that contradictions among the people are nonantagonistic and should be handled by persuasion, unlike contradictions between the enemy and ourselves, which are antagonistic and must be handled by coercion. The theory became part of the jargon of Chinese communism. In May 1989 Li Peng tried to make talismanic use of it by declaring that the regime would "strictly distinguish between the two different kinds of contradictions" in dealing with the democracy protesters, among whom the bad elements were "an extremely small, extremely small number."[6]

Saying so didn't make it so in 1989, or in 1957. Mao was radically overoptimistic about the loyalty of the intellectuals. When they finally accepted his invitation to criticize the Party, they unlocked unsuspected reserves of bitterness, in a process similar to that which occurred in Chinese cities in the spring of 1989. The criticism rapidly reached a hostile crescendo and had to be stopped. Several months later the official version of "On the Correct Handling of Contradictions" was published with heavy revisions which radically changed the ground rules of the campaign. Some 600,000 persons were labeled "rightists" for having gone beyond the rules. They were punished with up to twenty years of labor camp or internal exile.

One can glimpse the theoretical origins of both the Cultural Revolution and post-Tiananmen conservatism in Mao's 1957 analysis of the intellectuals' relationship to the Party. His decision to characterize the intellectuals' conflicts with the Party as a contradiction "among the people" is explicitly not based on a sense of identity with them—he estimates that fewer than 10 percent are really committed to socialism—but on a tactical judgment that they are now sufficiently cowed and isolated to go along with the regime. He states frankly in March 1957, "There is still class struggle, particularly in the ideological sphere, but we treat it as a contradiction among the people."

When the intellectuals betrayed him, he concluded in 1958 that "classes in terms of political thinking . . . are not easily abolished, and they have not yet been abolished—that is what we discovered during last year's Rectification [Hundred Flowers] Campaign." This spurred him to develop the theory of "uninterrupted revolution," which called for pushing ahead toward communism without giving "bourgeois ideology" a chance to take root—what he elsewhere referred to approvingly as "transition [to communism] in poverty." The idea that class struggle continues long past the abolition of the economic bases of class became the rationale for the Cultural Revolution. In the post-Mao era it justified the regime's assaults on "bourgeois liberalization."

The documents in the book skip over the second half of 1957 when the crackdown on the intellectuals occurred, and pick up again in early 1958 when the ebullient Mao is full of renewed confidence, this time in the peasant masses and their enthusiasm for socialism. Mao at this time sounds like a man on a caffeine high. Indeed, according to the memoirs of his bodyguard, he had no regular habits of eating, sleeping, or exercise. His body ran on a 28-hour day, so his sleeping patterns constantly changed. He might eat once or twice a day, depending on when he was hungry. When he was excited he would stay up for three or four days at a time, and then he had great trouble getting to sleep. He was addicted to sleeping pills, constantly drank tea, and ate the tea leaves to combat constipation. He was such a heavy smoker that many of his guards got stomach ulcers from the smoke.[7]

Mao relished the heaven-storming atmosphere of the Great Leap. A decade earlier, he told his colleagues at Beidaihe, his health had improved in Yan'an after the town was attacked by a Kuomintang general. Now he felt that the Western embargo of China was also a good thing, because it helped create a crisis atmosphere that "will mobilize all [our] positive forces." "To have an enemy in front of us, to have tension, is to our advantage." Earlier, in another passage excised from the official version of "On the Correct Handling of Contradictions," Mao said that he debated with Nehru over whether World War III would bring about the elimination of the human race. "I don't accept this argument. . . . As regards fighting World War III, I say that in the first place we do not welcome [it], [but] it's OK [too]." War "stimulates people's activism, arouses people's consciousness, makes revolution erupt."

In 1958, Mao was convinced that the masses had become aroused. Once they poured their huge energies into the task of production, all China's problems would be solved. China would become a great industrial power within "three, five, or seven years." There would be so much surplus grain that it would take three years to eat a year's crop; he worried that with such plenty people might quit cultivating the land. Excess population, which had concerned him as recently as 1957, was no longer a problem. "With many people, there's lots of power." More labor power would make for more wealth. Rural workers released from farming would be put to work in industry. The country would get so crowded that people would have to line up to go out on the street. "Every large commune will have highways constructed, wider roads of cement or asphalt, with no trees planted [alongside] so that airplanes can land—they will be airports."

The opportunity was ripe to strike toward communism. Mao warned his colleagues not to let the Soviet Union find out about this too soon, for they would be mortified to be left in the dust. The only worry was to find some tasks to leave for the next generation.

Mao's image of communism was drawn straight from Marx's enigmatic "Critique of the Gotha Program," which he took quite literally. People would work for the pleasure of it, not for wages, and would spend one-third of their time in leisure. They would eat without paying. Goods would no longer be produced for exchange but would be allocated on the basis of need, without regard to exchange value. The patriarchal family system would end with the availability of widespread social security; education and child care would be taken over by the community. Officials would engage in manual labor; military officers would spend time in the ranks; villages, schools, factories, and neighborhoods would be organized into communes that would combine governmental, economic, and military functions. The state would cease to have any role but national defense and the registration of births, deaths, and marriages.

It was easy for Mao to think of junking the commodity economy because he had little understanding of its workings. Until the early 1950s he and the other Communist leaders had lived under a "supply system" in which the Party provided directly for their needs. After taking power and assuming control over the vast bureaucracy already in place, the Party had to introduce a wage-grade system for officials. Mao himself received a salary of 530 yuan. But he hardly knew what to do with it. His bodyguard says he never touched money and hated it.

And for a farmer's son, Mao knew surprisingly little about agriculture. In December 1957, according to his bodyguard, Mao spent a sleepness night wondering why the peasants were still so poor; he saw no reason why socialism shouldn't already have made them rich.[8] At Beidaihe, he reminded the Party of his orders to enforce two innovations: deep plowing—better for eliminating weeds, he thought—and close planting, so as to get more plants per acre. In a later meeting he ordered close planting for fruit trees, too, because "when they all grow together, they will be comfortable." Deep plowing and close planting both turned out to be disastrous, although less so than his regime's stress on ill-conceived water conservation and land reclamation projects that did long-term environmental damage.

Mao claimed to be skeptical of reported super-high grain yields, but he had no idea of what a realistic figure might be. In November 1958 he discounted a claim of 450 million tons of grain to what he thought was a credible 370 tons—double the previous year's harvest. He believed that the communes could readily double agricultural output in one year by concentrating the labor force and land management. He told his colleagues that grain production would soon be so high that one-third of the land could be planted to fruit trees, one-third to grain, and one-third could be left fallow—a howler repeated to me with wonder by young Chinese economists in the 1980s, but never before documented on the public record. Mao claimed there would soon be so much grain that China would supply it free to other countries whenever they were in need.

Mao was a walking example of the danger of a little learning. His interests were wide-ranging, but his knowledge was unsystematic and inaccurate. He had enormous faith in the "Critique of the Gotha Program" and in a Soviet political economy textbook that he frequently quoted, remarking at one point that "dogs are superior animals quite capable of understanding human nature, but the only thing is that they don't understand Marxism, they don't understand steel production—more or less like capitalists." Yet Stalin's economic writings were too dispassionate for him. "In his economics, everything is cold and cheerless, wretched and miserable, and totally gloomy."

According to a recent book on Mao's reading habits, on one trip out of town in October 1959 he instructed his secretary to pack works by Marx, Engels, Lenin, Stalin, Plekhanov, Hegel, the utopian socialists; an anthology of Western philosophy; works of classic Chinese philosophy, including the Legalists and the Daoists; the twenty-four dynastic histories; and works of contemporary Chinese Marxist writers.[9] It was an ambitious reading program, but narrow and highly theoretical. His economic prescriptions at Beidaihe were theoretical in the worst sense—abstract, contradictory, and damaging. After twenty-seven years of rule, his legacy was an inefficient modern economic system that had been created at exorbitant cost sitting atop a backward rural economy.

Mao was deeply afraid of and contemptuous of intellectuals. "The trouble lies in the fact that whereas they have read a few books, we haven't. And because we haven't, they get so stuck up that it's really hard for us to deal with them." His talks are full of slighting references to professors in particular. In his ramblings before educated audiences on philosophy, history, literature, physics, biology, and chemistry, he self-consciously throws in peasant-like references, which seem intended preemptively to deflate his own intellectualizing while also establishing a superior claim to authority on the basis of materialist dialectics. Thus, in a disquisition on the sources of knowledge, Mao remarks, "the formula for protein has not yet been discovered, [but] the 167 types of reactive dyes have. The world's first, marsh gas, is H^4C; farts are H^2S."

Yet the intellectuals we encounter in these pages treat Mao with real deference. In several of the texts, groups of distinguished party and non-party intellectuals seek his advice on a wide range of issues, and he answers every question with self-assurance, although often delphically. The atmosphere is reminiscent of Confucius' dialogues with his disciples; Mao's dicta might as well be tagged "the Master said." Although his authority came partly from his ability to bully and humiliate others, it also drew from the prevalent belief that he really did have the correct answers to all questions. Few Chinese intellectuals, even inside the Party, knew enough about Marxism to challenge Mao's claim to interpret it. In fact, in an interesting sidelight, one of Mao's interlocutors in 1957 states that only about 47 percent of Marx's works have been translated into Chinese. Until the disaster of the Great Leap, Mao's political copybook was in fact unblotted by any major failure. He fostered the image of a sage-king, and for a long time his society was inclined to believe in his powers of vision.

Mao was a master of obfuscation masquerading as dialectics. He says that in writing newspaper articles, "[We] can combine stiffness and gentleness together." "[If] Lu Xun were alive, I think he'd both dare and not dare to write." "Our theory is different: . . . War turns into peace, peace turns into war, life turns into death, death turns into life." One of his favorite devices is to use his vision of the long term to deny the importance of problems in the short term. Arguing for the Hundred Flowers policy against those who fear that Marxism may come under challenge, he comforts them with the thought that "Marxism itself will come to an end some day. . . . The earth will rot one day. Humanity may also be negated." And he insists on the catch-22 proposition that the coercive history of his regime provides no excuse for people failing to speak up boldly. "The genuine Marxist [and] thoroughgoing materialist fears nothing, so he can write." Ignoring his regime's history of coercion, he urges, "We hope to make ours a lively country, where people dare to criticize, dare to speak, dare to express their opinions. [We] should not make people fearful to speak."

Once the Hundred Flowers were suppressed, of course, it was too late for this project to be achieved. The palmy period of the regime came to an end with the collapse of the Leap and the massive famine that followed—the largest in the history of the world. By 1976, when Mao died, the Party was widely unpopular. From 1978 on, Deng Xiaoping restored its authority by playing the economy like a slot machine, finding policy combinations that successively unlocked the suppressed productivity of the villages, underemployed urbanites, small town factories, and the coastal regions with links to the Chinese diaspora. But the payouts were all pocketed by the mid-1980s. The reforms seemed at a dead end and the regime's legitimacy began to slide. Unable to buy consent, Deng Xiaoping had to revert to rule by coercion.

Over its history one of the surprising features of the Chinese Communist regime has been its repeated ability to be surprised by its unpopularity with its own people—in the Hundred Flowers, the Cultural Revolution, the Democracy Wall movement of 1978–79, and the Beijing Spring of 1989. The dynamics of self-isolation and self-deception are clear in Mao's talks of 1957–58. At one meeting recorded in this volume he finishes a disquisition to a group of Party cadres in Tianjin and then asks for questions. There aren't any; they are afraid to talk to him. He misunderstood his people because he cut himself off from them by his brutality.

The same has been true of the Deng Xiaoping regime. Deng had to reconfront the contradiction that Mao was trying to resolve in 1957, between the coercive grounding of the regime and its need for the cooperation of the intellectuals. "Dictatorship, arbitrariness, and suppression cannot be applied to ideological problems," Mao warned in 1957. "[If you] want people to obey, [you] have to persuade rather than coerce [them]." It was advice he didn't follow himself. But at least when Mao tried to enforce ideological conformity there was some substance to his thought, however incoherent it may have been at a deeper level, and the intellectuals were disposed to have faith. Today when the regime demands that people "love socialism," the very concept is vacuous, having been sapped of all meaning by years of ideological revisionism. The terror that was imposed under Deng was more Stalinist than Maoist. Mao's terror, at least until the early 1970s, relied for its effectiveness on the ideological conviction of both its perpetrators and its victims. The terror in China after Mao was simply that of a police state, a much more fragile kind.

Who was Kang Sheng? Was he really, as *The Claws of the Dragon* claims, "the man Mao trusted more than any other," a man who could "control, even mesmerize Mao," "one of the most influential forces in modern China"? Is it really correct to believe that "next to Kang, Mao himself seems to shrink in importance and interest"?[10]

Starting in 1927, Kang was one of the leaders in the small Communist underground in Shanghai, placed by Zhou Enlai in charge of a secret service that fought a running battle with the Kuomintang's police and conducted assassinations of Communist defectors. When the Communists pulled out of Shanghai, Kang went to Moscow for ideological training and allegedly cooperated with the NKVD in purging "hundreds" from among the visiting Chinese Communist cadres studying there. In 1937 he returned to China, to become head of the Party School in Yan'an, the Communists' capital. A year later he was also appointed to head the intraparty security agency known as the Social Affairs Department, about whose work little is known.

The height of Kang's power as the Chinese Communist Party's secret police chief was past by the time the People's Republic was established in 1949. From 1949 to 1956, he was either physically or politically ill and out of power. By the time of Great Leap Forward in 1958, he had returned to Mao's side and although he did not occupy a high post, he was prominent in supporting Mao's call for the Leap. For the next several years he continued to serve as one of Mao's theoretical advisers, helping to devise the ideological rationale for the split with the Soviet Union and helping, with Mao's wife, Jiang Qing, to generate the critique of "revisionist" trends in literature and art that led to the Cultural Revolution. At that time he persecuted a novelist and a philosophy professor, each of whom had promoted ideas that he deemed retrograde; later hundreds of victims were hounded in connection with each of these cases.

Kang reached a brief second peak of influence during the Cultural Revolution, as a cat's paw of Mao's, without independent power. He was adviser to the Central Cultural Revolution Small Group and de facto head of the Party's Organization Department, reached protocol position number 4 in the Communist hierarchy, and was elected to the Politburo Standing Committee. He helped launch the Red Guard movement at the Party School and at Beijing University, exercised influence over the Party Investigation Department and the Ministry of Public Security, and (like several other CCP leaders) developed a private security force of 500 agents.

During this period, Kang took the lead in a number of intraparty persecutions, including those of Liu Shaoqi and Deng Xiaoping. Because of his knowledge of senior cadres' personnel histories, he knew whom to accuse plausibly of what, though the story is also told of his framing someone as a traitor simply because he thought the man looked like one. According to John Byron and Robert Pack, Kang "personally supervised ten special case groups that investigated the 'crimes' of 220 defendants from the very apex of the Communist Party." He also gave a talk to Red Guards from Inner Mongolia, who subsequently carried out a witch hunt that affected hundreds of thousands, and he had vaguely delineated ties to a purge in Yunnan Province that affected tens of thousands.

Byron and Pack conclude that more than 30,000 deaths were "directly attributable" to Kang, but it is not clear whether this number includes the deaths in Inner Mongolia and Yunnan, to which he is connected only indirectly, deaths that themselves exceeded 30,000 in number. Then in 1970 Kang was stricken with cancer. He was soon incapacitated and although continuing to hold high office ceased to play an important role. He died in 1975.

From these facts Byron and Pack—identified on the book jacket as a pseudonymous senior diplomat and a veteran investigative reporter—create a picture of Kang as "the creator of China's Gulag," the godfather of the Cultural Revolution," China's Beria, "a purveyor of terror to the largest nation in history," "the most callous and unrestrained" among China's Communist rulers. They base their account heavily on an officially sponsored *Critical Biography of Kang Sheng* issued for internal circulation within the Party in 1982. In turn, the *Critical Biography* is a popularized version of material compiled by a "special case group" charged with justifying Kang's posthumous expulsion from the Chinese Communist Party in 1980. Like the documentation released within the Party after the purge of Liu Shaoqi, the fall of Lin Biao, and the arrest of the Gang of Four, the Kang Sheng dossier was issued because the subject commanded substantial prestige. Drawing on the ancient tradition of Chinese "praise-and-blame" historiography, such materials seek to blacken the subject's reputation in every possible way. The *Critical Biography* portrays Kang as not just on the losing side, but as a thoroughly bad egg: a roué from a landlord background, a selfish materialist who lacked human kindness, engaged in sexual license, betrayed his friends, and may have been a hidden traitor to the Party.

In such works, the subject's crimes are separated from historical context and Byron and Peck perpetuate the error. Kang's relations with Zhou Enlai, his original patron in the Party, are hidden. Mao is portrayed as a victim, rather than as a beneficiary, of Kang's lies and deceits. Kang is made to appear a deviant from the Maoist system rather than a product of it.

Byron and Pack blacken the names of all those figures whom the CCP now blackens and paints in favorable terms the ones the Party praises. Zhou Enlai, Chen Yun, Peng Dehuai, and Liu Shaoqi receive sympathetic treatment, while Jiang Qing, Wang Ming, and Chen Boda are sneered at. These judgments are often conveyed through the use of potted physical descriptions. The propagandist Yao Wenyuan was "round-faced and rotund," and radical philosophy professor Nie Yuanzi was "a plump woman of 45." General He Long triumphs as "a heroic, dashing figure with a clipped mustache," and Deng Xiaoping is described favorably as "combative, energetic, and pushy."

The authors do supplement the *Critical Biography* with other sources, including interviews; but nearly all of them are with people who disliked Kang. Byron and Pack seem to believe that this adds to their informants' credibility. An interviewee who misremembered Kang's home province and his height is cited as the sole gospel for the controversial charge that it was Kang who betrayed five fellow-communists to the KMT police in 1931. An uncorroborated source subtitled *The Thief and the Prostitute* is used to prove that Kang was addicted to opium in the 1960s. And the authors labor even harder than their source to endow Kang with a deplorable sexual history.

Thus they expand two sentences in the *Critical Biography*, consisting of the Chinese equivalent of clichés like "Kang and his young friends painted the town red," into two pages filled with circumstantial detail of a "wild adolescence in Jiao county." They retail weakly founded rumors that Kang had an early sexual relationship with fellow Shandongese Jiang Qing. They call the rumors "plausible" because, "Jiang Qing was a precocious girl" and "Kang had a reputation for sexual escapades." Later they state gratuitously that "whether [Kang and Jiang] resumed or developed a physical relationship in Yan'an remains a mystery."

They cite an unreliable book in Chinese called *Personalities of the Red Dynasty* to assert that in the 1930s Kang was frequently in and out of brothels. They speak of "rumored amorous escapades" during the 1950s with no cited evidence. They make much of his watching "bawdy" traditional opera in the early 1960s, sometimes in the company of Jiang Qing, ignoring the fact that this was part of his job as head of the Theoretical Small Group and that even the bawdiest of Chinese operas is devoid of pornographic effect. They note insinuatingly that in the mid-1960s, when Kang helped Mao launch the Cultural Revolution, he was "aided by several women, including his wife and the ever present Jiang Qing and a university lecturer notorious for her sexual opportunism"—a woman who like many Chinese had divorced her spouse when he was labeled a rightist and who later married a highly placed cadre twenty years her senior.

The Claws of the Dragon often embroiders on the bare framework of Kang's curriculum vitae, which in many spots is all the *Critical Biography* provides. This makes the book slow-moving as we are treated to architectural detail on cities in which Kang lived, or accounts of historical events in which he played no direct role. The authors attribute states of mind to Kang without evidence. He is described as infuriated, fearful, carefully concealing his jealousy; as sensing, appreciating, enjoying; as being inspired by the exploits of traditional Chinese spymasters. His consistent and sometimes risky support for Mao's shifting line is portrayed as opportunism, part of "his quest for the unholy grail of total power."

If we are to have an imaginary Kang, I prefer a less banal one. Not knowing Kang's mind, I prefer to imagine it as Hannah Arendt imagined her totalitarians, as the mind of a fanatical ideologue who believed that all things are possible. When Kang justifies the brutality of the Cultural Revolution as a small price to pay for China's attempt to remake human nature, Byron and Pack see only nonsense. One might instead see the antiutilitarianism typical of totalitarian ideologies. It was an ideology not generated by Kang, but created by Mao and voiced at different times by the entire Chinese Communist leadership.

Some of the main Maoist techniques of terror as an instrument of rule were perfected during the Yan'an Rectification Movement of 1942–44. Byron and Pack follow the *Critical Biography* in blaming the mass-meeting denunciations, arrests, tortures, and executions on Kang. They leave Mao, the progenitor and beneficiary of the movement, in the background, ignore the collective involvement of the rest of the party leadership (some of whom are still in power), and overlook the complicity of the victims, without which the vortex of hysteria could not have been generated.

In any case, the Rectification Movement fits Byron and Pack's thesis poorly. It marked a shift from secret, professional anti-espionage work to the use of public spy hysteria as a tool to ensnare thousands of innocent victims and frighten masses of people into total compliance with the new ideology of "Mao Zedong Thought." For Kang it marked the end of whatever independent power he had and his enlistment as a loyal tool of Mao.

To say that Kang "used the security organs to turn China into a chamber of horrors" is thus erroneous in three ways. First, his victims were concentrated among the party and intellectual elite, not the whole of China. Second, the terror that swept both the elite and the entire population was not Kang's creation but that of Mao and the party apparatus, though Kang played his part in spurring the process along. Third and most important, the terror was not the product of the security organs, but primarily of other institutions in Mao's system of rule.

Mao's system was totalitarian, but it was not a "police state," as Byron and Pack call it. In a police state, the political police become a separate organization, more powerful than the regular police, the military, or the party organization. They operate without legal restriction, serve as the primary pillar of the regime, and have direct access to the leader. One thinks of Stalin's KGB, Hitler's SS, the Iranian Savak, Saddam Hussein's Mukhabarat, or the former South Korean Central Intelligence Agency. China had no similar organization. The Party never lost political control over the Ministry of Public Security, and its minister never ranked among the top figures of the regime. The Party's internal investigatory and disciplinary organs were independent from the police. So far as is known, these organs concentrated on intraparty and overseas intelligence work rather than domestic security, although information on them is extremely scarce. Under Mao, the military and rural and factory militias also served important security roles.

The huge bureaucracy of the Public Security Ministry reaches from the central government down to each neighborhood and village. Much of its work is public and nonpolitical: traffic policing, household registration, criminal investigations, fire fighting. Until 1983, it also ran the huge network of prisons and labor camps (since shifted to the Ministry of Justice), which is described in Hong-da Harry Wu's important book, *Laogai—The Chinese Gulag.*[11] A prisoner of conscience for nineteen years, Wu collected his information both during his imprisonment and during several risky return trips disguised as a Chinese-American businessman, one of them reported on "60 Minutes." Besides providing unique detail on the organization and distribution of the camps and life inside them, Wu incidentally provides proof of the export of labor camp products to the United States and other markets.

Like police anywhere, the Chinese police engage in some amount of surveillance, opening of mail, tapping of telephones, and infiltration of political groups, though not with great efficiency. But by far the major part of the job of political surveillance in Mao's time was performed by the hierarchy of work units—factories, communes, schools, neighborhood committees, military companies—in which most people were fixed for their entire careers. Each unit was dominated by its Party Secretary and controlled almost all aspects of its members' lives. The party apparatus and the security department within each unit took responsibility for the political lives of its members, as well as for most criminal problems, and maintained links with the local police. (This helps to explain China's extremely low crime statistics, because they include only those cases that get beyond the boundaries of the work unit and enter the regular police and judicial system.) The police were free to direct their attention to special targets, to organizations outside of work units, to circles of intellectuals, students, and workers in larger cities, to foreigners with whom Chinese citizens might have contact.

Political terror was delivered mostly through the unit. Terror commonly took the form not of jackboots on the stairs and the knock on the door, but a summons to a unit political study meeting. The life-long dissident Ni Yuxian, for example, constantly ran afoul of the regime. As Anne F. Thurston describes in her account of his life, *A Chinese Odyssey,*[12] Ni's oppressors were the political instructor of his high school class, his company commander and political instructor in the military, party officials in the college he attended, the worker propaganda team both in his college and in a factory he worked in, Red guards, and factory militia—in other words, control mechanisms within the unit. When Ni, like millions of others, was incarcerated during the Cultural Revolution, it was not in the prison system but in his own unit's "cow shed" (a broom closet, spare room, outhouse, or lavatory). He was never arrested by the police until after Mao's death, when he hung a wall poster on the side of one of Shanghai's major hotels.

Kang's trade was not in mass terror but intraparty terror. As the *Critical Biography* states with outrage, "Those he harmed were not ordinary people." (Kang also had links to some Red Guard groups during the Cultural Revolution. In Beijing and elsewhere, Red Guards may have been used occasionally both by special case groups and by the police to carry out searches or arrests, but almost nothing is known of this relationship, and *The Claws of the Dragon* does little to clarify it.)

Perhaps it was precisely because China lacked a highly developed and autonomous secret police apparatus, and relied so heavily for security on the party hierarchy in the units, that Mao and his allies had to turn to extraordinary methods in order to purge that very hierarchy. Kang's persecutions in the 1960s were conducted largely through entities called "special case groups." These were ad hoc groups of investigators, authorized by the Mao-controlled party center to investigate particular suspects. Their task was not to eliminate victims, but to conduct extensive investigations so that a plausible, if false, case could be put together to justify punishment—just as was done by the special-case group that produced the material for the *Critical Biography*. Many persecutions and tortures of secondary people had no other goal than to collect damaging information on major party figures. Whether police were among the case group members, and whether the groups had organizational links to the police, remain unknown, although it is plausible that the case groups borrowed professional staff from the police.

With the collapse of the old control mechanisms under Deng Xiaoping's liberalizing reforms, China came to resemble a classic police state more rather than less. Agencies dealing with counterespionage and border security were removed from the Ministry of Public Security to form a Ministry of State Security. Deng separated some military units involved in internal security to form the People's Armed Police (PAP). Elite counterterror and civil unrest units were reportedly established and received training in Eastern Europe. After Tiananmen, money was poured into the PAP to improve its technical surveillance capabilities, and control over it was shifted from the Ministry of Public Security to the more pivotal Military Affairs Commission. As work units increasingly refused to inform on their members or to conduct effective political campaigns, police surveillance and illegal police detentions increased.

Not every totalitarian state is a police state, and not every head of party security is a Beria. So far from being Mao's evil genius, the progenitor of the Cultural Revolution, or a man more interesting than Mao himself, Kang Sheng could have said in his defense what his colleague, Jiang Qing, said at her trial: "I was Chairman Mao's dog. When he said bite, I bit."

4

Maoist Institutions and Post-Mao Reform

If there was ever a regime in world history that came close to totalitarianism, Mao's China was it.[1] The concept of totalitarianism had its origins in the 1930s as an ideal of fascist ideologues who were seeking a political order able to provide total organization for society. After World War II, it was refurbished as a social science concept. One of the most influential definitions defines totalitarian systems by six characteristics: a totalist ideology, a single ruling party led by a dictator, a secret police that carries out political terror, a monopoly of mass communications, a monopoly of political organizations, and monopolistic state control of the economy. The classic totalitarian systems are usually said to be Hitler's Germany, Stalin's Soviet Union, and Mao's China.[2]

Mao's Regime as Totalitarianism

The Maoist regime departed in several ways from the classic concept of totalitarianism. The police played a less important role in creating political terror than in Stalin's Soviet Union or Hitler's Germany, since terror was created mainly through the work unit. The military was a more important factor in inner-party politics, serving as a trump card in the hands of Mao Zedong, while both Hitler and Stalin relied more on the loyalty of their secret police organizations to buttress their rule and kept the military effectively out of politics. Although Mao was the dominant Chinese Communist leader and the subject of a cult of personality, his power was intermittently checked by the authority of his colleagues among the top leaders. His power was based less on personal charisma than Hitler's and Stalin's and more on a combination of personal loyalty to him among the other leaders (especially the military) and his authority as an ideologist.

Some theories of totalitarianism claim that these societies are classless, because they reduce everyone to a mass. While this may not have been true of any such system, it is surely wrong in case of Maoism, which was highly stratified in several ways: by the class status system, by the system of bureaucratic ranks, and by the social cleavages between rural and urban residents and between state and nonstate employees.

Most versions of the theory of totalitarianism pessimistically saw these systems as unchangeable. In fact, they have proven rather fragile. In China, the breakdown had already gone far in the late Mao years, due to the ideological exhaustion of the population and the rise of corruption resulting from unchecked power. The exaggeration of the permanence of this kind of regime grew out of the ideological origins of the concept, which glorified these systems as something completely new and able to remake human nature.

Still, the concept highlights well several aspects of Mao's regime:

- The broad scope of its political control—the repression of all civil society and of nearly all individual autonomy. The system of control mechanisms (units, class labels, political campaigns, the party network) added up to a unique achievement in the social technology of control. While no control system is perfect, research has turned up little in the way of gaps in the Maoist system until its late years, when it began to decline in effectiveness.
- The monolithic nature of the political system. Political authority was highly centralized in the hands of a small number of people. No political system is ever totally centralized, and in Mao's China too the central authorities had to fight continuously against bureaucratic obstacles to their programs presented by the needs and procedures of bureaucratic hierarchies and local political units. But the center had ample power to override bureaucratic priorities when it wanted to.
- The centrality within the control system of both ideological belief and terror, with the two operating in a kind of symbiosis.
- The aspiration to remake totally not only society but nature and human nature.
- The aim not only to control, but to mobilize people.

Among totalitarian systems, Maoism most closely resembled Stalinism, which is not surprising considering Maoism's origins. The common points included exploiting the countryside to industrialize and creating a sharp urban-rural gap; establishing a command economy with huge, inefficient industrial enterprises; enforcing a rigid ideological orthodoxy; and creating a cult of personality.

But Maoism differed from Stalinism in having a less developed planning system with more economic decentralization and more small and local enterprises; in developing an ideology that was more voluntarist and more utopian: in the lesser role of the police and the different sociology of terror; in the creation of the unit and class status systems, both lacking in Stalin's Soviet Union; in Mao's relation to his colleagues and subordinates, which was never as absolute or as bloodthirsty as Stalin's except in 1966–68; in the relatively greater vigor of the Party; and in the greater influence of the military in politics.

After Mao's death, some Chinese writers referred to Maoism as a form of fascism. So far as this involves the idea that Maoism was a totalitarian system that was oppressive and unjust, it is true enough. But within the broad totalitarian type, Maoism and fascism are distinguished from one another by some important differences. Maoism's ideology was Marxist, while all forms of fascism have been based on self-styled fascist ideologies that usually included a myth of racial superiority. Fascist systems relied more than Maoism did on the police, police terror, and paramilitary organizations, and less on social and party organization. The class base of fascist regimes was the petty bourgeoisie, while Maoism was an avowedly proletarian movement that came to power with peasant support and, as a regime in power, created a broad base of support among a wide range of classes it labeled "progressive." Finally, although both Maoism and fascism were industrializing regimes, fascism was based on an alliance between big capitalists and the state, rather than on a state-owned economy that did away with capitalism.

Origins of Mao's Regime

When the Chinese Communist Party came to power in 1949, the new leaders faced the need to promote rapid industrialization in a continentally huge, backward agrarian economy, by relying mostly on capital drawn from within that economy. The Maoist regime can be understood as a unique ensemble of economic, social, and political institutions that resulted from a failed effort to impose a Stalinist development model on Chinese economic and cultural reality.

To understand why the Chinese Communist leaders first tried to adopt, and then modified, the Stalinist model, one needs to analyze the circumstances the new regime faced when it came to power.

First, the government faced a threatening international environment. As the two superpower blocs emerged after World War II, China found itself located on the boundary of their spheres of influence, so that any expansion of its influence would bring it into conflict with one or both. China was surrounded by countries that feared its potential, shared more land and sea borders with other countries and political entities than any other nation, and was highly vulnerable to invasion both by land and by sea, especially given its economic backwardness.[3]

The stronger of the two blocs, led by the United States, viewed Chinese communism with firm hostility, especially after American and Chinese troops fought in the Korean War. China turned to the other bloc, led by the Soviet Union, for protection against the American threat. But the overwhelming Soviet interest was to reach an accommodation with the United States rather than to protect China. These conditions dictated that the Chinese leaders' top priority was to build up the industrial base for a strong, militarily self-reliant, and secure national defense. They sought not just economic growth, and not entry into the Western-dominated world market as an exporter, but also industrial and military self-sufficiency.

Second, the new leaders faced a threatening security situation at home. The Chinese Communist Party (CCP) had come to power by winning a civil war, yet this victory did not give the regime a strong mandate for building socialism. Rather, its civil war victory reflected the disgust of broad sectors of the population with the corrupt Nationalist Party (Kuomintang, or KMT) rule. Many sectors of the population gave only weak loyalty to the new regime or opposed it. There were local insurgencies, subversion, bandits, KMT forces in the Southwest as well as in Burma and Taiwan. Tibet was still not under Chinese control. Landlords and businessmen formed a potential opposition force. And the regime had only cool support from the intellectuals, many of whom were hoping for intellectual freedom rather than for the discipline that the CCP hoped to impose.

The third condition facing the regime was that China was a continental country with a huge and poor population, having no real alternative to self-reliant development. The Soviet Union gave substantial economic assistance, but it faced a development crisis of its own and its means were limited, so this aid was limited; and it all came in the form of loans. Western aid was out of the question, and even had this not been the case, American priorities lay in the development of Europe and to some extent Japan. China in 1949 had only a small industrial sector. The rural agrarian economy was the only conceivable source of the massive capital needed for self-reliant, rapid industrialization.

Fourth, in the late 1940s in many parts of the world, capitalism commanded little respect as a development model while Stalinist socialism was considered to have scored remarkable achievements, bringing the Soviet Union from backwardness to the status of a world-class industrial power in three decades under wartime conditions. Not only the CCP leaders, but virtually the entire Chinese intellectual class, believed that capitalism was a wasteful and unfair economic system while state planning was an equitable, rational way to direct capital to serve national needs.

So the Mao regime aligned itself with the Soviet Union in international affairs and began to impose a Soviet model on its economy and society. The model involved establishing state control over the agricultural surplus and agricultural investment by organizing the peasants into collective farms, and using the capital accumulated from agriculture to invest in a relatively small number of large, vertically integrated heavy-industrial firms and infrastructure projects.

After a few years, however, the Chinese Communists began to turn away from the Soviet model and to experiment with their own variant of Stalinism. On the international scene, the Soviet search for accommodation with the United States, beginning with Stalin and becoming more pronounced under Khrushchev, left China feeling isolated in the face of its most potent and threatening enemy, the United States. In the domestic political arena, the Chinese leaders saw the Soviet Union as trying to subvert their autonomy by building up a pro-Soviet bloc within the Chinese regime. In response, they conducted a series of purges and political campaigns to wipe out pro-Soviet forces in the party and economic structure.

Economically, the Soviet model did not work as well as the Chinese leaders expected. Soviet aid, although substantial, was limited. The early years of rapid construction created their own bottlenecks in transport, energy, construction materials, and other areas. The agricultural surplus did not increase as rapidly as the leaders expected it to. Expecting more rapid growth, the CCP leaders were disappointed and resolved to try new experiments to produce the extremely rapid economic growth that they believed was possible. These experiments led into the disastrous Great Leap Forward (1958–1960).

Finally, intellectually, the Chinese leaders began to reassess the appropriateness of the Soviet model for China. Mao took the lead in this effort, developing a critique of the Soviet model as "revisionist" and articulating a separate model he deemed more suited to China, which depended

more on human willpower, on what he called "unbalanced development," and on political mobilization. These theories undergirded both
the Great Leap and the subsequent and also disastrous Great Proletarian
Cultural Revolution (1966–69). Mao's anti-Sovietism, adopted in the
search for autonomy, went hand in hand with the search for China's own
model. China found itself in international isolation, on terms of enmity
with both superpowers, and driven even further into the need for self-
reliant economic development.

The institutions of Maoist China thus become a hybrid between the
original half-realized Stalinist pattern and various other patterns, some
drawn from the Party's Yan'an experience, some from the KMT and
Japanese traditions, some developed as experimental, on-the-spot adjustments to immediate economic or political problems. This history
explains why Maoism as a regime partially resembles and partially differs
from Stalinism.

Characteristics of Maoism

The economic structure of Maoism consisted of repressing consumption
so as to raise state-controlled investment to high levels. Its social structure
forced individuals into dependency on party secretaries in their work
units in order to enforce social conformity despite these low levels of consumption. Its political structure penetrated society to provide a high
degree of social control, and centralized power in the hands of a few
decisionmakers at the top.

In the long run, the system generated strong social cleavages that
became axes of socio-psychological tension that broke out in the violence
of the Cultural Revolution.[4] It also permitted abuses of power at both the
unit and the national levels that ultimately led to a "crisis of faith" that
provided the impetus for Deng's reforms.

Ten features characterized Mao's regime.

1. *Capital for development was drawn predominantly from the domestic economy, with little coming from foreign aid or trade.* A very high rate of accumulation (forced savings) of about 30 percent of GNP was achieved
   by repressing consumption, with investment flowing from the countryside to the cities, from agriculture to industry. Many of the
   regime's key political and social institutions were adopted in order
   to make these high accumulation rates possible. In the early years,
   the accumulation came almost exclusively from the agrarian economy, through a mechanism called the "price scissors" by which the

state purchased agricultural commodities at low prices and sold agricultural inputs and consumer goods at relatively high prices. The exploitation of countryside by city gave rise to the major and still existing social gap in China, that between rural and urban dwellers.

The accumulation strategy thus consisted of pressing peasants to minimum living standards, at or below the average standards of the 1930s. Urban living standards were also kept low, although not as low as in the rural areas. The repression of living standards became the regime's largest political liability and the key reason why Deng's reforms were necessary after Mao's death.

The commune system—Maoism's most characteristic institution—was put into place, after several years of disappointment in the rural harvest, partly in an attempt to realize quickly what the leaders believed was the potential for increases in productivity, but even more importantly to assure state control over the surplus that existed, which the leaders thought was being squirreled away by the peasants.

2. *Forced rapid industrialization focused on a small number of huge, vertically integrated state-owned factories.* Efficiency was not a criterion. Major inputs were set at low prices to encourage the growth of enterprises. This left the legacy of the need for price reform, the rock on which the reform process foundered in 1988–89.

3. *A "command" or administered economy relied neither on a well-developed plan nor on market mechanisms for coordination but responded to orders from above.* This system enabled the leaders to make successive efforts at "breakthrough development." The lack of plan or market forms of coordination encouraged village and enterprise "cellularization," excessive local autarky, self-sufficiency, and vertical integration of enterprises, and left no real alternative to breakthrough development or what Mao called "creative imbalances."

4. *Rural-urban segregation, expressed in a household registration system, forbade rural residents from changing their place of residence.* Peasants were tied to the land in order to enforce the low rural standard of living and to prevent excess rural population from flooding the cities.[5]

5. *The "unit" system tied both rural and urban residents to a work or residential unit that controlled virtually all functions of their lives.*This included jobs, education, marriage, housing, medical care, recreation, and political education.[6]

In the countryside, the key kind of unit was the commune, with its subsidiary levels of the production brigade and production team. The functions of the commune system were to achieve state control of the surplus, to mobilize excess labor for investment, to achieve social control, and to spread technological innovation. In the cities, the major kinds of units were factories, schools, offices, and neighborhood committees. The functions of these urban units were to help with political and social control and to allocate jobs, housing, medical care, and other benefits, and thus help keep down the level of consumption so that funds could be directed to investment.

Because assignment to a unit was normally for life, the system provided the political authorities virtually complete control over individuals' geographic and social mobility. Dominant and unchecked power within the unit was normally exercised by the Party Secretary.

Political terror was implemented in China not through the police but predominantly through the unit. The unit system rendered each person vulnerable to the whims of the unit Party Secretary. The class status (*chengfen*) system created a permanent class of targets, to whom others could be added by the process of giving them negative political "labels." As in other socialist systems, the use of terror grew out of the siege mentality of the regime vis-à-vis real and imagined class enemies.

6. *The class status system assigned each individual a pair of labels.* One described his or her class origin (father's class), and one describing his or her own class (normally inherited from the father). The system originally grew out of the administrative needs of land reform teams who had to take land away from landlords and rich peasants and give it to poor, middle, and rich peasants. It was extended to cities gradually during the 1950s. Originally intended to be temporary, it became fixed in place as heightened political tensions especially after the Great Leap Forward led to a search for class scapegoats.[7]

Among competitive urban young people, the "good class" vs. "bad class" cleavage became a crucial dynamic in the factional struggles of the Cultural Revolution.[8]

7. *A high level of ideological mobilization* was carried out through political campaigns, study groups, and a massive institutional system of propaganda media and political-ideological education. The regime used ideology to legitimate itself, to provide a sense of identity and solidarity to citizens, to mobilize the population, and as a language for communicating policy priorities. Some CCP leaders believed in the possibility of using ideological indoctrination to remake human nature and create a new kind of citizen who was selflessly dedicated to socialism and the national interest.

Chinese communism was characterized by a distinctive mentality, involving the personality cult of Mao, asceticism and self-denial, definition of human value in terms of political virtue, and dehumanization of the class enemy. The fervor was such that for many years most acts of political repression were not carried out by police or Party cadres but by civilians acting against one another. The Maoist ideological system began to crumble in the late 1960s and early

1970s, as a result of the ending of the Cultural Revolution, the sending down of urban youth to the countryside, and the alleged coup attempt and death of Mao's chosen successor, Lin Biao.

8. *A Leninist-style system of single-party dictatorship was closely modeled on the Soviet system.* The elite party, comprising about five percent of the population, regarded itself as the vanguard of the proletariat and of the progressive forces generally. It was motivated by a strong sense of mission and of infallibility because of its command of an ostensibly scientific ideology. The Party exercised strong internal discipline over its members: the careers of both party members and nonmembers were controlled by the party organization department and its subsidiary organs via a Soviet-style nomenklatura (the list of jobs to be filled by party appointment).

The Chinese Communist Party penetrated society even more deeply than the Soviet Communist Party. It had members in all but the lowest levels of all kinds of units, and wherever they were located, party members were the dominant people in their units. The party thus had a low level of differentiation from other power structures in the civilian sector. Since the Party was located in virtually every unit, it was able to take over the administrative functions that might otherwise have been performed through other hierarchies. The Party not only reigned but also ruled, not only led society but actually ran most units in society.

9. *The supreme leader.* Power was not only concentrated in the Party, but also within the Party was highly concentrated in the party center. At its apex, the party center consisted of at most of thirty to forty individuals who had the authority to make all major decisions. Among them power was highly personalized, uninstitutionalized, and fluid. Mao was the dominant leader. He did not have absolute power and often had to struggle for his way, but he had predominant power, thanks to his compelling ideological vision, his record of leadership successes, his political skills, and his direct and exclusive control of the military.

Mao understood little about practical economics and was suspicious of intellectuals and experts. He had enormous self-confidence and nervous energy and enjoyed conflict and crisis. Over the course of time he was able to violate with impunity party norms that called for deliberate, collective decisionmaking among the top leaders, and to push his own vision in a series of economic and political experiments that were designed to prevent China from becoming revisionist and to lead the country rapidly into communism, which Mao identified with a high level of industrial development and public-spirited devotion to the collective welfare regardless of personal interest.

10. *An autonomous army, loyal only to Mao.* The role of the army in Mao's

China was distinctive among socialist states. Although, as in other socialist states, the Chinese army had a commissar system and a system of party organizations intended to assure party control, in fact the military reported only to the Military Affairs Commission, which in turn reported only to Mao. In political crises within the leadership, this was a crucial source of Mao's power.

Deng's Reforms

Mao died in 1976, and after an interlude of political maneuvering Deng Xiaoping acquired the leading role in Chinese politics in 1978. Chinese communism under Deng could no longer be called totalitarian, because it substantially relaxed political mobilization and terror, allowed the emergence of some independent groups and institutions in the economy and among intellectuals, gave citizens more individual freedom, and to some extent limited the exercise of power and made it more predictable. But it was still not a democratic regime because of the monopoly of power in the hands of a single political party, indeed, in the hands of a few top leaders.

The processes of reform in China resembled those in other socialist states. In each case reform aimed chiefly at improving economic performance and standards of living. It brought about reduced political mobilization, relegitimation of the regime on a technocratic rather than revolutionary-utopian basis, and a change in the makeup of the elite to bring in younger, better educated, more technically competent leaders at every level.

The legacy Deng inherited from Mao's regime was an economic, social, and political crisis. Economically, the Maoist development program had produced substantial results. Industry had grown at an average rate of 11 percent a year, China was industrially self-sufficient, and between 60 and 70 percent of GNP was produced by industry and commerce. However, the new industrial system was technologically twenty to thirty years behind the West, was extremely inefficient, and faced energy and transport bottlenecks. Because the Maoist economy grew by suppressing consumption, living standards had not increased since the 1950s, and there was a widespread popular impression that the Maoist program was an economic failure.

Socially, the political campaigns of the Mao years had created a huge number of "unjust, false, and wrong cases"—instances of political persecution, criminal convictions, demotion or loss of jobs, internal exile, erroneous application of class labels, denial of access to schooling, and so on—which led to a wave of demands for redress after Mao's death. These cases probably numbered in the tens of millions, enough to create vast social pressure for reform.

Politically, the regime was no longer able to legitimize its rule by appealing to a vision of communist utopia. People had become skeptical of the Party's programs and of its right to rule. The party leaders themselves, many of them victims during the Cultural Revolution, felt the need to make changes in the system to ensure that abuses of the Party's normal collective decisionmaking processes could not occur again.

The international environment was far less threatening to Deng's regime than it had been to Mao's. Thanks to Mao's opening to the United States from 1971 onward and the changes in American foreign policy resulting from the U.S. defeat in Vietnam, China no longer regarded the United States as a serious security threat except in the special area of Taiwan, where China continued to suspect the United States of encouraging Taiwan's de facto independence. The Chinese also evaluated the Soviet threat as receding under Mikhail Gorbachev from the mid-1980s on. Deng announced that China should take advantage of what he thought would be a prolonged period of international peace to solve its internal problems.

To resolve these problems, the regime undertook far-reaching reforms in Chinese communism.[9] Deng's regime tried to reform economic institutions so as to increase living standards and efficiency; to redress the grievances of individuals who had been harmed under Mao; to create a new legitimacy based on economic performance rather than a vision of a future utopia; and to institutionalize the Party's own decisionmaking processes to improve the quality of its leadership. Deng, however, made it clear that these reforms aimed to save, not dissolve, Chinese communism. He articulated "four basic principles" that reform should never challenge: socialism, dictatorship of the proletariat, Marxism-Leninism-Mao Zedong Thought, and Communist Party leadership.

In the first ten years of reform (late 1978 to early 1989), the Deng regime changed some of the elements of the Mao system more than others.

1. *While maintaining high rates of state accumulation and investment, the authorities relaxed the price scissors.* Peasants were allowed to sell much of their crop on free markets, and the state substantially raised the prices it paid for crops it purchased from the peasants. As a result, rural living standards increased and the peasants were allowed to set up small factories or migrate to cities and towns looking for work.

2. *More autonomy was given to large, state-owned factories in an effort to increase*

their efficiency. Initial steps were taken to raise the prices of industrial inputs like energy and steel to more realistic levels and to free the prices that industrial enterprises could charge their customers. Permission was given for the development of small- and medium-sized private enterprises (some of them labeled "collective").

3. *The regime took advantage of the more relaxed international environment to pursue an "open door" policy that drew in billions of dollars of foreign trade and investment.* It endeavored to move away from the "command economy" to a version of "market socialism" in which major enterprises would remain state-owned but would operate in a market environment. The market environment in turn would be guided by the state through its control of banking, taxation, and other "economic levers." During the era of reform the transition to market socialism was not completed, and there were periodic efforts to reassert and improve planning, as well as debate over the possibility of moving beyond market socialism to a true market economy based on privatized ownership of enterprises.

4. *Rural-urban segregation was substantially eased.* Although peasants were still forbidden to move permanently into cities, they were encouraged to move to small rural towns to work in factory jobs and were allowed to look for work (usually in construction) even in big cities.

5. *The "unit" system was virtually dissolved in the rural areas with the demise of the communes.* In the cities, it remained substantially in place except for self-employed entrepreneurs and workers in private enterprises. But the hold of urban units on their members was somewhat weakened by the decline of ideology and the rise of an embryonic labor market that gave people at least a possibility of switching to different jobs.

With the decline of both the unit and ideology, political terror greatly decreased. People were still punished for political deviance, and some leading dissidents, such as Wei Jingsheng, were jailed for long terms. But campaigns of political persecution within units fizzled out because neither party secretaries nor unit members were willing to disrupt normal routines for values that were no longer widely believed.

6. *The class status system was abandoned.*

7. *The regime continued its efforts at political education through political campaigns, study groups, and the propaganda media.* It no longer demanded a high level of participation from ordinary people, however. The regime tolerated people's opting out of politics to pursue private concerns, and it increasingly allowed intellectuals inside and outside the Party to debate sensitive issues publicly, although within limits. The goal of reforming human nature was pushed off into the distant future, and various philosophical and policy issues that had

been regarded as closed were reopened for discussion.

8. *The Leninist-style system of party dictatorship, constituting perhaps the most essential of Deng's four basic principles, was carefully maintained.* Reforms were made, however, to institutionalize the Party's internal procedures and to limit its interference in the work of government organs and economic enterprises.

9. *Deng Xiaoping tried to avoid becoming another Mao.* He restricted himself to relatively modest official posts (vice-premier, chairman of the Party's Central Advisory Commission, chairman of the Military Affairs Commission) and promoting others to the key posts of Party General Secretary and Prime Minister. Yet Deng never managed to shake the essentially personal nature of power in the CCP top command. Until his final illness he remained the supreme leader whose assent was needed for all crucial decisions, although he shared power somewhat more than Mao did with other senior leaders.

   Deng was not much more of an economist than Mao, but his instincts were pragmatic. In guiding the reform, he encouraged subordinates like Zhao Ziyang to present policy proposals formulated by experts from specialized institutes. But the advice of the experts often conflicted, and Deng often made compromise decisions in order to maintain a consensus among senior party figures, including both those in office and those formally retired. Because of these factors, the reform unfolded in an experimental, inconsistent way. It went furthest in the countryside, remained a mixed success in the urban economy, and made relatively few inroads into the structure of the Party.

10. *Under Deng, the army remained largely independent.* It reported directly to Deng as chairman of the Military Affairs Commission. The military accepted cuts in its budget and manpower in return for substantial modernization of arms and training. It proved its loyalty to the party elders in the operations of May and June 1989, putting down the democracy movement that almost toppled Deng's regime.

Deng's Regime as a Postmobilization Authoritarian Regime

China's evolution under Deng is well explained by the theory of post-mobilizational regimes developed by Richard Lowenthal, Chalmers Johnson, and others.[10] The theory argues that communist systems in their early phases are modernizing regimes that rely on mass political mobilization and state control of the economy to achieve industrialization. But such regimes cannot maintain a high state of revolutionary tension indefinitely. People become exhausted, and disappointed in the failure to realize the utopian vision. At the same time, the regime's success in creating modern, large-scale industry requires it to adopt more sophisticated economic structures, to rely more on technocrats, to adopt regular procedures and rational regulations, and to create a less politicized, more meritocratic and liberal society. Modernization thus imposes its own dynamic on the mobilization regime, ushering it into the "postmobilization phase" or phase of "mature communism."

What this theory failed to predict was that mature communist systems would prove to be as unstable as they were. In Eastern Europe in 1989, most of the postmobilizational Communist regimes collapsed. In China, Deng's regime confronted a series of crises. Economically, although the reforms succeeded in improving both living standards and economic performance, they failed to solve the key problem of the inefficiency of state enterprises. Meanwhile they generated both inflation and corruption, which aroused popular opposition.

Politically, people—especially urban residents, and among them particularly students and intellectuals—proved unwilling to settle for the limited political freedoms and rights they were granted under reform communism. After the repression of the Mao years, a desire for intellectual and political freedom became a political force of its own. In the spring of 1989, political demonstrations to commemorate the popular leader Hu Yaobang snowballed into a massive and prolonged nationwide urban movement that threatened the existence of the regime. This movement was crushed in June with military force.

The events of 1989 signaled that the legitimacy crisis inherited from Mao's regime could not be solved without fundamental political change. Deng and his senior colleagues had been unwilling to break with the most fundamental political characteristics of the old regime, partly because they were themselves of Mao's generation. Under the slogan of "socialism with Chinese characteristics," they looked for new solutions that would preserve the monopolistic authority of the Party. As it turned out, the regime could stabilize itself only temporarily by improving economic performance, but a legitimacy based solely on economic performance evaporated when performance faltered.

Most analysts had assumed that postmobilizational authoritarian regimes would stabilize themselves short of making a transition to democracy. In retrospect it appeared that analysts had underestimated the fragility of these regimes, overlooked internal forces that threatened their existence, and failed to investigate their possible paths of development after the phase of reform communism.

5

Chinese Democracy: The Lessons of Failure

China's experiments with democracy in this century have been few in number, short in duration, and limited in their democratic characteristics. Democratic institutions malfunctioned in numerous ways. Nine sets of causes for the failure of Chinese democracy can be suggested: ideology, internal and external war, military intervention, Chinese political culture, underdevelopment, a peasant mass, flaws in the design of Chinese constitutions, moral failures by democratic politicians, or the lack of transactional benefits for military-based elites in the process of democratic transition. Each of these factors is reviewed critically with an eye to its possible lessons.

In the summer of 1915 former Columbia political science professor Frank J. Goodnow wrote an essay for Chinese President Yuan Shikai exploring what kind of political system was best suited to Chinese conditions. "It is of course not susceptible of doubt that a monarchy is better suited than a republic to China," Goodnow wrote. "China's history and traditions, her social and economic conditions, her relations with foreign powers all make it probable that the country would develop . . . constitutional government . . . more easily as a monarchy than as a republic."[1] Goodnow's advice proved disastrous. Yuan made an abortive, and for him personally fatal, bid for the throne. Goodnow went down in history as a reactionary. Yet on their face, the failed experiments of the next 80 years showed Goodnow's concerns to have been justified.

But I shall argue that the lessons of the past are more ambiguous than they seem on the surface. Although my analytical categories are similar to Goodnow's, my conclusions are different.

Democracy in its most generally accepted sense has never actually been tried in China. Minimally, democracy means open, competitive elections under universal franchise for occupants of those posts where actual policy decisions are made, together with the enjoyment of the freedoms of organization and speech (including publication) needed to enable self-generated political groups to compete effectively in these elections.[2] Before Taiwan's 1996 presidential election, China never had a chief executive elected by direct popular vote. Until 1992 in Taiwan, it never had a national legislature elected by direct, universal franchise. Except for Taiwan since 1989, there has never been more than one strong political party running in an election. And, again with the exception of Taiwan since 1992, speech and organization have never been free of serious restriction.[3]

When we speak of democratic experiments in modern China we have in mind two things: efforts to establish legislatures that were chosen in relatively open, competitive elections, and that tried to exercise their constitutional powers; and efforts to establish freedoms of speech and organization. We can refer to these two kinds of efforts as the electoral and the liberal dimensions of democracy. When we speak of democratic failures, we mean that elected legislatures were unable to exercise the authority they were supposed to enjoy under the constitution and the laws; and that freedoms of organization and expression were subject to such severe limits, either legally or extra-legally, that they could not be used with much effect in political competition.

Specifically, China's main democratic experiments (leaving aside Taiwan) and their failures have been as follows:

1. In 1909, provincial assemblies were elected in all Chinese provinces, and in 1910 the Qing government convened a National Assembly half of whose 200 members were appointed by the court and half of whom were elected from the provincial assemblies. The franchise was limited to less than one-half percent of the population. The freedoms of organization and speech were limited in law, although they were fairly extensive in practice. Only the legislatures were elected, not the executive, and the legislatures were granted limited, essentially advisory, powers. These institutions were ineffective while in office and lasted for a short time, falling with the dynasty.

2. In 1912–1913 a Parliament was elected, consisting of a Senate elected by the provincial assemblies and a House directly elected by an all-male, economically elite franchise consisting of about 10.5% of the population. The election was attended with much corruption. The parliament had considerable powers on paper, including

the power to elect the president and confirm the cabinet. However, in practice the parliament was weak; the entire central government exercised little power. The constitutional system was interrupted twice by coups aimed at restoring the empire.

3. In 1918, a new parliament was elected which lasted until 1923. Again, the election, based on a limited franchise, was marked by corruption, and the powers of parliament were exercised weakly and intermittently, also with much corruption.

4. The "May Fourth" era of relative freedom of the press, political organization, and academic investigation and debate, dating roughly from 1912 to 1937, constituted another phase of democratic experimentation in the early Republic, aside from the elections just reviewed. The era of liberalism occurred more because of the weakness of government repression than because of a firm legal and customary basis for political freedoms, although these freedoms were listed in Chinese constitutions at the time.

5. In 1947–48, the National Government held elections in those areas it controlled for National Assembly, Legislative Yuan, and Control Yuan. Suffrage was universal, but due to wartime conditions and Kuomintang dominance of politics, the elections were neither complete nor competitive. Under the quasi-Leninist system of one-party dominance, these institutions did not begin to exercise their constitutional powers until recent years in Taiwan.

6. The People's Congress system of the PRC, which was put into effect in 1954, has democratic elements on paper, including universal suffrage, direct election since 1979 of the lower two levels of the four-level hierarchy of congresses, and constitutional powers for the legislature amounting to parliamentary supremacy. But the people's congresses have never exercised their powers in practice.

In sum, the democratic experiments were few in number, short in duration, and limited in their democratic characteristics. The democratic experiments were not robust on the electoral dimension after 1918, and on the liberalism dimension after 1937.

Democratic institutions malfunctioned in numerous ways. Elections were corrupt, parliaments were factionalized, the free press was irresponsible, political groups were unprincipled. Political actors outside these institutions refused to accept the outcomes of elections, did not obey laws passed by legislatures, and did not respect the legal freedoms of the free press or the organizational rights of legally constituted organizations. At base, the failure of democracy consisted in a failure of democratic institutions to acquire authority, or in Samuel Huntington's phrase, to become institutionalized.

To draw the lessons of failure, we need to know its causes. This is difficult because the causes were numerous and interactive. The saying that "Failure is an orphan, success has many fathers" applies well enough to political practice, but it often has to be reversed in political analysis. In politics as in biology, psychology, and engineering, failure is often overdetermined. It is impossible to identify distinct effects of each cause or to measure the relative importance of interacting causes. Moreover, the causes of failure exist on at least three analytical levels and thus potentially provide lessons of three types. Some involve conditions that democratic activists can do little to change. Others concern institutional arrangements that democrats might have a hand in affecting. Still others concern the democrats' strategy and tactics.

Nine sets of causes for the failure of modern Chinese democracy have been or can be suggested, each with its own possible lessons.

1. *Ideology*. Democracy in the sense in which we have defined it has not constituted the mainstream of modern Chinese political ideology. Almost every political movement tried to garb itself in the mystique of democracy, but what they usually had in mind by democracy was a mystical solidarity of state and people, in fact a kind of authoritarianism. The more powerful a political movement was, the less it looked to democracy for solutions to China's problems. One reason, then, for the failure of democracy was that most Chinese were not convinced it was the answer for China.

The implications of this lesson for today are not necessarily discouraging. The ideological landscape has changed enormously in the last twenty years. Since the Lin Biao incident of 1971, more and more Chinese have been rethinking the reasons for China's political misfortunes. By the time of the Democracy Movement in 1978–79, a small minority had groped their way toward a belief in pluralistic democracy as the kind of political system that could provide responsible and effective government. By the spring of 1989, this belief, in however vague a form, had spread to a wide section of at least the urban public.

Since its beginnings in the Tiananmen Incident of April 5, 1976, the contemporary democratic movement has been rhetorically effective in deploying the regime's democratic pretensions against it. Although this may have helped mobilize some support in society, it has proven a thin shield against repression. Strong voices within the ruling party have used Marxism-Leninism as a framework for arguing for press freedom and political competition. Many of these advocates have been expelled from the Party during periods of repression, but it appears that many who remain in the Party have been influenced by their arguments. Meanwhile, members of the Democratic Movement overseas are now exploring the relevance of human rights and political pluralism to China's cultural tradition and developmental needs. In Taiwan, democratic elements in the official ideology have proven robust and expandable, when called upon by both opposition and ruling party to justify and to some extent shape the transition toward democracy. A similar development of ideology might be possible in mainland China.

However, ideology alone cannot make democracy succeed. Democratic institutions have to prove themselves effective in solving China's problems in order to survive, or their attractiveness will remain only theoretical In this sense, ideology today provides a permissive environment for democratic institutionalization, but it does not guarantee success.

2. *National Security Problems.* Democratic institutions repeatedly failed in the face of internal or external war. Even when China was not actually fighting a war, its leaders and people perceived national security as severely threatened, by all the Powers in the 1910s and 1920s, by Japan in the late 1920s through the 1940s, by the United States in the 1950s, by the two nuclear-armed superpowers in the 1960s, and by the Soviet Union until the mid-1980s. Democracies seem able to wage foreign wars effectively, and can sometimes survive civil wars, but the Chinese experience confirms the often-drawn conclusion that war is not a conducive environment for building democratic institutions.

The implications of this lesson for Chinese democrats today are encouraging. China faces the most peaceful, unthreatening international environment it has enjoyed in a century and a half, with little prospect that it will be disrupted. Civil disorder is a possibility and a succession struggle among leadership factions a near certainty, but civil war is unlikely to occur. No group can mount a civil war so long as the military remains united, and military breakdown is unlikely for a number of reasons to be discussed below.

Chinese democrats, however, can do little to affect the international or domestic security environments, at least until they take power and establish strong democratic institutions. So the lesson of the past in this respect, while encouraging, is not particularly practical.

3. *Militarism.* The Chinese experience at several points supports the widely accepted view that military intervention in politics undercuts democracy by undermining civilian authority. The failures of several of the early democratic experiments were linked to military coups and warlordism. The failure of democracy under the Kuomintang coincided

with Chiang Kai-shek's increasing reliance the military as the basis of his regime. The lesson is less obvious in the case of post-1949 China, where the conventional wisdom has it that "the party controlled the gun." In fact, Mao's power was based to an important degree on his exclusive control of the Chinese military machine through his chairmanship of the central Military Affairs Commission, so that his was also a sort of quasi-military regime.

Many believe that a military coup or a recurrence of regional militarism is a possibility today. My reading of the tea leaves is different. First, China lacks a Latin American-type tradition of military rule, or "guarantism," which would make coup legitimate in the eyes of the people, the civilian leaders and bureaucrats, or in the eyes of the military itself. Second, Chinese military people appear reluctant to take responsibility for solving China's political and economic problems since they do not believe they have solutions for them. Third, the enormous size of the Chinese officer corps would make it difficult to coordinate a coup without leaks and intra-military opposition. A military coup would benefit some commanders—probably certain department heads in the central Military Affairs Commission and the Beijing Garrison Commander and Beijing Military Region commander—more than others, creating jealousy among those left out, who might even be more senior and command larger forces than the members of the coup coalition.

Fourth, historically one of the factors facilitating regional militarism was the existence of foreign spheres of interest. Contrary to popular images, the Western powers were not opposed to democratic institutions in Republican China, did not take direct steps to frustrate them, and gave but slight support to the warlords. In fact, the foreign powers offered consistent diplomatic recognition to China's successive central governments and provided important financial support through loans and the customs and salt revenues. Still, the foreign presence helped warlords even if only marginally by arms sales, by providing the occasional haven of the foreign concessions, and by whatever it contributed to the weakness of the central government. This historical element, of course, is absent today.

Finally, the most important factor militating against a coup is that the PLA already exercises strong influence on central party politics through its direct representatives among the Elders and in the Politburo. In the past, the military's interests were represented by leaders like Mao, Lin Biao, and Ye Jianying, whose roots were as much in the military as in the Party. In this way, the military was able to have its say without directly taking power, as in the arrest of the Gang of Four and the fall of Hu Yaobang and Zhao Ziyang. This tradition was carried on by Deng and Yang Shangkun. Since Deng's death, the military no longer has senior leaders, whose careers have followed a dual military and civilian track, who can wear two hats as central party leaders and representatives of military interests. But instead of directly taking power, future military and party leaders will probably agree on some senior officers who can formally or informally enter the highest levels of government to represent military interests.

What are those interests? Given its national security mission and the increasing professionalization of the military, the officer corps appears to give priority to political stability, economic development, and the technical upgrading of the economy. The officers probably disagree about how to achieve these goals, but younger officers seem to favor following reform wherever it leads, even if it involves abandoning traditional ideas of socialism. If democratization could promote stability and reform, they would have no reason to oppose it.

The lesson of history, then, is that democrats must find ways to keep the military out of politics. But the strongest force for achieving this will be the vigor and legitimacy of civilian political institutions, whether democratic or not. This again is a lesson that provides no direct guide to action, but that also offers no reason to be discouraged.

4. *Political Culture.* It is often argued that Chinese political culture is inhospitable to democracy. Lucian Pye, for example, has argued that Chinese political culture embodies an intolerance for conflict, a yearning for authority, and a stress on personal loyalty that all lead to factionalism, which in turn destroys the functioning of democratic institutions.[4] It is a view widely held among Chinese democrats themselves.

This is a difficult argument to evaluate historically. Without direct data to tell us what the political culture of the past was, we can only infer culture from historical behavior (including written texts). But this makes the argument that culture causes action circular, because culture and action are measured by the same evidence.

But the more we learn about late-nineteenth and early-twentieth-century Chinese political behavior the less warranted seems the argument that Chinese of any class were culturally unable to organize self-interested action in an open, competitive public sphere.[5] It is true that democracy failed, but it is fallacious to attribute the failure to culture. One could equally well argue that culture is in good part the product of institutions.[6] When institutions do not work, they produce a culture of despair. If elections do not count because important issues are not raised or because elected officials have no power, people will not go to the trouble of voting seriously. If a legislature has no power, legislators will not treat their jobs seriously. If earlier democrats had been able to institutionalize democracy, a more democratic political culture would have been engendered. Working to change culture, then, is not necessarily the most cost-efficient way to institutionalize democracy and may even be the wrong way.

In any case, China's political culture today is different from what it was earlier in this century. Thanks to economic and social development (further discussed below), the spread of mass education and the mass media, as well as the deep social penetration of Chinese political institutions and the broad social impact of government policies in China, politics have become more salient to the average Chinese citizen than they were before, and citizens are better informed and more interested. Because of the experiences of the Cultural Revolution, which affected virtually every Chinese family, easy acceptance of authority is less widespread than it was before. Circumstantial evidence and preliminary survey data suggest that at least some of the characteristics of a democratic political culture—perception of the salience of government, belief in one's own ability to understand and affect government, tolerance of different opinions—are more widespread in China today than they seem to have been historically.[7]

Until they take power, it is difficult for democrats to do much about culture except talk about it. Thus we confront another lesson that offers little guidance for practical action, although it also gives democrats no reason to be discouraged.

5. *Underdevelopment.* It is well-established that the level of development affects a country's ability to practice democracy. The theory is disputed, the minimum level of development needed for democracy is ill-defined and probably not very high, and the development-democracy relationship may not be a direct or linear one. But until recently, China was so poor and underdeveloped that the theory in its most brutal form probably did explain much of China's difficulty in establishing democratic institutions. But its explanatory power for the past is limited, and its predictive power for the future is nearly nil.

The most obvious relationship is that the majority of the population was too ill-educated and poverty-stricken to take an interest in politics. Whatever democracy existed was thus elite democracy. But this consideration cannot explain the failure of the early Republic's limited-franchise institutions to function well or to become institutionalized. Historically elite democracy in many countries was a step toward full democracy because it allowed competitive institutions to become established before mass participation began.

A second argument involving underdevelopment is that an underdeveloped country faces urgent developmental problems, which do not brook the disunity and slowness of democratic policymaking. The argument for developmental dictatorship was used as an ideological rationale, and may have been to some extent a real motive, for both the Nationalist and the Communist regimes in limiting democracy. But in fact, dictatorships cost more in famines and ecological disasters than they gain in development. The estimated 50 million Chinese dead at the hands of their own governments in this century (not counting the 27 million killed by the government-caused famine of 1958–61) testify to this fact.[8]

A third argument relates underdevelopment to the weakness of civil society. To some extent democracy depends on the existence of independent social forces and groups that demand access to policymaking, and that have enough financial and other power to force the state to respect the rules that grant them this access. In this view, democracy gets institutionalized when there are social forces that have an interest in defending democratic procedures. In a backward society these forces are weak. This argument applies well to late Qing and Republican China. Civil society was not absent in those years, but it was relatively weak compared to the countries where democracy established itself.

Whatever the force of these three developmental arguments in explaining past problems, socioeconomic development in China is far more advanced today. China's GNP per capita places it already above the minimum level at which democracy has been reasonably successfully practiced in some other nations. And because of low prices of housing, basic foods, and medical care, GNP per capita figures understate the average level of welfare in China. A more meaningful measure of development is the Human Development Index developed by the U.N. Development Program. By this index, China ranks in the middle level of countries, along with many that practice democracy.[9] Since development is thought to impact on democracy via such mediating factors as geographic mobility, mass media reach, organizational and economic participation, and political information, political interest and other public attitudes, this measure of development is more relevant to political analysis than straightforward GNP per capita figures.

Here is still another lesson from the past that offers little guide to practical action by democrats, since they, like other Chinese, are already committed to development as a goal, aside from whatever impetus it may lend to democratization. Our reflections on this variable once again suggest, however, that at least the failures of the past are not a premonition of what will happen in the future.

6. *Peasant mass.* Some Chinese argue that it is difficult or impossible to build democracy in a society with a peasant mass. This argument is often simply a restatement of theories we have already considered: either the theory that Chinese political culture, here seen as a peasant culture, is inhospitable to democracy; or the argument that developmental backwardness, seen as a feature of a peasant society, is adverse to democracy. Sometimes, however, the peasant society argument has a distinct meaning—that peasants, as a majority social group, if given the chance to vote, will vote against liberalism, cosmopolitanism, and competitive institutions, and will use their democratic access to reinstall dictatorship. The argument is that the peasants are anti-city, anti-foreign, anti-intellectual, and authoritarian.

This argument is difficult to defend. Several functioning democracies have large peasant populations. In modern Chinese history, the peasant masses had little to do with failure of democracy. Moreover, the Chinese peasants today are more modernized, literate, urbanized, mobile, industrialized, and cosmopolitan than the proponents of this theory give them credit for. It is more appropriate to call them farmers than peasants.[10] Chinese farmers have proven capable of operating simple democratic institutions at the village and township level. They have considerable access to mass media, are sophisticated about market opportunities nationwide, and understand well the impact of national policies on their immediate interests. It seems likely that if Chinese farmers had the chance to vote in meaningful elections, they would vote a well-informed version of their interests.

There are, to be sure, contradictions between rural and urban Chinese residents in their economic and political interests. The impact of democratizing the system so that peasants can affect policy will be adverse to some urban interests. Chinese democrats, who are overwhelmingly urbanites, may fear this. But the fact that farmers have strong policy interests constitutes a favorable condition for institutionalizing democracy, not an unfavorable one. The lesson of these reflections is that democrats must be prepared to see other social groups benefit from the opening of the political system that they alone are currently pushing.[11] Democratization will not hand control over policy to the proponents of democracy.

7. *Flaws in the constitutions/institutions.* One might argue that earlier Chinese constitutions failed because they were ill–designed. I do not reject this argument in principle, but for most Chinese constitutions it is impossible to sustain it on the basis of the historical record. Political conflicts that ended in the failure of democratic experiments usually took two forms: either struggles among parliament, cabinet, and president, or subversion of constitutional principles by military- or party-based dictatorship.

The Provisional Constitution of 1912, under which most government business was conducted from that year until 1923, was criticized for ambiguity that permitted conflicts among the branches of government to develop. But the other failures did not seem to arise from constitutionally engendered paralysis, but rather from politicians ignoring and circumventing the constitution.

In fact, China's major constitutions all seem to have been fairly good ones, although they were quite different from one another. The constitutions of 1923 and 1946 have been especially praised by legal scholars. The 1923 constitution was never really put into effect because the government that promulgated it was almost immediately overthrown. The 1946 constitution proved to have had some remarkable strengths in Taiwan; the reform so far has done away with the Temporary Provisions that were added to it and changed the method of presidential election, although discussions have been initiated about altering the five yuan structure and the method of presidential election and clarifying the relationship of presidential and cabinet power. The PRC constitutions of 1954 and 1982, which are quite different from the 1923 and 1946 constitutions but similar to one another, offer on paper a workable set of institutions for moving China toward democracy: a series of four levels of people's congresses from the local to the national level, exercising popular sovereignty. What has undermined the democratic potential of these constitutions is domination by the CCP.

The lesson for democrats today is that China's constitutional tradition offers as good a starting point as any for building democratic institutions. No conspicuous mistake made in the past stands as a guidepost to what should be avoided. Since none of the previous Chinese constitutions experimented with federalism or with judicial review, we have no reason to conclude either that these institutions would not work, or that they are needed. As a practical matter, it may be most realistic to build democracy on the existing PRC constitution, with its provisions for NPC supremacy and its strong rights articles. But history offers no lessons as to what kind of constitution is definitely unsuited to China, or which constitutional arrangements are most suited to China in the abstract. Constitutionalism of whatever sort has not yet really been tried beyond Taiwan.

8. *Moral failures of the democrats.* Many Chinese historians write as if China's democratic experiments failed because the participants abused the process. Analogously, many democrats argue today that the democratic movement is weak because of the failure of its members to unite, to handle funds well, to establish an attractive image, and so on. But this moral argument is like the political culture argument on a smaller scale: it is hard to distinguish preexisting moral weakness from the behavior induced by being placed in institutions that do not work. In fact, some of the behavior deemed to be moral failure would be good, competitive, democratic behavior within working democratic institutions.

In reflecting on this purported lesson of history, one is caught between two irreconcilable truths. On the one hand, to paraphrase Rousseau, if democratic institutions are to function well, they have to take human beings as they are and not as they ought to be. On the other, pervasive moral degeneration can undermine any system of political institutions. The mystery is that when institutions work, they work morally as well as in other ways, and when they fail, they fail in many ways at once, including morally. The fact that moral failure is part of general failure does not mean that moral exhortation is an effective avenue to institution building.

Not only is this lesson of history ambiguous, but its practical implications are once again unactionable. Moral behavior can be wished for, asked for, and encouraged by mechanisms of reward and oversight, but it hardly seems a viable point of access to the problem of democratic institution-building.

9. *Elite transactions theory.*[12] This body of theory works at a different level of analysis from those discussed so far. It concerns not environing conditions for democracy, but the ways in which the success or failure of institutions come about through the interactions of political elites, operating in pursuit of what we assume they perceive as their political interests. This approach leads us to look at faction leaders, militarists, Yuan Shikai, Chiang Kai-shek, Mao and other major actors, to see where they thought their political interests lay, and try to figure out why they behaved as they did.

This line of thought leads to something like the following formulation. China was an empire that broke up, leaving in place military elites and civilian elites with power bases in the relatively weak, localized, civil society. Since the empire did not evolve but broke down, there were no rules of the game in place. Democratic experiments represented an initial consensus that seemed attractive because of the prestige of the Western model, which military elites thought they could adopt to legitimate their rule, and which civilian elites hoped to use to gain a greater share of power. However, once these institutions were in place, military-based elites did not see benefit in sharing power with electorally based elites, who lacked sufficient financial or other resources to compel such power sharing.

The lessons of this line of analysis are familiar from the literature on democratic regime transitions. Democracy will be firmer if it evolves from the current system rather than being set up on the shards of a broken system. It will be better established if it evolves gradually. It can become institutionalized if it serves the interests of all or most of the powerful social and political forces in the society. Its survival will be helped by moderate, compromise-oriented leadership. Once again, these lessons are hard for democrats to put to use in practical politics for the time being, because for now and in the foreseeable future the fate of Chinese politics depends on many large forces that they do not control.

Our investigation has proven inconclusive. Democracy did not work, but it is hard to disentangle specific reasons why. We have explored a list of possible lessons. Were the earlier failures due to wrong institutions, to wrong leadership, to insufficient civil society, to foreign intervention, to problems of political culture? But the nature of history is so complex that it does not permit us to identify a single or a small number of key causes of democracy's failure. Democracy failed across a broad front.

History does, however, give Chinese democrats reasons for courage. In the past few Chinese really wanted democracy. Today many of them do. In earlier years, authoritarianism seemed more likely to solve China's pressing problems—weakness and division. Today, democracy seems more likely to solve the pressing problems—dictatorship and political stagnation. In the past, political institutions lacked authority and administrative capability. Today the Chinese bureaucracy is large and strong. The regime's legitimacy is compromised, but many of its institutional procedures seem well-accepted. The situation, then, is different, and more favorable to democracy. History does not promise that democracy will work if tried, but neither does it warrant the conclusion that past failures prove China to be unsuited for democracy. Unfortunately, however, the historical record is not generous with practical guidance to democrats on how to bring about a transition to democracy or how to make it work once it begins to take shape.

6

The Democratic Vision

From China a friend elliptically writes, so as to avoid alarming the postal censor, "I remember what you said in your letter of June 1989 about 'I still believe that in the long run. . . .' I think you were right because I myself still believe that in the long run. . . ." Scholars in China privately continue projects that were canceled after the crackdown, believing that their recommendations on political reform will be heeded later. Local party officials around the country make fun of the latest campaign to emulate a revolutionary model hero. A university refuses to turn in students who participated in the democracy demonstrations.

The Chinese, in short, are outwaiting their rulers. In 1988 the controversial television series *River Elegy* likened Chinese civilization to the stagnant Yellow River that must find its way to the cosmopolitan blue sea. Today the Chinese Communist Party is no longer the river god that it once was, able to turn back the current. It issues directives on vigilance against foreign ideological subversion, but they are like paper boats that face upstream and float downstream. China is finally joining the world—economically, culturally, and politically. It will, eventually, become a democracy. But of what sort? New documentation on the movement for democracy that stirred the world in 1989, in the volumes published by M. E. Sharpe, provides a clearer idea of what the movement stood for, of its limits, of its prospects.[1] And the views of three of China's most influential prodemocracy intellectuals can now be read in English.[2]

Fang Lizhi, a physicist and academic administrator, was expelled from the Chinese Communist Party in 1987 because his campus speeches in favor of academic freedom were deemed largely responsible for the stu-

dent demonstrations of December 1986 and January 1987. Fang's continued criticisms of the regime helped create the atmosphere for the
movement of spring 1989. Although he played no direct role in it, the
government was poised to arrest him as a "backstage manipulator" when
he took refuge in the American Embassy in Beijing. He was released after
about a year, and is now conducting his research in the United States.

Yan Jiaqi, founder and former head of the official Institute of Political
Science in Beijing, was a high-level political adviser to reformist Party
Secretary Zhao Ziyang when the democracy movement broke out. He
tried to encourage the government to accede to the demands of the students for dialogue. When this failed, he sided with the demonstrators
and had to flee China after the crackdown. He now lives in New York.

Wang Ruowang is a senior Shanghai writer. Although relatively little
known in the West, he was important enough to share the distinction
with Fang and the journalist Liu Binyan of being among the first victims
of Deng Xiaoping's purges in January 1987. (Only one prominent intellectual, Ruan Ming, now at Princeton, had been expelled earlier under
Deng for dissidence. Scores, of course, were purged subsequently.) Wang
had already been expelled once before, during the anti-rightist movement of 1957. In both cases, his crime was writing honestly. He, too, now
lives in New York.

China is one of the great world civilizations, but one whose integration
with modern international culture has been most protracted and
painful. It is engaging it slowly and on its own terms. It will eventually produce a version of that culture that is distinctively its own. What Chinese
culture will look like is partly visible in Taiwan and Hong Kong, but the
mainland is much vaster and internally more diverse. It is likely to
Westernize less. The shape of Chinese democracy is not easy to detect
from the universal-sounding slogans—science, democracy, human
rights—that its advocates employ. The sameness of language, itself a phenomenon of the international culture, masks significant differences in
assumptions and values.

Considering the national scope of the 1989 movement, we generalize
about its meaning at risk. There were not scores of localities where
demonstrations occurred, there were hundreds. Except for the Sichuan
city of Chengdu, about which both *The New York Times* and Amnesty
International reported, almost nothing is known about any location
beyond the ten described in *The Pro-Democracy Protests in China*. All of
these are big cities, except for one small town in Hunan province whose
story Anita Chan uncovered through interviews in Hong Kong. The

reports give some sense of variation. In Chan's small town, a local school-teacher advocated direct elections of central government leaders, a proposal not heard in Beijing so far as I know. In Xi'an, as reported by Joseph Esherick, a mixed crowd of demonstrators became unruly in a way that did not happen in Beijing, where the students by and large kept the movement under tighter control. In tropical Fujian, obsessed with business across the Taiwan Strait, as Mary S. Erbaugh and Richard Kraus report, the demonstrations were low-keyed, and the demands even vaguer than in Beijing.

In Beijing itself, as the Australian scholar Geremie Barmé observes about the Beijing scene of May and June 1989, there was predominantly a movement of intellectuals (a term that in China includes college students). Barmé saw a cohort of writers who "had draped ribbons across their chests like contestants in a beauty pageant and had written on them their names and most famous works." Demonstrators in Tiananmen Square collected autographs from the most famous student leaders and from any foreigner whatsoever, including Harrison Salisbury (who, Barmé devastatingly notes, was under the illusion that they wanted his signature because they admired his book on the Long March). As the hunger strike dragged on, and martial law signaled the hardening of the official position, students dreamed of dying in the poses of the revolutionary heroes immortalized on the Monument to Revolutionary Martyrs where they were gathered. Floral offerings were placed on a makeshift altar before an immobilized bus that sheltered the students who refused food and water. The hours that they had fasted were posted on the side of the bus.

Other social groups were more or less rigorously excluded by the student leaders. Esherick tells of young men from the countryside who joined the crowds in Xi'an, and the same thing must have happened elsewhere, since the Chinese cities are full of young men from the villages looking for work. Still, we have little sense of how deeply into the countryside the movement penetrated, or what the peasants thought. No peasant organizations are known to have been formed. To differing degrees in different places, the demonstrations were joined by workers and *getihu*—the new class of small-scale individual entrepreneurs spawned by the reforms. Lawrence Sullivan, in Tony Saich's collection, refers to these forces as an emergent civil society; but they do not yet have the level of coherence and social autonomy that that term implies.

The intellectuals tried to limit the agenda to their own issues of freedom of speech and dialogue with the government. Frank Niming explains the exclusion of other social groups as one of several expedients that demonstrators adopted to avoid provoking the government. They kept the focus initially on mourning for Hu Yaobang, a leader symbolizing not opposition to communism but the good side of communism, and later they shifted to the equally mom-and-apple-pie question of the health of young, hunger-striking students. They preferred nonstudents to play the role of supportive bystanders rather than the more confrontational role of demonstrators. When nonstudents did demonstrate, moreover, they marched mostly in formation with their work units rather than as a mass of individuals, again signaling the lack of challenge to the social order. As one wall poster said, the Party is like a donkey, which should be prodded to move forward but not poked so hard that it kicks.

Barmé notes that although some of the lower-class demonstrators referred to themselves as *shimin*, as urbanites or "civilians," a term that is still fairly new in China, the intellectuals continued to call them by the old communist terms "masses" and "common people." In view of all this, Erbaugh and Kraus charge that the democracy movement was "an elitist movement." In Fujian, they say, many of the activists seemed to equate democracy with little more than the recruitment of educated people into government on the basis of merit rather than political connections. As Yan Jiaqi's editors David Bachman and Dali Yang put it, the intellectuals have accepted the "self-defined mission of saving China," intending not to distribute power but to exercise it. The intellectuals in sum, want democracy without the demos.

This charge draws support from the fact that the theory of "new authoritarianism" continues to be actively promoted by some among the democrats now in exile. One section of Michel Oksenberg and Marc Lambert's collection is devoted to documents that illustrate this theory, which was originally associated with thinkers around Zhao Ziyang and endorsed by Deng Xiaoping. Its proponents argue that China can move toward democracy only by passing through a phase of authoritarianism, during which painful economic and political reforms will be accomplished by strong-arm methods. Such authoritarianism would be "new" because its goal would be democracy. Many analysts have concluded that the theory was a tool in Zhao's bid for greater power in the Deng regime, but its persistence in China and among the exiles suggests that it draws on a deeper ambivalence among the intellectuals about democracy.

When the transition to democracy in China starts, the other social classes will face a long struggle to establish their place in it. And they will be further impeded by the fact that China's democrats have devoted little effort to designing the institutions of a democratic China. Among the numerous wall posters, speeches, and poems in *Cries for Democracy,* one finds almost no discussion of electoral systems, of the division of powers, of the role of parties, of the judiciary.[3] During his service as a political adviser, Yan Jiaqi limited himself to a handful of modest proposals, especially fixing terms of office for government officials, involving technical experts in decisionmaking, and strengthening the people's congress system and proceduralism in policymaking, no matter what the procedures might be. He devoted more attention to arguing what democracy could do for China than to discussing what it would be or how to introduce it.

Keeping the institutional vision of democracy vague was, again, partly a tactic. It did help to disarm the regime for a while. *Beijing Spring, 1989* provides the full texts of the "dialogues" granted to the students by State Council spokesman Yuan Mu and by a group of officials headed by Premier Li Peng. The government men all insisted that the regime shared the students' concerns, that a free press and dialogue channels already existed, and that any crackdown that might be necessary to preserve social order would affect only a handful of bad elements who had wormed their way among the patriotic students. But as Melanie Manion points out in her introduction to the book, overlapping terms and symbols disguised divergent stances. The Party could accept the students' slogans, but could not compromise on power.

A noteworthy exception to the dearth of practical proposals was the last-minute call by followers of Zhao Ziyang, who lost power with the declaration of martial law, to summon an emergency meeting of the National People's Congress or its standing committee to rescind martial law and dismiss Li. Yet the ineffectiveness of this effort shows well enough why such steps were not tried earlier or more often. The main organizer of the attempt, Cao Siyuan, was jailed without charges for a year, and was then for years prevented from traveling outside of China.

But the avoidance of institutional proposals was, unfortunately, more than a tactic. It was also a consequence of deeper habits of thought, particularly of the idea that democracy is something much more and much greater than an improvised and unstable and flawed compromise among competing forces that can never be satisfied. Chinese democrats dream of something better than what Winston Churchill called "the worst political system except for all the others." Three times in his collection of essays and speeches, Fang recalls an incident that occurred while he was a visiting scholar at the Institute for Advanced Study in Princeton, a year before he was expelled from the Chinese Communist Party. "I was obviously neither an immigrant nor a citizen," Fang remembers, "but nonetheless I received a report from my congressman giving an account to the citizens of just what he'd been up to." This showed that "in democratic countries, *I* am the master and the government is responsible to *me.*" It may be hard for Americans to suppress a smile at Fang's response to a newsletter. But we should remember that while members of China's National People's Congress sometimes make "inspection tours," they never even pretend to account to their constituents.

Nowhere are the hopes placed on democracy higher than in the largest country that doesn't have it. According to Fang, if democracy were implemented in China, policy would reflect public wishes, decisions would be implemented smoothly, corrupt leaders would be removed from office, government would serve the interests of all classes and nationalities. Yan Jiaqi believes that democracy would unleash creativity and initiative, allow for social trust and cooperation, create "love for the collective," and promote modernization. The "New May Fourth Manifesto" issued by the Beijing Students' Federation in 1989 declares that democracy would bring to bear the collective wisdom of the people for modernization while allowing the full development of each individual's abilities and the protection of each individual's interests.

This view of the potentials of politics has roots in early Chinese thought, in which the human world was seen as an integral part of a cosmos ordered by moral rather than physical consistency. Cosmic harmony was thought to descend from the heavens to the natural world to human society and finally to the mind of the individual—and then to extend back, for the Chinese saw the entire cosmos as responding to the moral or immoral behavior of human beings, especially the ruler. So strong was this belief in the cosmic unity of the human and natural worlds that Fang uses it to explain why the Chinese failed to develop science. He points out that they did not expect nature to exhibit physical regularity. Since they could explain such anomalies as floods, earthquakes, epidemics, eclipses, and shooting stars as responses to moral irregularities at court, there was no need to chase down the complicated physical explanations that produced the scientific breakthroughs of Galileo, Newton, and Einstein.

In the same way, when Chinese in the late nineteenth century began to ponder the international strength of democratic countries, they explained it by saying that democracy was a political system in tune with the order of the universe. As Hao Chang of Ohio State University has shown in *Chinese Intellectuals in Crisis*,[4] the seminal thinker Kang Youwei

(1858–1927) declared that the ideal society, which he called the Great Unity, would be a democratic, federal welfare state of material abundance and technological advancement, devoid of private property, free of inequalities based on class, gender, and race, and unified by the innate moral consciousness shared by all its members.

Kang's influence on Mao Zedong is obvious. Through Mao, if not directly, Kang and his generation have also influenced the current generation of thinkers. Given the continuing link between the cosmos and the polity in Chinese thought, it is no coincidence that one of China's leading democratic thinkers is a professional cosmologist, and that James Williams, a graduate student at Berkeley specializing in the history of science, begins his collection of Fang's essays with selections from Fang's cosmological writings.

Fang was trained as a physicist, but he turned to cosmology during the Cultural Revolution, when he was deprived of laboratory facilities. In the early 1970s he was criticized for advocating the Big Bang theory of the origins of the universe, which was labeled "bourgeois idealism" by Chinese ideologues. The experience of battling interference in his scientific work confirmed Fang's commitment to academic freedom, but the impact of this episode went deeper. Fang was both a Communist and a cosmologist, and he believed in both bodies of theory.

Chinese Marxism has never admitted to being what the West calls an ideology. As a field of study, it was referred to as "philosophy" in the schools. This term was not meant to convey the Western sense of speculativeness, or a divorce from reality. It denoted a master science—"dialectical materialism"—which could guide the development and integrate the findings of all other sciences. Fang's conflict with the ideologues led him to conclude that "philosophy is constantly withdrawing from areas that were once within its domain, while natural science moves into them one by one."

I do not think that this was just a politically cautious way of saying in 1982, while he was still a party member, that philosophy is bunk. It reflected a particular conception of science as being able to provide certain knowledge about an ever expanding circle of issues. So far as one can tell from the nontechnical excerpts provided here, Fang's view of science is not at all Popper's or Kuhn's; he does not construe science as an approximation, as provisional knowledge that is true only to the extent that it has not yet been falsified, as a constructed paradigm that will hold sway for a limited historical period. For Fang, science is able to make the same kinds of all-embracing claims to certainty as did the dialectical materialism that it displaces. Even the old idea of cosmic harmony reappears when Fang argues that the beauty of a certain mathematical concept is evidence for the inevitability of democracy, on the grounds that both the formula and democracy demonstrate the principle of harmony that is the essential nature of the universe.

In the 1980s, under Deng, "philosophy" retreated not only from the realm of natural sciences, but also from the fields of economic and social policy, from foreign policy, to some extent from literature, and, cautiously, from discussions of how to reform China's political institutions. Many Chinese believed, like Fang, in the ability of science to move in where philosophy moved out, not only in dealing with questions of the natural world but in solving those of the human world as well. Fang writes that "the basic principles and standards of modernization and democratization are like those of science—universally applicable. In this regard there's no Eastern or Western standard, only the difference between 'backward' and 'advanced,' between 'correct' and 'mistaken.' "

A similar faith is expressed by Yan Jiaqi. Yan studied physics in college, then transferred into the field of dialectical materialism. It was not until the reform period that he was assigned to establish the new field for China of political science, a term intended even more literally there than here. Like Fang, Yan considers that political problems are subject to scientific solutions. In the 1978 essay that first made him widely known, Yan uses the device of fictional time travel to contrast the "court of religion" in seventeenth-century Rome, the "court of reason" in Enlightenment France, and the "court of practice" in a futuristic China. Galileo, Voltaire, and Deng were his heroes, because each defended the sovereignty of science against dogmatism. When Yan says that "for science, all that is not understood can be understood," he does not refer only to the physical world. He means that democracy springs as much from objective truth as does $e = mc^2$.

And many of China's other proponents of democracy have also come from scientific backgrounds. Lu Xun, the famous left-wing writer of the 1930s, was trained as a physician. Wang Juntao, sentenced to thirteen years as the alleged backstage eminence of the Tiananmen incident, graduated in physics from Beijing University. Chen Yizi, former head of a major reform think tank, studied physics before he was sent down to the countryside during the Cultural Revolution. (He now heads the Center for Contemporary China in Princeton, which produces policy papers for post-Deng China.)

Nor is the scientism of the democrats a recent phenomenon. The May

Fourth Movement of 1919, conventionally viewed as the beginning of China's democratic revolution, was based on the slogan of "science and democracy." In *Cries for Democracy*, the "new May Fourth manifesto" alludes to democracy as "the spirit of science." A poster at Beijing University called for a government with science as its "sole guiding ideology." When Chinese democrats speak of democracy as scientific, or defend it as mandated by "natural law," they mean that democracy is the only ontologically correct political system, the only kind of system that is compatible with the nature of the universe. Institutional questions are secondary, because democracy carries the inevitability and the perfection of science. In retrospect, one can see that Mao's anti-intellectual policies grew out of a well-founded fear of science as the only ideology prestigious and ambitious enough in China to challenge Marxism for hegemony.

In contrast to the Soviet Union, the idea of human rights has so far been less corrosive in China. As a scientist who traveled from an establishment position to dissidence, Fang has often been called China's Sakharov. But the Fang we meet in this book is more like Dorothy addressing the Wizard of Oz. While Sakharov tangled with the Soviet leadership over nuclear weapons, the invasion of Czechoslovakia, political trials, religious repression, the falsification of history, and other issues, Fang got into trouble just by saying that "Marxism is no longer of much use," or that people suspected the Chinese leaders of putting money into Swiss bank accounts, or that a Beijing deputy mayor who accompanied a scientific delegation overseas was unqualified. In December 1988 he wrote a short letter to Deng suggesting the release of political prisoners.

Fang has bravely demonstrated the solvent effect of plainspeak on dictatorship, but neither he nor other leading democrats confronted the regime with a firm idea of human rights as something inherent and inalienable. Yan, in office at the time and perhaps constrained in his speech, states that the content of human rights "varies according to country and time." Fang defends rights as universal and grounded in scientific truth, but then falls right into the Marxist trap of saying that rights are granted in exchange for a citizen's exercise of his or her duties.

Chinese thought has always proceeded from the premise that society rather than the individual is primary. The few Chinese who have looked carefully into Western thought see mostly nonsense in the Hobbesian or Lockeian notion that man is, in some original way, an isolated individual. Any Chinese can see that this is not true, that people are born into society, that from the beginning they have social values and goals. It remains a real question for Chinese, perhaps especially for those committed to democracy, how it is that human rights can become so important that, in Ronald Dworkin's term, they can "trump" other social values.

Regardless of the lack of a rights-oriented philosophical tradition, Chinese are as strongly motivated by the desire for personal liberty as people anywhere. And nowhere has this impulse been more eloquently expressed than in the life and the writings of Wang Ruowang. Although abstractions like science, democracy, and human rights may have different meanings in China than in the West, a stubborn 73-year old who wants to say what he thinks is the same everywhere. Wang was expelled from the Party, first in the 1950s, for describing the "conceit and arrogance" of party members toward nonparty intellectuals, and then again in 1987, for calling for liberty when the Party was criticizing "bourgeois liberalization."

Wang treats eloquently the meaning of freedom in *Hunger Trilogy*, his memoir of three encounters with extreme hunger. His translator, Kyna Rubin, shows how Wang uses the battle with hunger as a symbol for the process of discovering truth, and food as a symbol for the freedom to express it. In his first chapter Wang and his cellmates conduct a winning hunger strike against their Kuomintang jailers in the 1930s; in his second chapter, still animated by patriotism and Communist ideals, they keep up one another's spirits as they face starvation in the wilderness while fleeing from Japanese invaders in the 1940s; in his final chapter, Wang returns to the same Shanghai jail, where he is imprisoned as a counterrevolutionary during the Cultural Revolution. He discovers that conditions are worse than they were under the Nationalists, that a hunger strike cannot succeed against a regime that no longer cares whether prisoners live or die.

In the course of his meditations on food, Wang uncovers two senses in which food is like freedom. It is a source of satiety and satisfaction, and it is a focus of self-control and moral identity. He comes out of his last experience of hunger with no more compelling goal than to tell what he has seen. In Wang's case, as in Fang's, truth-telling proved mortally threatening to the regime, which detained him without charges for a year after the demonstrations in 1989, and for years kept him under a version of house arrest in Shanghai, unable to accept invitations to leave the country. He was given a passport in 1992 and came to live in New York.

The democracy movement's abstention from institutional proposals was matched by the paucity of its criticism of existing institutions. Instead the movement chose to focus its attack on Chinese culture. Fang blamed China's "feudal culture" for the country's absolutism, narrowmindedness, and love of orthodoxy. Yan blamed what he called China's "dragon culture" for the persistence of autocracy and personalized authority. A poster-writer in *Cries for Democracy* stated that "the character of the Chinese consists of two outstanding traits: slavishness and sectarianism." And the democrats in exile since 1989 have been conducting an inquest on "Communist culture" and "Communist discourse."

To some extent the attack on culture, like the avoidance of a multi-class alliance, was a tactic to discourage government repression: culture was a euphemism for political institutions that were too dangerous to attack openly. Still, euphemisms sometimes become habits of thought. The obsession with culture has been characteristic not only of the Deng era, but also of democratic discourse in China throughout the century. The early-twentieth-century democrat Liang Qichao, for example, argued that the trouble with the Chinese was that they were slavish, ignorant, selfish, dishonest, cowardly, and passive. Lu Xun personified his countrymen by the self-deceiving braggart and weakling Ah Q. The May Fourth democrats called for a "new culture."

The criticism of Chinese culture usually starts as an attack by cosmopolitan Chinese on parochial Chinese, develops into a savaging of the intellectual class by its own members, and spirals back into merciless individual introspection. All three stages were encapsulated in a remarkable essay by the young literary critic Liu Xiaobo, written just before he returned to China from New York in May 1989 to join the demonstrations (and translated by Barmé in *Problems of Communism*). Liu writes:

> I face an agonizing dilemma. I now know that in using Western values to criticize Chinese culture I have been attacking an ossified culture with only slightly less ossified weapons. I am like someone who, though partially paralyzed himself, mocks a paraplegic. Having transplanted myself into a completely open world, I am suddenly forced to acknowledge that not only am I no theoretician, but I'm not a famous person anymore. All I am is a normal person who has to start all over again from the beginning. In China, the backdrop of ignorance highlighted my wisdom. My courage was thrown into relief by the cowardice of others. I appeared healthy in comparison with the congenital idiocy of my surroundings. Yet, in the United States, now that this backdrop of ignorance and failing has disappeared, so has my wisdom, courage, and vigor. I have become a weakling unable to face myself.[5]

The final hunger strike declaration issued by Liu and three colleagues on June 2 is reprinted in *Cries for Democracy*. (After June 4, Liu spent about a year in jail, then was unemployed in Beijing.) Issued when the original hunger strike was petering out, it has been interpreted as an attempt to breathe new life into the confrontation with the regime. On rereading, however, it is a document of Calvinist severity. It begins: "We protest! We appeal! We repent!" It criticizes the intellectuals for spinelessness, the students for disorganization, emotionalism, and elitism, the government for autocracy and inflexibility, and all Chinese for a mentality of mutual hatred and violence. Calling for "the birth of a new political culture," the document ends by saying that "We all must carry out a self-examination!"

The intellectuals' criticism of national character sometimes becomes so intense that it ironically aligns them with the official view that the people are too backward to deserve the democracy that the intellectuals are demanding. After all, democracy would entail the exercise of power by peasants and workers who might turn out to be anti-Western, anti-scientific, anti-intellectual. This is another reason why discussion of specific political institutions is deemed premature.

As capitalism and democracy sweep the world, there are only two governments crowing that their policies have been right all along: the Americans, for promoting democracy, and the Chinese, for staving it off. In the eyes of the Chinese leaders, everything that has happened since Tiananmen confirms the wisdom of their authoritarian ideology. The free fall of the Soviet economy, the agonies of transition in Poland and East Germany, the political disorder in Albania and Yugoslavia, the assassination of Rajiv Gandhi, the collapse of the Marxist regime in Ethiopia —almost anything that occurs in a world of rapid change shows to their satisfaction the overweening importance of order. And attacks on China's human rights record in Congress and in the media, and even the Presidential defense of extending most-favored-nation treatment as the best way to promote Chinese human rights, demonstrate to Chinese leadership that the West still seeks to subvert their society.

Shortly after his flight from China, Yan predicted that the regime of Li Peng and Deng Xiaoping would fall within two years. His optimism was widely shared among his colleagues. But today the exile movement is at a low point. Membership has eroded, funding is hard to find, the movement is fragmented into scores of organizations. The younger leaders are learning English and entering graduate school, while many of the older ones are living from year to year on fellowships. Many in the overseas community criticize the movement as divided, demoralized, rudderless, even corrupt. But this harshness is misplaced. The democracy movement abroad needs to be evaluated for what it is: not a political party with a program to hasten the fall of the Deng regime, but a community of intellectuals who are suffering the personal frustrations of exile yet also taking advantage of the opportunity to rethink. They are not the ones who will overthrow the regime, but they will be prepared with new ideas when it finally falls.

Yan Jiaqi, Fang Lizhi, and Wang Ruowang, and many other democrats are more or less heavily marked by the ideas of the CCP out of which they came. The movement includes some more radical thinkers (the best example is Wei Jingsheng), but with the breakdown of the old order, ex-Communists have become the main force. Their most subversive ideas—the hegemony of science, the yearning for liberty, the faith in the ability of democracy to create a vital collective, the claim of a special mission for the intellectuals—are only loosely Western as they interpret them. And that is what accounts for their appeal in China. In this sense, the regime's accusation that these dissidents are "total Westernizers" is unfair. Nobody need fear, or should hope, that China will become less Chinese for becoming more democratic.

7

The Decision for Reform in Taiwan

Written with Helena V. S. Ho

In March 1986 President Chiang Ching-kuo launched a dramatic political reform which marked a shift from gradual liberalization under a regime of "soft authoritarianism" to the beginning of what seems to be a process of democratic transition.[1] Within four years this process had achieved or facilitated, among other things, the lifting of martial law, the legalization of opposition parties, a smooth constitutional transition of political power after Chiang's death, a marked freeing up of the print media, and the invigoration of the electoral arena—all substantial moves in the direction of democracy.

This chapter seeks to analyze Chiang Ching-kuo's motives for launching the reform at the time that he did, in the context of the theory of democratic transitions. The focus on Chiang is appropriate because the available evidence (some of it reviewed in the section on "party renewal" below) supports the conventional wisdom that the reform decision was Chiang's and Chiang's alone. This does not gainsay the fact that he took the decision in response to conditions at home and abroad; it is these conditions and his response to them that this chapter seeks to analyze. But it is easier to identify these surrounding conditions than to figure out what Chiang made of them. To the limited extent that we can clarify Chiang's calculations and motives, our findings will be of historical and biographical interest, enriching our understanding of the political goals and style of this little-known and elusive political leader, and to some extent helping us decipher his vision for Taiwan's future.

In addition, such an investigation has a contribution to make to theory. A reform leader's motives are only part of the total story of a political reform, but they are an important part of it from the perspective of the transitions literature, which tends to focus on elite motives and strategies.[2] We will argue that Taiwan's experience, like Spain's in the 1970s, fits into Alfred Stepan's "Path 4a" ("redemocratization initiated by the civilian or civilianized political leadership"), but that it also differs from Spain's in some interesting respects. Comparing this case to the model and to the similar case should help clarify both the Taiwan case and the theory.

The dating of the reforms from March 1986 refers to the meeting that month of the Third Plenum of the KMT's 12th Central Committee. Chiang, as party chairman, called on the delegates to make stepped-up progress toward the party's long-standing goal of constitutional democracy. Not much was accomplished on this task at the session, so in early April Chiang appointed a twelve-man task force, which he charged with framing reform proposals to solve four specific issues: how to lift the ban on formation of new parties, how to lift martial law, how to revise the Taiwan Provincial Government Organization Law, and how to reform the Legislative Yuan and National Assembly.[3] The task force made its first report in June. In October, the President informed Katharine Graham of the *Washington Post* of his intention to lift the martial law decree and legalize opposition parties. Formal lifting of the martial law decree occurred in July 1987, followed by other reform measures. Meanwhile, in September 1986 the opposition had already formally established its own political party, which the regime tolerated even though it was at first still illegal.[4]

This chapter will not seek to analyze President Chiang's choice of reform tasks, because there was little ambiguity or controversy over what the initial steps of reform would involve when and if they were taken. Taiwan was ruled under a constitution promulgated in mainland China in 1947, modified by "Temporary Provisions" that had come into effect on that island in 1948 and under which various martial law provisions were enacted. Given the commitment of the ruling Kuomintang (KMT) since its founding to "constitutional government and democracy," the initial agenda for political reform inevitably involved lifting the martial law decree and moving toward fuller implementation of the constitution.[5] Given the rapid rate at which old mainland-elected members of the national representative bodies were dying off, "renewal" of these bodies was inescapably high on the agenda. And given the opposition's insistent and widely supported demand for more press freedom and more electoral competition, so too was removal of the bans on newspapers and new political parties. There was room for disagreement about the details of these steps and what would follow them, but most of these issues did not come up for decision until after Chiang Ching-kuo's death in January 1988.

Nor do we attempt to analyze the conditioning factors making this democratic transition possible. They have been elucidated by Tun-jen Cheng, among others. First, Taiwan had reached a socioeconomic level that fulfilled the precondition for democracy; e.g., high per-capita income, relatively equitable income distribution, high educational levels, and a high proportion of citizens identifying themselves as members of the middle class. Second, specific features of Taiwan's class structure helped make democratization easier: the lack of landlords and big capitalists and the cross-cutting nature of political and economic cleavages. Third, the regime's constitutionalist and prodemocratic ideology, strong liberal-technocrat faction, deep roots in society, and substantial legitimacy and organizational strength facilitated reform. Fourth, Cheng emphasizes the importance of elections and the pressure from a maturing opposition in encouraging the KMT to reform.

But, as Cheng points out, "the actual decisionmaking process of the democratic breakthrough in 1986 is yet to be studied."[6] This is the focus of our analysis. We cannot weigh the relative importance of the leader's decisions as against the permissive conditions, because such an evaluation, if it is possible at all, would require a broader study. We assume that socioeconomic conditions and leadership factors are both important in some way. Even if conditions are the more important of the two in determining whether a democratic transition will take place, political leadership is crucial in influencing the timing of the transition, its smoothness, the order in which transition measures are taken, and the type of institutional structure toward which the reform at least initially moves. In the case of Taiwan, socioeconomic conditions for democratization had been ripe for at least ten or fifteen years, and the domestic opposition and foreign critics had been pressing for change for an equal length of time, before Chiang Ching-kuo made his decision to allow the process to move forward.

It turns out that the question of why the leader acted when and as he did is hard to answer in Taiwan's case; this is probably why it remains the least studied aspect of the story. CCK (as he was often called) cultivated a populist image, but he kept his personality and his motivations to himself. The *Asian Wall Street Journal* reported in November 1987, "The reason for the democratic turn is a mystery. . . . Mr. Chiang is in no hurry to shed light on these events. He hasn't written about his life and has declined to cooperate with biographers. In answering written questions submitted by the Asian Journal, he ignored an invitation to talk about himself. . . ."[7] Chiang's public statements were usually couched in a hackneyed Confucian phraseology which—however sincerely he meant it, and we will argue that he probably did—tended to deter analysis. He listened to many different opinions, but even his close subordinates apparently did not know how he put the information together. Since he encouraged his aides to imitate his reticence in speaking both about him and about their roles with him,[8] even after his death those around him revealed relatively little about his thinking during the time the reform decision was made. As Tillman Durdin had written earlier, "The cult of concealment that surrounds the personal life of this shy and wary man . . . make[s] him something of an unknown quantity to the world at large."[9]

We have scrutinized each factor that appears likely to have influenced his reform decision, examined how this influence might have worked, and marshalled whatever evidence is available to help clarify whether this factor really did play a role in his thinking. For ease of exposition we have ordered the factors roughly in narrowing concentric circles around Chiang, looking first at two international factors, then at two in the sphere of Taiwan, and finally at two pertaining to Chiang himself. In each case, we examine how the factor in question may have appeared to Chiang and may have influenced his decision. The ordering is meant to imply nothing about the relative importance of the factors, since we have no way to measure this.

Although the result of this analysis is inconclusive, we hope it gives a relatively plausible reconstruction of Chiang's motives and sharpens issues for further research, which might be conducted if more presidential papers become available or if further interviews can be carried out with President Chiang's colleagues and subordinates.

International Pressure

Martial law had long been an embarrassment to Taiwan in its international relations. For example, in a 1983 interview with *Der Spiegel*, President Chiang confronted a number of sharp questions. He was told, "Never before in modern history has there been a country as long under martial law as Taiwan." The interviewers asked when martial law would be lifted, and also "Why is Taiwan so slow in democratization?" The President's answers showed that he did not find it easy to answer such questions. As to martial law, he confessed, "This is indeed a dilemma," then stated both that martial law was needed to defend Taiwan from the communists and that its effect was extremely slight. On democracy, he argued that Taiwan was already quite democratic without an opposition party, but also acknowledged that "No political party can maintain its advantage forever if it does not reflect the public opinion and meet the people's demand."[10]

According to CCK's long-term chief secretary, Wang Chia-hua, Chiang, even before becoming president, was frequently embarrassed in this way. When foreign visitors asked him, as Taiwan's premier, why Taiwan still had martial law, he had to answer that Taiwan really didn't have martial law because there was no curfew and no troops were in the streets. Chiang more than once asked Wang to read him the emergency decree (*chieh-yen ling*) and explain whether, if the decree were lifted, the legal basis would still exist to reimpose it if needed. "So I think," Wang stated, "that the President's first priority was to lift the state of emergency so long as the premise could be assured that no damage would be done to national security."[11]

Wang's reminiscences accord with the account of Ma Ying-jeou, Chiang's English-language secretary during the years in question. Although Ma judged that the pressure of international public opinion was not the main factor in the reform decision, he recalled that as early as 1984 CCK asked him to gather materials on how Westerners understood Taiwan's *chieh-yen*.[12]

The issue of martial law was particularly galling in Taiwan's relations with its intrusive and self-righteous ally, the United States, especially after the murder of writer Henry Liu in California in 1984 by gangsters hired by Taiwan's military intelligence authorities. The Formosan Association for Public Affairs (FAPA), an organization of Taiwan-born U.S. residents and citizens, became highly effective as a political lobby after its founding in 1982, and gained several important congressional allies including senators Claiborne Pell (D-R.I.) and Edward Kennedy (D-Mass.) and representatives Jim Leach (R-Iowa) and Stephen Solarz (D-N.Y.).

Also setting the scene for CCK's reform decision was the wave of democratic transitions which started in Southern Europe and Latin America in the mid-1970s and spread to South Korea and the Philippines in the 1980s. After the fall of Marcos, the opposition in Taiwan raised the slogan, "Why is it that the Philippines can, and Taiwan can't?" However, we have not found any evidence about what CCK specifically thought of these events.

The PRC Factor

The rival regime across the Taiwan Strait presented a growing threat to Chiang's regime in several ways, and political reform can be understood partly as a response to each of them.

First, the perceived PRC threat to Taiwan's security was increased by the breaking of U.S.-ROC relations by President Jimmy Carter in 1979. As CCK told a German reporter, "President Carter has repeatedly emphasized that the establishment of U.S.-communist bandit relations will not create any threat to our people's prosperity, security, or welfare. But if we look at Carter's public statements on the 'normalization' of relations with the Chinese communists, the U.S. has no clear arrangements for guaranteeing the security of the Taiwan area after the establishment of U.S.-bandit relations; they just proceed on the basis of the American hypothetical judgment that the bandits 'have no intention' and 'have no capability' to invade Taiwan. This kind of hypothesis is very dangerous."[13] The PRC followed up their normalization breakthrough by launching a campaign to induce Taiwan to accept peaceful unification. Beijing offered Taipei the right to keep its own political, social, and economic system under the formula of "one nation, two systems." The PRC campaign gained added force when the Reagan administration agreed to the 1982 Shanghai communiqué promising gradually to decrease the quantity and quality of U.S. arms supplies to Taiwan, and in 1984 when China and Britain signed an agreement on the future of Hong Kong that provided for using the one-nation/two systems formula there.

KMT political concessions to the native Taiwanese population had long been linked with PRC pressure. As Hung-mao Tien wrote in 1975, "The party leadership has been compelled by the disheartening diplomatic events [like expulsion from the UN in 1971] to undertake measures for the purpose of fortifying internal solidarity and to pacify discontented Taiwanese."[14] These measures included recruiting increasing numbers of Taiwanese into the ruling party and into high positions in government, increasing the number of locally elected ("supplementary") seats in the Legislative Yuan and National Assembly, and allowing the nonparty opposition (Tang-wai, or TW) more freedom to compete.

As detailed below, derecognition brought a temporary halt in the reform process that was already slowly getting under way in the late 1970s. But in a longer time perspective, CCK's subsequent decision to resume and accelerate political reform may be interpreted as an attempt to strengthen the KMT's ability to survive on Taiwan after derecognition.

As CCK told a Spanish reporter in April 1979 when asked what would happen if America ceased to supply weapons to Taiwan, "A nation's defense strength does not rely on weapons. More important is to firm up our faith in and will for freedom."[15] By increasing the party's staying power in its Taiwan base, the reforms would signal that the KMT was not to be forced into negotiations with the CCP at a time not of its own choosing, that it intended to survive and prosper as long as necessary in Taiwan in order to reunify China on its own terms. Such a signal would also serve to reassure the local population that no sell-out of their interests was imminent, thus further increasing the regime's domestic security, and would disabuse the mainland authorities of any overoptimism about their prospects for easily enticing KMT-ruled Taiwan into the motherland's embrace.

Second, CCK's reforms appear to have responded not only to the PRC political-diplomatic offensive against Taiwan, but also to the threat to Taiwan's image as the freer of the two Chinas that was presented by political events in the mainland. These events included Democracy Wall (1978–79), the promulgation of a new and ostensibly more liberal PRC Constitution in 1982, the first and second rounds of direct elections of county-level people's congresses (1979–81 and 1984), the progressive liberalization of the PRC media, and Deng's licensing of discussion of political reform in 1986. Deng Xiaoping's picture appeared twice on the cover of *Time* magazine in the 1980s, and he was widely hailed in the West as leading China into an era of freedom and, some said, capitalism.[16]

On the other hand, CCK insisted that the mainland regime had not changed its spots. He told Katharine Graham of the *Washington Post*, "There are certain changes taking place. But they are cosmetic. The essence of communism remains the same."[17] He seemed to believe that the communist regime was bankrupt and making superficial concessions in order to retain its hold on power. Even so, his remarks seemed to imply that PRC democratization initiatives posed a challenge which Taiwan had to answer. For example, he stated in 1981, "Especially today when the communist bandit regime is near the end of its road, with its vile reputation known to everyone, and the communist system has been proven a total failure . . . it is more important than ever for us to strengthen the construction of constitutional government to demonstrate clearly that the strong contrast between the two sides of the Taiwan Strait is basically due to the fact that one side has implemented a constitution based on the Three People's Principles while the other has not."[18]

Third, CCK's statements indicate not only that did he not intend to negotiate a surrender to the communists, but also that he actually believed the KMT would eventually recover the mainland through political means. In 1979 he told a German reporter, "The late President Chiang [Kai-shek] used to say that recovering the mainland depended on '70% political, 30% military.' . . . We are going to use our achievements in building a democratic and free society on Taiwan based on the Three Principles of the People, to exert a strong political influence on the Chinese people on the mainland. . . . So long as our actions [in recovering the mainland] receive the warm support of the mainland compatriots, they won't lead to a world war."[19] The achievement of prosperity on Taiwan under the Three People's Principles, he told a KMT party plenum the same year, "has established a good model for the future construction of a free, peaceful, strong, and unified modern China. We have established an unbeatable position in our struggle to the death with communism!"[20]

Even when the CCP regime in the mainland was as weak as it had ever been, such reasoning seemed unrealistic to most observers. Yet it may have played a part either in Chiang's thinking about reform or at least in his ability to persuade more conservative forces in the party to accept reform. In his October 1986 interview with Graham, he stated, "Abolishing the emergency decrees is for the purpose of speeding up democratic progress here. We must serve as a beacon light for the hopes of one billion Chinese so that they will want to emulate our political system."[21]

Ma Ying-jeou recalled in an interview after Chiang's death, "He felt at the time that the domestic conditions were mature. [This was the main point.] But also, strengthening democratic politics was an important step for improving our international image and appealing to the mainland brethren. We had a saying that the mainland should emulate Taipei in politics, but what in our politics should they emulate? If our level of democratization was insufficient, did that mean we wanted them to emulate our use of martial law? President Chiang was perfectly clear about this point."[22]

Opposition Pressure and Election Timing

In explaining the need for reform, CCK often stressed the maturity of social conditions, stating that thirty years of peace and prosperity and the spread of education had raised the people's demands on the government for opportunities for political participation.[23] As we read them, these statements did not so much reflect a social-scientific analysis of pre-conditions for democracy as refer to the outcome of a complicated history of "transactions" (to adopt the term recommended by T. J. Cheng) between Chiang and the opposition over the course of a decade or more. Through these transactions—some public and some probably secret and still unknown—CCK and the opposition found their way to a mixed relationship of conflict and compromise that made the reforms possible. This dramatic record of conflict and cooperation included some sharp clashes, but ultimately led to the creation of sufficient common ground to enable CCK to manage his reforms successfully. That the reform did not occur either sooner or later than it did appears to have had much to do with this interaction.

The nascent opposition first entered the electoral arena in 1969 in the shape of a few non-KMT independents, when K'ang Ning-hsiang and Huang Hsin-chieh were elected respectively to the Taipei City Assembly and the Legislative Yuan. In the early 1970s, CCK tried and ultimately failed fully to coopt the emerging Taiwanese political elite into the KMT.[24] People like Chang Chün-hung, Hsu Hsin-liang, and Su Nan-ch'eng got started as promising young KMT members but broke away from the party either because the rules of party life frustrated their ambitions or because they could not accept the limits the party set on their political views. Other future leaders of the opposition like K'ang Ning-hsiang and Yao Chia-wen never joined. The KMT was no longer able to absorb all the aspiring participants into its own ranks.

In 1977 the non-KMT made a breakthrough and began to take shape as a real opposition rather than as a congeries of independents. Opposition candidates won two county magistracies and two mayorships, and did well also in the polling for the Taiwan Provincial Assembly (other local posts were also elected at the same time). The KMT handled relatively mildly a riot in Chungli triggered by a dispute over the balloting. The opposition geared up strongly for December 1978 elections for National Assembly and Legislative Yuan supplementary seats. According to one observer, "It seemed as if Taiwan had reached the threshold of a multiparty system."[25]

But the December 1978 elections were canceled, the reason given being Carter's recognition of the PRC. The TW split into a moderate and a radical faction, the former committed to electoral politics, the latter to mass action. Frustrated members of the opposition tried to step up pressure on the KMT, founding *Mei-li-tao* magazine and mounting mass meetings and demonstrations. The confrontation culminated in the

Kaohsiung Incident of December 10, 1979, and the jailing of eight opposition politicians for long terms.

The impetus toward gradual political change resumed a year later.
The elections delayed from 1978 were carried out in December 1980
under a new election law administered by a new election commission.
They were deemed reasonably fair, although the KMT did better than
before.[26] Through the 1980s, the KMT made gradual concessions while
the TW leaders not in jail stepped up their challenge. The TW developed
the posture of a somewhat loyal opposition within somewhat stable rules
of the game, campaigning hard in elections while constantly criticizing
the unfair aspects of the electoral system.

In the mid-1980s, demands within the TW to organize a political party
grew stronger. The opposition needed a party or party-like organization
for several purposes: to gain legitimacy, to channel financing, to seek
agreement on issues, to arrange for cooperation during campaigns, and
most importantly, to negotiate the coordination of candidacies in order
to avoid undercutting one another under the rules of Taiwan's "single-
vote multi-member" (SVMM) electoral system (see chapter 8). In 1980
the TW formed an electoral assistance association (*hou-yuan hui*). In
1985 they organized a TW Central Election Assistance Association (*Tang-
wai hsuan-chü chung-yang hou-yuan hui*) and produced a common electoral platform, which included the demand for formation of a new party.
TW-KMT relations became tense as the TW increased pressure in late
1984 and 1985.

CCK had authorized a number of informal contacts (*kou-t'ung*) with
the opposition, first via newspaper publisher Wu San-lien in 1978. In
1985, right after the founding of the Tang-wai Research Association on
Public Policy (TRAPP) and of the radical Editors' and Writers'
Association (*Pien-lien hui*), four professors (Hu Fu and others) on their
own initiative spent several months mediating to prevent the KMT from
cracking down on these organizations. Not long after, the liberal senior
KMT politician T'ao Pai-ch'uan came back from overseas and got CCK's
blessing for another stage of *kou-t'ung*.[27]

The timing and character of the 1986 reforms was crucially affected
by the relationship that the two sides had arrived at through a process of
mutual testing. The opposition was neither weak and disorganized like
that in mainland China and many other socialist states in the late 1980s,
nor was it armed and antisystem like many of those in Latin America in
the 1960s. Rather, it was a relatively strong, fairly well organized, ambitious and aggressive movement which was, nonetheless, basically nonvio-

lent, semi-loyal to the system, and willing to play within, or around the edges of, the rules of the game even as it challenged and tried to change some of them. It was an opposition that used the legal system, the electoral system, the public opinion system, even street demonstrations, but which after extended internal debate, and numerous arrests at the hands of the government, had decided to abjure systematic violence. By 1986 the opposition CCK faced was at the same time one that was putting enormous pressure on him and one that he could talk to. That he faced this sort of opposition is a key factor for explaining both how he was able to make the reforms that he did and the fact that he felt it necessary to do so.

Just as the opposition differed from oppositions in the socialist and Latin American examples, so CCK's regime differed from those models. It was neither ideologically and financially bankrupt, as were many of the socialist regimes of the late 1980s, nor was it as repressive as those regimes or as the Latin American military and corporatist regimes of the 1960s. CCK used police powers not to eliminate the opposition but to set limits to it—specifically, in an only partly successful attempt to deter it from raising the issue of Taiwan independence and from using the tactics of street violence or insurrection—and to induce it to accept his regime's rules of the game. His selective resistance to the TW and intermittent use of repression forced the TW to go through a long process of internal struggle which ultimately gave rise to its broad internal consensus to play more or less by the rules of the game. That the reforms did not occur earlier may have been partly due to the time consumed in this process of shaping a more acceptable opposition, although it is probably equally true that the long delay in reform helped to fire the determination of the opposition's more radical wing.

In any case, by 1986, CCK and the more moderate TW leaders understood one another well and were moving, with or without conscious coordination, in such a way as to outflank together both the KMT conservatives and the TW radicals.

At the time of CCK's reforms, important elections were in the offing. Scheduled for December 6, 1986, they would fill seats in the Legislative Yuan and National Assembly. By getting reform under way before these elections, CCK could seize credit for the KMT and improve its electoral performance. As James Soong stated in an interview after CCK's death, "There wouldn't be another election for three years after that, and Mr. [Chiang] Ching-kuo hoped that the KMT could do its preparatory work well and could do so on its own initiative, rather than being led by the

nose by others. This doesn't mean that Mr. Ching-kuo hadn't been thinking about these matters earlier, but now he felt the time was becoming
more and more ripe. It was necessary to break through all difficulties and
to move as fast as possible."[28]

At the same time, the prospect of elections had caused the opposition
virtually to make up its mind to organize a political party even before it
was legal to do so, in order to provide the organizational resources it
needed to perform well against stiff KMT competition (after having
done relatively poorly in 1983). The decision by the exiled opposition
politician Hsu Hsin-liang to organize a party abroad also stimulated the
in-island politicians to do so before they were outflanked from abroad.

Toward the end, Chiang and the TW got into a race to the finish line.
Chiang may have hoped that he could preemptively announce the
prospective legalization of the inevitable new party and thus avoid an
ugly confrontation. But with CCK moving in the direction of legalization,
the TW politicians for their part could not afford to wait for him, lest they
be viewed as timid creatures of the ruling party. So the TW won the race;
the party was established in September 1986 before Chiang had made his
intentions clear, leading to a brief period of concern lest he authorize
the arrest of those who had participated in the founding.

Chiang's response, however, was typical of his transactional style of
dealing with the opposition. In his October 1986 interview with Graham,
while stating that permission to form new parties would be announced
soon, he also gave a negative evaluation of the newly established DPP,
stating that the party lacked a "concept of the nation" and had failed to
include the policy of anticommunism in its party charter. In effect, he
was telling the DPP what conditions it would have to meet to enjoy the
benefits of legalization—inviting DPP to the negotiating table and giving
them the opening bid.[29] Chiang's subsequent behavior was in the same
vein—declaring the DPP illegal but not arresting its members, warning
against advocacy of Taiwan independence, and including in the draft
civic organizations law the three conditions of anticommunism, non-
advocacy of separatism, and loyalty to the constitution. All this put the
burden on the DPP either to fit within the framework Chiang was establishing or to take on the risks of challenging the framework.[30]

It is often argued that opposition pressure forced CCK to reform.[31]
This analysis is true as far as it goes. Had the opposition been weaker,
Chiang might not have undertaken the reforms despite the existence of
other factors we have identified as pushing him toward change. However,
we can also say that had the opposition been substantially more aggres-

sive than it was, the reforms might also not have been feasible, or at least might not have unfolded as smoothly as they did. Equally, had CCK been less skillful, the opposition might not have been induced to play as constructive a role as it did. Also less often noted is the way in which Chiang and the opposition mainstream helped each other in dealing both with anti-reform forces within the KMT and with more radical forces in the opposition.

The Need for Reinvigoration of the Ruling Party

Reviewing the events of the year before CCK's reform decision, James Hsiung wrote, "An eerie sense of crisis, at the start of the year [1985], hung over the open trials of the principals charged with the murder of Henry Liu, a Chinese-American writer in California [murdered in 1984]. Then came the collapse, in tandem, of the Tenth Credit Cooperative, a big-name savings and loan institution, and its sister investment outfit, Cathay Investment and Trust Co. A number of ranking government officials were implicated in the failures, which victimized numerous creditors. These, plus other mishaps . . . generated a momentary aura of doom. . . ."[32]

Whether Chiang Ching-kuo shared in the sense of doom is not known, but there is some evidence that these events—as well as others that had accumulated earlier such as the murder of three relatives of TW personage Lin Yi-hsiung in 1980 and the death in police custody in 1981 of Ch'en Wen-ch'eng, an American professor of Taiwanese origin—convinced him that the ruling party was losing its revolutionary élan and needed to renew itself. The Henry Liu incident cut especially close to Chiang because his son, Hsiao-wu, was widely accused of being the man behind the murder (an accusation that has never been proven). The Tenth Credit incident involved KMT Secretary-General Chiang Yen-shih, a close Chiang adviser, who resigned in its aftermath. Both the Ch'en Wen-ch'eng incident and the Henry Liu incident also led to increased criticism of the KMT in the United States. And both were mistakes committed by the security apparatus, which Chiang had virtually built in the 1950s.

Chiang may have felt that subjecting the ruling party to more media and electoral oversight and to increased political competition would revitalize its sense of mission, help get rid of some incompetent people, strengthen the party's image, and improve its links to the people. The party's victories over the opposition in the semi-open elections of the late

1970s and early 1980s showed that it had strong organizational roots and substantial public support. This was not a party that would collapse at the first breath of challenge but one that had the resources to rise to the challenge. As stated by K'ang Ning-hsiang, not a Chiang intimate but a close observer, "The KMT's strongman era was coming to an end. If they wanted their third generation to continue ruling Taiwan, they had immediately to adjust their relations with Taiwan society or suffer severe problems. . . . The question of foreign evaluations and the international situation was secondary. If they could get good international reviews while guaranteeing the survival of their regime, so much the better."[33]

According to Ma Ying-jeou, "I believe he was very grieved that things like this [Henry Liu and Tenth Credit] had occurred during his second term as president. That was why he decided to hold the Third Plenum. Although there was no clear declaration, the comrades inside the party knew that 'although it will not be called an overhaul (kai-tsao), it will be an overhaul in effect.' "[34] (The term kai-tsao evokes major personnel reshuffles in KMT history such as the purging of the communists in 1927 and the party reorganization in 1949 after defeat on the mainland.)

At a conference of the KMT Standing Committee on October 15, 1986, which endorsed CCK's reform policy, CCK said (using a phrase that was much quoted from then on), "The times are changing, the environment is changing, the tides are also changing. To meet these changes the ruling party must adopt new concepts and new methods and on the basis of the democratic and constitutional political order, push forward measures of reform and renewal. Only in this way can we link up with the tides of the times, only in this way can we remain forever at one with the people." In the same speech he stressed the need for the ruling party to maintain a constant attitude of self-criticism and to have the courage to make the necessary changes in itself.[35] While these phrases were typically vague and formulaic, they seem to have referred to the need to revitalize the party.

The reforms suited the interests of members of the KMT's so-called "young Turk" wing (shao-chuang p'ai), people like Chao Shao-k'ang whose careers depended on winning elections rather than on bureaucratic promotions within the party machine. There is no reason to think that this group had enough clout to pressure the President. But the fact that it existed presumably made it more possible for CCK to contemplate reform, since his own party had within it the kind of personnel it would need to respond successfully in a more competitive political environment.

On the other hand, "The opposition to reforms from the right wing of Chiang's ruling party is so strong that only a leader of his standing is likely to be able to bring even the beginnings of meaningful change."[36] As we will argue in the next section, the very strength of the party's conservative faction may have been one consideration motivating Chiang to undertake the reform, knowing that if he did not do so, his weaker successors would have a hard time doing it themselves. Also, since both the Ch'en Wen-ch'eng and Henry Liu incidents involved the security-military sector, these events may have weakened the political influence of this sector or may have helped persuade CCK to decrease his reliance on them.

Health and Succession

CCK had long suffered from diabetes. He was 60 when he took the office of president in 1978 for a six-year term. In 1981 and 1982 he underwent eye surgery for retinal bleeding, and in 1985 he had cataract removal surgery. Both conditions were connected with his worsening diabetes. Also in 1985, according to *Newsweek*, he had a pacemaker implanted. Describing his appearance at Katharine Graham's October 1986 interview with him, *Newsweek* said that Chiang "moves slowly, with apparent pain, and his hands tremble."[37]

In 1983 CCK had demoted the second most powerful man in his regime, Wang Sheng, head of the military's political warfare department, to the post of ambassador to Paraguay. It is generally believed that he did so because Wang had been acting too independently and challenging the President's power. His heir apparent, the popular and able Prime Minister Sun Yun-suan, suffered a cerebral hemorrhage in 1984. Also in 1984, when accepting his second term as president, Chiang chose Lee Teng-hui as his vice president and hence constitutional successor should he die in office.

These events, especially the state of CCK's health, brought the sensitive succession problem into the realm of public debate.[38] Although CCK's second term ran until 1990, speculation about his plans for succession was frequent in the early 1980s. He addressed these concerns for the first time in a *Time* magazine interview published in September 1985, stating that he had "never given any consideration" to the possibility that he might be succeeded by a family member and that the succession would be handled in accordance with "democracy and the rule of law."[39] Chiang gave a still more unambiguous statement of his position on

Constitution Day, December 25, 1985, when he said that members of the Chiang family "could not and would not" (*pu-neng yeh pu-hui*) run for the office of president and that military rule "could not and would not" take place either. (Although Chiang did mention in this short speech that his health was not as good as it used to be, from the context it appears that he was not expecting to die in office but meant to suggest that he would not be a candidate for a third term; although the constitution allowed only two terms, this provision was suspended under the Temporary Provisions.)[40]

There is no direct evidence as to why he took this position against family succession. It may be significant that he made his statement not long after the reputation of his second son, Hsiao-wu, was damaged by charges that he had given the order for the murder of Henry Liu. (The eldest son, Hsiao-wen, was chronically ill; the third son, Hsiao-yung, was a businessman who had never been seriously involved in politics. CCK also had a younger half-brother, Wei-kuo, whom some had regarded as a potential successor. The two had been political rivals in the past; we do not know what CCK's attitude toward Wei-kuo was in the 1980s.) The public discussion of the succession issue had revealed widespread distaste for a family succession, articulated especially strongly by the opposition press.

The succession issue may have affected Chiang's thinking on political reform in two ways. First, with his retirement or death the political system would lose a popular leader whose personal legitimacy (derived from a mix of family heritage, connections, and political skill) was important to bolster the regime. Chiang may have wished to begin the process of giving that regime greater long-term security based on its ability to win competitive elections. Since he had decided for whatever reasons that he could not be succeeded by a family member, a collective leadership of KMT oligarchs, or a military man, he may have felt that only democratic political reforms could give his civilian, non-Chiang successor, whoever he might be, a good chance to consolidate power. As a "foreign observer" told Daniel Southerland of the *Washington Post* in October 1986, "Chiang wants in his final years in office to bequeath some kind of stable, lasting system, and has concluded that the only way he can do this is to invite broader participation in the political process."[41]

Second, insofar as implementing constitutional government was his goal (as we argue below), Chiang probably realized that it would be harder for a successor to implement reforms over the opposition of conservative forces in the KMT and the military than for him to do so himself. If reforms were to have a good chance of success, he would have to initiate them, which in view of his health gave him little time to act.

We have uncovered no direct evidence on these points. But in any case Chiang acted as if reform were a matter of special urgency as his health deteriorated. During 1986, in public statements to party organs charged with reform tasks, he frequently urged rapid action.[42] James Soong recalled that after the Third Plenum Chiang "expressed himself very urgently and clearly" on the issue of reform.[43] According to Ma Ying-jeou, the day before his death CCK asked Party Secretary Li Huan whether the CEC meeting at which parliamentary reform would be discussed was scheduled for the next day. "The impression he gave me," Ma recalled, "was that he was in a big hurry, probably because he knew about his health situation. . . . One can say that ever since the Third Plenum, he had been hoping for reform extremely urgently."[44]

The succession problem may have affected not only CCK's calculations but also those of the TW and hence the challenges with which CCK had to contend. According to one contemporary report, "TW personalities figure that the TW camp has to get a party organized while CCK is still alive; only in this way can they avoid another big wave of political arrests or even bloodshed. Otherwise, it will be hard to predict the attitudes of the authorities in the post-CCK era toward a TW political party."[45] If, as we argued earlier, the threat of an impending TW party organization was one of the forces that pressed Chiang to act, then this threat in turn may have been partly a result of the succession crisis.

CCK's Political Values and Sense of Mission

CCK's reform decision was dramatic and surprised many both abroad and in Taiwan. Yet it was not a sudden decision. Preparation for it went back a long way—to the values of "constitutional government and democracy" always espoused by the KMT; to values long voiced by CCK himself; to years of opposition demands; and to earlier CCK policies.

In his early years on Taiwan, CCK played a very tough role. He served as head of the General Political Warfare Department of the army, where he installed a Soviet-style commissar system, established the China Youth Anti-Communist National Salvation Corps to control youth, and became the head of the regime's National Security Bureau and, in Edwin A. Winckler's phrase, its "security czar." According to Tillman Durdin, "operating in the shadows, CCK became one of the most feared men in the leadership. He had no apologies for the repression that went on well into the 1970s."[46]

But either then (as he insisted) or some time later, democratization also became one of his long-term goals. From the time he became premier in 1972, if not earlier, the regime began gradually to liberalize, allowing more participation, recruiting more Taiwanese to party membership and government posts, and allowing somewhat more freedom of speech. All the same kinds of factors we adduced above for the 1986 reform decision probably played a role in this series of gradual reform measures—PRC and international pressure, the rise of the opposition, and so forth. In addition, however, his words and actions reveal an orienting set of values behind his political strategies.

In April 1975, Chiang Kai-shek died and Ching-kuo, serving as premier, became the top leader. In a speech to the National Assembly on Constitution Day, December 25, CCK affirmed his commitment to the goals of "democracy and legal system, and full implementation of the constitution," and said, "We have already established an excellent basis for putting democratic politics into effect in the recovery base [Taiwan]. Five days ago we smoothly completed the election for supplementary Legislative Yuan members. In this election, not only did the election organs fulfill the requirements of 'fair, just, and open,' but also we could see from the candidates' excellent political comportment and the voters' enthusiasm that our citizens are full of keenness for political participation and concern for national affairs, and that they have a high level of commitment to electing virtuous and capable candidates that a democratic country's citizens should have when they exercise their citizens' rights."[47]

As we have seen in many quotations adduced earlier, Chiang constantly referred to Sun Yat-sen's Three Principles and to the long-term party program of moving from tutelage to democracy. For example, in his speech on Constitution Day (December 25) 1973, Chiang stated, "We have now implemented the constitution for half of our republic's 72-year history. In the first 36 years our nation suffered internal rebellion and external invasion, yet in the midst of blood and tears we still bravely persisted in carrying forward the steps laid down in our National Father's [Sun Yat-sen's] *Outline for Nation-Building* (Chien-kuo ta-kang), moving from military rule, through tutelage, into the stage of constitutional rule. In the second 36 years the full-scale implementation of constitutionalism was impeded by communist rebellion and the fall of the mainland, but we made a brilliant success of carrying out construction of democracy and constitutional government in the recovery base."[48]

Without mentioning CCK's name, Arthur Lerman argued in a 1977 article that Taiwan's "national elite" (the mainlanders) "felt a deep commitment to democracy"—which they understood, in Lerman's words, as "liberating the energies of the people and channeling them into public affairs; disciplining the energies of the people; [and] orderly discussion in search of a unified general will."[49] Lerman's portrayal of the elite view of democracy fits CCK well, to judge by his public statements. For example, in 1975 CCK said, "As President Chiang Kai-shek used to say, 'The basic nature of democracy is equality and freedom, and the spirit of freedom means obeying the law and performing one's role [*shou-fa shou-fen*].' Thus the concept of rule by law is the core entity of democratic politics."[50] In 1976 he said, "The most important thing in politics is that the government should understand the people, and the people should trust the government."[51] In the same year he said that, thanks to the government's construction measures of the last three years, "the masses and the government have united together, our wills are concentrated, the people are stimulated to a spirit of struggle, their spirits are high."[52]

"When I go to the countryside on a visit," he told a group of American newspaper people, "it is to hear the people's opinions in order to understand deeply their difficulties and their needs. During the visit I do not make any immediate administrative decisions, but take what I have heard and seen back to my office to serve as reference material as I implement policy. These visits also serve to increase good feelings between government and people."[53]

There is no way to prove that such quasi-Confucian jargon is meaningful. But it fits well with two other leading themes in our analysis—the transaction model of relations between CCK and the opposition, in which he wants to give them space to operate but also wants to lead them into a law-abiding form of oppositional behavior; and the competition with the mainland regime in which CCK uses democratization to strengthen the competitiveness and fighting trim of his own political system against its rival. Since CCK's rhetoric seems to fit in well with his pattern of action, we had best take it into account in analyzing his motives for reform.

Findings and Theoretical Implications

The evidence we have been able to gather gives a better picture of CCK's probable motives than has been available before in one place and may contribute something to our understanding of his motives and style as a political leader. But because of data limitations our account is not definitive. As far as we could determine, all the factors we have considered seem to have influenced CCK's decision for reform to some extent. No single factor seems to have been decisive, and we have not seen any way even to try to weigh the relative importance of the different factors. Nor have we tried to evaluate the relative importance of "conditions" versus leadership decisions. Nothing we have discovered leads us to doubt that the ripeness of socioeconomic conditions was important for the reform. Nor does our analysis do anything to derogate from the importance of the TW role, despite our chosen focus on the choices made from the top down by CCK.

We selected this focus in order to contribute to the recent literature on democratic transitions in authoritarian regimes, a literature which eschews the "macro-oriented focus on objective conditions" in favor of a concentration on "political actors and their strategies."[54]

The Taiwan case confirms some of the axioms of this literature—for example, that a democratic transition is initiated to resolve a legitimacy problem, and that the regime that undertakes it gives up some measure of political control in the hope of improving its ability to survive. The transition is undertaken in order to increase the regime's ability to win allegiance from the citizens with reduced reliance on coercion.

More specifically, many of our findings conform to observations made by Alfred Stepan about what he calls "Path 4a," or "redemocratization initiated by the civilian or civilianized political leadership." Stepan's main example of this path is the case of Spain. According to him, this path has the best chance of being followed:

(1) the more there are new socioeconomic and political demands from below or from former active supporters, (2) the more there is doubt or conflict about regime legitimacy rules (especially among those who have to enforce obedience), and (3) the more there is the chance that the power-holders will retain and ratify much of their power via competitive elections.

Stepan further points out that in this path, "the military-as-institution is still a factor of significant power. Thus the civilian leadership is most likely to persist in its democratizing initiative (and not to encounter a military reaction) if the democratic opposition tacitly collaborates with the government in creating a peaceful framework for the transition."[55]

This model fits Taiwan fairly well. One especially important area of fit is in the role of the opposition in both keeping pressure on the regime and cooperating with it. A second parallel is the existence of "doubt about regime legitimacy rules," although in Taiwan's case this doubt came not from the ruling party's loss of faith in its ideology, but in the long-standing conflict between this ideology and the authoritarian realities which the regime had always labeled as temporary.

Taiwan, however, differs from Spain in several ways. For one thing, the leader of the old regime did not have to die before the transition started; he started it himself, for reasons we have tried to investigate. Second, this fact in turn dictated that the military was a much less serious potential challenger to the reform, at least during its early phase when CCK was still alive, and even after his death so long as the ongoing reform could continue to carry the mantle of Chiang's blessing. Third, the cooperation provided to the reformist regime by the opposition came about in Taiwan through a long and difficult process of internal struggle within the opposition and between opposition and regime.

The fourth, and perhaps most important, way in which the Taiwan case differs is in the existence of the mainland factor in the Taiwan reform. Among nations that have begun democratic transitions, only South Korea and Taiwan are parts of divided nations. (East Germany might also be cited, but it is doubtful whether the "transition to democracy" literature is intended to apply to the breakdown of communist regimes.) In both cases, and in contrast to all other nations studied in the transitions literature, competition with the other regime has provided a key motive for democratizing reform. This motive has had two related components: the need to improve domestic legitimacy in order to create a political basis for a more effective defense capability; and the need to create a stronger political appeal to the nation's citizens on both sides of the dividing line.

Of course, the confrontations between North and South Korea and Taiwan and mainland China had been going on for forty years before the phase we are identifying as democratic transition began. Thus a full analysis of how the "divided-nation" factor operates would require looking at the changing international environment and, again, at the always-important factors of domestic social, economic, and political conditions. But the point here is only that, given permissive conditions at home and abroad, the divided-nation factor enters the reformers' calculations of potential benefit and cost on the reform side of the ledger.

In the case of Taiwan this presents a double paradox. First, the opposition, many or most of whose members are motivated in part by the desire to assure that Taiwan never comes under mainland control, can thank the looming and threatening presence of the mainland for making their transactions with Chiang Ching-kuo more successful than they probably would have been otherwise—since, we have argued, this looming presence provided Chiang with one of his important motives for accommodating the opposition, however reluctantly. (Probably detailed research on the opposition's behavior during the reform process would show that they, too, were pushed toward more moderate and constructive behavior by the existence of the mainland threat, thus making them more acceptable to Chiang than they otherwise might have been.) Second, a democratization which was initiated to some extent because Taiwan was part of a larger China seems to be leading to Taiwan's increasingly well-established and irreversible *de facto* separation from that China, as the island's politics become more and more responsive to the preferences of the majority.[56]

8

Electing Taiwan's Legislature

In the most democratic election in the history of any Chinese society, Taiwan voters went to the polls on December 19, 1992, and elected a new Legislative Yuan. This body occupies an important place in the Republic of China's (ROC) constitutional structure, with powers to pass laws, review the budget, approve the nomination of the premier, and interpellate cabinet members. The full Legislative Yuan was last elected in mainland China in 1947, and all elections since then had been for "supplementary" members, never constituting a majority, so that the Yuan operated essentially as a rubber stamp. With its complete reelection in 1992, the Yuan's whole membership for the first time was directly accountable to the residents of Taiwan and the Pescadores, the territory actually administered by the Republic of China.

The ROC's political system was not yet fully democratic. The president was not popularly elected, the electronic media remained government-controlled and biased against the opposition, and the central and local election commissions were stacked with ruling party members—although these commissions seem to have operated fairly in this election. However in 1992, in contrast to earlier Legislative Yuan elections, no one was excluded from candidacy for political reasons (there were age and educational limits), and candidates' freedom of speech was virtually unlimited. There were no charges of interference with the secrecy of the ballot, and the only charge of vote-rigging arose in one district in Hualien County. The ruling Kuomintang (KMT) won 60.5% of the vote and 103 of 161 seats; the opposition Democratic Progressive Party (DPP) won 31.9% of the vote and 50 seats; and minor parties and nonparty candidates won 7.6% of the vote and 8 seats.[1]

As Taiwan's political system becomes more democratized, it is appropriate to turn attention from the process of transition to the dynamics of the institutional system that is emerging.[2] The electoral system used to produce the Legislative Yuan is an unusual one in comparative perspective. It belongs to a type which so far as I know is found elsewhere only in Japan, called a "single-vote, multi-member constituency" (SVMM) system.[3] In this system most electoral districts have more than one representative, but each voter has only one vote. Although based on the Japanese model, the ROC electoral system has a higher maximum number of representatives per district—sixteen compared to a maximum of six in Japan where most electoral districts have three to five lower house (Diet) representatives. Japanese and Taiwanese districts have similar sized electorates, averaging about half a million, although in both places the electorates range widely in size from district to district. The ROC's restrictive campaign laws also follow the Japanese example.[4]

This type of system differs both from the single-vote, single-member (SVSM) constituency system found in the United States and Britain, in which each district elects the one candidate with the highest number of votes, and from the proportional representation systems found in some parts of Western Europe and elsewhere in which each voter has as many votes as there are seats. The ROC system produces strategic calculations for candidates, parties, voters, and incumbents that are different from those produced by other types of electoral systems, and that are similar but not identical to those found in Japan. These calculations were fully on display for the first time in the 1992 elections. This analysis of the consequences of Taiwan's electoral system is a preliminary one, based on field observation and simple post-election statistics. Its findings are subject to revision on the basis of more sophisticated voting and survey data that will become available later.

ROC Electoral System

In the 1992 elections, 119 legislators were elected from 27 territorial districts.[5] Unlike in Japan, Taiwan's electoral districts conform to administrative lines, being identical with counties or cities except that the two largest cities are each divided into two districts, North and South. Depending on population size, these districts elected from one to sixteen legislators (see table 8.1). In addition, six legislators were elected by aboriginal voters, who are allowed to cast their ballots anywhere in Taiwan on the strength of their

TABLE 8.1

Lowest Winning Vote in Territorial Districts, 1992 Legislative Yuan Elections

District	Number Seats	Number Candidates	Total Vote	Lowest Winning Vote	LWV as % of Total Vote
Taipei city N.	9	28	603,766	21,060	3.49
Taipei city S.	9	40	588,930	28,048	4.76
Keelong city	29	5	145,817	37,418	25.66
Yilan county	2	5	207,853	56,005	26.94
Taipei county	16	48	1,390,498	36,845	2.65
Taoyuan county	7	13	628,305	50,279	8.00
Hsinchu county	2	7	185,081	57,231	30.92
Hsinchu city	2	10	136,005	29,810	21.92
Miaoli county	3	10	261,884	56,355	21.52
Taichung county	7	16	616,542	58,501	9.49
Taichung city	4	11	332,624	57,206	17.20
Changhua county	7	16	605,489	59,496	9.83
Nantou county	3	7	243,346	48,253	19.83
Yunlin county	4	8	344,045	49,147	14.29
Chiayi county	3	6	278,353	53,905	19.37
Chiayi city	1	2	116,079	58,145	50.09
Tainan county	5	11	502,215	49,235	9.80
Tainan city	4	13	341,480	50,721	14.85
Kaohsiung county	6	13	534,430	40,252	7.53
Kaohsiung city N.	6	14	350,102	33,027	9.43
Kaohsiung city S.	6	13	306,175	32,456	10.60
Pingtung county	5	11	398,989	48,339	12.12
Taitung county	1	7	67,474	35,657	52.85
Hualien county	2	8	122,928	26,667	21.69
Penghu county	1	3	44,393	20,641	46.50
Lienchiang county	1	2	2,807	1,648	58.71
Chinmen county	1	3	20,531	10,926	53.22

Source: Calculated from *Tzu-li tsao-pao*, December 20, 1992, p. 8; *Lien-he pao*, December 20, 1992, pp. 3, 9.

identification-card status as aborigines. All other voters must cast ballots in their residential districts; there is no absentee voting.

Besides territorial-district and aboriginal representatives, the ROC system provides for two proportional-representation (PR) lists, one for thirty "national at-large delegates," notionally representing the mainland areas of the ROC over which the government claims sovereignty but not control, and the other for six overseas Chinese delegates. Each party gets a number of seats on these two lists proportional to the total vote cast for that party in the territorial districts. Thus KMT won nineteen at-large seats, the DPP eleven; the KMT won four overseas Chinese seats and the DPP two. Functional constituencies used in earlier Legislative Yuan elections were abolished for the 1992 election.

In five small territorial constituencies that elect only one delegate each, campaign dynamics fit the winner-take-all model familiar to American voters, but the strategic focus of the election falls on the large constituencies that elect multiple delegates. The largest number of seats are won in such districts as Taipei County with sixteen seats, Taipei City North and South with nine seats each, Taoyuan, Taichung, and Changhua Counties with seven seats each, and Kaohsiung City North and South and Kaohsiung County with six seats each. In these districts not only are there more seats to be won, but also the larger number of votes more heavily influences the distribution of seats from the two PR lists.

Given the system, a candidate in a district with many seats can win with a small percentage of the vote cast, the exact amount depending on how many seats and candidates there are, and on how lopsidedly the top winners win. Mathematically, the number of votes needed for victory in any district by the last winning candidate is the total number of votes, minus the sum of the votes won by the other winning candidates, divided by the total number of remaining candidates, plus one. If there are ten candidates for five seats, and they divide the vote nearly equally, a candidate who gets slightly more than one-tenth of the vote will win. But if the top candidate draws substantially more than one-tenth of the vote, candidates near the bottom of the winners' list will need even less than one-tenth to win. The actual lowest winning votes for each district in 1992 are shown in table 8.1. The minimum winning percentage is even smaller if expressed as a percentage of registered voters. Turnout varies from district to district, averaging 72 percent in the 1992 election. In a total registered electorate of 13,421,170, the smallest number of votes needed to win amounts to as few as 20,000 to 50,000 votes in many districts.[6]

Electoral Strategies: Candidates

The electoral system creates an incentive for anyone with a voter base of roughly 20,000 or more to stand for election.[7] The more candidates there are, the fewer votes are needed to win and the greater the incentive for additional candidates to join the race. To discourage frivolous campaigns, the electoral law calls for confiscation of the deposits of candidates who receive less than a certain minimal percentage of the vote. In the 1992 election, 144 candidates lost their deposits,[8] which is a sign of how strong an incentive the system creates for people with small electoral bases to run for a seat.

Once declared, the obvious strategy for each candidate is to solidify a particular electoral base (*p'iao-yuan*) of which there are several identifiable types. One is local factions, found mostly in rural areas, although there are some urban factions. According to Ming-tong Chen of National Taiwan University, of 165 Kuomintang members competing in the campaign (including those nominated and unnominated by the party), 72 were supported by local factions.[9] A second type of electoral base is provided by the votes of retired military personnel and their dependents who live in special compounds in major cities; this is supplemented by the votes of serving military personnel loyal to the KMT, many of whom are sent home on leave at election time. Residentially concentrated, with a high turnout rate and a high rate of loyalty to the KMT, the veterans and their families are estimated to cast roughly one million votes— referred to as "iron votes" (*t'ieh-p'iao*). Again according to Chen, 56 KMT candidates were supported by the military in this election.

Sub-ethnic constituencies provide a third type of electoral base in some districts. Taipei City, highly urbanized Taipei County, and Kaohsiung City—all districts with large numbers of seats—have heavy populations of migrants from other parts of the island. In Taipei, organized same-place associations (*t'ung-hsiang hui*) from Yunlin, Chia-yi, Changhua, and elsewhere, which have memberships in the tens of thousands, supported specific candidates; in Kaohsiung, different candidates appealed to the mainlander vote, the Hakka vote, and the votes of people from Penghu and Tainan.[10] A fourth kind of electoral base consists of the employees and retainers of major enterprise groups (*ts'ai-t'uan*), which have large concentrations of voters in certain cities. Candidates with this kind of backing, usually enterprise owners or their scions, are derogatorily referred to as golden cows (*chin-niu*).[11]

The support of such constituencies is solidified through constituency service and vote buying. Many candidates maintain a network of service centers (*fu-wu ch'u*) in their districts, through which they maintain contacts with local neighborhood heads and other network leaders. During the 1992 election vote-buying was widely reported, with prices said to range from NT$500 to NT$2,000.[12] But candidates thought to be connected with vote-buying performed less well than expected, according to most press commentators, and a large proportion of voters who accepted money, gifts, or banquet invitations apparently cast their votes independently. This may have reflected both the effectiveness of the anti-vote-buying campaigns mounted by the government and the opposition, and the voters' sense of high stakes in the outcome of the election.

An alternative to the electoral-base strategy is mobilization based on image and ideology. In this strategy candidates reach out through the mass media, handbills, and rallies to try to swing voters with whom they have no network-based connection. In 1992, this type of strategy worked well for two types of candidates. The first was relatively conservative mainlander candidates in Taipei City and Taipei County whose campaigns stressed their educational qualifications, incorruptibility, and willingness to stand up against the party machine and politics as usual. Many of them had been passed up by the ruling party for nomination in favor of factionally supported candidates. The two biggest vote-getters, former environmental administrator Chao Shao-k'ang and ex-Minister of Finance Wang Chien-hsuan, had not been nominated because they were in the cabinet at the time of the nomination process. They then resigned and ran against the party machine with great success (Chao had been the top KMT vote-getter in the 1989 Legislative Yuan elections). The initial impression from street interviews was that Chao, Wang, and other conservative mainlander candidates in Taipei drew their support from the middle class, both mainlander and Taiwanese.

A second kind of image- and ideology-based strategy was used by opposition candidates, stressing their heroic records of political dissidence, past victimization by the regime, willingness to stand up for Taiwanese interests against the mainlander-dominated regime, their commitment to social welfare, women's rights, and Taiwan independence, and their expertise in foreign affairs gained from years of (voluntary or involuntary) residence overseas. Some of these individuals are charismatic, and they attracted large, excited crowds. As part of their strategy, they sometimes engaged in street politics, such as leading groups of supporters to demonstrate and hurl eggs at KMT or government offices. Street interviews suggested that these candidates' base was drawn predominantly from urban workers and rural farmers, and was chiefly male. Several DPP candidates stated that their party is supported by 60 percent of male but only 10 percent of female voters. Despite their lower-class electoral base, DPP campaigners placed about as much stress as do KMT candidates on their educational backgrounds, often including Ph.D.'s earned at overseas institutions.

The traditional constituency-based electoral strategy naturally tends to be preferred by candidates who have a solid electoral base on which to rely. Given the history of the authoritarian regime, these are almost exclusively ruling-party candidates, often incumbents. Their campaign literature stresses sincerity, service, and endorsement by popular leaders like President Lee Teng-hui. They avoid contamination from controversial issues such as Taiwan's international status and often do not bother to display the KMT logo prominently in their campaign material. Their appeal is personal and their goal is to protect their minimum winning vote.

In contrast, candidates using a mobilizational strategy make heavy use of issues like Taiwan independence (for DPP candidates) or corruption (for insurgent KMT candidates) and, in the case of opposition candidates, of the party logo featuring a green silhouette of the island of Taiwan. Instead of seeking to protect a minimum vote base, mobilizational candidates appeal to their supporters to elect them with the highest vote count in their district (*tsui-kao-p'iao*), making the argument that this will send a strong message to the government and will strengthen the candidate's ability to represent his or her supporters in the Legislative Yuan. Lacking an organizational base, they have no way to know whether their projected vote count is in the safe range. Public opinion polls provide little useful information as a majority of Taiwan voters report themselves undecided throughout the campaign. By calling for a high vote count, a candidate hopes to overcome the voters' tendency to vote for their second preferred candidate when they believe that their preferred candidate is safely in the lead. Since many of the image-based candidates are insurgents against or loners within their party, they are not concerned that their high-vote strategy may knock a second candidate of their own party out of the race.

In some ways, the campaign rules are unfavorable to mobilizational campaigning. The campaign is limited to ten days, TV news coverage and television advertising are limited, and spending restrictions are severe although widely ignored. But many candidates have long-established public images based on previous public service or activism in the opposition, and many in both parties rely heavily on newspaper advertising and attractive printed handbills. The literacy rate in Taiwan is high, and the novelty of this first fully democratic election seemed to catch the voters' attention. Some rallies drew audiences of close to 10,000. In general, the campaign seemed to mark one stage in a long and perhaps partial shift from faction to image. One sign of this was that, according to one study, more than 80 percent of candidates who ran campaign advertisements on underground cable TV stations were victorious.[13]

The system tends to generate intraparty feuds. Candidates who think they are losing have a better chance to save themselves by attacking those of their own party who seem to be winning—in order to peel away party loyalists' votes from them—than by trying to win votes away from candidates of the other party. Last-minute charges against a leading candidate's character by a member of the same party were a feature of campaigns in several districts and by both parties. Since the campaign period is short, there is not enough time for the press to investigate such charges and the targeted candidates have to respond very quickly.

Party Strategies

Under this electoral system, it is rational for a party to nominate the number of candidates that it expects to be able to elect with the number of votes it expects to have, and then to use party organization to allocate its votes among the candidates so that each gets just a little more than the minimum number needed to win. The process of spreading the party vote among a party's candidates so that few votes are wasted on the top candidates is called "vote allocation" (*p'ei-p'iao*). Only the KMT has the organizational capability to do this. In each electoral district, KMT candidates sit down with local party officials to decide which candidate will concentrate on which organizations (e.g., the farmer's association, veterans' association, irrigation association) and areas (neighborhoods, villages). Leaders in those organizations and areas are then assigned to deliver quotas of votes to the designated candidate. Party loyalists are discouraged from voting for the candidate they prefer in favor of voting for the candidate that the party organization assigns to them.

The combination of strategic nomination and vote allocation practiced by the KMT is referred to as "organizational warfare," as distinguished from the more mobilizational style used by the opposition DPP. More a congeries of like-minded notables than an institutionalized party, the DPP lacks the capability for organizational warfare.[14] Still, its nomination strategy in the 1992 election reflected the logic of the electoral system. The party put forward only 59 candidates for the 125 territorial constituency seats in the election, nominating in each district only the number it thought that it could elect and avoiding the more adventurist strategy of fielding additional candidates at the risk of dividing the party vote among too many aspirants. Also, the DPP's most famous senior figures came forth as its nominees. As a result, 63 percent of the DPP's nominees in territorial constituencies (37 of 59) were successful.[15] But given the size of the total vote the party's candidates attracted, some districts might have elected an additional DPP legislator had the party been capable of dividing its vote organizationally.

On the other hand, the KMT's rather similar victor-to-candidate ratio of 58 percent (73 of 125) must be read as signaling a decline in its historically strong party discipline. In many districts, KMT candidates who were denied the party nomination ran anyway, some of them supporters of the KMT's "non-mainstream faction" rather than of the group that controlled the party machinery. When such candidates lost, they carried significant numbers of party votes away with them. Among 43 insurgent KMT candidates, only seven were successful, but some of them were high vote-getters.[16] These candidacies made it difficult for the party to allocate votes reliably. It was also considered an indication of the decline in voter discipline that the vote totals of candidates supported by KMT-affiliated enterprise groups were lower than expected, even though 27 of 38 such candidates were elected.[17]

The KMT faced the dilemma of whether to endorse popular insurgent candidates who ran despite the denial of party nominations, thus rewarding their insurgency but gaining the benefit of their votes for its two PR lists. The party offered insurgent candidate Wu Tzyy (Wu Tzu) endorsement but he refused it; it expelled candidate Ch'en Che-nan from the party but still got the benefit of his vote in its PR columns because he had been a KMT candidate when the ballots were drawn up. Many of the non-nominated candidates came from a group called the New KMT Front, which has called for party reform. According to post-election press commentary, the message to the party organization was that it needs more qualified candidates, and the message to candidates was that they have to count more on themselves.

Voter Strategies

The dilemma facing voters in such a system is that while most districts have more than one seat, each voter has only one vote, and that vote cast for a preferred candidate may be wasted if the candidate is widely popular. But if the voter switches to a candidate who seems less likely to win, the risk is that the preferred candidate may lose. To counter voters' temptation to switch in this way, many leading candidates on the last two days of the ten-day campaign advertise that they are in danger of losing, a tactic that looks odd to observers familiar with the American single-winner system in which it makes more sense to claim to be winning, even while warning one's supporters against complacency.

In this context, party-coordinated vote allocation serves the interests of those voters who want the KMT to win the maximum number of seats.

Vote allocation assures them that the maximum number of their pre-ferred candidates will win so long as these like-minded voters observe party discipline. Many independent and opposition voters engage in what is called "automatic vote allocation" (*tzu-tung p'ei-p'iao*), or family-level allocation of the vote[18] in which members of a family agree among themselves to divide their votes among candidates they like. This family-level division is encouraged by the DPP, which lacks the organizational network to engage in more structured vote allocation. The strategy seems to be useful, judging by the party's ability to distribute votes among its candidates in such large districts as Taipei North and South, Kaohsiung North and South, Pingtung, and Tainan County and City.

On the other hand, some voters may be less concerned with the dis-tribution of seats in the Legislative Yuan than with sending a strong sig-nal to the government by piling up votes on a candidate who they believe carries a certain symbolism. The enormous votes for Chao Shao-k'ang (KMT insurgent) and Lu Hsiu-yi (DPP) in Taipei County, and for Wang Chien-hsuan (KMT insurgent) and Ch'en Shui-pien (DPP) in Taipei North sent such messages. But it is in the nature of the ballot that the message it sends can be both strong and vague. High votes for insurgent KMT candidates, for example, were clearly votes against the so-called "KMT mainstream" of President Lee Teng-hui and Party Secretary-General James C. Y. Soong, but they also seemed to be votes in favor of personal probity, courage, high educational qualifications, and substan-tial political experience. Beyond this their meaning was open to inter-pretation.

A number of voters told me that they were voting for the DPP to cre-ate a force to check and balance the KMT. The DPP made this more fea-sible by moderating its platform in comparison to its position in the National Assembly elections in December 1991 in which it performed relatively poorly. The party replaced its 1991 "Taiwan Independence Platform" with an umbrella position of "One China, One Taiwan." Although it foreclosed reunification, this slogan was vague enough to accommodate a variety of positions from Taiwan independence to main-tenance of the status quo. The party also developed a series of positions on welfare statism, lower taxes, women's rights, and so forth, that enabled its candidates to escape from the single-issue trap of 1991. Of its 78 candidates, 62 belonged to moderate factions.[19] Voters in 1992 seemed to view the DPP less as a revolutionary force and more as a bal-ancing partner in a stable democratic system. Since this was the third election in which the DPP participated as a party, they may also have been encouraged to support it by the experience of previous elections carried out without excessive violence or post-election retribution from the mainland.

Voters with whom I spoke were also aware that, for the first time, they were electing the entire Legislative Yuan and not merely supplementary members, as in the past. The election outcome would directly affect the conduct of government. Thus empowered, the voters apparently wanted to send a message of caution to the KMT without throwing it out of office. In a similar spirit, some who voted for KMT insurgent candidates may have wanted to balance the KMT mainstream faction within the party without intending to reject its leader, President Lee Teng-hui.

The election also represented another step in the process by which the native Taiwanese majority has been taking over power in the island's political institutions from the previously dominant mainlander elite. Mainlanders, who made up 60 percent of the membership of the former Legislative Yuan, have now been reduced in number to 22 percent,[20] and mainlander politicians campaigned mostly in the Taiwanese language. One result of the election was the appointment of the first Taiwanese premier, former Taiwan Provincial Governor Lien Chan. Some DPP candidates won on strong Taiwanese-identity campaigns, but this was not always a winning card. A number of candidates of the insurgent KMT "wisdom coalition" ran campaigns based on Taiwanese identity, which were not successful, and in Taipei City, twelve of the eighteen successful candidates were mainlanders, even though the mainlander population of Taipei is only 27 percent.[21] The voters showed that they had more than ethnic identity on their minds, and fears of Taiwanese-mainlander polarization were eased.

Incumbent Strategies

The newly elected legislators have relatively short three-year terms, so incumbents will need to cultivate their local constituencies continuously. Those who ran constituency-based campaigns will work hard to channel central government project funds and social services into their local bases. Those who ran image- and ideology-based campaigns will compete for media attention and, in the case of opposition legislators, engage in street politics to show that they are serving the values of the constituencies that elected them. Each type of candidate may also try to diversify his or her base, with constituency-based candidates trying to polish their

images for honesty or issue commitment, and issue-based candidates trying to provide local services, help constituents with government bureaucracies, and attend more weddings in their districts.

The Legislative Yuan is expected to play a larger role in policy-making
than it did in the past. As the only directly elected organ of ROC government, it is the one with the most popular legitimacy. Legislators are
now more answerable to their constituents than to party leaders, and
with the disappearance of the rubber-stamp majority of elderly mainland-elected legislators, the Yuan's bargaining power vis-à-vis the cabinet
will be at a new high. In a political culture that values consensus, the
DPP's 31 percent of the seats (50 of 161) entitles it to be consulted
extensively by the government. Some DPP members even believe it entitles the party to seats in the cabinet.

Although the ruling KMT has 64 percent of the seats (103 of 161),
the poor performance of "organizational warfare" in this election weakened the ability of the party to control its members' votes in the legislature. On issues ranging from mainland and foreign policy to social welfare and administration of the six-year infrastructure program, the
administration will reach out for support in the Legislative Yuan where
it can find it, which will not always be along party lines. On a number of
these issues, the interests of the "mainstream" (pro-Lee Teng-hui) KMT
faction converge more closely with those of the moderate or "Formosa"
faction of the DPP than with the "non-mainstream" minority faction
within the KMT. Legislators seeking to prove their worth to their constituents will exercise the interpellation power more aggressively than it
has been used in the past. Party discipline is likely to be relatively inef-
fectual in overcoming the priority of local interests in legislative politics.
In short, the election produced what can be called a locally penetrated
center.[22]

Although the candidate who ran on the slogan "Taiwan priority," Wu
Tzyy, failed to be elected, his slogan reflects the direction in which the
Legislative Yuan will probably push government in the coming years.
Since the voters did not vote on strict ethnic lines, Taiwan priority does
not necessarily mean Taiwanese as opposed to mainlander priority. But
the interests of the residents of the island, Taiwanese and mainlander
alike, will dominate the legislators' concerns. One obvious consequence
is that the chances for reunification on the terms currently being offered
by the PRC are dimmer than ever, and the ROC's "flexible diplomacy" is
likely to become even more flexible in the search for the international
respectability that Taiwan's residents crave.[23]

Winning seats did not require candidates to build coalitions across the electorate to "aggregate interests." Local factions, sub-ethnic constituencies, enterprise groups, and issue- and ideology-based groups were all able to place their representatives in the Legislative Yuan. From now on, the Yuan is likely to reflect the shifting levels of ideological and ethnic polarization among voters. The 1992 election seemed to reveal a moderate electorate, but one containing some polarized groups. Voters crossed ethnic lines to vote for candidates with images of personal probity, and they rewarded the DPP for moderating its party platform on independence. But some mainlander candidates came to power chiefly with mainlander votes, and some groups of voters supported fiery DPP politicians who have devoted their careers to pushing aggressively for political change and who openly favor Taiwan independence.

Now that the government has ceased to use the criminal law to censor political discourse, the electorate is the only arbiter of what can be discussed and how. Since the electoral system makes it possible for different groups of voters to reward different types of politicians, we can expect Taiwan's politics to continue to be as lively as ever. Politicians of all shades of opinion will compete for the public ear, and while the danger of polarization is always present, powerful forces are pushing the electorate toward an aggregate preference for moderation. The most important of these forces are Taiwan's growing wealth and its vulnerability to military and political pressure from the mainland.

Conclusion

The 1992 Legislative Yuan election solidified a tacit pact of peaceful coexistence and peaceful competition between a former authoritarian ruling party and a former anti-system opposition movement. Opposition leaders who were in prison or exile just a few years ago took seats in the nation's highest elected body. Despite the bias of the electronic media, the dominance by KMT officials of central and local election commissions, stringent campaign limits, and widespread charges of vote-buying, the electoral system was sufficiently acceptable to both parties so that each participated in it with full energy and each accepted its verdict. The ruling party hailed the election as a step toward two-party democracy, acknowledging the possibility of a future peaceful transfer of power. The DPP stated its intent to "fulfill the responsibilities of an opposition party in a modern democratic state."[24] In short, after years of struggle between regime and opposition, the opposition has been granted legitimacy within the system and has accepted the legitimacy of the system. In retrospect, it was a remarkably peaceful transition, despite some large street demonstrations, political arrests, and the breaking of some desks and chairs in the Legislative Yuan over the preceding few years.

Not only is the ROC electoral system unusual in comparative perspective, but its relationship to the party system reverses a common historical pattern. Most party systems were shaped through history by their countries' electoral systems, among other factors. In Taiwan, the party system was formed in the absence of national-level elections, although Taiwan has been holding hard-fought local elections for years. Now for the first time the electoral system has started to affect the party system.[25] Its initial impact appears to be to promote internal fragmentation in the ruling party, while encouraging a fragmented opposition party to remain so. Other forces are also at work, so the outcome is by no means predetermined.

Indeed, the electoral system itself is subject to change at the parties' initiative. A relatively minor reform that has been discussed would allow each voter two votes, one for a local candidate and the second for the two proportional-representation lists. Such a change would probably favor the opposition because it would allow voters beholden to ruling-party candidates to cast a second, balancing vote for the opposition. It would also create an incentive for each party to pay more attention to its platform and to its image as an organization. A bolder reform would be to shift to the single vote, single member system, with one legislator per district and smaller districts. Such a change would offer potential gains and risks to each party. Although the current system allowed an opposition with less than one-third of the vote to establish a strong foothold in the Legislative Yuan, it also enabled the ruling party, with its strong local bases, to maintain a majority position that will be difficult to shake. For the opposition to move from a minority to a majority under the current system, it would have to recruit scores of additional attractive candidates and painstakingly build local party machines that could compete with local pro-KMT factions. If just one seat per district were to be filled, the DPP could field its strongest candidates in one-on-one battles with KMT nominees, and it might be able to break out of what now looks likely to be protracted minority status. But under such a system, the KMT would be able to turn its 60 percent electoral majority into a near-100 percent control of the Legislative Yuan if it could get more than 50 percent of the vote in each district.

The complexity of the system makes it difficult to say unambiguously whose interests it favors. It also creates numerous vested interests among currently elected politicians with their small electoral bases, and the constituencies they serve. So far, neither party has decided to support change in the system, and it may be difficult to construct a consensus for change in the foreseeable future.

9

The Struggle for Hong Kong's Future

Hong Kong's 6 million people, 98 percent of them ethnic Chinese, have the world's tenth largest trading economy, a 5.5 percent annual growth rate, and a GDP per capita in excess of Mother England's. Compared with Britain, Hong Kong also has a better infrastructure, better social services, cleaner streets, and a better-educated population.

Queen's Road Central bustles with young executives—sleek, smart, with foreign MBA's, many of them women, many running family firms that manufacture in South China and sell in Paris and New York. Multistory malls such as Pacific Place and Ocean Terminal display Chinese dried mushrooms and Rolex watches, antique calligraphy and Hermès scarves, Scotch whiskey and dried tiger's penis. Hong Kong residents worship at the world's largest outdoor Buddha; attend classes at some of the world's most sophisticated universities; bet at the race track and dress up in black tie and ball gowns for the Annual Ivy Ball, attended by hundreds of U.S. university graduates.

A taxi ride from Central brings you to mountain paths threading through the woods of Tai Tam Reservoir. On the back of the island, beaches look out on scores of small rocky islands whose fishing villages and seafood restaurants can be reached by ferry. Seagoing cargo ships thread their way into the deep-water harbor. The harbor draws Victoria Island together with Kowloon peninsula in a living sculpture of glittering skyscrapers, decorated with ferries, freighters, and planes moving in and out of Kai Tak Airport.

Frank Welsh, an English businessman and writer, has written a history not so much of Hong Kong as of British rule there, a study in colonial rather than in Chinese history.[1] Drawing chiefly on British archives and memoirs, he presents a parade of merchants, generals, ambassadors, financial secretaries, governors and the men's wives, showing them as alternately affable, pompous, visionary and eccentric. I have always wondered about Nathan Road, Kowloon's main commercial street. It turns out to be named after its builder, Sir Matthew Nathan, governor from 1904 to 1907, bachelor engineer and also founder of the Kowloon-Canton Railway.

Welsh gives about 300 pages to the colony's first fifty years, the remaining 250 to a gallop through the twentieth century. He tells an affectionate story of foibles and follies, half-intended wars, business ventures, hot weather, fever, gambling, prostitution, and public works. The book is a parade of the droll and the quotable, except for episodes of war and diplomacy where the tone becomes appropriately sober. Welsh has used only a few Chinese sources, spelling Chinese personal and place names wrong almost as often as he spells them right.

Welsh puzzles over how Britain got involved on this "barren rock" and how it made a go of it. The colony remained until the 1950s "a colonial backwater," a trading post linking the Chinese and British economies. The international order that emerged after World War II was marked by a growing international division of labor in manufacturing and by burgeoning international trade. It was the fall of China to communism that made it possible for Hong Kong to take advantage of those trends with a combination of cheap refugee labor and entrepreneurs from Shanghai and Ningbo.

While China isolated itself under Mao, its exiled capitalists in its lost territory built a paradigm of an export-oriented economy, of the sort that the mainland now wants to emulate. Hong Kong started with textiles and other low-quality goods and followed Japan up the value-added ladder, moving ahead of competitors into more capital- and technology- intensive products. After Deng Xiaoping opened up China, Hong Kong shifted its sweatshops to the mainland, while retaining engineering, design, and marketing functions in the air-conditioned towers of Central and Kowloon. And as the rest of East Asia boomed, Hong Kong took advantage of its location, facilities, and freedoms to become the center of regional banking, lawyering, shipping, and media, to develop a major stock market and to nurture some of the biggest global investors.

The Crown Colony consists of three parts. Victoria Island, 32 square miles, was ceded in perpetuity in 1841 (with treaty confirmation in 1842) after a handful of young British merchants and naval officers picked a fight with the Chinese empire and won what became known as the Opium War. This displeased Prime Minister Lord Palmerston, who wrote, "You have obtained the Cession of Hong Kong, a barren island with hardly a house on it. . . . Now it seems obvious that Hong Kong will not be a Mart of Trade." In 1860, after another clash, Britain acquired the peninsula of Kowloon, comprising nearly four square miles, aiming to protect the island from pressure from other foreign powers. In 1898, during the "scramble for concessions," the colony added the 365-square-mile New Territories, again with a view to buffering the existing territory from outside pressure.

The New Territories, however, were not acquired outright, but by a ninety-nine year lease, in the style of fin-de-siècle imperialism. Hence the magic date 1997, which was at the center of the Sino-British troubles marking the end of Hong Kong's colonial life. They stemmed from the same source as the Opium War at its beginning—in Welsh's words, "a clash of cultures [that] was inevitable . . . given the supreme self-confidence of both parties."

If Britain had not raised the issue of 1997 in 1979, the Chinese might not have done so, either. They considered the Unequal Treaties, as they called them, illegal anyway. This meant they could take back Hong Kong whenever they wanted, which was no time soon as long as the colony kept producing foreign exchange for the motherland. As T. L. Tsim, a Hong Kong columnist, put it, the Chinese view was, "We don't think there is a problem. If you still think there is a problem, it is your problem."[2] But the British feared declining business confidence due to uncertainty about 1997. So a few years after Mao's death in 1976, when Sino-Western relations were warming, they privately offered to stay in Hong Kong beyond the end of the lease and continue to run the territory in the mutual interest of London and Beijing. Deng Xiaoping had to say no.

In 1982, Mrs. Thatcher visited Beijing fresh from her Falklands victory, aiming to talk sense into the old man. She took the line that the original treaties were still valid, apparently angling to prolong the British presence indefinitely. Deng found this infuriating. The Hong Kong stock market plunged. The late, legendary David Bonavia of *The Times* wrote of Thatcher's visit, "Seldom in British colonial history was so much damage done to the interests of so many people in such a short space of time by a single person."[3]

After two more years of negotiations, the Chinese and the British issued a Joint Declaration in 1984, which they hailed as guaranteeing the stability and prosperity of Hong Kong. China would resume sovereignty in 1997. Until then, Britain would govern. In 1997, Hong Kong would become a Special Administrative Region (SAR) under a Basic Law to be written by China's national legislature. For at least fifty years beyond that, Hong Kong would enjoy "a high degree of autonomy" and maintain its social system unchanged, under Deng's concept of "one country, two systems." (By separate agreement with Portugal, tiny neighboring Macao reverts to Chinese control in 1999.)

"The runup to '97," however, revealed misunderstandings buried in the Joint Declaration. For Britain, exit with honor from its last colony required "mak[ing] possible the widest democratic participation by the people of Hong Kong in the running of their own affairs," in the words of Hong Kong's last Governor Chris Patten.[4] This was in keeping with the British practice of decolonization elsewhere and with democratizing trends in the post-Cold War era.

Moreover, the previously apolitical residents of Hong Kong wanted political reform. Until then always psychologically on the way from someplace to someplace else (as Welsh's title suggests), the people of Hong Kong were shocked that the Joint Declaration and the Basic Law were written without any real input from them. The prospect of merging into the chaotic mess north of the border concentrated their minds on the value of their security, prosperity, and freedom. On vacation trips to China, they found themselves treated as future wards by scruffy mainlanders. Hong Kongers responded with a mix of "fear, hostility, condescension and aversion," in the words of Hong Kong sociologist S.K. Lau.[5]

The killings in Beijing on June 4, 1989, sparked vast anti-China demonstrations in Hong Kong. When the PRC's National People's Congress adopted the Basic Law in 1990, it contained numerous provisions designed to keep power in the hands of Beijing. A pro-democracy group swept twelve of the fourteen seats it contested in Hong Kong's 1991 Legislative Council elections, the first in which any LegCo members were directly elected. Meanwhile, Beijing's reluctance to approve financing for an expensive new Hong Kong airport undermined the conciliatory policy of Britain's hitherto dominant China-policy "mandarins," Sir Percy Cradock and then Hong Kong Governor Sir David Wilson.

A few weeks before the newly arrived Governor Patten introduced the most sweeping of a series of British reform proposals, he told some visitors, including me, that he intended to persuade Beijing that accountable government would make Hong Kong easier rather than harder to rule after 1997. Welsh points out that the shift in 1971 from appointing governors with Colonial Office careers to appointing those with Foreign

Office backgrounds reflected a change in priorities from administering Hong Kong to dealing with Beijing. By the same token, the appointment in 1992 of Patten, a former M.P., former minister of environment, former chairman of the Conservative Party, talented campaigner and close ally of Prime Minister John Major (and early in his career, an aide to New York Mayor John Lindsay), reflected the importance in British politics of a graceful departure from Hong Kong, as well as the fact that such a departure would need the Hong Kong people's support.

No one who met Patten doubted his commitment to democratic government, except the Chinese leaders. Where Britain saw honor, the Chinese saw perfidy. Their view was described in the serialized memoirs of Xu Jiatun, Beijing's chief representative in Hong Kong from 1983 until his defection shortly after the 1989 crackdown. China expected the British to return power in Hong Kong "to China, not to the people of Hong Kong." (Hong Kong, after all, had no sovereignty.) That which China was planning to keep unchanged for fifty years was not a new democracy created during the waning years of British rule, but the same executive-led system that the British found adequate for 150 years and that would have been as easily dominated from Beijing as it had been from London.

The Chinese suspected Britain of using democratic reform to sow dragon's teeth of chaos, nurturing in Xu's words "pro-British forces which could be relied on to continue to rule Hong Kong after 1997 as a regent of London even in the absence of British rule." They feared people such as Martin Lee, the leader of the United Democrats, a ramrod Lincoln's Inn barrister with a clipped British accent, who had given up drinking tea and coffee to get in shape for the political imprisonment he anticipated after 1997.

In the eyes of the Chinese, Patten violated previous understandings and common sense. He reversed the practice of consulting the Chinese in advance of major decisions and denied them the veto they felt was implicit in the concept of "convergence" between the pre- and post-1997 systems. He spoke with irony, understatement, and logic, and acted as if he thought words meant what they said, in Beijing's eyes signs of weak reason or bad will. Beijing called Patten in ascending order a "political prostitute, a "two-headed snake," and "the triple violator" (for violating the Joint Declaration, the Basic Law, and some pre-Patten diplomatic letters).

Patten proposed to transform the Legislative Council from an appointed advisory body into an autonomous legislature, with a majority of its members accountable to the electorate through competitive elections in geographic and functional constituencies. He envisioned LegCo functioning on the Whitehall model of public debate and legislative supremacy. Chinese leaders wanted elections in which party-selected representatives would be confirmed in a display of public consensus. They expected LegCo to serve as a "flower vase" akin to Beijing's National People's Congress. Patten argued that the choice was his and LegCo's, since Britain still ruled Hong Kong and his proposals were not inconsistent with the letter of either the Joint Declaration or the Basic Law. The Chinese answered, in effect, that it was their Basic Law and they knew what it meant. The contretemps revealed two different concepts of "a high degree of autonomy," two different concepts of law, and two different concepts of national honor.

China's leaders had large interests at stake. Reform in Hong Kong (as in Taiwan) increases pressure for democratization in China. The prosperous province next door, Guangdong, may be the place where domestic political control comes unbuttoned. Other restless regions, such as Tibet and Xinjiang, may ask for democratic self-rule on the Hong Kong model. Abroad, a weak response in such a crucial place to a challenge from a weak power would reduce the credibility of Beijing's demands that countries such as France and the United States respect Chinese sensitivities in Taiwan and Tibet. The Sino-British agreement granted Hong Kong a quasi-independent foreign policy in technical areas such as aviation, GATT (WTO) membership, attendance at international trade meetings, Interpol membership, Olympic membership, and so on. In 1992 the U.S. Congress adopted the McConnell Act, expressing an American national interest in Hong Kong's freedom and prosperity. A democratic Hong Kong is more likely to invite foreign interference in internal disputes with the home government in Beijing.

To stave off such problems, the Chinese leaders preferred to confront Britain sooner instead of the people of Hong Kong later. Beijing's chief policymaker for Hong Kong, Lu Ping, warned residents in 1994 that "the value of Hong Kong to China has been and will be its economic value. . . . Of course there are always a handful who are so naive [as] to think that they can turn Hong Kong into a political city in order to influence the mainland in the sense of politics. If that were the case, Hong Kong would be of negative value instead of positive value to China. This [would be] disastrous for Hong Kong."[6] Inside the colony the confrontation produced strange partnerships. In the words of the sociologist Paul C. K. Kwong, "on one side is a peculiar alliance of high official[s] and Chinese tycoons which is trying to maintain a colonial structure encrusted until recently in a polity featuring a political appointment-cum-consultative system. . . . On the other side is a lameduck colonial government which is wooing the public, the middle class, the smaller businessmen, and international capital to support its hastily drawn up blueprint of quicker democratization."[7]

"We're all investing in China," an elegant businesswoman told me at a dinner in Hong Kong in 1994, adding with a wrinkled nose, "We don't like Patten." Hong Kong's "property boys," as some call them, encounter the corruption, lawlessness, and arbitrariness that are part of doing business in China but tell themselves that "things in China are done on a handshake," "I have connections that will protect me," and "the most important human right is to have enough to eat." They persuade themselves that China's current 12 percent growth rate will continue, the Chinese army won't split after Deng, the collective party leadership will hold together, economic growth will improve human rights, and outside investment will subvert the police state from within. The Hong Kong elite expresses more anxiety about the economic consequences of American human rights pressure on China than about the impact of human rights violations themselves on political stability in China and Hong Kong.

The property boys are in some ways more intimately involved in China's economic development than the reformers in Beijing. It is not merely the magnitude of the investment funds passing through Hong Kong that matters, although the amounts in transit constitute two-thirds of direct foreign investment in the mainland. More important is the alchemy that occurs when tens of billions of dollars from China flow into the thousands of Hong Kong "shell companies" (also known as "false foreign devils") set up by Chinese enterprises and government offices in Hong Kong, and are then reinvested back in China in private companies or joint ventures. In a dialectic worthy of Marx, the pass-through transforms money-losing socialist capital sodden with pension obligations, central government quotas, investment controls, and profit remittance requirements into money-making capitalist capital responding with robber-baron keenness to domestic and international markets.

The result is an ambiguous kind of "property-rights reform," to borrow a euphemism beloved by both economic theorists and Chinese reformers. Just as the ancient Daoist philosopher Zhuangzi did not know whether he was a philosopher dreaming he was a butterfly or a butterfly dreaming he was a philosopher, so China's state enterprises do not seem to know—or do not want others to know—whether they are socialist firms employing market techniques or capitalist companies renting government doorplates. In either case, Chinese state enterprises are eating their "stateness" away from within under the ardent tutelage of Hong Kong's patriotic capitalists.

Patten was unable to convince Beijing that the secret of Hong Kong's success is the rule of law, which would depend on a democratically elected, independent legislature (and an independent judiciary, another focus of debate). Having been rebuffed by Beijing in a series of talks that collapsed in 1994, he moved with LegCo support to implement his proposals without Chinese approval. Beijing in turn threatened to dissolve LegCo and two other tiers of elected bodies in 1997 and start over. The stage was set for repression. Patten's gamble in this sense had already failed. He ultimately could not win unless Beijing changed its mind about Hong Kong democracy.

But neither could he lose. A possible future British Prime Minister, Patten had gained an international reputation standing up to China and had no incentive to back down. He chose to place plates of glass around Hong Kong, in the words of an American diplomat, so that if the Chinese shattered them, at least the world would hear.

Should the glass shatter or slowly crack, Americans will become more aware of our interests in this once-borrowed place. Hong Kong is one of our major trading partners, and the center of our business presence in China and the Asia-Pacific region. A healthy Hong Kong is a strong force for the "peaceful evolution" of China. Its successful integration into China would establish a worldwide precedent for the peaceful settlement of territorial issues, the coexistence of different social and economic systems and the solution of political and ideological issues by open competition. The crushing of Hong Kong's freedom would damage the post-Cold War momentum toward democracy, hurt economic growth and political stability in the region, and destroy a valuable way of life that embodies entrepreneurship, personal freedom, and cultural pluralism.

There is, unfortunately, almost nothing America can do to avert a Hong Kong "train wreck." Expressions of concern are cheap, MFN trading privileges have already been abandoned as an instrument for influencing China and Beijing's leaders have shown they will pay any economic price to keep power. The only hope is that the modernization of China will bring wiser, more tolerant leaders to power in Beijing.

Yet the biggest threat to Hong Kong's future prosperity is not political repression, which the economy can survive within limits. Nor is it that Beijing will violate the principle of "one country two systems" as it understands it—as keeping a market system open and "letting the horses keep racing and the dancers keep dancing." It is that Hong Kong will be infected with the mainland's corruption. Xu Jiatun stated that, in the late 1980s, 200 sons and daughters of high-ranking mainland cadres were doing business in Hong Kong. Many mixed public and private money, led extravagant lives, and used their influence to gain positions and pay-offs from Hong Kong businesses.[8] Some "worms turned into dragons," that is, became rich; others went bankrupt and fled. Hong Kong investors, traders, publishers, and officials began their accommodations with people in power in Beijing and Guangdong the moment the Joint Declaration was signed. They started paying a tax in money and freedom that could easily grow large enough to undercut Hong Kong's competitiveness.

Hong Kong's hotel rooms were fully booked for June 30, 1997. At midnight the Union Jack was lowered at Government House. The next morning, the city looked as beautiful as ever. Hong Kong had survived. But barring unlikely changes in China, Hong Kong has made an invisible transition, from a stable member of the developed world to an emerging market in a Third World dictatorship.

10

Is Chinese Culture Distinctive?

Anyone who works in the field of area studies knows from experience that cultures are different. Indeed, the effort to understand the distinctiveness of cultures in comparative perspective is a central undertaking of the modern humanities and social sciences, not only in Asian studies but also in studies of other parts of the world. But works on the subject seldom discuss the conceptual and methodological issues involved. What do we mean by culture in the context of comparative statements? How can a culture's distinctiveness be conceptualized? What is required to demonstrate that such distinctiveness exists, what it consists of, and what influence it has on the performance of societies? In the case of Chinese studies, how far have we come in establishing that Chinese culture is distinctive, in what ways, and with what consequences?

It is helpful to discuss these issues in terms of two bodies of literature with different ways of conceptualizing culture and its distinctiveness, although I intend to blur the distinction at the end.[1] Following Ying-shih Yü, I will label the two approaches hermeneutic and positivistic.[2] I do not argue that one of the approaches is better than the other; each achieves goals that the other does not. The real problem is lack of clarity about the different logical statuses of the kinds of findings that typically emerge from the two approaches. This can lead to problems when insights are transposed from the hermeneutic approach into positivistic language or vice versa.

Although I will suggest two meanings of distinctiveness, both involve identifying a culture's differences from another culture or cultures along one or more dimensions. In analyzing differences, two operations are involved: abstraction (of a characteristic to be compared) and comparison. These moves are often made in order to take a third step: to use the differences in culture to explain a difference in some societal outcome, such as economic development or democratization.

In the course of these operations, knowledge about a single culture is sometimes restated as knowledge about two cultures, hermeneutic knowledge as positivistic knowledge, insight about what makes a society unique as comparison of differences among cultures. A reverse error is made when comparative differences among cultures are treated as absolute differences that place each society beyond comparison. In either of these cases, we learn something about what Chinese culture is like, but gain unreliable information about its distinctiveness. In this review essay, I will argue that we can enjoy the potential benefits of living in two methodological worlds, but only if we avoid pitfalls in negotiating back and forth between the two.

Hermeneutic Approaches to Distinctiveness

The hermeneutic approach views culture as a historically shaped, socially shared set of symbols, concepts, and ways of organizing them. The major concern of hermeneutic works is interpretation. Hermeneutic methods vary, but have in common the attempt to elucidate meaning in a text or a text-analogue (such as a pattern of belief or belief-revealing behavior) by paying attention to the text's context and its inner structure. This family of methods seeks to understand culture by exploring its "pattern of meanings," in the phrase of Clifford Geertz, or by sympathetically entering what Benjamin Schwartz calls its "world of thought" to explore the "problematiques" of its thinkers and discover their "shared cultural assumptions."[3] The approach predominates in all but two of the books reviewed here, reflecting the fact that the positivistic approach remains relatively underdeveloped in Chinese cultural studies for a variety of reasons.

A common theme of hermeneutic works is cultural identity, which is the chief subject of two works under review here. Wang Gungwu's book, a collection of sixteen previously published lectures and essays, describes "the Chineseness of China" from many angles, as a civilization, a place, a society, and a people.[4] The book contains chapters on Tang geopolitics, historiography in the imperial and communist periods, China's relations with its neighbors, the roles of Chinese intellectuals, and Mao Zedong. Wang builds up a picture of Chinese identity as ever-changing but rooted in an awareness of its own past. He concludes that "the Chineseness of China" is whatever went on among Chinese, so that "there is nothing absolute about being Chinese" (p. 266).

Much of the material in "The Living Tree" likewise addresses the question of what it means to be Chinese.[5] In his introductory essay, Tu Wei-ming argues that the qualifying factor is participation in the "symbolic universe" of Chinese civilization, even if the participant is living in the diaspora or is ethnically non-Chinese. The nine essays range from Mark Elvin's evocation of "the inner world of 1830" to meditations on the roles of the intellectuals and the overseas Chinese communities in what one author calls "the construction of Chinese identity." Chinese identity proves to be so elusive that the participants conclude that "the only relevant criterion of identity is the self-identity perceived by a person" (Hsu Cho-yun in end matter, no page). In Myron Cohen's words, where once there was a common Chinese culture, today the identity of "being Chinese is no longer buttressed by a firm sense of cultural participation in something Chinese," so that Chineseness has become "as much a quest as a condition" (p. 133).

If cultural identity is a subjective psychological affiliation that members of a society can accept, reject, or change, one can validly make only certain kinds of comparative statements about it. One can say, as Tu Wei-ming does, that identity has been more of a problem for Chinese than for Indian intellectuals (p. 2), or that Hong Kong people's Chinese identity is stronger than Singapore people's (p. 11). But one cannot lay out objectively what Chineseness consists of and say who is more Chinese than whom. For example, we should not read literally Wang Gungwu's statement that "The most Chinese thing about Mao Tse-tung was his poetry and his loyalty to its traditional forms" (p. 261), as if Wang were suggesting that a person who considered himself Chinese but was less loyal to traditional poetry than Mao would actually be less Chinese. For, as Wang says a few pages later, "an American-educated engineer who subscribed to Jeffersonian democracy and loyally served the Canton Government under Sun Yat-sen [was not] any less Chinese than Mao" (pp. 265–66). Like Tu and his contributors, Wang builds a mosaic of ways of being Chinese rather than a list of Chinese characteristics.

The hermeneutic approach also can be used to compare cultures objectively, as it is in two other books under review. Benjamin Schwartz's book consists of two lectures given at the University of Arizona in 1982.[6] In the first, in order to explore the "qualitative differences between cultures, which endure over time" (p. 3), he compares the civilization of ancient China to those of ancient India, the Middle East, Greece, and the Jewish world. As distinctive features of Chinese civilization, he identifies, among others, ancestor worship, the "religious quality of Chinese familial life," the theme of universal kingship, the familial model of the Chinese socio-political order, the unity of ruling and teaching, the "primacy" and "sacred" quality of the political order, the "faith that the good order had been realized in the past," and a sense of total order. The second lecture explores continuity and change in Chinese culture from the ancient period to the modern.

The other, Lucian Pye's book, is an effort to identify attributes of Chinese political culture that help explain why China has had a harder time with political development than some other countries.[7] He put his classic work back into print, with two new chapters, with the conviction that "the special importance of political culture for understanding China . . . lies in the ways in which China is unique at both the collective and the individual levels" (p. ix). To understand political culture, he uses an approach that he describes in a later work as "interpretive political culture studies."[8] As he explained in *Spirit*'s original preface (not reprinted in the new edition), in this method "our concern is to describe the constellation of sentiment and attitudes that we feel must have existed for the Chinese political system to have developed as it has. We are not concerned with questions about the actual distribution of attitudes and feelings throughout the Chinese population" (orig. ed., p. viii).

As with the works on identity, comparative statements in these works should be read in light of their conceptualization of culture. Although their approaches differ in many ways, Schwartz and Pye have in common that they conceptualize culture as a complex of attributes defined so specifically that they are not found in the same form anywhere else. When Pye speaks about the management of aggression as a central problem in Chinese political culture, he does not mean that aggression is unique to China, but that in China the problem is "particularly acute . . . because the impact of the modern world . . . disrupted the elaborate mechanisms by which the drives of aggression had been traditionally repressed" (pp. 33–34). When Schwartz singles out as distinctive "the religious quality of Chinese family life," he does not mean that in no other ancient civilization did family life have much of a religious quality at all, but that no other ancient civilization had a religious quality of family life quite like China's.

Similarly, when Schwartz argues that ancestor worship was a distinctive characteristic of ancient Chinese society, the statement should be under-

stood in the following sense, as no doubt it was intended. Religious worship exists in all societies. Ancestor worship is a form of religious worship
that exists in many societies. Specifically Chinese-style ancestor worship
existed only in China. The finding of China's distinctiveness is a function
of the level of specificity at which Schwartz has conceptualized his object
of comparison, Chinese-style ancestor worship. By the same token, one
could go on to say that ancestor worship in the Qing was different from
ancestor worship in the Ming, and ancestor worship in Guangdong during the Qing different from ancestor worship in Hebei during the Qing,
and so on.

Comparison rests on a prior operation of classification. Objects can
properly be compared only with objects belonging to the same class,
except to make the trivial point that they belong to different classes. If
that class is populated in one society and empty in others, then the object
is properly said to be unique, i.e., "distinctive" in the first of two senses of
that word that I want to identify. But this finding is dependent on the
level of generality at which the class is defined. A sugar doughnut is different from a jelly doughnut, but both are doughnuts, and doughnuts
are cakes, and cakes are sweets. Although each object is unique, it can
also be conceptualized as belonging to a class within which it is not
unique.

Uniqueness is thus a function of location on what Giovanni Sartori has
called the "ladder of abstraction." Moving up the ladder is a process of
simplification, reducing the number of definitional attributes. Moving
down the ladder is a process of complication, rendering the object more
complex and hence more specific.[9] For a given object, at a given level on
the ladder, a finding of uniqueness is preordained. In this sense it is true
by definition, not in the sense that it is obvious to the ignorant but in the
sense that it is a consequence of conceptualization. In effect, such finding of uniqueness is not a finding about a society's culture in comparative perspective, but a finding about one's way of defining the cultural
complex one has selected for comparison.

We already knew that two cultures were not identical when we identified them as two cultures rather than one. A true-by-definition finding of
uniqueness tells us in more detail how the two cultures are not the same.
This is often worthwhile. But it may not take us as far as we often want to
go. For a variety of reasons (discussed further below) we may also need
to ask how much the two cultures differ, how they compare rather than
how they are unique; in other words, how they are "distinctive" in the second sense of the word. In this second sense, unlike the first, the attribute

exists in both cultures. We want to know about the degree of difference between the two in the attribute's quantity (extent, degree, etc.), quality (intensity, functional importance, etc.), distribution (sector of society, geographical location), or relationship (pattern of association with other attributes). From the level of abstraction at which one makes a finding of uniqueness, one has to move to a higher level of abstraction to make such findings about difference.

To anticipate a point developed further below, it would be fallacious either to restate a finding of uniqueness as a finding of difference, or to restate a finding of difference as a finding of uniqueness. To say Chinese aggression expresses itself in unique ways is not to say the Chinese are more aggressive than others; to say the Chinese are more aggressive than others is not to say they are unique in possessing the psychological drive of aggression.

Perhaps because so many of the contrasts noted in hermeneutic works are true by virtue of conceptualization, they are seldom given close specification as to time, place, and social group. Schwartz warns that culture is not unitary or changeless, that the existence of "dominant" and "persistent orientations" does not rule out the existence of alternative views, that there are class differences and differences between high and popular cultures. Yet he, along with others using this approach, seldom states explicitly which class or group of people he believes held which attitude at what time.[10] In addition, many writers in this tradition treat similarities across time as continuities, without attention to the alternative possibilities that they are parallel developments or not even really similar, and without asking how continuity was created.[11] Authors often discuss institutions as if they too were culture, setting up a tautological relationship between beliefs and behaviors, in which the behaviors are both the evidence for the attitudes and their purported consequence.

In many hermeneutic works the comparison culture—the object of contrast—is not seriously analyzed and is reduced to a stereotype. Wang Gungwu's chapter on "Power, Rights, and Duties in Chinese History" is an exception; it pauses to give nuanced, if brief, definition to the Western versions of the concepts with which he contrasts Chinese ideas. An even more fully developed example of such an exception is Rodney Taylor's careful comparison of the ideas of the Confucian sage and the Christian saint, in which he uses careful hermeneutic analysis to show that, although the two concepts are different in specifics, at a higher level of abstraction they have enough in common to support the view that Confucianism has an important "religious dimension."[12] By developing both sides of a comparison, such works use hermeneutic methods to achieve findings about difference rather than findings of uniqueness.

Positivist Approaches to Distinctiveness

Positivist approaches to cultural distinctiveness produce not better but different answers, having their own limitations. Contrary to caricatures by some critics, the kind of positivism influential today is not the version that flourished through the early 1960s, which sought natural science-like laws of history and behavior based on the comparison of epistemologically unproblematic, objective facts. It is a diminished positivism that requires only that any proposition be precisely specified (for example, with respect to time frame, social actors, geographical location, and indicators of amount or degree), that it be stated in a form that is potentially disprovable by reference to empirical evidence (the falsifiability criterion), and that it be treated as unproven until empirically proven. In order to meet these requirements, positivists conceptualize culture as a distribution among a population of specifiable and identifiable attitudes, values, and beliefs.

For cultural comparison, positivist approaches have advantages and disadvantages. The differences between the two approaches can be illustrated with examples from some recent studies that use survey research, a popular positivist method that has recently come into use in Chinese studies, to investigate some themes that are also treated in the hermeneutic literature.

For example, one of the most common hermeneutic findings about the distinctiveness of Chinese culture is that it lays greater stress than other cultures on the use of *guanxi* (personal connections), the Chinese term for certain kinds of particularistic ties between pairs of people. In the Tu volume, Ambrose King argues that "to know and practice *guanxi* is part of learned behavior—of being Chinese" (p. 79). Fei contrasts Western societies based on organizations with the Chinese pattern, in which "our social relationships spread out gradually, from individual to individual, resulting in an accumulation of personal connections [which] form a network" (p. 70).[13] Survey research in both the United States and China included the following question: "From time to time, most people discuss important matters with other people. Looking back over the last six months, who are the people with whom you discussed matters important to you?" By collecting data on the backgrounds of these people, researchers were able to compile information on social networks in the two societies. Among other findings, Chinese persons' networks are twice as large as Americans'; Chinese are more likely to associate with people of the same age and educational level; and Chinese are less likely than Americans to mention kin as important associates. In explaining these differences, the researchers referred to the importance of the work unit in Chinese society, which dictates that most Chinese have constant, intimate, and important relations with colleagues at work.[14] The findings tend to support the notion that *guanxi* are more important in China than in America, but also reveal that these ties are more instrumental than personal in nature.[15] Although China-U.S. differences exist, the comparison also demonstrates that networks built out of personal relationships are not unique to China.[16]

Another theme treated in both hermeneutic and positivisitic studies is personalistic factionalism, or the use of *guanxi* in politics. Pye, for example, considers *guanxi* to be "the key ingredient of [Chinese] factions" (p. 212). In a 1985 Hong Kong survey by S. K. Lau and H. C. Kuan, respondents were asked to name effective ways to influence government policy. One-point-eight percent spoke of making use of relatives who are officials; 18.1 percent mentioned writing letters to officials or meeting them in person; 25.7 percent mentioned mobilizing and organizing the people affected; 14.7 percent mentioned exercising influence through political parties and other political organizations; 3.8 percent said they would demonstrate and protest; 1.8 percent gave other methods, and the rest said there was no way or did not answer. This can be compared with data from the 1959–60 *Civic Culture* surveys in five countries in which citizens were asked what they would do to try to influence their local government. None of the respondents mentioned working through relatives who were officials; the percentages in the U.S., U.K., Germany, Italy, and Mexico who said they would organize an informal group of friends and neighbors ranged from a low of 7 percent to a high of 56 percent depending on the country; the percentages who spoke of directly contacting elected officials or the press ranged from 12 percent to 45 percent; and a range of other items was mentioned.[17] The findings show that the cultural options for political action are distinctive in each of the six places, yet the range of possible approaches to political influence is basically similar. The distribution does not support the idea that the Chinese in Hong Kong are partial to the use of *guanxi* in politics to a striking degree.

A third theme treated in both kinds of literature is intolerance. Pye argues that Chinese political culture demands obeisance to whatever ideology is espoused by the current rulers (pp. 13–16). In a 1990 national survey in mainland China,[18] the following situation was posed: "There are some people whose ideology is problematic; for example, they sympathize with the Gang of Four." The respondent was then asked whether he or she thought that such people should be allowed to express their views in a public meeting, as a teacher in college, and by publishing articles or books. This can be compared with a question about "people who want to overthrow the government by revolution" asked by the International Social Survey Program in 1985 in six countries.[19] Fewer than one-fifth of the Chinese respondents were willing to allow sympathizers of a deviant viewpoint to express their views in a meeting, as compared with two-fifths to three-quarters of the populations in the ISSP survey. Much of the Chinese "intolerance edge" was accounted for by differing educational levels in the comparison countries. Among respondents with some college education, over 50 percent of Chinese respondents would tolerate deviant speech at a meeting, compared with anywhere from 59 percent to 84 percent of college-educated respondents in the other countries. In short, Chinese were less tolerant than residents of six other countries, but the differences among Chinese and others were less substantial among people of similar educational levels.

In each of these three examples, the fit between hermeneutic generalization and positivist test is less than complete. The social networks measured in the Tianjin survey are a pale reflection of the rich concept of *guanxi* presented by Fei Xiaotong or Ambrose King. The idea of influencing government policy hardly describes the wealth of purposes for which factions are supposed to operate, and intolerance for dissident speech only scratches the surface of what Pye means by the demand for consensus. This is partly because the survey literature is still underdeveloped. For example, it might be better to test Pye's idea about *guanxi*-based factions with mainland data, but for now only Hong Kong data are available. The question about sympathizers of the Gang of Four may not be the best way to measure intolerance, so different measures need to be tried in future surveys.

Even when these inconveniences are overcome, however, positivist tests of hermeneutic insights will continue to display a certain meagerness compared to the original insights. In order to have validity (the ability of an operational measure to tap the attribute it is supposed to measure) and reliability (the measure's ability to measure that attribute accurately), a questionnaire item must be limited to a single carefully defined variable, not a complex of attributes. The insight being tested loses in complexity what it gains in specificity. Of course, additional questions can be asked to gather data on more variables making up the complex, but often the original insight is either too elaborate or too vague to be adequately represented by any practical number of measurable variables.

Moreover, in survey research across cultures, care must be taken to provide an equivalent stimulus in each setting.[20] A valid comparative survey must ask questions that can be meaningfully asked in all the settings the research is taking place. To ask Americans about *guanxi*, a term they do not understand, would be as meaningless as asking Chinese about their participation in school board elections. Whatever is truly unique, such as a linguistically distinctive way of referring to a cultural attribute or the name of a particular institution, has to be squeezed out of a question before it can be asked in more than one society. Most of the hypotheses stated in the hermeneutic literature are stated in forms that are inherently untestable across cultures, and have to be abstracted to be tested.

Here, from another angle of approach, we reencounter an earlier conclusion: A culture's uniqueness or nonuniqueness is not a characteristic of the culture itself, but of the way its attributes are conceptualized. As an attribute is abstracted to be measured cross-culturally, it loses the uniqueness it possessed when it was located lower on the ladder of abstraction, where it was described in a more complex, specific form. It now becomes by definition an attribute that all cultures possess, differing only in degree.

This does not mean that the positivistic approach is incapable of finding uniqueness among cultures. But the uniqueness it can discover consists not in the possession or nonpossession of a particular cultural attribute or cultural complex, but in the pattern of distribution of an attribute among the population, or in its pattern of association with other (cultural or noncultural) attributes. For example, in China the expectation of fair treatment from government authorities is strongly affected by respondents' educational levels. In this respect China is similar to five other countries where the same question was asked. Where China is unique is in the shape of the curve: only in China do those with college educations have a lower level of such expectation than those with no formal education.[21]

Yet after all the caveats have been entered about positivist findings, they still remain robust enough to raise doubts about the distinctiveness of Chinese culture. In the examples we have been using—*guanxi*, factions, and intolerance—the question the positivist findings raise is not whether these phenomena are important in China, but whether they are either more important in China than elsewhere, or important in different ways. The positivist literature, limited though it is, leaves doubt about whether there is an empirical basis for any strong claim of Chinese distinctiveness in these three areas, other than to say that the Chinese on the average have somewhat larger *guanxi* networks or are somewhat more intolerant than members of certain other cultures at certain points in time. The hermeneutic literature makes bolder claims, but usually offers little clarity about what it is claiming and little empirical evidence to back up its claims.

Survey research is not the only positivist approach, but other works within the same tradition lead to similar doubts about Chinese culture's distinctiveness. For example, Richard Wilson's *Compliance Ideologies* makes positivistic use of comparative history in the sense that Wilson uses historical data to test clearly specified propositions.[22] He starts with an innovative definition of political culture as a dominant ideology justifying compliance with a society's institutional system (p. 19). He conceives of two general types of compliance ideologies, which he calls contractual and positional, the first stressing compliance based on individual rights and obligations, the second stressing compliance based on one's place in society (p. 89). He abstracts the sets of ideas that would characterize each of these two types of political culture at each of four historic stages in the life of a society (p. 91). The resulting eight categories offer a grid within which societies can be placed and compared. In this conceptual scheme no culture is unique: each box in the grid potentially contains more than one case. However, the scheme does highlight important differences among societies. Wilson looks at monographic studies, especially on the United States and China, for evidence that each displays the characteristics suitable to its type. The methodological difference between a work like Wilson's, which I here classify as positivistic, and the work by Taylor, which I classified above as hermeneutic, is not sharp. Both use a typology and both look at evidence. Wilson's typology is more formally constructed and the evidence he uses depends less than Taylor's on the interpretation of states of mind. As I argue in the conclusion, ultimately the most successful works combine insightful interpretation and careful empiricism. The boundary between the two approaches is made to be crossed.

Although less formally conceptualized, Fei Xiaotong's book serves as an example of comparative anthropology used in a positivistic way.

Originally published as a series of magazine essays in the 1940s, the book aims to describe the rural Chinese society of the day to Chinese urbanites who were out of touch with rural society. Much of it consists of an elementary description of rural life, some of it touching and true, some repetitive and simplistic. In light of recent research on the commercialization of late traditional Chinese rural society, Fei's picture of a timeless, changeless, tradition-bound rural society (p. 57) seems exaggerated; perhaps this reflects the fact that he conducted his fieldwork in the 1930s, partly in remote Guangxi and Yunnan, while during the war his students did their fieldwork in Yunnan.[23]

Whether Fei's argument is right or wrong, however, it is positivistic in form. Citing Toennies and Durkheim, and influenced by Redfield, Fei argues from two universalistic ideal types (confusingly and inconsistently referred to, respectively, as "rural" or "Chinese" and "modern" or "Western") (pp. 41, 61ff.). The former type is conditioned by poverty, physical immobility, a simple division of labor, and clustered dwellings; the latter type by the opposite characteristics. Each set of social conditions generates corresponding cultural features, such as different types of personal relationships, different senses of time, and different modes of exchange. In other words, like Wilson, Fei presents a typology of societies and shows where China fits. The attributes of Chinese culture, while unique in their particulars, are characteristic of societies of the relevant type.

Uniqueness, Difference, and Hypothesis-Testing

One of the most important and common uses of cultural comparison is to use culture as an explanation for certain societal outcomes, among them economic development versus stagnation and democracy versus authoritarianism. Pye, for example, says in another work, "Briefly put, my thesis is that political power is extraordinarily sensitive to cultural nuances, and that, therefore, cultural variations are decisive in determining the course of political development."[24]

Logic says that a causative proposition cannot be proved with a by-definition finding of uniqueness. To test a hypothesis about the effect of culture on a social outcome, it is necessary to define cultural attributes in a way that is cross-culturally valid in principle.[25] Weber would have argued fallaciously if he had tried to prove that the notion of Original Sin was essential to capitalism because capitalism developed only where this idea existed. His theory of the Protestant Ethic was convincing because he abstracted from the Protestant mentality the idea of an acquisitive ratio-nality that he said was crucial to capitalism, and which might have existed elsewhere but apparently did not. Only because Weber built his argu-ment at this level of abstraction, was it possible for Thomas Metzger later to argue that neo-Confucianism contained a concretely different but abstractly similar kind of transformative tension.[26] If we find that a cul-tural attribute that is supposed to affect a particular outcome is absent in one place and uniquely present in the other, the logic of the investiga-tion is flawed if this finding is an artifact of conceptualization.

Comparative propositions in the hermeneutic literature are often stated at the wrong level of abstraction for hypothesis-testing. For exam-ple, Pye proposes that in China, "more than in most countries, politics revolves around clashes of ideas and sentiments that have to be played out in the context of exaggerated notions of authority, on the one hand, and straitjacket controls on dissent, on the other" (p. ix). How could this hypothesis be tested? In a later book, Pye argues that "cultural factors dominate public life in China more than in just about any other coun-try."[27] What might this mean in operational terms?

In statements like these (which are not limited to Pye's work), an author takes an interpretive insight into a unique complex of attributes in Chinese culture and restates it in the guise of a comparative statement about the different magnitude, extent, or influence of a cultural attribute in two or more different cultures. Such a transposition turns what may have been a valuable insight into the web of meanings within a culture into an untestable proposition about two or more cultures. This is what I meant earlier by saying that it is fallacious to restate a hermeneu-tic finding of uniqueness as if it were a positivistic finding of difference. When the goal is to frame comparative propositions that are meaningful for testing the kinds of explanatory hypotheses that the literature con-tains, we cannot transpose findings of uniqueness from the hermeneutic approach into findings of difference stated in positivistic language.

Equally, it is fallacious to restate a finding of difference as a finding of uniqueness. This is the transposition conducted by Gary Hamilton and Wang Zheng in their translators' introduction to Fei Xiaotong's book. As noted earlier, Fei places rural China into a category of societies in which relationships are predominantly parochial and personalistic. He labels this cultural complex *chaxugeju*, or network structure, as distinct from the organization-based structure that he believes to be typical of modern Western society. In effect, Fei is referring to the familiar concept of *guanxi*.

While Fei states that Western and Chinese society both contain mixed patterns, and that the difference is that in Chinese society the network pattern is "predominant" or "more important" (pp. 80–81, although he offers no guidance as to what this means), Hamilton and Wang turn this comparative statement into a statement about China's uniqueness, proposing that "Chinese social structure is unlike Western social structure." And although noting that Fei himself does not claim the patterns he describes are unique to China, Hamilton and Wang argue further that "there is sufficient evidence to indicate that the network patterns described by Fei are distinctively Chinese," even in comparison to other Asian societies. In the large literature on *guanxi*, Hamilton and Wang may be the first to make such far-reaching claims for its importance: they see it as the root of differences between China and the West in the concept of the self, sex roles, and family functioning (pp. 25–33).

Such statements might be a case of overlooking nuance in order to stress a main point, yet they promote a major misunderstanding. They place us in the presence of a homogeneous, classless, stateless China, which is contrasted with an equally caricatured "West" that stretches, presumably, from Scandinavia to Sicily and relies entirely on organizations without networks. Hamilton and Wang have reified Fei's already oversimple typology of societies, essentialized his concept of culture, and restated his insight into what makes China different from some other societies as a claim that China is unique.

The Fallacy of Conceptual Relativism

Hamilton and Wang do not merely offer the factual (if false) proposition that "Chinese social structure is unlike Western social structure" (p. 32). They also make a meta-theoretical claim: "There are . . . no universal social patterns and no universally valid principles by which all societies are held together" (p. 16), and therefore "Western concepts did not work well" in studying China (p. 12). "What passes in the West for general social theory," they conclude, "is often, in fact, local knowledge" (p. 34). If this claim is acceptable, the problems I have addressed in this essay disappear. Cultural comparison will consist of using different concepts to describe different cultures. We will see cultures as different not in the degree to which conceptually abstracted attributes are present, nor even in the possession of unique complexes of attributes, but in the very concepts needed to grasp them.

In making this claim, Hamilton and Wang part company with their translatee. As I pointed out earlier, Fei uses universal categories to explain to his Chinese readers what is distinctive about the rural Chinese society of their day. In a Chinese book for Chinese readers, he of course uses Chinese terms. But this is a choice of language, not a methodological position. His method is functionalist like that of his teacher Malinowski, and hence dependent on universal concepts. Fei's intellectual biographer David Arkush states that one of the main achievements of this book was to introduce "to a wide Chinese public the basic categories and ideas of Western social science."[28]

Hamilton and Wang, however, use Fei to revive the old debate about whether there can be culturally universalistic concepts in social science. The use of culturally "local" concepts as tools for analysis may have its attractions as a strategy for single-country hermeneutic insight (although I think they are limited), but it is self-defeating as a strategy for cross-cultural comparison because it deprives us of concepts that can mark off for comparison comparable entities in different societies.[29] The insistence on the ineffability or incommensurability of cultures would solve the question of distinctiveness by fiat while preventing actual comparative investigation of cultures.

To say this is not to claim that there is such a thing as a floating vantage point above culture.[30] The vantage point that comparison requires is no doubt culturally rooted, and members of different cultures may adopt different vantage points. Chinese social scientists, for example, may choose to compare American and Chinese society using concepts derived from Chinese tradition or from Marxism. But in any case, they will need to use a single set of concepts to grasp comparable entities within the two societies.

Hamilton and Wang themselves use, as they must, the universal concepts of "class," "state," "network," "family," "the self," and so on, to express their views as to what China has and the West does not and vice versa.[31] Indeed, "Fei's sociology" could hardly "demand that we in the West rethink ourselves" (p. 34) if all social knowledge is only local knowledge. Their emicism thus contains its own negation. It leads to the statements that "in China the state does not exist as an organization" (p. 29) and that "China should be considered not a class-based but a network-based society" (p. 33). As empirical claims, such statements are false; as conceptual claims, fallacious. A culturally particularist social science will never be able to go beyond the limited and in many senses trivial finding that all cultures are at some level by definition unique. From this position, it cannot engage in explanations based on culture.

Conclusion

While we have learned a great deal about Chinese culture, successful comparative work remains rare in both the hermeneutic and positivist traditions. One reason is practical: good comparison requires extended conceptual and empirical study of both entities being compared, which is time-consuming and difficult. The second reason is methodological: the failure to gain the benefits of both approaches by learning how to combine them in valid ways in comparative studies.

Hermeneutic insights that are useful for comparative studies are those that anchor their propositions in specific persons, times, places, and groups, that deal conscientiously with evidence that might disprove their arguments, and that avoid true-by-definition claims of distinctiveness by paying attention to the ladder of abstraction. Good positivist work makes use of hermeneutic insights both to develop hypotheses, concepts, and measures and to interpret findings. Interpretation is an essential phase of the positivist method: no findings are self-evidently meaningful, as shown in the examples from survey research discussed above.

Is Chinese culture distinctive? Although anyone who studies it must be convinced that it is, we have far to go to state clearly how it is distinctive and to prove it empirically.

11

Cultural Requisites for Democracy in China

Written with Tianjian Shi

Chinese political culture is often cited as an obstacle to the realization of democratic aspirations.[1] Its undemocratic attributes are generally thought to include authoritarianism, passivity, ignorance of politics, fear of politics, and intolerance. The first national sample survey of Chinese political culture allows a more nuanced look at some related attributes and their distribution among the population. Some of the specific findings are surprising, and the overall pattern suggests that political culture may affect democratization in more complex ways than usually acknowledged.

Until now, evidence concerning the nature of Chinese political culture has been drawn from interpretive studies.[2] We use this term to describe studies that are characteristically based on documentary sources, interviews, and field observation. Interpretive studies seek to identify complex sets of attitudes, or syndromes, of values, beliefs, and practices, which are thought to be distinctive of, or even unique to, a given culture, or to a broad section of its population, often over a long span of time.[3]

When implemented well, the interpretive approach to the study of political culture has marked strengths. These include the ability to characterize the culture of a whole people or of large social segments; the ability to attend both to broad themes in a culture and to nuance, contradiction, levels of meanings, and dialectical relationships; and the capability to use documents and other historical evidence to retrieve information about the belief and value systems of the past.

The approach also has weaknesses. These include a tendency to imprecision when specifying referents (what the belief or attitude in question consists of); frequent ambiguity of propositions (who is said to have believed what at what time, and with what effect); an inability to provide rigorous, intersubjectively reliable evidence that the propositions are more true than alternative propositions (are the Chinese really more authoritarian than some other people?); a tendency to tautological arguments about the effects of culture on behavior, since behavior itself is often used as an indicator for the existence of a belief or attitude; the inability to describe with precision the distribution of attitudes among the population; and the inability to carry out analytical procedures to distinguish the effects of sociodemographic attributes on cultural attitudes or the effects of attitudes on behavior. In short, even the best interpretive work consists of broadly stated, loosely specified insights using ill-defined terms, meaning different things to different readers, and making statements that may or may not be true.

These weaknesses multiply when a cross-cultural comparison is attempted. For example, Chinese are said to be more collectively oriented, Americans more individualistic. But interpretive studies cannot give precise or reliable answers as to what this means, how large the difference is, whether the contrast really exists, and how different sectors of the two populations vary among themselves.

An alternative to the interpretive approach, the survey approach, has been widely applied to the study of democratic political systems, but has not been used very much in the study of Chinese culture.[4] Its research tool is the sample survey, whose use requires precise sampling methods, sophisticated interviewing techniques to assure reliability, scoring and scaling techniques to sort and organize responses in categories related to theoretical variables, and statistical analysis and inference.[5] In this approach, political culture is conceptualized as the distribution of values, attitudes, and beliefs toward politics among a population.[6] The unit of observation is the individual. Culture is an aggregative concept referring to the pattern of attitudes among the population or a specified subset.

When implemented well, the survey approach has certain advantages. These include clear specification of referents, disambiguation of propositions, empirical reliability of findings, the ability to measure variation in cultural attributes among a population, the potential ability to measure change over time if serial surveys are done, avoidance of tautology in the specification of relations between culture and behavior, and the ability to perform a wide range of statistical analyses, including analyses of the effects of sociodemographic variables on culture, and of cultural variables on political behavior.

The method also has disadvantages. Aside from its technical difficulty, these include the inability to go back in time except under special circumstances, the technique's flattening or simplifying effect on the cultural attributes which can be measured, and the intrinsic inability to identify attributes which are or might be culturally unique, except in a trivial sense. We discuss these advantages and problems later.

Prior to the study reported here, no one had done a survey of Chinese political culture that was based on a random sample and hence permitted statistical induction.[7] A few studies by foreign scholars employed multiple émigré interviews, but the numbers of respondents were too small and the samples too unrepresentative to make induction possible.[8] In the 1980s, scholars in China began to conduct surveys, some of which touched on political-cultural topics. According to Dong Li, during the period from 1979 to 1991, Chinese scholars conducted at least 181 surveys concerning political attitudes.[9] Only one was national in scope, Min Qi's *Chinese Political Culture*, carried out in 1987 under the auspices of the Beijing Social and Economic Research Institute.[10] All the Chinese surveys on which we have information, including Min Qi's, were methodologically flawed in terms of sampling, question formulation, and interview techniques. Min Qi's study, for example, severely undersampled women, older citizens, rural residents, and other key sectors of the population.

This chapter reports some results from a survey conducted in China in 1990 which is, so far as we know, not only the first scientifically valid national sample survey done in China on political behavior and attitudes, but also the first valid national-level sample survey on the political behavior and attitudes of the general populace ever done in a communist country.[11] (See the Appendix to chapter 12 for details.)

The survey assessed approximately fifty political-cultural variables, too many to examine in a single essay. As a first step, we have selected for discussion certain items which involve the cultural requisites for democracy, and which were designed to permit cross-national comparison. Most of them were adapted from two classic studies—Gabriel Almond and Sidney Verba's *The Civic Culture* and the International Social Survey Program (ISSP).[12] We are comparing China in 1990 to other countries in 1959–1960 and 1985 respectively, and to countries that were democratic at the time of their surveys.[13] These time gaps and system differences present no obstacle to comparison as long as we take account of them in the analysis.

The study of political culture emerged from curiosity about the prerequisites for stable democracy, especially the relationships between citizens' subjective orientations and democratic stability. Theorists have stressed the importance to the democratic process of such values as the belief in popular sovereignty, commitment to the equality of citizens, and the principle of majoritarian decisionmaking with adequate protection of minority rights.[14] In a recent study of Russian political culture, James Gibson and Raymond Duch identified five values conducive to democracy: (1) the belief in the legitimacy of democratic institutions; (2) beliefs about authority relationships between government and the governed; (3) confidence in the capacity of the government; (4) political and interpersonal trust; and (5) the belief in the possibility of cooperation and the legitimacy of conflict.[15]

We focus here on three dimensions of political culture which we believe are fundamental to democracy: First, do citizens perceive the government as salient to their lives, as having an impact on themselves and their families? Second, do people believe that they have the capability to understand and engage in politics? Third, to what extent are citizens prepared to be tolerant of those who hold different political beliefs?

We show that while some of the attitudes associated with democracy are less prevalent in China than in some other countries, Chinese political culture is neither especially traditional nor especially totalitarian. Our findings lead to two kinds of concluding reflections: on the prospects for democracy in China and on cultural distinctiveness—not only China's cultural distinctiveness, but the notion of cultural distinctiveness as it appears from the perspective of the survey approach to culture.

The Perceived Impact of Government

One of the cultural requisites commonly cited for democracy is that citizens perceive the actions of government to be salient to their lives. An awareness of the impact of government is thought to generate interest in politics and a desire to participate in the political process. The classic question to assess this attitude was asked by Gabriel Almond and Sidney Verba, authors of *The Civic Culture*, who separately measured citizens' perceptions of national and local government impact. We asked the same two questions in China.[16] Our results are displayed with Almond and Verba's in Table 1 and 2.

It is striking that so few Chinese citizens perceive their government as having an impact on their daily lives. Whether China's system is now or ever was totalitarian is a subject of debate,[17] but few would question that the Chinese government is more intrusive in citizens' lives and deals with

TABLE 11.1

Estimated Degree of Impact of the Local Government on Daily Life, by Nation

Percentage who say local government has:	China	U.S.	U.K.	Germany	Italy	Mexico
Great effect	5.4%	35%	23%	33%	19%	6%
Some effect	18.4	53	51	41	39	23
No effect	71.6	10	23	18	22	67
Other	—	—	—	—	2	—
Do not know	4.6	2	3	8	18	3
Total percentage	100.0	100	100	100	99	100
Total number	2896	970	963	955	995	1007

Actual text of the question used in *The Civic Culture*: "Now take the local government. About how much effect do you think its activities have on your day-to-day life? Do they have a great effect, some effect, or none?"

Actual text of the question used in China: "Now let's discuss the local government. How much effect do you think its activities have on your day-to-day life? Do they have a great effect, some effect or none?"

a broader scope of policy than most other governments. Yet, approximately 72 percent of Chinese citizens stated that both national and local governments had no effect on their daily lives, figures comparable in the Almond and Verba data only to Mexico. As in most of the other nations, slightly more Chinese attributed the influence to local rather than to the national government, but the difference was not great.

TABLE 11.2

Estimated Degree of Impact of the National Government on Daily Life, by Nation

Percentage who say local government has:	China	U.S.	U.K.	Germany	Italy	Mexico
Great effect	9.7%	41%	33%	38%	23%	7%
Some effect	11.7	44	40	32	31	23
No effect	71.8	11	23	17	19	66
Other	—	0	—	—	3	—
Do not know	6.7	4	4	12	24	3
Total percentage	100.0	100	100	99	100	99
Total number	2896	970	963	955	995	1007

Actual text of the question used in *The Civic Culture*: "Thinking now about the national government [in Washington, London, Bonn, Rome, Mexico City], about how much effect do you think its activities, the laws passed and so on, have on your day-to-day life? Do they have a great effect, some effect, or none?"

Actual text of the question used in China "Now let's now discuss the national government in Beijing, about how much effect do you think its activities have on your day-to-day life? Do they have a great effect, some effect or none?"

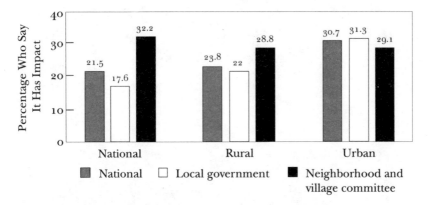

FIGURE 11.1 Perceived Impact of National and Local Government and Neighborhood or Village Committee on Daily Life by Type of Household Registration

Do differences in the structure of public administration in China help explain the low salience of national and local governments? Unlike the five nations referred to in *The Civic Culture,* the structure of government in China extends below the local (provincial and county) levels to the urban neighborhood and rural village committees, the so-called "grassroots level of government," and below these to the work units which are officially nongovernmental.[18] Even if Chinese citizens are unaware of the impact of the national and local government, they may perceive the impact of the village/neighborhood level of administration, which performs many distributive and redistributive functions important to local residents. FIGURE 11.1 reveals that, indeed, a higher percentage of respondents perceive an effect on their lives from the village/neighborhood level of administration than from the national or local levels. But the numbers are still remarkably low.

It is also possible that the low Chinese totals result from different groups of citizens paying attention to the impact of different levels of government, each focusing on the level that most concerns him or her. If a different group of citizens were aware of the impact of each level of the government, then the groups added together would make for a widespread awareness of government at one level or another. However, FIGURE 11.2 shows that this is not the case. Nearly 60 percent of the population attributes no impact to any of the three levels of government.

In any society, awareness of the government is likely to vary with such individual attributes as urban residence and education. If the population is heavily weighted toward persons who are less likely to be aware of the impact of government, the overall level of awareness might be low in the

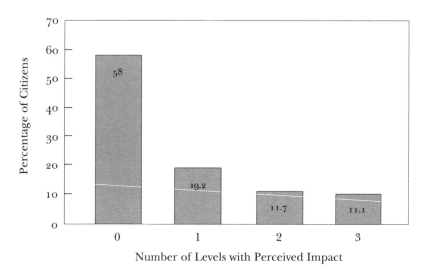

FIGURE 11.2   Perceived Impact of Government

population as a whole because of the population's composition rather than because of the nature of the culture. Modernization theory suggests that urban Chinese might be more aware of the impact of government on their lives than rural residents. According to this theory, economic development expands the proportion of higher status roles in a society, involves tensions and strains among social groups, produces an expansion of the functions of the government, and raises the saliency of an individual's identity as a member of the national state. These trends usually lead to higher levels of political mobilization.[19] Since urban China is more developed than rural China, urban residents might be more aware of the impact of government than their rural cousins.

When we subdivided our sample into urban and rural sectors as shown in Figure 11.1, we found that, as expected, more urban than rural residents attributed some influence to the national and local governments.[20] But the urbanites did so at levels below all the *Civic Culture* nations except Mexico. Unlike rural residents, urban residents perceived no substantial difference in the influence of the three levels of the administration.

In the *Civic Culture* nations, awareness of the government's impact varied with educational level. Italians and Mexicans without formal education had a very low level of awareness of the impact of the national and local governments.[21] In China, 25.7 percent of our sample was illiterate and another 30 percent had educations at or below the primary level.[22] This suggests that the differing aggregate levels of awareness among the

TABLE 11.3

Educational Differences in the Perceived Impact of the National Government, by Nation

Percentage who say national government has:		None	Primary or less	Some Secondary	Some University
China	Some effect	12.0%	17.2%	27.4%	61.2%
	No effect	75.3	77.1	68.1	36.1
	Other	0.0	0.0	0.0	0.0
	Do not know	12.7	5.7	4.5	2.3
	Total percentage	100.0	100.0	100.0	100.0
	Total number	687	869	1276	64
U.S.	Some effect		73	89	96
	No effect		17	10	4
	Other		0	0	0
	Do not know		10	1	0
	Total percentage		100	100	100
	Total number		339	443	188
U.K.	Some effect		70	76	92
	No effect		25	21	8
	Other		0	1	0
	Do not know		4	2	0
	Total percentage		99	100	100
	Total number		593	322	24
Germany	Some effect		69	83	92
	No effect		18	14	8
	Other		0	0	0
	Do not know		14	2	0
	Total percentage		101	99	100
	Total number		792	123	26
Italy	Some effect	24	48	72	85
	No effect	17	20	19	13
	Other	6	3	2	2
	Do not know	53	29	7	—
	Total percentage	100	100	100	100
	Total number	88	604	245	54
Mexico	Some effect	25	30	35	57
	No effect	65	68	62	41
	Other	—	—	2	—
	Do not know	10	2	1	3
	Total percentage	100	100	100	101
	Total number	221	656	103	24

six countries might be due to differences in the educational makeup of national populations. Table 11.3 shows that in China, as elsewhere, the perceived impact of the national government varies substantially with the level of education, with less-educated respondents less likely to perceive an impact by the government on their daily lives. In both China and Mexico, the high proportion of less-educated citizens in the total population partly explains why the aggregate estimate of the impact of the government is low.

But the data also reveal that at each educational level, Chinese respondents are less aware of the impact of the government than similarly educated respondents in the other five nations. About half as many Chinese with no formal education perceive the national government to have an impact as do uneducated Italians and Mexicans. For those with primary educations, the gap was 55.8 percent between Chinese and Americans, 52.8 percent between Chinese and Britons, 51.8 percent between Chinese and Germans, 30.8 percent between Chinese and Italians, and 12.8 percent between Chinese and Mexicans. Even among persons with university educations, the Chinese are substantially less likely to perceive a national government impact, with gaps ranging from 20 to over 30 percent. The sole exception is Mexico: Chinese with university educations are slightly more likely than similarly educated Mexicans to perceive an impact of the national government on their daily lives.

The initial impression remains unshaken: compared to citizens in the five democratic nations studied in 1959–1960 in *The Civic Culture*, Chinese citizens in 1990 were relatively unaware of the impact of the government on their daily lives even when education is held constant. But the Chinese profile did not depart far from that of the Mexicans thirty years earlier, when Mexico was already considered a democracy, although not yet a highly developed one. In Almond and Verba's terms, Chinese citizens today are still relatively parochial;[23] the workings of even the grass-roots levels of administration remain obscure to the majority.

According to conventional wisdom, the state in communist systems exercises close control over society. Our data are not about the objective role of the state, but about the subjective perceptions of ordinary citizens. We seem to have found a gap between the two. Although the regime in China controls the daily lives of citizens more totally than was the case in the five nations studied by Almond and Verba, fewer citizens are able to identify such control. We do not know what mechanisms are at work to produce this paradox—whether the regime manages to make its subjects overlook its control over their daily lives or whether the citizens contrive to ignore the regime's control as a way of managing the psychological tension that it induces. In any case, the finding suggests that the Chinese regime enjoys a "safety cushion" of popular underestimation of its role, which may to some extent blunt demands for democracy.

Political Efficacy

The sense of efficacy is a powerful determinant of people's involvement in politics. Whether or not citizens can influence politics, their beliefs about whether they can do so help guide their political behavior. Feelings of efficacy motivate people to engage in political activities, while the absence of these feelings evokes political apathy and withdrawal. Some researchers consider efficacy a key indicator of the health of a democratic system.[24]

Political efficacy was originally defined as "the feeling that individual political action does have, or can have, an impact upon the political process."[25] Two different operationalizations of the concept have been popular in the literature. Almond and Verba concentrated on whether citizens believe that they have the capacity to wield influence. They differentiated political efficacy into subject and citizen "competence." The former refers to a person's awareness of his or her rights to fair and equal treatment from the government, the latter to his or her awareness of the ability to influence the government.[26] The approach associated with the Survey Research Center (SRC) of the University of Michigan puts more emphasis on the perceived responsiveness of political institutions than on the respondent's sense of his or her own capabilities.[27]

Subsequent research demonstrated that both approaches are valid. Political efficacy is a multidimensional phenomenon containing two separate components. One is internal efficacy, which consists of beliefs about one's competence to understand and participate in politics. The other is external efficacy, which refers to beliefs about the responsiveness of the government.[28] Internal efficacy in turn contains two subdimensions: the belief in one's ability to understand complicated political issues and the belief in one's ability to act politically. The former component affects the likelihood that people engage in politics; the latter affects the level and patterns of participation.

Some measures of internal efficacy in China are displayed in Table 11.4. The table shows that slightly less than half (47.3 percent) of our respondents deemed themselves able to understand work unit issues as well as other people. In relation to the national government, the percentage of persons with a sense of efficacy dropped to 31.9 percent.[29]

TABLE 11.4

Internal Efficacy

Percentage who report they:	Understand work unit affairs as well as others	Understand national affairs less well than others	Can be as good a unit leader as any others	Can be as good a government leader as any others
Strongly agree	17.6%	16.5%	8.4%	6.1%
Agree	29.7	32.6	14.1	10.7
Not sure	5.5	4.7	4.2	3.3
Disagree	24.6	23.3	29.9	27.3
Strongly disagree	8.0	8.6	24.8	32.3
Do not know	14.6	14.3	18.6	20.2
Total percentage	100.0	100.0	100.0	99.9
Total number	2896	2896	2896	2896

Actual text of the question: Do you strongly agree, agree, disagree or strongly agree with the following statement: "I think that my understanding of the situation in our work unit is no worse than other people's"; "I think that my understanding of national affairs is not as good as ordinary people's"; "I think that I would not be a worse work unit leader than other people"; "I think that I would not be a worse government leader than other people."

About 20 percent of the population believed that they could be as good a leader in their work unit or village as others, and 16.8 percent had confidence in their ability to serve as government leaders.

Table 11.5 shows the results from a similar but different question, which asks the respondent to rate his or her understanding of the issues facing the nation, the local government, and the unit. Self-rated understanding

TABLE 11.5

Understanding of National-Level, Local, and Unit Affairs

Percentage who say they:	National affairs	Local affairs	Unit affairs
Understand very well	0.9%	1.9%	15.4%
Understand relatively well	17.0	18.0	31.9
Understand poorly	37.5	32.7	23.0
Do not understand at all	41.5	44.8	25.9
Do not know	3.1	2.7	3.9
Total percentage	100.0	100.0	100.0
Total number	2896	2896	2896

Actual text of the question: "Regarding the important international and domestic issues facing our country, how well do you think you understand them? How about the important issues facing the city (county, or district)? How about the important issues facing your work unit (village), do you understand them very well, relatively well, not very well, or not at all?"

TABLE 11.6

Understanding of National-Level Affairs

Percentage who say they:	China	U.S.	U.K.	Germany	Italy	Mexico
Understand very well	0.9%	7.2%	8.0%	13.1%	6.6%	1.5%
Understand relatively well	17.0	37.9	36.3	35.1	19.9	6.4
Depends on the issue	—	2.1	1.8	7.5	4.1	—
Understand poorly	37.5	37.0	35.5	24.3	23.7	44.8
Do not understand at all	41.5	14.6	15.5	14.7	33.7	44.4
Do not know	3.1	1.1	2.9	5.3	12.0	2.8
Total percentage	100.0	100.0	100.0	100.0	100.0	100.0
Total number	2896	970	963	955	995	1008

Actual text of the question used in *The Civic Culture*: "Thinking of the important national and international issues facing the country — how well do you think you can understand these issues?"

Actual text of the question used in China: "Regarding the important international and domestic issues facing our country, how well do you think you understand them?"

of unit affairs is again higher than self-rated understanding of local or national-level affairs. Nearly 50 percent of the respondents felt that they understood the "important issues facing [their] work unit" very well or relatively well, compared to 19.9 percent for local issues and 17.9 percent for national-level issues. Taken together, the figures from Tables 11.4 and 11.5 demonstrate a substantial gap in internal efficacy when one moves from the grassroots level of administration to formal government institutions.

Tables 11.6 and 11.7 place these Chinese figures in the context of comparable figures from *The Civic Culture*. Chinese citizens generally scored lower on this measure than citizens of other nations, but they did not lag

TABLE 11.7

Understanding of Local Affairs

Percentage who say they:	China	U.S.	U.K.	Germany	Italy	Mexico
Understand very well	1.9%	21.0%	17.5%	24.8%	15.0%	5.4%
Understand relatively well	18.0	43.5	36.8	36.8	23.3	13.4
Depends on the issue	—	1.0	1.0	7.6	3.3	0.1
Understand poorly	32.7	22.9	25.2	17.9	19.3	47.2
Do not understand at all	44.8	10.2	14.2	7.1	26.5	32.9
Do not know	2.7	1.3	5.2	5.8	12.6	1.0
Total percent	100.0	100.0	100.0	100.0	100.0	100.0
Total number	2896	970	963	955	995	1008

Actual text of the question used in *The Civic Culture*: "How about local issues in this town or part of the country. How well do you understand them?"

Actual text of the question used in China: "How about important issues facing the city (county or district), how well do you think you understand them?"

TABLE 11.8

Expectation of Treatment by Governmental Bureaucracy, by Nation

Percentage who say:	U.S.	U.K.	Germany	China	Italy	Mexico
They expect equal treatment	83%	83%	65%	57.0%	53%	42%
They do not expect equal treatment	9	7	9	24.2	13	50
Depends	4	6	19	—	17	5
Other	—	—	—	9.1	6	—
Do not know	4	2	7	9.8	11	3
Total percentage	100	98	100	100.1	100	100
Total number of cases	970	963	955	2876	995	1007

Actual text of the question used in *The Civic Culture*: "Suppose there were some question that you had to take to a government office—for example, a tax question or housing regulation. Do you think you would be given equal treatment—I mean, would you be treated as well as anyone else?"

The text of the question used in China: "Suppose there were some issue that you had to take to a government office. Do you think you would be given equal treatment? I mean, would you be treated as well as anyone else?"

behind the Italians and the Mexicans in all respects. Although fewer Chinese than Italians or Mexicans claimed to understand either national-level or local issues "very well," the sum percentage of Chinese under-standing national-level issues "relatively well," "depends," and "poorly" was higher than in Italy and Mexico, and the percentage claiming to understand national-level affairs "not at all" was lower than in Mexico.

Turning to external efficacy, the best-established measures would have been too sensitive to ask in China.[30] As a surrogate, we used Almond and Verba's measure of "output affect," which, besides feasibility, offered the opportunity for further comparison with the *Civic Culture* countries. The question asks about the respondent's expectation of equal treat-ment at a government office. In view of China's reputation for govern-ment corruption and abuse, it comes as a surprise to find in Table 11.8 that Chinese citizens in 1990 were not very different from Germans, Italians, and Mexicans at the time of *The Civic Culture* surveys in their expectation of equal treatment. The percentage of Chinese who expected equal treatment was a little lower than the Germans and a little higher than the Italians. Overall, a majority of Chinese respondents thought they would be treated equally by a government office.

Most political culture variables are strongly affected by respondents' educational levels.[31] Output affect is no exception. In China, education's impact on the expectation of equal treatment displays an unusual pat-tern. Figure 11.3 shows that in four of the five *Civic Culture* nations, the

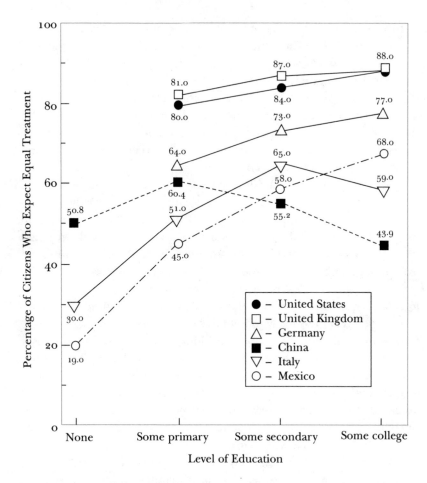

FIGURE 11.3 Expectation of Equal Treatment by Government Authorities, by Education

expectation of equal government treatment increases with the level of education. In the United States, Britain, and Germany, although education has a positive impact on people's expectation of fair government, the less educated do not expect to be treated categorically differently from the more educated.[32] In Italy and Mexico, the overall percentage of those expecting equal treatment is lower, and the differences between the more educated and the less educated are more marked. In Mexico, only 19 percent of the people with no education expect equal treatment compared to 68 percent of those with a university education: a spread of 49 points. In all six countries, except China and Italy, the expectation of equal treatment increases linearly with every step in the educational ladder.

In China and Italy, the relationship between education and output affect is curvilinear. The expectation of equal treatment increases with respondents' educational levels up to a certain point and then reverses itself. In Italy, in 1959, 30 percent of the most disadvantaged group expected equal treatment by the authorities. The expectation increased with each increase in education up to the level of secondary school. But the expectation of equal treatment among the most advantaged group, people with some college education, was 6 percent less than among those with secondary school education.

The shape of the curve in China is remarkable. Slightly more than half of the most disadvantaged group expect equal treatment by the government, a figure much higher than that of Italy and Mexico. The figure increases slightly with the level of education, but only up to the primary school level. Beyond this level, the advantage imparted by education not only disappears but becomes negative. Those with some secondary education are 5 percent less likely than those with some primary education to expect equal treatment, and those with some university education are nearly 17 percent less likely to hold this expectation.

In short, while the least-educated Chinese have the strongest output affect among the nations studied, the best-educated Chinese have the weakest. The decline associated with education is so sharp that Chinese with college educations are 6 percent less likely than their most educationally disadvantaged countrymen to expect equal treatment. Compared to college graduates in other countries, Chinese college graduates are more than 44 percent less likely to expect equal treatment than Americans and Britons, 33.1 percent less likely than Germans, 24.1 percent less likely than Mexicans, and 15.1 percent less likely than Italians.

When a person feels he cannot achieve his goals through conventional participation, one logical choice is to turn to unconventional political activities—either to oppose the political system, take advantage of its loopholes, or simply to express frustration and dissatisfaction. Findings from a 1988 survey in Beijing showed that political activities of these types are indeed associated with college education in China.[33] Our findings on output affect help to explain why.

The findings also show how a cultural attitude considered conducive to democracy may also help buttress authoritarianism. The relatively high Chinese figures on output affect dovetail with findings from the 1988 Beijing survey that many Chinese citizens have developed a range of techniques for exerting influence on the bureaucracy despite the authoritarian nature of China's political system.[34] This sense among ordinary people of having access to the system may help explain why political dissatisfaction among intellectuals has not struck many sparks among the broader population, especially in rural areas where the less-educated are concentrated. Together with the widespread ignorance of the government's impact noted above, the reservoir of confidence in the government among less-educated Chinese may have helped the authoritarian regime to survive. But the implications of the high system affect are not necessarily adverse to democracy. It might also help to stabilize the society during a transition to a more open system and give a new democratic system a grace period to establish itself.

Political Tolerance

Political tolerance is associated with two principles underlying the democratic process: the commitment to the equality of citizens and the protection of minority rights. Both require tolerance for the viewpoints and political activities of one's opponents. Some students of democracy consider tolerance the essential ingredient of democratic politics. As pointed out by Gibson and Duch, "without tolerance, widespread contestation is impossible, regime legitimacy is imperiled, and a numbing conformity prevails."[35]

Interpretive studies have portrayed Chinese political culture as intolerant. According to Lucian Pye, for example, "the dominant emotion of modern Chinese politics has been a preoccupation with hatred coupled with an enthusiasm for singling out enemies." Pye states that Chinese political culture knows no equals, only superiors and inferiors, and that the Chinese perceive a sharp divide between friend and foe.[36] Using the survey technique, we can compare Chinese levels of intolerance to those elsewhere, compare intolerance in different domains (speaking, teaching, and publishing), and determine which sectors of the Chinese population are more or less intolerant.

Since *The Civic Culture* contains no measure for tolerance, we selected a series of items from the ISSP for comparison. The position presented in the 1985 ISSP survey was, "There are some people whose views are considered extreme by the majority. Consider people who want to overthrow the government by revolution."[37] The respondent was then asked whether he or she thought that such people should be allowed to express their views in a public meeting, express their views as a teacher in a college, and express their views by publishing articles or books. We adapted the question to the Chinese setting by stating, "There are some people

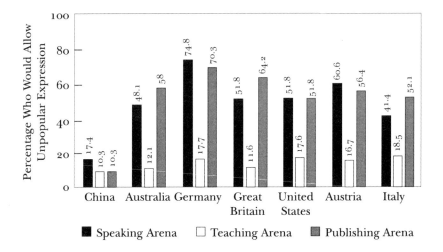

FIGURE 11.4   Political Tolerance

whose ideology is problematic, for example, they sympathize with the Gang of Four."[38] We then asked the same three questions.

Figure 11.4 presents the figures for China and for the six highly developed democratic ISSP countries. It reveals that the Chinese are indeed the least tolerant among the seven nations. Fewer than 20 percent of the Chinese respondents were willing to allow sympathizers of a deviant viewpoint to express their views in a meeting, as compared to 40 to 75 percent of the populations in the other countries. When asked about teaching, Chinese tolerance levels were even lower, standing at 10.3 percent of the population, but the gap between China and the other countries was not as large. Tolerance for publishing unpopular ideas was again low in China (10.3 percent), with the range in the other countries extending from 51.8 percent to 70.3 percent.[39]

Political tolerance is normally associated with education: the less educated are less tolerant and more authoritarian.[40] Are the lower levels of tolerance in China attributable to generally lower levels of education, or does the tolerance gap remain when educational subgroups are compared across nations? Figure 11.5 breaks down tolerance for speaking at a meeting, by level of education. As in other countries, in China education has a strong positive impact on tolerance. But at each level of educational attainment, Chinese respondents are less tolerant than people in other countries.

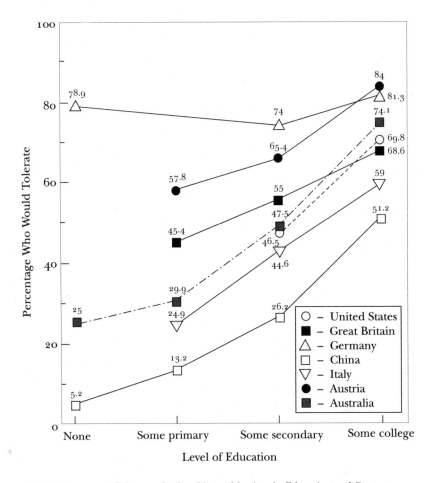

FIGURE 11.5   Tolerance for Speaking at Meeting, by Education and Country

By far the most intolerant group in all the countries studied were the Chinese illiterates.[41] Figure 11.6 provides a profile of this group. It shows that illiterates are heavily concentrated among persons above age forty (that is, who were born in 1950 or before), and that within this group illiteracy is especially widespread among females resident in rural areas.

Figure 11.6 demonstrates how survey research can allow us to look some distance into the past. The curves give insight into the distribution of educational opportunities in China from 1920 to 1972. They confirm that most urban male children and many rural male children were given some education in the early Republican period, show that virtually no education was given to rural females until about 1930, and suggest that a fraction of urban females were given some education starting about

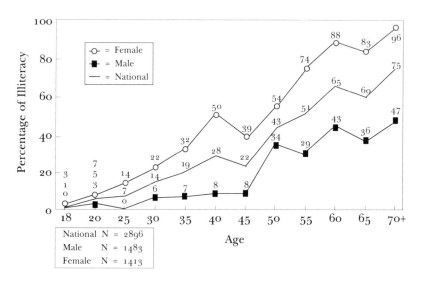

FIGURE 11.6   Illiteracy Rates, by Gender and Age Group

1920.[42] A number of refinements of this analysis are possible, but these rough figures are sufficient to illustrate the retrospective use of survey data.[43]

The data suggest that average tolerance levels in China are likely to increase as older illiterates are replaced by later-born, better educated citizens.[44] Even so, Figure 11.5 shows that even the better-educated in China are less tolerant than their opposite numbers in the other countries studied. Tolerance levels in China may remain lower than those in democratic countries for some time, even with changes in the educational makeup of the population.

Prospects for Democracy

We have presented data on only three sets of attitudes out of many that are theoretically related to democracy. Political scientists have established no minimum thresholds for perceived saliency of government, internal and external efficacy, and tolerance in democratic societies. And political culture is but one of the several sets of conditions that affect the prospects for democracy. So our data justify no sweeping conclusions.

Some patterns in the data suggest potential difficulties if the Chinese political system begins to democratize. Relatively low levels of awareness of government's impact, system affect, and tolerance may pose impediments to democratization. People may be unmotivated to engage in politics and may favor the repression of ideas that they do not agree with. It is not clear whether the educated elite have sufficiently high levels of political tolerance to set an example for the rest of the population. Although educated Chinese are more likely to be aware of the impact of government, to feel able to understand and influence government, and to tolerate political speech by disliked groups, they are substantially less likely to hold democratic orientations than people of the same educational levels elsewhere.

The distribution of output affect in relation to other variables gives cause for both concern and hope. Although educated people are most likely to be aware of the influence of government and are more confident of their ability to understand and engage in politics, they are least likely to expect fair treatment from the government. They know that government policy can have a great effect on their lives, but they do not expect government officials to treat them equally. This contradiction may create psychological tension akin to what Ted Gurr calls "status reversal," an attitude Gurr considers conducive to outbreaks of rebellion.[45] If so, it helps to explain why this group has been the most likely to engage in regime challenging activities and why they may do so again.

The cultural profile of the rest of the population is virtually the reverse. They have a relatively low sense of the government's impact, relatively low internal efficacy, and relatively high system affect. In short, they are somewhat insulated from and satisfied with the government. The contrast between the two patterns suggests that if a political crisis between the regime and the intellectuals occurs again, the majority of the population may once again not offer much backing for the demands for democratic change. But if this is true, the implications for a democratic outcome are uncertain. The attitudinal gap between the educated and the uneducated that now helps to stabilize the regime may moderate the violence of a regime transition and provide a reserve of deference to help an infant democracy survive.

Nothing in our data supports the theory that Chinese political culture is an absolute bar to democracy. When compared to residents of some of the most stable, long-established democracies in the world, the Chinese population scored lower on the variables we looked at, but not so low as to justify the conclusion that democracy is out of reach. In general, as theory predicts, the more urban and educated sectors showed more democratic attitudes, supporting expectations derived from modernization theory that China's culture will move closer to the patterns characteristic of democratic countries as the economy grows. Once in place, a democratic regime could speed the pace of cultural change by actively inculcating the popular attitudes it needs to survive.

Conclusion: Cultural Distinctiveness and Universal Attributes

Because this chapter is concerned with questions of cultural distinctiveness and universalism, we have selected for analysis a few attributes for which comparative data are available. In each case, the distribution of attitudes in China both resembles and differs from the distributions in other countries. The data show China's culture to be distinctive, but only distributionally, not categorically. The attributes are universal, only the distributions are particular.

This finding, however, is in a sense an artifact of our approach. The survey method inevitably illuminates how Chinese citizens stand, compared to citizens of other countries, along universal or potentially universalizable dimensions of analysis, as well as how Chinese vary among themselves. In contrast to the interpretive method employed by most other research on Chinese political culture, survey results can never take the form of generalizations about all Chinese and how they differ from all non-Chinese. Surveys measure attributes which exist (whether they have been measured or not) in some degree everywhere, and they assess variation in the distribution of these attributes within and across one or more populations.

Of course, it is possible to ask a survey question that makes sense in only one culture, thus demonstrating the uniqueness of the culture. But this uniqueness would be an artifact of the way the question was asked and in that sense trivial. What is universal about a given norm or attitude is that which can be expressed in universal language (i.e., translated from language to language in a form that is understood within each language); what is distinctive about it is that which is expressed in a way that is understood in only one language. The norm or practice itself is intrinsically neither universal nor particular. An attitude can be shifted from the category of the unique to that of the universal, either linguistically or by going up or down the ladder of abstraction. *Guanxi*, for example, is culturally unique, but particularism (of which *guanxi* is an example) is universal.

By the same token, findings of cultural distinctiveness are equally an artifact of the interpretive approach. In this approach, cultural attributes are conceptualized with such specificity or complexity that what is portrayed is by definition unique. Ambrose King's informative discussion of *guanxi* and network building in an earlier issue of *Daedalus* provides an example.[46] If we were to ask Americans whether they function through *guanxi*, they would say no, because they would not know what we were talking about. If we were to ask them whether they sometimes get things done through networks or connections, or whether they consider it proper to help a relative or friend under certain circumstances, or whether it is important to cultivate personal relations with people from whom one wishes to get favors, many of them would say yes, perhaps as many in the United States as in China.

If King is describing something distinctively Chinese, it is not because the component cultural attributes are distinctive to China, but because the author has formulated a complex of attitudes and behaviors which is unique as a whole and by definition. Such a claim of uniqueness is not accessible to proof by survey research, because the survey technique of measurement requires the breakup of a cultural complex into measurable components. Since such components are cross-culturally measurable, they are bound to some degree to be cross-culturally existent. Cultures, then, are unique synthetically, universal analytically. Both the distinctiveness and nondistinctiveness of cultures are not facts about cultures, but artifacts of the ways in which cultures are studied.

12

Left and Right in Deng's China

Written with Tianjian Shi

In the 1980s, the first decade of Deng Xiaoping's reforms, Chinese society became wealthier and more complex, and state control of ideology weakened. As public attitudes diversified, new ideological alignments took shape. This essay explores the ideological landscape in the aftermath of the 1989 Tiananmen pro-democracy demonstrations. It uses data from a 1990 national sample survey that interviewed 2,896 adults throughout the country, except for Tibet, to provide a statistically accurate picture of mass attitudes. The technical details of the survey are described in the appendix.

Chinese society in 1990 was split along ideological lines into two large, loose groups, each with distinctive sociological characteristics. One group had more liberal attitudes toward public issues, the other more conservative attitudes. In Western terms, both Chinese issue constituencies stood on the left, in the sense that both demanded big government and egalitarianism: the liberals wanted government to fight against special privilege and economic inequality, and the conservatives wanted government to take responsibility for citizens' welfare.

The difference between the groups centered on attitudes toward reform and its consequences. Chinese liberals, who were concerned with the effects of reform on the moral state of society and on good government, thought the way out of China's difficulties was to push forward with economic and political reform. Chinese conservatives for their part worried more about the negative impact of reforms on their personal welfare and thought reform should be slowed or reversed.

We explore the extent to which the dynamics that divided the Chinese population resemble the dynamics of ideological polarization in the West. We choose the West as the case for comparison because that area has been the focus of most of the research and theory on mass ideology and its determinants. We find that in China, as in the West, class, as measured by education, income, and occupation, has a strong effect on issue priorities and democratic values. The urban-rural cleavage is also important, although for reasons that differ somewhat from those that operate in the West. In China one finds some influential social divisions that are not found in the West: that between party members and non-party members and that between employees of state and nonstate units. Nonetheless, the ways in which these attributes affect the individual's ideological standpoint can be understood in terms of the same logic that explains the impact of sociological attributes on attitudes in the West.

In short, the Chinese ideological spectrum is distinctive in substance but universal in the dynamics that shape it. In light of the cultural and institutional differences between China and the West, that is, by the logic of a most-different-case comparison, this finding supports theories of mass ideology hitherto grounded chiefly in studies of the United States and Europe.

Ideological Polarization in the West

Two issues have dominated the ideological space of the West: the role of the state and the conflicting norms of equality and achievement in the distribution of goods. The left generally favors more government intervention in the economy and more egalitarian income distribution; the right typically stands for relative freedom of private enterprise from state intervention and toleration of higher levels of income inequality. But left and right have accumulated additional meanings as well. According to Seymour Lipset and Stein Rokkan, the political cleavages embodied in European party systems crystallized the results of four major historical struggles: between center and periphery, church and state, town and country, and owners and workers.[1] Arend Lijphart suggests seven dimensions of ideology: socioeconomic, religious, cultural-ethnic, urban-rural, regime support, foreign policy, and postmaterialism.[2]

The polarity of left and right emerged from a synthesis of these different cleavages, taking different form in each country. Each country varied in whether issue preferences and party loyalties were dominated by class alignments, or by religious, regional, ethnic, or other ones, or by distinctive combinations of several.[3] There was no tight relationship among positions on all these issues. Yet people usually thought of themselves as liberal or conservative because they leaned one way or another on a series of value dilemmas that characterized their nation's political culture. In the postwar era there emerged a new cleavage dimension—called materialism-postmaterialism by Ronald Inglehart—that generated the "new politics" of the environment, women's issues, and the peace movement. Even though older parties and issues tended to be more closely aligned with the left-right scale than the parties and issues of the new politics, citizens still thought of the new issues roughly in terms of a left-right dimension.[4]

Different people may combine these value choices in different patterns.[5] Left-right self-placement may reflect a mix of abstract thinking about issues and favorable and unfavorable feelings toward groups and issues.[6] Yet, according to John Zaller, "[A]lthough there are numerous 'value dimensions' between which there is no obvious logical connection, many people nonetheless respond to different value dimensions *as if* they were organized by a common left-right dimension."[7] Thus, in the "political action" study of four European countries and the United States done in the early 1970s, respondents were able to locate themselves on the left-right dimension in numbers ranging from a high of 92 percent of the respondents in Germany to a low of 68 percent of those in the United States.[8]

Ideas of left and right remain broad and vague in the minds of most Western citizens. Depending on the country, only 11 percent to 30 percent of the political action respondents were able to say what the terms meant. "A sizable proportion . . . either could not give any meaning of the terms or else completely reversed their meaning."[9] In America, the country where mass attitudes have been most intensively studied, few citizens are able to relate their overall ideological self-identification to their opinions on particular issues.[10] Still, no matter how vaguely comprehended, many citizens use these general categories to help orient their ideas about politics.

Western respondents align along the liberal-conservative dimension chiefly in response to the combined operation of two forces, social position and cognitive sophistication. Members of different social groups have different economic and other interests, which partly determine their positions on the ideological spectrum. Attitudes on the left tend to be preferred by the working class, urban residents, young people, and members of minority ethnic and religious groups, because they are dissatisfied with their share of benefits in society and think they would be better off if the state intervened to redistribute resources. People who are more satisfied (or less dissatisfied) with the status quo tend to take a more conservative stance toward government activism, social change, and redistribution. In Western societies these groups usually include white-collar workers, suburbanites, middle-aged people, and members of dominant ethnic and religious groups.[11]

While cognitive sophistication is affected by many factors, including education, media exposure, political campaigns, and government propaganda efforts, it is usually measured by education.[12] Cognitive sophistication has mixed effects on left-right self-placement. Greater knowledge is associated with higher socioeconomic status, which makes people more conservative. But education also increases openness to change and thus helps to move people toward the liberal end of the spectrum. Education may have different effects on people's left-right positions on different issues in different countries: in the United States, for example, liberal social values are promoted in schools and better-educated citizens tend to be more liberal than those who are less-educated.[13]

Whatever the ideological direction of its impact, however, greater cognitive capacity allows citizens to approach issues in a more abstract, generalized, and interrelated way.[14] Without necessarily making citizens less self-interested, political knowledge enables them to see how " 'roundabout' routes . . . will better secure ultimate gratification."[15] As a result, educated and knowledgeable sections of Western publics are more likely than are less educated groups to think about political issues in terms of an explicit ideology or broad policy choices as distinct from immediate self-interest. While the ideological position of a less sophisticated constituency tends to be a direct reflection of its social position, that of a more cognitively sophisticated constituency reflects the combined influence of social interest and an abstract conception of the issues.

Left and Right in Communist China

Under Mao, the meaning of the liberal-conservative dimension was decreed from above. Mao accepted Stalin's scheme that history moved from primitive communism to feudalism to capitalism to communism and that whatever pushed things in that direction was "progressive" and hence leftist. Class became a question of one's stance toward historical change rather than a matter of objective economic interest. And class was a label formally assigned to each citizen by the party authorities, rather than a self-chosen identity.[16]

Mao labeled as "left" those who stood on the side of what he considered progress. Those who went too far in advance of history he designated ultraleft deviationists or adventurists. Those who failed to push historical progress at the appropriate speed were right deviationists guilty of class compromise. The position Mao occupied at any moment defined the magic place that constituted the authentic left between the ultraleft and the right.[17]

After 1949 Mao moved this point of reference steadily in a radical direction, speeding the pace of change toward an egalitarian, state-dominated society. In a series of mass campaigns the Communist Party targeted as enemies all those defined as occupying positions on the right—landlords, counterrevolutionaries, "bureaucrats," and "sectarians." In the mid-1950s Mao accelerated agricultural collectivization and launched the Great Leap Forward. He accused party colleagues who failed to keep up of "tottering along like a woman with bound feet."[18] An estimated three-quarters of a million people fell victim to charges of rightism. In the 1960s Mao carried out the Great Proletarian Cultural Revolution to make sure the revolution continued uninterrupted.

With Mao so impatient for historical progress, hardly any space remained to the left of him on the spectrum. The rare exceptions were certain allegedly ultraleft organizations that arose during the Cultural Revolution, organizations like the Hunan Provincial Proletarian Association (*Shengwulian*), which called for virtual anarchy, or an alleged anti-Mao conspiracy called the "May 16th Group," which supposedly was prepared to challenge Mao's dominance.

China was like a ship whose passengers all rush to port. During the Cultural Revolution every organization proclaimed its progressiveness with names like "Red Guards" and "Revolutionary Rebels." Street names (Anti-Revisionism Street), markets (East Wind Market), and personal names ("Defend-the-East" Zhang) crowded the left side of the symbolic space. For a time the Beijing Red Guards even forced cars to drive on the left side of the street and to stop on green and go on red.[19] In effect, the ideological spectrum collapsed, and ideology ceased to be a meaningful concept because all views came cloaked in nearly identical terminology. When Mao's chosen successor, Lin Biao, fell from power, the Party announced that Lin, who had always been praised as the leftest of the left, was really "left in form but right in essence." In the bankrupt terminology of the day, this meant that Lin had pretended to be a good man but was not. Left and right had become devoid of substance.[20]

A multidimensional ideological landscape reemerged after Mao's

death. The official debate over the speed and content of reform continued to orient itself to the presumed direction of the march of history and
to speak partly in terms of left and right. But Deng Xiaoping's regime was
no longer able to monopolize public debate. In addition, two unofficial
ideological dimensions emerged, one focusing on mass grievances
toward a variety of targets and the other on ideas of democracy. Attitudes
to reform, attitudes of grievance, and attitudes toward democracy constituted the three dimensions of ideology in Deng's China.

The ideas of left and right were used in the official reform debate
more in attack than defense. Each side claimed to be on the left in a good
sense and accused the other of being in some sense conservative.
Advocates of reform tried to deny critics access to the progressive and
socialist side of the rhetorical spectrum by presenting reform as the self-
perfecting mechanism of socialism. Deng claimed to be "building socialism with Chinese characteristics" and to be guiding reform with the "four
basic principles" of socialism, proletarian dictatorship, Communist Party
leadership, and Marxism-Leninism-Mao Zedong Thought. Critics of
reform labeled the reformists "bourgeois liberals" and accused them of
fomenting "spiritual pollution," which by implication located them on
the right.[21] Reform advocates labeled conservative values ultra-left or
"left" in quotation marks.[22]

A second ideological dimension was discernible in the unofficial
media and in the liberalized official press. We call it the grievance dimension, but it consisted of many elements: a mix of economic grievances,
nostalgia for the past, moral condemnation of social and political corruption, opposition to change, traditionalism, and antiforeignism. Deng
Xiaoping had allowed the weakening of Party control over ideology and
the rise of a partial civil society. Newspapers, magazines, and book publishers eluded tight oversight by the propaganda departments.[23] Public
opinion polling appeared, providing leaders and to some extent the public itself with information about mass attitudes, even though polls conducted by Chinese organizations fell short of international methodological standards.[24] Unofficial and private channels of communication came
into existence—open letters, underground publications, foreign and
Hong Kong-based books and magazines that made their way into China,
and a vast realm of private conversation and rumor.

Dissatisfaction focused on a seemingly contradictory mix of targets:
the ruling clans, the party and state bureaucracies, nouveaux riches
entrepreneurs, dissident intellectuals, and foreigners. Despite their suffering under Mao, many Chinese remembered that era as a time when

they could leave their front doors and bicycles unlocked, when prices were stable, when everyone had a job, when officials were honest, and when China was not afraid of war with the West. The new phenomena of inflation, economic inequality, corruption, personal insecurity, and cosmopolitanism seemed part of a general decline of values. Ordinary people were liable to complain about the rise of a new Mercedes-riding class of "bureaucratic capitalists" and "compradores" (*maiban,* an old term for Chinese who served as agents for foreign firms). The bustle of downtown construction prompted complaints that officials were "selling out the country like Li Hongzhang," the nineteenth-century negotiator who ceded Chinese territories to Japan. Dissidents and foreigners were perceived as collaborating with, rather than opposing, corrupt bureaucrats and party ideologues, all undermining what was native and true to China.[25] People complained that even *guanxi*—personal connections, the cement of human relations in Chinese society—no longer carried its overtones of friendship and moral obligation but had become instead cynical instruments in a marketized but lawless system.[26] The popular mood was essentially "anti."

The third ideological dimension was shaped by a broad group of prodemocratic intellectuals. They ranged from Wei Jingsheng, the selftaught dissident, to Wang Meng, a Communist Party member and government-supported writer of fiction and essays who had once served as minister of culture. They included world-class scientists like Fang Lizhi and Xu Liangying and teachers in provincial party schools; academic philosophers and senior party thinkers; private-venture entrepreneurs and poets. Despite its diversity, this group agreed on a central point: that China had a historic obligation to learn from the tragedies of the past in order to prevent the reemergence of a Maoist-style dictatorship. Their prescriptions varied from immediate democratization (Wei Jingsheng) to an interlude of authoritarianism (the "new authoritarians"); from civil service reform to Western-style democratization; from "rule by law" to human rights. The core issue across this band of debate was "preventing another cultural revolution."[27]

Although Chinese ideas of democracy are shaped by the heritages of Confucius and Marx, they also bear an essential similarity to Western concepts. The parallel is partly due to the direct influence of Western ideas, but more importantly it stems from the universality of the problem of making government accountable.[28] The Party tried to deal with the lessons of the past in its resolution on the Mao years: it acknowledged that Mao had made ideological errors but asserted that the Party had now corrected them.[29] This failed to satisfy many Chinese intellectuals, however. By the late 1980s the influence of the liberal intellectuals had gone so far on the subject of democracy that some observers argued their ideas enjoyed a hegemony in unofficial discourse.[30] Pro-democratic ideas were also widespread among the general population.[31]

Issue Priorities and Agendas

Our survey data enable us to analyze how attitudes toward these three issue dimensions were distributed among the population in 1990. They also help us probe beneath the surface similarity of Chinese ideological issues to liberal-conservative ideas in the West, to see whether the two sets of ideological dimensions reflect the operation of the same social and cognitive forces.[32] We draw our evidence about the reform and grievance dimensions from a question about citizens' concerns with public issues. Another question, on which we report below, included items relevant to the democracy dimension.

The public-issues question asked, "Nowadays, our government is facing many problems, and to solve these problems is not easy. For each of the following problems that I mention, please tell me on which problems you think the government has spent too much effort, on which problems it has spent the appropriate effort, and on which problems it has spent not enough effort." The results are displayed in Table 12.1.

The question was not designed to uncover issues of public concern that we did not already know about. Rather, it assesses the relative degree of priority the public places on a predetermined list of issues.[33] The first column displays the issues in the order in which the public ranked them as getting "not enough" government effort (this was not the order in which they were listed in the questionnaire).

Not surprisingly, the two top issues—inflation and corruption—were the same concerns that dominated the 1989 Tiananmen demonstrations. The next four items—crime, bureaucratism, inequitable income distribution, and inadequate government investment in education— were also prominent among the complaints of the 1989 demonstrators. The rank of these six items at the top of the table is consistent with our sense that the public felt beleaguered by the collapse of public and official morality and the rise of self-seeking materialism. It turns out therefore that the concerns of the urban, student demonstrators were widespread across the national sample, which included urban and rural residents, young and old, educated and uneducated. Remarkably high

TABLE 12.1

Attitudes Toward Government Handling of Issues (%)

Issue[a]	Not Enough Attention	Just right	Too Much Attention	No Interest[b]
Inflation and complaints				
Price control	55.7	19.7	1.9	· 22.7
Oppose corruption	53.8	17.9	3.0	25.3
Oppose crime	47.1	28.6	3.0	21.4
Oppose bureaucratism	46.8	16.8	1.8	34.6
Economic welfare				
Income distribution	42.5	15.0	1.7	40.8
Education	42.1	35.6	3.8	18.5
Unemployment	37.8	20.6	1.5	40.0
Housing	34.2	29.0	3.0	33.8
Consumer protection	33.6	21.7	1.7	43.1
Environment protection	33.6	30.3	2.6	33.5
Subsidies	27.9	21.7	7.4	43.0
Population control	24.7	50.4	12.8	12.2
Reform				
Anti-bourgeois liberalization	21.2	25.2	5.2	48.4
Private enterprise	18.2	25.4	9.4	47.1
Economic reform	17.9	28.6	4.1	49.4
Political reform	17.6	26.6	2.8	52.9
Foreign policy				
Taiwan	17.0	32.5	4.0	46.5
Opening	12.6	34.4	5.5	47.4
Defense	9.8	33.4	3.2	53.6
Foreign aid	5.7	20.0	8.1	66.1
N=2,896				

Source: China survey (1990)

a. Issues were: price control; opposing bribery and corruption, and rectifying party work style; opposing crime; opposing bureaucratism; solving the problem of inequitable income distribution; raising the education level; solving the employment problem; solving the housing problem; protecting consumers' rights; protecting the environment; subsidizing the basic necessities of life; population control and family planning; opposing bourgeois liberalization; encouraging the development of individual or private enterprises; economic system reform; political system reform; reunifying with Taiwan; opening to the outside world; national defense; and foreign aid.

b. No interest equals don't know plus no answer.

percentages of respondents of all kinds said that the government was not doing enough to solve the same problems that had motivated the demonstrators in Beijing.[34]

The table goes on to reveal how much priority the public placed on greater government effort on other issues. From one-quarter to two-fifths of the respondents wanted the government to do more to solve problems of daily life, including those related to jobs, housing, shoddy goods, environmental pollution, subsidies, and population pressures. These represent a variety of demands that the government was expected to satisfy in the former socialist society. Now that the socialist system was giving way to a market-based system, a substantial portion of the public seemed to deplore the weakening of government effort in these areas of traditional state responsibility.

The next four items relate to reform. Fewer than one-fifth of the respondents indicated a positive attitude toward reform, by stating that the government should do more to promote economic and political reform. A slightly larger percentage expressed a negative view of reform through their concern that the government needed to do more to stop bourgeois liberalization, a term used by critics of reform to refer to its negative ideological and cultural effects.

Finally, foreign policy ranked at the bottom of the public's list of priorities, as it does in most countries. Among foreign policy issues, the heavily propagandized, nationalistic issue of Taiwan stood above the rest.

The public may assign a low priority to an issue for either of two reasons: because it does not have much interest in the issue[35] or because it feels that the government is already handling the issue adequately. The second and fourth columns in Table 12.1 help clarify which of these two attitudes applies to each issue. "No interest" is the label we have assigned to the summed percentage of "don't know" and "no answer" responses. Lack of interest generally increases as one moves down the list of issues. It strongly marks the foreign policy domain and also characterizes public attitudes to reform and to certain economic welfare issues like subsidies and consumer protection. Thus, the fact that the public did not demand more government action in these areas does not represent a vote of confidence in policy. But for issues higher on the list, such as price control, corruption, bureaucratism, and income distribution, dissatisfaction seems to be a better explanation than low interest for the public demand for greater government effort. "Just right" responses, which show the proportion of the public that was satisfied with the government's handling of the issue, are generally lower than both "not enough effort" and "no interest" responses.

"Too much effort" plays a substantial role in the public pattern of response only toward population control. This was the issue on which the fewest respondents felt no interest, the issue on which the largest number of respondents thought the government was already doing enough, and also the issue on which the highest percentage thought the government was doing too much. The pattern suggests that many people were concerned about population pressure and approved the government's strong policy to limit population growth, yet many were unhappy with the impact of population control policies on their own lives.

The main message of the table is that Chinese citizens were dissatisfied or uninterested in the government's handling of most issues. Only in the area of foreign policy was there a satisfied plurality, and its size was small.

The rank ordering of public concern about the issues given in Table 12.1 is not a test of how the public perceived the links among them. A factor analysis, which we display in Table 12.2, provides such a test. This procedure sorts the issues into groups according to the frequency with which respondents who answer "not enough" with respect to a particular set of issues will also answer "not enough" with respect to another given issue. In other words, factor analysis identifies clusters of issues (we label them agendas) that are related to one another in the response patterns of our respondents.[36]

Table 12.2 shows that the issues were associated in the public mind in much the way our analysis of three issue dimensions would lead us to expect.[37] Following the usual standard in interpreting factor analyses, we concentrate on items with loading scores above 0.5. Items that fall below this level are not closely linked to other sets of issues in the public mind. For example, "opening to the world" was of roughly equal (and as Table 12.1 suggests, relatively low) concern to everyone, regardless of respondents' patterns of concern with other sets of issues.

Corruption, crime, bureaucratism, and price control cohere in factor 1 to constitute what we can call the *Tiananmen Agenda*. They represent an interrelated set of issues that implies a critical view of regime performance. The second factor identifies a *Reform Agenda*, which includes economic and political components. People who wanted the government to pay more attention to economic reform also wanted it to pay more attention to political reform, and vice versa. Although the factor loadings of "encouraging private enterprise" and "opening to the world" are too low to justify a strong statement of their relationship to the factor, they also make sense as reform-related issues.

The third factor separates economic and quality-of-life issues as a distinct agenda, which we label *Economic Welfare*.[38] The fourth factor constitutes a *Foreign Policy Agenda*. As we saw in Table 12.1, only a small number of people assigned high priority to this last set of issues. The factor analysis shows that there was no strong tendency to link foreign policy issues with any of the other three issue agendas.

These findings deepen our understanding of two of our three sug-

TABLE 12.2

Factor Analysis of Issue Priority[a]

	Tiananmen Agenda	Reform Agenda	Economic Welfare Agenda	Foreign Policy Agenda
Oppose corruption	.78	.02	.00	-.02
Oppose crime	.75	-.05	.07	.02
Oppose bureaucratism	.65	.07	-.09	-.02
Price control	.59	-.05	-.13	-.03
Education	.35	-.01	-.22	.12
Antibourgeois liberalization	.32	.19	.05	.10
Political reform	-.03	.82	.00	.02
Economic reform	-.01	.81	.00	-.03
Private enterprise	.03	.30	-.18	.09
Opening to world	.07	.25	-.07	.21
Unemployment	.02	.04	-.66	.01
Housing	-.06	-.03	-.65	.04
Income distribution	.21	.05	-.50	-.01
Subsidies	.01	-.00	-.49	-.01
Environment	.10	.17	-.36	.07
Consumer protection	.23	.18	-.35	-.01
National defense	.04	-.04	.05	.79
Foreign aid	-.04	.01	-.03	.51
Percentage of variance	32.5	8.6	6.6	5.8
Eigenvalue	5.9	1.5	1.2	1.1

Source: China survey (1990).

a. The factors are derived from a principal axis analysis of "not enough effort" responses to issue priority question in oblique rotation. Population control and reunifying with Taiwan loaded weakly on factors 1 and 2 respectively, and a slightly clearer factor structure emerged when they were excluded. This is reported here and used in the correlations and regressions that follow.

gested ideological dimensions. The Tiananmen and Economic Welfare Agendas both reflect elements of what we called grievance. The Reform Agenda corresponds to our reform dimension. Foreign Policy emerges as a separate agenda that is not important enough to generate a major ideological cleavage in the population.

All the agendas call for government action, since that was the subject of this question. But the agendas differ in the type of government role they envision. The Tiananmen Agenda calls for government moral leadership as well as a degree of economic intervention to control inflation. The Reform Agenda calls for government leadership to change the system. The Foreign Policy Agenda calls for government attention to foreign policy issues.

The Economic Welfare Agenda alone calls for direct government intervention in the distribution of goods in order to solve the problems that individual citizens confront with jobs, housing, wages, and subsidies. This is the only one of the four agendas that seems on the face of it to resemble the classical Western left-right dimension. To say in Deng's China that the government should do more about jobs, housing, and income distribution was to say that it should create more jobs in the tens of thousands of enterprises that it owned, build state-owned housing to rent at subsidized rates, and raise the salaries it paid to tens of millions of officials, teachers, technicians, factory workers, and other state employees. It is in this sense that the Economic Welfare Agenda resembled the agenda of the Western "left." It was also "left" in the Chinese context—or "conservative" according to the label reversal common in postsocialist and reforming socialist countries—in the sense that it ran counter to the reform effort to reduce direct government participation in the economy and to create more autonomous enterprises operating under market conditions.

Issue Constituencies

Face comparisons of the left in the West and China take us only partway toward knowing whether they reflect similar or different ideological structures and mechanisms. Deeper insight can be gained by identifying which kinds of citizens are most concerned with which agendas. We cannot expect to find the same constituencies as in the West any more than we find the same issues, since neither China's issue space nor its sociological structure is a copy of the West's. The deeper question is whether the issue constituencies in China reflect patterns of social interest in interaction with cognitive sophistication that are intelligible in terms of the theories that explain ideological alignments in the Western case.

Table 12.3 presents correlations of selected respondent attributes with the tendency of respondents to give high priority to each issue agenda. Some of the attributes we look at are the same as those found in the West, such as sex, education, income, and age. Others, though different from the West, have a sociological logic similar to that of attributes studied elsewhere. For example, being a party member is a measure of elite status. Membership in a state unit is an indicator of economic privilege and high social status. Urban household registration signals the right to live in the cities, where conditions are better and most residents have access to social services not available in the countryside.[39]

For each attribute, the size of the correlation coefficient is a measure

TABLE 12.3

Correlations Between Respondents' Attributes and Issue Agendas[*]

	Tiananmen Agenda	Reform Agenda	Economic Welfare Agenda	Foreign Policy Agenda
Household registration[a]	.17	.20	-.33	.09
Sex[b]	.24	.20	.22	-.16
Age	-.18	-.17	-.17	.15
Education[c]	.38	.37	-.44	.26
Family income[d]	.15	.16	-.21	.12
Party member[e]	.16	.14	-.16	.12
Occupation[f]	.19	.25	-.25	.13
State unit[g]	.21	.23	-.32	.13

Source: China survey (1990).
[*] All correlations are significant at the .001 level.
a. Household registration: one if urban household registration, 0 if rural household registration.
b. Sex: 1 if male, 0 if female.
c. Education: by years of formal schooling.
d. Family income: by yuan.
e. Party member: 1 if member of Communist Party of China, 0 if not.
f. Occupation: 1 if white collar, 0 if other.
g. State unit: 1 if respondent reported working at state organization or state-owned enterprise, 0 if working at collective or other kind of enterprises.

of how strongly the attribute influences a respondent's tendency to be concerned with the items that make up each agenda. The stronger the correlation, the more intense the social cleavage around that issue agenda, that is, the more sharply persons who differ along the particular social dimension differ in the priority they assign to the issue agenda.

All the correlations are statistically significant, and several are strong. Education is the most powerful predictor of issue priorities. Type of work unit is the second strongest correlate. Household registration, sex, and the other variables also have moderate effects on the choice of issue concerns.

However, there is a tendency for many of these factors to reinforce one another. For example, a person with more education is more likely to be young, male, and have more income. A multiple regression analysis, shown in Table 12.4, distinguishes how each attribute functions separately. The standardized regression coefficients (betas) measure the relative strength of each variable in affecting respondents' choice of issue agendas. Education is the attribute that most strongly influences the choice of issue agenda, and it does so consistently across all four agendas. This suggests that differences in cognitive sophistication play a major role in determining the ideological alignments of Chinese citizens, even after taking account of the privileged social position of many educated citizens.

TABLE 12.4

Multiple Regression Analysis of Respondents' Attributes on Issue Agendas

	Tiananmen Agenda		Reform Agenda		Economic Welfare Agenda		Foreign Policy Agenda	
	Coefficient	Beta	Coefficient	Beta	Coefficient	Beta	Coefficient	Beta
Household registration[a]	.07	.03	.12	.06**	-.35	-.18***	-.03	-.01
Sex[b]	.28	.15***	.20	.11***	-.16	-.07***	.15	.09***
Age	-.00	-.06***	-.00	-.08***	.01	.13***	-.00	-.09***
Education[c]	.06	.25***	.05	.20***	-.05	-.24***	.03	.15**
Family income[d]	.00	.03	.00	.04**	-.00	-.03*	.00	.05**
Party member[e]	.21	.07***	.17	.05***	-.18	-.06***	.21	.07***
Occupation[f]	.07	.02	.29	.10***	-.11	-.04**	.07	.26
State unit[g]	.11	.05**	.11	.05**	-.13	-.07***	.07	.03
Constant	-.45		-.41		.60		-.11	
R Squared	.17		.17		.24		.08	
N = 2,727								

Source: China survey (1990).
*=significant at .1 level, **=significant at .05 level, ***=significant at .01 level.
a. Household registration: one if urban household registration, o if rural household registration.
b. Sex: 1 if male, o if female.
c. Education: by years of formal schooling.
d. Family income: by yuan.
e. Party member: 1 if member of Communist Party of China, o if not.
f. Occupation: 1 if white collar, o if other.
g. State unit: 1 if respondent reported working at state organization or state-owned enterprise, o if working at collective or other kind of enterprises.

The next three most influential variables reflect the importance of social interest. Different variables more strongly affect different agendas. Sex is the second strongest factor affecting adherence to both the Tiananmen and Reform Agendas; men are more concerned with these sets of issues than are women. Household registration and age are the second and third strongest factors influencing adherence to the Economic Welfare Agenda; rural residents and older people place relatively high priority on this agenda.

When the four variables mentioned so far are controlled, the effects of the remaining variables are nearly all statistically significant. Some of them are quite strong, in particular, the tendency (1) of party members to be more concerned about all four agendas, (2) of persons in more prestigious occupations to be strongly concerned with the Reform Agenda, and (3) of employees of state units to be concerned with the Economic Welfare Agenda.

The most important feature of Tables 12.3 and 12.4 is the sign of the coefficients. A positive sign indicates that those concerned with the given agenda tend to measure one way on that attribute; a negative sign indicates that they measure the other. Thus, a positive sign on household registration indicates urban registration, a negative sign rural; a positive sign on sex indicates male, a negative sign female; a positive sign on age indicates an older group, a negative sign a younger group; and so on. For each variable in both tables (except for age and sex in Table 12.3 and the statistically insignificant relationship between foreign policy and household registration in Table 12.4),[40] the sign for the Economic Welfare Agenda is the opposite of that for the other three agendas. This means that with respect to the four agendas, the Chinese public divides into two constituencies with opposite characteristics.

One of the constituencies is predominantly urban, male, young, and well educated; it has above-average family incomes, contains more party members than the other constituency, tends to work in white-collar occupations and to be employed in state units. This group is disproportionately concerned with the Tiananmen Agenda and the Reform Agenda. It wants more government leadership in attacking the problems of corruption, crime, bureaucratism, and inflation, and it favors more attention to economic and political reform. This constituency is critical of government performance yet supportive of reform. In the Chinese context, it is relatively liberal. (It is also interested in the Foreign Policy Agenda. But we know from Table 12.1 that interest in the Foreign Policy Agenda is not strong, and Table 12.3 shows that this agenda divides the two constituencies more weakly than the other two. We therefore drop it from the rest of the analysis.)

The second constituency has relatively more members with the opposite characteristics: rural, female, older, less educated, with lower incomes, without party membership, and working in nonstate units. This group is most concerned with the Economic Welfare Agenda. It is uneasy about the impact of reform on jobs, housing, incomes, and subsidies, and it does not support accelerated reform. In the Chinese context, it is relatively conservative.

The attributes that divide the two constituencies are partly the same as and partly different from those that divide left and right in the West. But more importantly, the divisions make sense in terms of the same theory that explains ideological alignments in the West.

First, socioeconomic interest explains why the constituency for the Tiananmen and Reform Agendas consists of the relative winners from reform, while backers of the Economic Welfare Agenda are those who have been most vulnerable to the costs of reform.[41] Although inflation, corruption, and the decline of government services have affected everyone (as Table 12.1 shows), they hit hardest those of lower social and economic status, who perceive themselves as more in need of the kind of government protection characteristic of the old system and who are less equipped to take advantage of the market economy that is emerging under the reforms.

Reform dissolved the rural commune system and left village residents to fend for themselves in the market, while urban residents continue to have access to social benefits denied rural residents. Women lost some of the protection they had enjoyed under the old system, in which the government supported relative equality of the sexes; they are now openly discriminated against, especially in the growing private and collective enterprise sector. Older people have seen their guarantees of lifetime employment threatened and their pensions eroded; many lack the energy and skills to take advantage of the new opportunities that reform offers.

Persons with lower educational levels lack the training and connections to get ahead in the new order. Those with lower incomes lack the capital to get started in business. Party members have the connections to get ahead, and some can use their positions to benefit from the corruption that reform has generated. Members of state units, with their privileged employment status, have less need to worry about jobs, subsidies, housing, and the like. The fact that those without privileged access to state benefits show greater concern with the Economic Welfare Agenda reflects the fact that reform has subjected them to risk and deprivation. In short, those social groups who have been relative gainers in the reform process are more concerned with the general public agendas of Tiananmen and Reform. Those who have been relative losers because of the reform process have been more concerned with the personal damage they have suffered.

As sometimes happens in the West, cognitive sophistication reinforces the operation of economic interest by making those who are likely to be liberal even more likely to be liberal. While both constituencies are critical of the present state of affairs, the better educated tend to look at the problems generated by reform in a way that goes beyond immediate personal interest and to see them in terms of broad public issues. They are more likely to understand how indirect measures like further reform can over the long run solve immediate problems like housing, jobs, income distribution, and satisfaction of consumer needs more effectively than

TABLE 12.5

Opinions on Democracy (%)

Issues	Pro-democracy	Antidemocracy	Don't know
More democracy will lead to chaos (disagree)	37.7	22.4	39.9
Multiple parties will cause political chaos (disagree)	29.5	35.7	34.7
Different thinking will lead to chaos (disagree)	32.2	43.0	24.8
Heads of cities should be elected (agree)	67.8	21.6	10.6
China needs more democracy now (agree)	54.8	6.0	39.3
China's democracy depends on CCP's leadership (disagree)	1.7	76.1	22.2
N=2,896			

Source: China survey (1990).

can state intervention aimed directly at these issues. The better educated—more advantaged by reform and so more liberal—are also more willing to trade material benefits for ideological values and to trade immediate benefits for long-term benefits.

In short, there were two distinct issue constituencies in the Chinese mass public in 1990. Although they were not replicas of the classic Western left-right constituencies, they resembled them in certain ways. To the extent that they differed from Western constituencies, they did so in ways that can be explained by the same logic of interest and cognition that explains ideological alignments in the West.

Democratic Values

We turn finally to our third ideological dimension, attitudes toward democracy. Does the pattern of cleavage over democratic values fall along the same ideological spectrum just identified or crosscut it? Our data permit us to answer this question by looking at democratic attitudes and also at two related sets of attitudes, social liberalism and procedural liberalism.[42]

Using an agree-disagree format, we posed six statements about attitudes toward democracy.[43] The pattern of responses is displayed in Table 12.5. We also asked six questions about attitudes toward women (social liberalism) and two about criminal procedure (procedural liberalism),

TABLE 12.6

Social Attitudes (%)

Issues	Liberal	Conservative	Don't know
Would you allow son to marry a divorced woman (yes)	46.0	38.5	15.6
Do you mind if supervisor is a woman (no)	81.2	5.3	13.5
Wife's educational level should be lower than husband's (no)	70.3	17.4	12.3
Wife's income should be lower than husband's (no)	75.0	15.5	9.5
Do you care if you do not have a son (no)	63.8	27.1	9.1
Should couple be able to divorce (yes)	55.0	33.8	11.2
N=2,896			

Source: China survey (1990).

some of them in agree-disagree format.[44] The pattern of responses is shown in Tables 12.6 and 12.7.

The responses to these questions contain several points of interest. On democracy, the public's responses would be unexpected in the West but make sense in China. Democracy is understood by most Chinese not as a system of competition and participation, but as a term for the good polity, one that is fair, egalitarian, stable, and honest. What legitimizes government is not pluralism and participation but moral rectitude and administrative performance.[45] The majorities who want "more democracy" want government that is more honest and responsive. They would like top city officials to be elected instead of appointed, because current mayors are often viewed as remote and corrupt. But at the same time substantial minorities fear that too much pluralism will give rise to ideological and social disorder. And only a tiny number are willing to dispense with CCP leadership.[46]

Social attitudes show a consensus on liberal values that is surprisingly

TABLE 12.7

Attitudes Toward Due Process (%)

Issues	Pro-due process	Ignore due process	Don't know
Punish without legal procedure	43.2	40.7	16.1
Judge solicit opinions of local government	22.6	57.3	20.1
N=2,896			

Source: China survey (1990).

TABLE 12.8

Correlations Between Respondents' Attributes and Degree of Democratism

	Political	Social	Procedural
Household registration[a]	.25	.23	.23
Sex[b]	.28	.16	.18
Age	-.28	-.17	-.10
Education[c]	.49	.39	.34
Family income[d]	.21	.15	.17
Party member[e]	.14	.13	.16
Occupation[f]	.25	.19	.21
State unit[g]	.29	.22	.23
N=2,896			

Source: China survey (1990).
*All correlations are significant at the .001 level.
a. Household registration: 1 if urban household registration, 0 if rural household registration.
b. Sex: 1 if male, 0 if female.
c. Education: by years of formal schooling.
d. Family income: by yuan.
e. Party member: 1 if member of Communist Party of China, 0 if not.
f. Occupation: 1 if white collar, 0 if other.
g. State unit: 1 if respondent reported working at state organization or state-owned enterprise, 0 if working at collective or other kind of enterprises.

strong in light of the poor social and economic status of Chinese women.[47] Most people say they are willing to have a female supervisor and to allow their son to marry a divorced woman. Few say that they think a wife's income or education should be lower than her husband's. Since the Chinese population is still largely rural and has relatively low average educational levels, we suspect they have expressed politically correct responses rather than deeply rooted beliefs.[48]

By contrast, procedural liberalism is relatively weak. Faced with what they see as a crime wave, Chinese are not immune from the tendency found in mass publics elsewhere to be less liberal when they think about the rights of suspected criminals than when they think about other issues.[49] This fits with Chinese attitudes of intolerance toward proponents of unpopular political attitudes, which we have discussed elsewhere.[50] In short, liberalism in China is no more consistent a belief system than it is in the West.

In order to discover which sections of the public hold democratic and liberal values, we scaled respondents according to the number of democratic or liberal answers they gave for each set of issues[51] and then correlated the strength of pro-democratic attitudes with the same respondent attributes used in Table 12.3. The results are displayed in Table 12.8.

TABLE 12.9

Multiple Regression Analysis of Respondents' Attributes and Degree of Democratism

	Political Coefficient	Beta	Social Coefficient	Beta	Procedural Coefficient	Beta
Household registration[a]	.31	.09***	.34	.10***	.14	.09***
Sex[b]	.58	.19***	.24	.07***	.14	.10***
Age	-.02	-.15***	-.01	-.05**	.00	-.02
Education[c]	.10	.27***	.11	.29***	.04	.23***
Family income[d]	.00	.05**	.00	.01	.00	.04**
Party member[e]	.19	.04**	.26	.05**	.15	.06***
Occupation[f]	.22	.05**	.09	.01	.09	.04*
State unit[g]	.27	.07***	.09	.02	.07*	.04*
Constant	1.41		2.9		.15	
R Squared		.29		.17		0.15
N=2,896						

Source: China survey (1990).
*=significant at .1 level, **=significant at .05 level, ***=significant at .01 level
a. Household registration: 1 if urban household registration, 0 if rural household registration.
b. Sex: 1 if male, 0 if female.
c. Education: by years of formal schooling.
d. Family income: by yuan.
e. Party member: 1 if member of Communist Party of China, 0 if not.
f. Occupation: 1 if white collar, 0 if other.
g. State unit: 1 if respondent reported working at state organization or state-owned enterprise, 0 if working at collective or other kind of enterprises.

Table 12.8 displays the same pattern of correlations as the Tiananmen and Reform Agendas in Table 12.3. All three kinds of democratic/liberal attitudes are powerfully affected by education. Urbanites, males, and younger people tend to be more liberal on all three dimensions. Income, party membership, occupation, and unemployment in a state unit also contribute. The cleavage patterns on political democracy and social and procedural liberalism are thus isomorphic with those on the reform issue dimension: the same kinds of people tend to array themselves in the same way along both dimensions. A pro-reform, pro-democratic constituency of the relatively privileged finds its complement in a relatively disadvantaged constituency that wants a return to state responsibility for economic welfare and withholds support from democratic values.

The multiple regression presented in Table 12.9 shows that all the variables have distinguishable effects but that education is by far the strongest, with sex, age, household registration, and party membership following. As in the United States, cognitive sophistication appears to play an even more important role in the choice of democratic/liberal attitudes than it does in the choice of issue agendas, with social interests having correspondingly less influence.[52] Respondents who are better educated, male, younger, more urban, and members of the Party tend to be at once more knowledgeable about politics, better trained in official norms, and more tolerant and less authoritarian in their values. Even though most members of this group are relatively privileged under the current political system, they probably expect Chinese-style democracy to open the system to even greater influence by people like themselves.

Conclusion: An Emerging Cleavage Structure

Both constituencies we have identified were nostalgic for some aspects of the Maoist past, but the first group wished for the era of honest government and stable prices, the second for the time when government provided jobs, housing, and incomes. Liberals tended to blame the government for corruption and inflation; were eager to see more progress on reform; and held relatively tolerant, pro-democratic political, social, and procedural attitudes. Conservatives were dissatisfied with the shrinking role of government in solving citizens' individual economic and social problems; did not place a high priority on reform; and held relatively nondemocratic and nonliberal attitudes.

Socioeconomic interest and cognitive sophistication explain how citizens aligned themselves on the issues that confronted them. The predictor variables do not work exactly as they do in the West. The impact of education on issue priorities and values is so powerful that it should be understood as not just a surrogate variable for class and cognitive sophistication, as in the West, but as additionally marking a status and role gap between the mass of people and the educated minority that the Chinese call "intellectuals." People in this category, conventionally including anyone who went to college, consider themselves collectively responsible for the fate of the nation. Their sense of a special role probably shapes their response to questions about issues facing the nation.

The urban-rural gap is also especially important in China, defining a wider range of differences than it does in the West. Mao's regime created a castelike division between rural and urban residents to make possible the accumulation of capital from the rural sector for industrial development. Rural residents remain radically disadvantaged today. The role of work-unit type and party membership also reflect distinctive Chinese institutional dynamics—the tradition of lifetime employment in state units with cradle-to-grave benefits, and the small size and total political dominance of the Chinese Communist Party. But however distinctive they are, the impact of all the predictor variables can be deciphered with social-interest and cognitive logics that are as valid in China as in the West. We found no parallel for Lipset and Rokkan's center-periphery cleavage when we coded respondents on a coastal-inland dimension. Since regional identities are important in China, this deserves further research; different coding might produce stronger results. Nor are religious cleavages important in shaping the distribution of political attitudes across the population as a whole. Although religious issues animate political movements in Tibet, Mongolia, and Xinjiang, and there are sizable Catholic and Protestant communities at odds with the state, 92 percent of our respondents described themselves as not religious.

The attitudinal and sociological structure of the Chinese mass public today provides the context within which future political change will take place. As in Europe in the eighteenth and nineteenth centuries, and as in Russia and Eastern Europe in the twentieth, so in China in the twenty-first, the social cleavages of the past are likely to shape the political system of the future. The cleavages we have described are statistical tendencies rather than structured groups. As China moves toward more openness, the issue agendas are likely to become contested issues and the issue constituencies are likely to become interest groups. When and if a multiparty system forms, the constituencies may form party coalitions. With appropriate adjustments, the issue agendas may become their platforms. Deng Xiaoping's reform may thus have bequeathed to China not only a soft transition to the market but also the beginnings of relatively clear, institutionalized, interest-based cleavages that can either shape a post-Deng authoritarian-corporatist structure or undergird a democratic party system if one should emerge.

Appendix

The analyses in Chapters 11 and 12 are based on a survey conducted in December 1990, in cooperation with the Social Survey Research Center of People's University of China (SSRC). The sample was designed to be representative of the adult population over eighteen years old residing in family households at the time of the survey, excluding those living in the Tibet Autonomous Region.[53] A stratified multistage area sampling procedure with probabilities proportional to size measures (PPS) was employed to select the sample.

Since the political structure in the rural areas is different from that in urban areas, political culture and behavior in the countryside were expected to be different from those in cities and towns. In order to obtain separate estimates for rural and urban areas, we divided the whole population into two domains: the rural domain and the urban domain. Because only about 20 percent of the population hold urban household registrations, they were oversampled, and rural residents were undersampled. Poststratification weighting technique was used to correct for household registration, age, and sex, while preserving the original sample N. This created a valid national sample consistent with the 1990 census 10 percent sample.[54]

The primary sampling units (PSUs) employed were *xian* (counties) for the rural domain and *shi* (cities) for the urban domain. Before selection, counties were stratified by region and geographical characteristics and cities by region and size. The secondary sampling units (SSUs) were *xiang* (townships) in rural areas and *qu* (districts) or *jiedao* (streets) in urban areas. The third stage of selection was villages in the rural domain and *juweihui* (residents' committees) in the urban domain. For both domains, households were used at the fourth stage of sampling.

In the selection of PSUs, national population data for 1986 acquired from the Ministry of Public Security were used as the database to construct the sampling frame.[55] The number of family households for each county or city was taken as the measure of size (MOS) in the PPS selection process.

For the subsequent stages of sampling, population data were obtained from local public security bureaus or governments. At the village and residents' committee levels, lists of *hukou* (household registrations) were obtained from police stations. In places without household registration, lists were obtained by field count.

The project interviewed 3,200 people, and 2,896 questionnaires were collected, which represents a response rate of 90.5 percent.

The survey instrument was constructed in the United States and pretested in Beijing in December 1988. After thorough analysis of the pretest, we revised the questionnaire. College students of sociology and statistics were employed as field interviewers. Before the fieldwork, project members went to China to train the interviewers in field interviewing techniques.

13

The Place of Values in Cross-Cultural Studies

The proper role of the investigator's values in social scientific and historical studies is no longer as intensely debated as it once was. So far as I know, no one now seriously disputes the view, prominently identified with Hume and Weber, that fact and value statements are different in kind and need to be based on different kinds of arguments. But the strict behavioralism or "naturalism" that argued that social-science inquiry, to be valid, must be entirely value-free, has yielded among most practitioners to the acknowledgment that the investigator's values unavoidably influence at least the choice of topic and approach and the language of description and analysis. Beyond this, many historians and social scientists believe that value judgments may legitimately be made in the course of an inquiry, as long as they are clearly expressed as such and are separated from statements of fact. Some argue further that social inquiry is incomplete without an ethical dimension and that reasoned argument about value issues should be a standard part of social science research. Some even hold that ethical judgment constitutes social science's main reason for being and the ultimate source of its meaning. In one way or another, all these views recognize that values play a legitimate role in social science inquiry alongside empirical analysis.[1]

Scholarship in cross-cultural studies is capable of being as value-free and empirical as scholarship in which the investigator studies people or events within his or her own culture—which is to say, value-free and empirical within the limits of the human sciences. This is true even in the limiting case of works whose main subject is the values of another culture, provided that they treat the values they are describing in an objective way, in the sense that they describe them comprehensively, fairly, and with insight.[2] To be sure, the fact that an author is describing another culture's values in the language of his own culture introduces special problems of translating and interpreting value-laden concepts, whose meanings are in some sense changed just by being rendered in another language. Yet the challenge this presents is one of translation in its broadest sense rather than of evaluation.

But as students of foreign cultures, we often reach the point at which, for one reason or another, we wish to make an explicit value judgment. Sometimes it is precisely because cultures differ about the values concerned that cross-cultural study of a particular issue is intellectually compelling in the first place, or has practical significance. We may study another culture to seek new ethical and moral perspectives for ourselves, or because we hope to influence others to accept our values. At the same time, citizens from the country the area specialist is studying often invite dialogue by showing a lively interest in our judgments of their country's political, legal, social or economic performance.

The problem the area specialist confronts at this point is whether the values that form the ultimate ground of judgment in a given study ought to be those of the culture being studied or those of the investigator. Actually, value judgments made in the course of scholarship on one's own culture also face this problem whenever the values of the judger and the judged are different, as can easily happen in societies of any complexity. What I have to say will apply to this situation of what we might call domestic cross-cultural judgment as much as to the problem of international cross-cultural judgment, but it is in the latter that the issue is especially sharply felt.

To be more precise, two possibilities confront an investigator who wishes to make an explicit, reasoned value judgment as a component of scholarly research about a foreign society. The choice which I will argue for is to base the judgment on values in which the investigator believes. Even if the values chosen have some supporters in the subject society, the investigator choses them because he or she believes in them. These are most likely to be values based in his own society, although that is not strictly necessary to my analysis of the problem. This choice is founded on the claim that values which the investigator believes to be valid can validly be applied to societies other than his own—what might be called evaluative universalism.

The second choice, which I think is the one in principle preferred by most area specialists, is to base the judgment on values the investigator finds among those indigenous to the subject society. Even if he shares these values, he choses them because they are native to the society he is judging. These may be among the dominant values there, or they may be the values of a minority. In either case, their choice as the standard of evaluation is founded on the claim that a society can validly be judged only by values that are among its own. I label this position cultural relativism, narrowing that term for the purposes of this essay to one of its meanings.[3]

The problem of evaluative universalism versus cultural relativism as methodologies of evaluation in cross-cultural studies should not be confused with a separate difficulty that has more often been discussed: whether and how members of one culture can understand, or interpret, the ways of thinking of other cultures.[4] This is a question of how to know or understand, rather than how to evaluate or judge. Evaluation and understanding are intimately related in several ways, one of which I will discuss later, but the two procedures are different and so are the problems of carrying them out cross-culturally. Similarly, the question whether it is appropriate to apply foreign value standards to another culture is not same as whether it is appropriate to apply foreign analytical frameworks—whether it makes any sense to refer to the Chinese National People's Congress as a legislature, or to speak of it as performing the rule-making function; or to refer to the casting of ballots in China as voting or as the performance of the interest-articulating function.[5] The use of such concepts might sometimes be a prelude to evaluation, and may even tend to create a bias toward either positive or negative evaluation depending on how they are used. But the problems of categorizing and evaluating remain separate ones.

Nor, third, do I wish to discuss in detail whether value judgments may be made at all in social science inquiry (although many of the arguments adduced below pertain to this broader problem as well as to the narrower one on which I wish to focus) or whether value statements can be epistemologically meaningful. I address myself to the area specialist who has made an empirical study of some aspect of a foreign culture, in the process overcoming to the extent possible the problems of translation, understanding, interpretation, and analysis, who now wants to make a value judgment, and who assumes at least for the time being that such a judgment conveys some kind of meaning. In short, I wish primarily to discuss not why we want to make value judgments or whether we are allowed to do so, but how to do so: to give not so much a philosopher's account of the problem as a practitioner's.

Cultural relativism has its roots in the aspiration of the modern social sciences to treat a diverse humankind with an equalizing objectivity.[6] In its effort to rise above racism, modern anthropology adopted the theory that each society's culture serves its own functional needs. Functionalism in turn became the basis of modern sociology and political science, and through them of area studies. As a professional tool of post-World War II American area studies, relativism especially recommended itself as a corrective to our society's nineteenth- and early-twentieth-century missionary impulses. The pioneers of area studies believed that Americans must reconcile themselves to the fact that their way of life was not going to sweep the world. Other cultures must be understood on their own terms in order to avoid confrontations that no one would profit from. In China studies in particular, relativism represented an attempt to temper the nativism which from the 1950s on threatened to produce disastrous misunderstandings of Asian communism.

John K. Fairbank, for example, worried that "[the] difference in values between Chinese and Americans makes it easy for each to regard the other as essentially immoral. Our great power rivalry can be superheated by the moral righteousness that is second nature to both peoples."[7] He warned the American public in 1946: "It is because we apply our political faith to China directly, with no allowance for Chinese conditions, that our thinking has become confused. . . . We cannot expect democracy in China soon or on our own terms, but only on terms consistent with Chinese tradition, which must be gradually remade."[8] Reaffirming this argument with characteristic wryness nearly forty years later he commented, "Liberals do get themselves between fires! I was committed to viewing 'communism' as bad in America but good in China, which I was convinced was true. This led me to claim China and America were different 'cultures' or 'social orders'—also true. It followed that area specialists like me had esoteric knowledge of these cultural-social differences between China and America. The question was whether we could impart it to our fellow citizens. . . . It was a tall order but the only way to keep American policy on the right track."[9]

Throughout the postwar era, practitioners of China studies have continued to see themselves as needing constantly to correct the culturally biased misunderstandings and impatient judgmentalism of nonspecialists. For example, a 1971 collection of essays by younger China scholars opened with the declaration: "One frequent reason for the inadequacy of our policies is that they are based on assumptions that grow out of the application of norms external to China. Negative judgments are rendered because the questions asked and the norms applied are derived from other civilizations. Thus the politics of the People's Republic is decried because it fails to conform to cherished Western notions, like the rule of law, separation of powers, and institutional pluralism. . . . For a new generation this will not do. . . . We must try to come to an understanding of modern Chinese history which appreciates the Chinese understanding."[10] Similarly, a 1979 symposium of essays sponsored by the Asia Society was based on the premise that "a judgment about China's human rights record must be made, but only after choosing our yardstick with care. It is no good looking at our own cherished values, labeling them universal values, then asking if the Chinese are human enough to adhere to such 'universal values.' . . . A billion people live in China—and we don't. . . . Ultimately the values of the Chinese people—their priorities, views about the world, and ultimate beliefs—must be a key testing ground of any theory about China."[11]

Perhaps, as Paul Hollander has argued, the call for cultural relativism in many cases masked what was really the projection of personal values, critical of American society, onto the Chinese revolution under the claim that they were Chinese values.[12] In this sense it was not authentic relativism, but instead a convenient mask for what was, in the terms of this essay, actually a universalistic but negative evaluation of one's own society. But the fact that a relativist disguise was deemed useful for such a critique is tribute to the fact that relativism had become the conventional wisdom of area studies. As such, relativism existed before and lasted after the era of American self-disillusionment during the Vietnam war, and its influence has extended to virtually all points of the political spectrum.

Thus, relativism has largely survived the turn toward negativism which American feelings about China took shortly after the purge of the "Gang of Four."[13] The new negativism was fueled in part by gradually increasing (although hardly complete) Chinese honesty about the past, by revelations that became available because of improved Western access to China,[14] and by the increased sophistication of China specialists about the actual functioning of Chinese society.[15]

The earlier paradox of the West praising China most warmly just when it least deserved it was replaced by a new paradox: Skepticism and disillusionment grew widespread just as Chinese-Western relations were improving and China was ending the worst abuses of the Maoist era. Some commentators deplored China's backwardness or authoritarianism, while others expressed pessimism about the prospects for modernization. Some criticized China from the left for abandoning Maoism. By the late 1980s, the mood of American China specialists was sufficiently critical to permit some 160 scholars to sign an open letter protesting the removal of Hu Yaobang from the post of Party General Secretary and the purge of three leading intellectuals from the Chinese Communist Party, an act of adverse public judgment on the actions of the Chinese Communist Party so far as I know unprecedented among such a broad spectrum of China scholars since at least the 1950s.[16]

But these developments constituted only a modest, and mostly inarticulate, shift in the direction of what I have labeled evaluative universalism.[17] This is perhaps partly because the Chinese have been making negative judgments of their own errors and shortcomings at the same time as Westerners have been doing so, with the result that many of the values involved (e.g., development) and many of the evaluations (e.g., that Mao behaved tyrannously) appear to be shared, at least at a certain level of generality, by both sides. To the extent that American critics confirm what Chinese critics have said, a clear clash of value premises is avoided and with it the need to clarify the problem of which set of values is being used as a basis for judgment. In addition, evaluative works by political scientists and economists in particular often sidestep the issue of value selection by applying criteria of "growth" or "performance," derived from their disciplines, which are putatively accepted by and thus applicable to all cultures.[18]

But much of the apparent new agreement on values is merely verbal, and disappears when broad concepts like development, democracy, or human rights are analyzed more closely for their specific meanings within different cultures. Similarly, many apparently universalistic values describing such economic or political "system outputs" as welfare, security, equity, freedom, or justice are not understood or ranked the same way in different societies. In many areas, such as the proper limits of state power or the role of law, the differences between the two cultures' preferences are too obvious to be papered over by any formula. Thus the problem remains, because in many respects the values of the two societies remain different, even if they no longer seem to be as different as they once were.[19]

Before the choice that is faced in making value judgments about another society can be explored further, it is necessary to be precise about what it consists of. It is often conceived as a choice between applying Western values to a foreign country and applying its own values. But this way of stating the problem ignores the likelihood that there is a diversity of values on the question at issue within the culture of the judger, within that of the judged, or within both. Taking this fact into consideration, the choice between universalism and relativism can only be defined as I did at the outset—as a choice between values in which the investigator believes and values that are found in the subject society.

The problem takes the simplified our-culture-versus-theirs form only if two conditions exist. The first is that the cultural mainstreams of the two societies are distinctly identifiable and fundamentally opposed on a given issue. To be sure, this is not an uncommon situation. It is certainly the case with the example of democracy and China. The mainstream democratic values of both China and America are relatively easy to identify, and they are different. What is called democratic pluralism (defined further below) is recognized by its critics and supporters alike as the dominant conception of democracy in the West.[20] And in China even most critics of the official notion of socialist democracy share some of the core values embodied in that concept, for example, that democracy should be conducive to social harmony.[21]

The second condition is that the outside analyst choses to apply the mainstream values of his own society. This is also a common situation, but not inevitable. I can illustrate with two examples. Maurice Meisner in *Mao's China* operates as an evaluative universalist, but he does not apply the dominant values of his own society to China. He evaluates the performance of the Chinese political system against standards of humanistic socialism which he applies not because of their Chinese provenance (although he argues these values are grounded in Chinese communism) but because he believes in their validity himself.[22] Otherwise, he would not be able to continue to evaluate Chinese socialism by these values even as he marks an almost complete erosion of commitment to them on the part of most Chinese. On the other hand, in a recent article Thomas A. Metzger employs essentially Western values to evaluate Chinese politics, but feels able to do so only because he is able to locate their proponents within the Chinese context. He argues that "one cannot expect a society to realize options not clearly conceptualized by a good number of its more influential members."[23] In other words, one's standard of evaluation should be chosen from among those available within the society being evaluated, although the outsider has the latitude to chose for this purpose whichever of the indigenous outlooks most closely resembles his own.

The point of these examples is that standards applied under the rubric of evaluative universalism need not be those that are dominant or even widely influential in the analyst's own culture, nor need the standards applied by the cultural relativist necessarily be unpopular ones in his own society. And although cultural relativism is often linked with a positive evaluation of a foreign culture and evaluative universalism with a negative one, these linkages are not inevitable either.

Three arguments are usually given against the rendering by a foreigner of judgments on aspects of another society based on his own values. First, to judge by other than native values is arbitrarily to impose an outside standard without moral justification. We have no right to do this; it is a form of interference or cultural imperialism. Second, it makes no sense to the people being judged. The values applied have no intellectual foundation in the society they are being applied to, because such societies lack a tradition of these values and the values are not widely supported there (although there may be a few supporters, out of tune with their own society). The outside values are abstract words, with no cultural referents. Third, applying outside values exerts no useful effect. Since the values we seek to impose have no roots and few supporters in the target society, insisting upon them is an empty exercise that is not going to persuade anyone or change behavior. Indeed, our values would not even work if transplanted to most other societies, because most non-Western societies lack the prerequisite cultural, economic, and social conditions. For example, people in poor countries lack the economic security, educational backgrounds, and sense of individuality necessary for Western standards of human rights or democracy to function successfully.

The first argument is apparently based on a misunderstanding of what making a value judgment entails. The metaphors of imperialism and sovereignty are inappropriate. Evaluation is an intellectual act, not an act of coercion; an act of communication, not of excommunication. It is the opposite of the kind of denigration labeled by Edward Said as "Orientalism."[24] A value judgment is a way of respectfully sharpening and focusing discussion, not ending it. It involves defining, defending, and applying a value so that others may become informed of it and may respond if they wish. Applying values in which one does not believe, were it even intellectually feasible to do so, would defeat the process of communication.[25] As Gerald James Larson has pointed out, "The glossing over of important differences in the name of civility may, in fact, be the worst kind of uncivilized behavior."[26]

In fact, evaluative universalism amounts to little more than the almost tautological position that a value is a standard in the validity of which the person holding it believes. As both Bernard Williams and Geoffrey Harrison have pointed out, the opposite position is both incoherent and contradictory: first, it derives from the fact that different cultures' values are different an injunction for moral relativism which does not logically follow; then it contradicts itself by applying this injunction universally.[27] By contrast, evaluative universalism is logically consistent. It does not make the untrue claim that one's values are or must be universally accepted, but only states the intention to apply them oneself in a consistent manner, both inside and outside one's own society. A certainty of having absolute answers is thus no more a prerequisite of rendering a judgment for advocates of evaluative universalism than it is for advocates of cultural relativism. If anything, the opposite is more nearly the case: the more controverted one recognizes the issues to be, the more appropriate evaluative universalism becomes, because it is all the more important to communicate clearly and to explain to those who apparently disagree with us what we really think.

Nor is the application of one's own values an exercise in arbitrariness. As noted earlier, it is generally accepted that evaluative or moral reasoning is different in kind from empirical or scientific reasoning. But this does not mean that values are simply a matter of taste about which no argument is possible. There are standards of logic and reasoning that are applicable to ethical or evaluative argument.[28] Frank Fischer, for example, following Paul Taylor,[29] identifies four stages in evaluation—verification, validation, vindication, and rational choice. Some of these stages involve the empirical assessment of a situation against value-derived criteria, others the derivation of the criteria themselves or the defense of the values on which they depend. Thus valid evaluation entails both careful argumentation about the values involved and empirical research about the situation to which they are being applied. One need not accept Fischer's highly articulated version of what evaluative reasoning entails to agree that people can discuss value issues more or less reasonably.

If this were not the case, then to be sure the argument for evaluative universalism would fail. For then there could be no logical warrant for applying one's own values to a foreign culture, or even for applying them within one's own culture to groups or individuals who do not happen to share them. No reasoned discourse about values would be possible among those who disagreed. This indeed seems to be the ultimate, if normally unacknowledged, argument of the relativist. It is a counsel of intellectual despair that suggests that values are so irrational or immutable that only people who already agree on them have any business discussing them.[30]

Indeed, in the hands of some of its practitioners cultural relativism goes even further than this. It requires the application of value standards from the subject society not only when the evaluator finds some he is able to agree with but even when he does not. The prerequisite for discussion, then, is to give up whatever there is to discuss. For example, the reporter Hans Koningsberger in his widely read *Love and Hate in China* wrote, "What right to we Westerners have, freshly back home from plundering the world for four centuries, fat and rich and worried about calories, what nerve do we have really, to poke around here and see if there's dust on the political piano, and worry so nobly whether these people, whose former drowning or starving by the millions didn't make our front pages, have enough democratic rights?"[31] And a Quaker delegation of the early 1970s argued, "The American social experience of pluralism and diversity and the relatively ungoverned U.S. economy do not constitute a lens through which Americans can successfully examine the basis of Chinese society."[32] What such viewpoints forget is that, in the words of Bernard Williams, "*De gustibus non disputandum* is not a principle which applies to morality, [and] 'When in Rome do as the Romans do' . . . is at best a principle of etiquette."[33]

Besides the difficulties with cultural relativism already mentioned, such judgment by abdication of judgment carries insoluble methodological problems. The more authoritarian a society is, the less we know about any differences that exist within it about value issues; the more united it appears. By no coincidence, objections to foreign value judgments are voiced most often and most loudly by authoritarian governments, not by private citizens under authoritarian regimes nor by the citizens or the governments of open societies. Since modern societies are seldom unanimous on value questions, which values from the subject society should we select to apply to it? How does one apply standards one does not find convincing? What does one achieve by doing this? The relativist position provides no independent footing from which to call into question whether the standards promoted by the dominant forces in a society are in fact generally accepted there.

For example, in the Mao period most cultural relativists acknowledged that the Chinese system appeared totalitarian to Western eyes, but in their view it was inappropriate to take account of this in our analyses because the perception itself was based on Western individualism. This was a value that the Chinese were thought not to share because no Chinese at the time dared to express it. On the one hand, a truthful book by Ivan and Miriam London about violence and subsequent disillusionment among the Red Guards was widely disbelieved by China specialists because of the apparent anti-communist stance of its authors.[34] On the other, Western scholars attempting to evaluate China by what they thought were Chinese standards reached a series of erroneous conclusions: One scholar found that "May 7 cadre schools are reasonably successful in revolutionizing many cadres";[35] another that "[Chinese industries] have equaled the most progressive and democratic experiments taking place in various corporations of western Europe";[36] and the Quaker delegation concluded that "[China's] political system . . . is willingly supported, in our opinion, by the great majority of the Chinese people."[37]

Objective information thoroughly understood is obviously a prerequisite to a meaningful value judgment. But less obviously, the relationship can also run the other way. Evaluation can serve as an aid to understanding by spurring skepticism.[38] By contrast, suspending one's standards of judgment in order to try to evaluate another society by what we take to be its standards can lead us to lose our critical footing in dealing not only with values but also with facts.

Cultural relativism, in short, led into not only a moral but also a cognitive dead end. The relativist position adopted in order to prevent missionary zeal from clouding our understanding of the non-Western world led in some cases to an equal but opposite kind of self-deception. Precisely when, as we know now, the Chinese people's alienation from the Maoist system reached its height, so did the vogue of Maoism among China specialists in the West. The lesson we should draw from this experience is that so far from there being no moral justification for applying one's own values to another society, there really is no justification, moral or intellectual, for applying any values but one's own to any society.

Strictly speaking, this line of thinking disposes of all three arguments against evaluative universalism. For if there is no choice but to apply the values one believes in, then it does not matter how difficult it is to make oneself understood to persons in the subject culture (the second argument)—although we should do our best to overcome obstacles to understanding—or how remote are the values being applied from those that have any realistic possibility of being realized (the third argument). A value judgment, after all, is not a prediction. For example, to argue that Chinese democracy is inadequate by some chosen standard does not require proof that an adequate form of democracy is actively possible there. If it is indeed the case that a better form of democracy is not an available option, this fact confirms the evaluation instead of altering it, and perhaps helps to explain why an inadequate form of democracy persists. There are other logical weaknesses in these two arguments as well. The second seems to exclude the possibility that, through communication across cultural lines, people might come to understand something for the first time; the third appears to deny that societies change or respond to international opinion.

But it may be interesting to address directly the factual assumptions at the base of these two remaining arguments. How often is it the case that an outside evaluation actually holds a society to a value standard that we know for certain its members can neither understand nor achieve? It is of course impossible to answer this question for every possible case of a society evaluated along some dimension by a foreigner. The example of a Westerner's evaluation of Chinese democracy may continue to serve as an example. Because it is a "hard case," it suggests how rarely it can be true that a set of outside values on an important human issue are completely irrelevant to a given society's thinking and possibilities. Another good example would be the application to China of the idea of human rights as embodied in the Universal Declaration of Human Rights.[39] The arguments for that example would be closely parallel to the ones presented below.

The evaluative standard which I applied in *Chinese Democracy* is "pluralist democracy," a concept that traces its lineage to Joseph A. Shumpeter's *Capitalism, Socialism, and Democracy*.[40] It is an avowedly minimalist standard that defines democracy as government which is rendered at least potentially responsive (or accountable) to the public by means of three institutions: open, competitive elections; freedoms of speech and publication; and the right to organize politically. In Schumpeter's sense of the term, political systems as structurally diverse as the American, British, Indian, and West German are democratic because each has an open competition for political office; on the other hand, a society might be quite open and free, and might be ethnically, economically, or culturally pluralistic, like Yugoslavia, without being deemed a pluralist democracy in Schumpeter's sense.

Some have argued that pluralistic democracy is not really very democratic.[41] Several quite different but still Western conceptions of democracy have been offered in its place, including notions of corporatist democracy, participatory democracy, and socialist democracy, all of them gaining substantial scholarly and political support.[42] Even though this debate is unlikely ever to be settled, for the purposes of the present essay the discussion can proceed on the basis of the fact that the writer believes that pluralism is the form of government most efficacious in protecting individual rights and achieving responsive government.[43] Since pluralism is reasonably easy to apply as an evaluative standard (it is not hard to determine whether its three defining conditions are present or absent), and it is a realistic rather than utopian standard (quite a few countries in the world fulfill it), nothing seems to stand in way of applying this standard to China if one believes in it, unless we find that it is blocked by the force of the remaining two arguments against evaluative universalism.

The second argument would hold that China lacks the cultural and intellectual foundations for pluralist democracy. In fact, however, we know now that interest in pluralist democracy is strong there. The Democracy Movement of 1978–81 first revealed the existence of a small number of serious thinkers who advocated in China what amounts to the pluralist theory of democracy. There is no evidence that they read Schumpeter or other contemporary Western democratic theorists, nor was their vision of democracy a fully Americanized one.[44] Nonetheless, through a combination of some familiarity with Western texts and concepts on the one hand and, on the other, by dint of their own thinking about the political situation they faced, they came to the view that free elections, freedom of political organization, and the right of free speech are the necessary minimal institutions needed to render leaders accountable. Public expression of these notions was initially limited to a small circle of students and workers. But support for them steadily widened, so much so that, by the mid-1980s, the notion that Western-style democracy suits China had become almost faddish, especially among intellectuals and younger, urban party members.[45]

Some of the more conservative party elders tried to stem this development. For example, the attack on pluralism was a major theme in the Anti-Bourgeois Liberalization Campaign of 1987. Senior party leader Peng Zhen stated that the bourgeois liberalizers "advocated something called 'pluralism,' which in reality is a negation of [communist] party leadership. They wanted to organize a political party that opposed socialism, that stood against the Communist Party."[46] *Guangming ribao* carried an article entitled "The Two-party System Is Not Suited to China's National Conditions."[47] Yet, even the official notion of political reform contained some elements of Schumpeterian pluralism—among them, the idea that government should be accountable to the people, and the insight that the mechanisms necessary for this included meaningful elections at least at the local level and an active press functioning independently of those it was licensed to criticize. By early 1989, however, the official vision of political reform remained limited to such measures as political consultation, decentralization of administrative powers, and the establishment of a civil service system—all "under the leadership of the Communist Party." As then Party Secretary Zhao Ziyang stated at the Thirteenth Party Congress in November 1987, "We will never abandon [the advantages of our own system] and introduce a Western system of separation of the three powers and of different parties ruling the country in turn."[48]

The fact that few, if any, foreign specialists on China anticipated before 1978 that Western-style democratic ideas would gain the degree of importance in China that they did warns against a closed, deterministic view of what outside ideas members of a culture are capable of understanding. In any case, our knowledge of premodern Chinese culture and modern intellectual history should have deterred us from arguing that pluralist democracy has no potential cultural roots and no possible intellectual future in China. After all, what is required in the realm of culture or ideology for democracy to flourish are not replicas of specific Western values, but values that perform similar functions in supporting democratic institutions. J. Roland Pennock, for example, suggests in *Democratic Political Theory* that democracy requires widespread acceptance of such values as dignity, autonomy, and respect for persons; belief in individual rights; trust, tolerance, and willingness to compromise; commitment to democratic procedures and values; public spirit; and nationalism, among others.[49] In this perspective, the question is not whether key Western values find exact equivalents in China, but whether the Chinese tradition contains values that can potentially serve as their functional equivalents in supporting political institutions that—although they too may not be cognate to Western ones—fulfill the criteria of pluralist democracy.

Recent scholarship has revealed or reemphasized the existence of a number of proto-modern, proto-liberal, and even proto-democratic values in the Chinese tradition which could conceivably serve as some of the building blocks of a Chinese democratic political culture.[50] They include such ideals as the morally autonomous individual, the absolutely just ruler, the responsibility to protest injustices at any personal cost, the responsibility of the government for people's welfare, and the ordinary person's responsibility for the fate of the nation. In imperial times, these values were not used to shake China's autocracy. But, in modern times, they have been used quite directly—with little, if any, Westernization—to justify resistance to both the Kuomintang and the CCP. We learned recently that such values motivated at least a few Chinese to resist the Maoist dictatorship at its height. For example, Liu Binyan's controversial reportage, "The Second Kind of Loyalty," told the story of two men who insisted on protesting injustice under Mao at great personal cost.[51] Liu's own career as an investigative reporter, for which he was purged from the party in 1987, provides another example. The vitality of these ideas in the

1980s was further demonstrated by student demonstrations, insubordinate writings and actions by ideological theorists and literary and art workers, and pressure by journalists for more freedom to write critically. In these events, Western rationales for intellectual freedom—for example, as an innate human right, or as contributing through a marketplace of ideas to the discovery of truth—were relatively unimportant.[52] Instead, traditionally based values served as the main justification for the growth of a pressure movement demanding democratization in a Schumpeterian direction. Thus, while the Chinese tradition does not necessarily contain functional equivalents of all the values needed for democracy, it contains strong versions of some of them.

Nor, of course, is the Chinese tradition a stagnant reservoir. In "responding" to the West, Chinese thinkers neither discarded nor blindly reaffirmed tradition, but created a synthesis by absorbing selected but numerous elements from Western thought into conceptual patterns already in existence or in the process of coming into being. Thus, when a concept like human rights was adapted into the Chinese framework, although it lost its Western associations of uninfringeable, legally based individual claims against the state, it gained strength from Chinese notions of personal sacrifice in the cause of justice and truth. Similarly, democracy, originally a Western concept, is today a cherished Chinese value. Although its meaning is sharply contested and few Chinese understand it in the Schumpeterian sense, almost all Chinese throughout the century have understood it to include such ideas as governmental responsiveness, just government, and the right of ordinary citizens to be informed and express opinions about politics.

Even Chinese Marxism—a separate tradition which China adopted from outside—is not devoid of notions that can be interpreted to support pluralistic political institutions. Marx himself and many of the early Marxists envisioned the politics of the socialist period as democratic in the Western bourgeois sense.[53] Although Marxism in China today is officially used only to support the nonpluralist concept of socialist democracy, a number of Chinese thinkers have explored its democratic implications. For example, the theorist Wang Ruoshui was criticized and fired from his job in 1983 because, his critics claimed, his exposition of the concepts of alienation and socialist humanism had politically pluralist implications.[54] Fang Lizhi, an astrophysicist and university administrator, was purged from the party in early 1987 after giving a series of lectures which allegedly offered encouragement to the student demonstrations of late 1986. The transcripts of the lectures show Professor Fang, then still a party member, arguing from a Marxist standpoint for, among other things, complete freedom of thought and speech; exclusion of the party from most policy decisions; resistance to the Party by intellectuals when it makes errors; and the idea that democratic rights are inherent and not given by the state.[55]

That both Chinese traditions, the domestic and the imported, are capable of reinterpretation and development in pluralist-democratic directions is also suggested by the late 1980s political reforms in Taiwan. Although the Kuomintang, the ruling party there, did not espouse Marxism, it was structurally modeled on the Communist Party of the Soviet Union and until recently made claims, similar to those of the Soviet and Chinese Communist Parties, to the right to exercise undivided and uncontested rule. To this degree, the Kuomintang was, like the CCP, a Leninist party. But in 1986–87, the Kuomintang allowed the formation of several opposition parties, most importantly the Democratic Progressive Party, and took a series of other significant steps to ease restrictions on freedoms of the press and political organization. For the time being at least, the Kuomintang retained unchallenged electoral dominance, which left the reformed system well short of full pluralist democracy by Schumpeter's definition, but the changes it made were in the pluralist direction.[56] The Taiwan experience demonstrates that a society within the Chinese culture area, with political institutions not unlike those on the mainland, is capable of evolving in a pluralist direction.

The Taiwan example may seem irrelevant, however, because Taiwan's level of economic and educational development is much higher than that of the mainland. This brings us to consideration of the third argument against evaluative universalism, that it is futile to apply standards that the subject society lacks the preconditions to fulfill. In his classic article "Economic Development and Democracy," Seymour Martin Lipset has shown that democracy is closely correlated with several indicators of economic development—industrialization, urbanization, wealth, and education.[57] According to G. Bingham Powell, Jr., democracies with lower levels of economic and social development are less stable.[58] Since China is one of the poorest countries in the world, it may seem clear that it lacks the preconditions for stable democracy. Many Chinese intellectuals appear to believe this. While struggling for more freedom for themselves, they oppose any reform that would put substantial power into the hands of the peasants, who they feel are so superstitious, anti-intellectual, and anti-foreign that their rule would be disastrous for intellectual freedom and modernization.[59]

But China's economy is growing. GNP per capita was $300 in 1980, already above the level found in the three poorest stable democracies in the 1970s, and, if the goal of quadrupling national income by the year 2000 is achieved, GNP per capita will match or exceed the level enjoyed by the eight poorest democracies in the early 1970s (India, Sri Lanka, the Philippines, Turkey, Costa Rica, Jamaica, Chile, and Uruguay in ascending order of wealth).[60] China's level of literacy in the 1982 census was already as high as that of several democracies (India, Sri Lanka, the Philippines, and Turkey), and the 1985 decision to extend compulsory education to nine years, despite difficulties in implementing it, suggests that the educational level of the populace will continue to rise.

How tight, in any case, is the relationship between democracy and a specific level of economic development? In Lipset's argument, development was thought to support democracy not so much because of the direct effect of wealth on politics but because a more developed society had a higher degree of stability and consensus, less polarization, and more involved, participant citizens. China appears to have achieved many of these preconditions at a lower level of GNP per capita than has been required in some other countries. China, for example, has a relatively equitable distribution of wealth, excellent means of political communication which reach even its illiterate citizens, and strong police and military institutions that are more than equal to the task of controlling civil disorder. Although poll data are lacking to prove it, China also appears to have many of the elements of a "civic culture" (that is, a set of public attitudes conducive to the stable functioning of a democratic regime). These include a relatively high degree of consensus on some basic political values (including nationalism, modernization, and the desire for order); widespread acceptance of the Communist regime as legitimate, although it may not be especially well liked; and a certain degree of alienation from politics, which reduces expectations directed at the political system.[61] Even if one argues that all this was achieved because China has had an authoritarian regime, the fact that such conditions now exist suggests that a democratic transition is not out of the question.

In short, a Western-based evaluative statement about Chinese democracy is not only valid on its own, as I argued in the first half of this essay, but is relevant to the Chinese situation. Perhaps the foregoing discussion has illustrated one dimension of this relevance—in stimulating a critical analysis of the factors in the empirical situation that seem to favor or to block development in the valued direction. More directly, Western values are relevant to China because they are of interest to the intellectuals there and have played a role in the party's internal discussions about political reform.

In the end, it is the view that holds that one culture's values are not relevant to another that turns out to be insular, because it blinds itself to the reality of a cross-cultural dialogue that it thinks ought not to occur but does. It is those who hold Western-style rights or democracy irrelevant to China who are behaving prescriptively rather than those who acknowledge that democracy has been declared relevant by the Chinese themselves, whatever they make of it in the end. If there is any cultural arrogance at play, it is not on the part of those who enter into international dialogue in good faith.

That evaluative universalism seems to make more sense today than it did forty or twenty years ago is no doubt as much a creature of historic context as the dominance of cultural relativism has been. This essay is written in an era of resurgent American self-confidence and of transitions to democracy in Asia and Latin America. My arguments may be used to justify the promotion by America of democracy abroad or to support the international lobbying of human rights organizations. But whatever philosophical validity universalism has extends beyond its historical context. And its policy implications are not fixed. The New Left among social scientists in the 1960s called for the freedom to evaluate in order to attack, not defend, the institutions of American democracy. The policy implications of evaluative universalism depend on the values that are applied.

Evaluative universalism by no means requires a return to the missionary mode of promoting Western values. It is not a call for proselytism but an expression of the belief, first, that value differences when they exist can, and can only, be honestly expressed, and second, that beliefs originating in different societies can fruitfully be confronted with one another, compared, and judged, even though disagreement is expected to persist. Just as Western values are a valid basis for a judgment of Chinese society, Chinese values are valid for those who believe in them to apply in judging Western society. "Those who do not like [intellectual] prisons," says Karl Popper, ". . . will welcome a discussion with a partner who comes from another world, from another framework, for it gives them an opportunity to discover their so far unfelt chains, to break them, and thus to transcend themselves."[62]

This call for dialogue, however, should not be read as a last-minute concession to the relativist position that all values are equally valid. One can favor dialogue about democracy while still holding that one form of democracy is superior to other forms. One can recognize that this is not a question that will ever be settled conclusively for everyone while holding, without inconsistency, to the view that there are a preponderance of arguments in favor of one position. Again to quote Popper, "From the fact that we can err, and that a criterion of truth which might save us from error does not exist, it does not follow that the choice between theories is arbitrary, or non-rational."[63]

The implications of this conclusion trespass beyond the boundaries of my original topic to suggest an anti-relativistic point of view that applies as much within as between cultures, as much to scientific as to moral reasoning, and as much to the problems that I said I was not going to discuss in detail (understanding, interpretation, the validity of making value judgments at all) as to the practioner's issue of how to make cross-cultural value judgments that I have attempted to focus on. This was unavoidable, because the problems we face as practitioners of area studies are, after all, at bottom the same as those faced by searchers after knowledge generally, even within cultures. Our problems are only a special, and perhaps in some respects an especially clear, case of everyone's problems. Perhaps it is precisely in area studies, where both the obstacles to and the achievements of understanding are so conspicuous, that we have earned the right to affirm most strongly the potentialities of understanding.

The major issues of the Western tradition—democracy, rights, individual, and society—are no longer the West's alone, if they ever were. Benjamin I. Schwartz has always argued that on the great questions the answers may have varied, but the questions are transcultural. After two centuries of intense contact, the language of political discourse around the world has become Westernized; or to put it in a better way, once-Western issues have become part of international discourse. How non-Western thinkers deal with originally Western ideas has become an important part of the history of these ideas. The "foreign areas" are part of the world—they are the greater part. For this reason, area studies cannot treat itself as detached from the great issues. A major task of area studies is to learn enough of the language and cultures of other societies to carry out cross-cultural discussion of common concerns with minimal misunderstanding. What is at stake here ultimately is the value Benjamin Schwartz holds most dear, "the possibility of a universal human discourse."[64]

14

The Chinese Volcano

The West alternates between seeing China as weak and friendly and fearing it as strong and dangerous. The notion of China as a threat revived after Tiananmen, and today it is nourished by Beijing's upgrading of its navy and air force, its sales of arms around the world and its assertiveness in making territorial claims to parts of the South China Sea. China-threat theory is congenial to the defense bureaucracy, to American industries threatened by Chinese exports, and to some sections of the labor movement.

Two recent books usefully confuse the debate. They portray China as booming and collapsing at the same time. Orville Schell, our most durable China observer, describes the events he witnessed in Tiananmen Square in 1989, the desolate aftermath, the economic boom since 1992, and its puzzling accompaniment of "heterodox ideas, weird fads, errant cultural tendencies and unorthodox economic hustles."[1] Nicholas Kristof and Sheryl WuDunn, the energetic married team who won a Pulitzer Prize for their reporting in *The New York Times*, write about their five-year tour of duty, marked by economic dynamism and continuing political repression.[2]

Of course, we have heard about China waking before, during the reforms of the late Qing in 1900–1910 and the Kuomintang revival of the 1930s—episodes that scholars often compare to Deng Xiaoping's reforms—and during the early years of Mao's reign. In each episode, political wreck brought economic ruin. On the whole, both books give more testimony against a brilliant future for China than in favor. If Deng's regime proves to have been a collapsing dynasty, a monarchical metaphor that both books use, then China should face several more decades of chaos and poverty before it can make another attempt to fulfill its potential as a world power.

On the other hand, powerful forces are pushing China toward "peaceful evolution," which is what Chinese reformers want, and what Chinese conservatives fear. Economic reform is ushering in the rule of law; modernization is creating social pluralism; prosperity encourages the assertion of individual interest; and the post-Deng political succession is likely to expose the need to find a new basis for legitimizing the regime. And yet, as the political scientist Adam Przeworski has argued, liberalization never saved a dictatorship. In Eastern Europe and Latin America, liberalization was always a way station to popular mobilization followed by renewed repression, or to authentic democratization.[3] China has already had the former experience, and it could have it again. Or it could democratize.

Both books trace the current Chinese boom to Deng's "talks on a Southern tour" in early 1992. During visits to Shanghai and the Special Economic Zones, Deng made a series of pronouncements, among them, "Only development is hard logic," "Anyone who doesn't reform can get out of office," and "Policies are good if they are good for liberating the productive forces, increasing comprehensive power of the socialist state and raising the people's living standards." These slogans became the mantras of provincial officials and enterprise managers in their race for growth.

Twelve percent growth has brought goods to the markets, construction cranes to the streets and tales of giddy achievement to the official press. The numbers are real, if rough; but much of what they measure is fake. Some state enterprises consist of waste piles of spoiled goods surrounded by subsidized workers on permanent smoking break, but the output, jobs, and cigarettes increase the respective national numbers. Pirated CD's, counterfeit jeans, and poisoned medications count in production statistics. Investment capital that flows into the country is tallied, but capital flight is not. The economy is bloated with unrecoverable state-bank loans, "triangle debts" among enterprises and their suppliers, and "black" and "gray" speculative capital.

Some Chinese economists believe that, as one of them told me, "those who think Russia is in worse shape than China are wrong. We have a larger population, a lower ratio of industrial to agricultural employment, weaker institutions of macroeconomic control, and fewer social-welfare programs. After forty-five years of socialism, we still need to industrialize."

China has been industrializing for a long time, but the task only gets more pressing. Mao's policy of breakthrough modernization, which was inaugurated in the 1950s, left the peasants to raise themselves by their bootstraps while putting state resources into large factories. This gave China a big industrial sector, but left 80 percent of the population living on the land in poverty. Deng's reforms in the late 1970s and early 1980s freed the peasants from the collectives in order to raise rural living standards. This brought brick homes and television sets to the villages, but it also meant diminishing returns once the land was made as productive as possible under the given technology.

Today Chinese reformers believe that neither strategy any longer meets China's needs. One told me, "Now we see the problem in terms of employment structure. If we let our growth rate go below 6 percent, we cannot keep up with the demand for jobs and will fall into social disorder due to unemployment." Actually, even at 12 percent growth it's hard to see how the economy can ever provide enough good jobs for the several-hundred-million strong army of the underemployed bequeathed to China by its socialist past.

Eight hundred million Chinese rural residents live on about half as much arable land as about some 5 million farming Americans. Eighty million to 120 million, depending on whose figures you choose, are stuck in poverty that is irremediable unless they move, because their soil, water, and transport resources are too meager to support them. Even those living in fertile areas farm an average of only 100 days a year because their plots are so small. Reformers estimate that to transfer enough people from the land to make agriculture efficient will require from 150 million to 300 million new jobs in other fields. From 40 million (officially) to 100 million (unofficially) peasants are already roaming the country looking for work in factories, construction sites, private households, or as farm hands. The higher estimates amount to 5 to 8 percent of the country's population.

Many workers in the cities are also underemployed or unemployed. The streets are filled with peddlers and bicycle- and shoe-repairmen. Factories and schools run small shops to employ staff or dependents as clerks. On the Gate of Heavenly Peace, a soft-drink vending machine is staffed by two young women who take your coins, drop them in the machine and hand you the can. The reformers are like Buster Keaton on the railway tracks: no matter how fast they run, the population keeps gaining on them.

In the days of the command economy, the regime provided full employment (more precisely, fully disguised unemployment) without inflation; it did so by controlling prices, at a high cost in inefficiency. Deng's reforms dismantled most of the command mechanisms. China's leaders now maneuver between inflation and unemployment as leaders in democratic countries do.

Events like Tiananmen—or the peasant uprising in Renshou County, Sichuan, in 1993, or rural protests and spontaneous factory strikes, each recently reported to number in the thousands each year—are China's moral equivalent of off-year elections, but they are a lot scarier and less predictable. This is one reason (along with the weakness of the central bank) that inflationary and deflationary policies oscillate more violently in China than in the West. A large instance of this oscillation in 1988 lay behind the demonstrations in 1989.

The major divide between reformers and conservatives in Beijing in the 1990s has been over whether faster or slower growth is more risky to the regime. Inflation in 1994 was said to be around 20 percent. Some said 30 percent, and it was far more in the foodstuffs sector, which is especially visible because most people pay little for housing. Yet real incomes in the cities grew in 1993 and 1994. People may complain, but they have more money than they can spend (not least, because there are so few good things to buy). Savings deposits have surged, and money has flowed into two new official stock markets and many unofficial ones, bidding prices to ridiculous heights. Rural real income growth is slow, but the peasants are too dispersed to present much of a threat. Reformers believe the party can survive inflation as long as winners substantially outnumber losers in the cities.

Conservatives see inflation as the main threat. The unemployed can be scattered and suppressed. Inflation upsets everyone: even the winners see other people getting ahead faster than themselves, and the government's share of the pie seems to take more diverse, unfair, and irritating forms even as it shrinks in relation to GNP. If the government tries to smooth imbalances by helping the losers, it moves toward indexation and hyperinflation. But if it lets the winners win, those who benefit most are private and semiprivate entrepreneurs who can never be firm allies of the regime.

Conservatives point to a second cost of the reformers' strategy of stimulating growth by weakening state control: a scramble to privatize state assets. When state enterprises set up subsidiaries and subsidiaries of subsidiaries, the government ends up with an empty shell whose contents have slipped into the hands of the managers and their friends and relatives. The same thing happens when a government enterprise's money is sent abroad to be invested, or is put into the stock market to "stir-fry stocks" (the Chinese financial though not culinary equivalent of "churning"). Land-use rights are also stir-fried. Since all urban and most rural land belongs to the government, people with official connections can acquire such rights, get development licenses, and raise investment money from government organs and state enterprises looking for fast returns. They don't necessarily develop the land. All these devices lead to assets moving beyond state control.

The reformers know these tricks; but they see them as necessary methods of transition to a more efficient property rights system, like the Enclosure Movement in eighteenth-century England. Scams grow faster than laws, so it is seldom clear what is illegal. Many entrepreneurs brag about the social wealth and the jobs they create, and their public-spiritedness in working closely with local officials. Because the current state of Chinese law leaves private capital legally and politically insecure, many of the purloined assets are consumed in the form of cars, housing, and foreign trips instead of being reinvested. This creates an expense-account frenzy that makes the American two-martini lunch look like the cottage cheese diet plate at a local diner.

The third cost the conservatives see in all-out growth is the decay of moral values. Their idea of decay consists of one part traditionalist revival (old novels, Daoist fortune-tellers, Mao images used as lucky charms), one part foreign influence (rock music, porn videos), one part human nature. A Communist official who specializes in ideological education for a large government bureaucracy explained that "for several decades we were able to keep China the cleanest society in history. Now that we have reduced control to let the economy grow, human nature being what it is, unclean things have developed, like drugs, gambling and prostitution. If we're going to bring in foreign capital we have to accommodate the Westerners' life styles. After all, they can't bring their wives with them to China." Deng belittled such trends as "flies coming in an open window." Schell is a skillful entomologist of such flies. His chapters on publishing and music sketch a popular culture that is vulgar, vibrant and despairing.

Finally, the conservatives fear the growth of an independent legal system. The reformers think the growth-generating benefits of entrepreneurship can be reaped only if the government protects the rights of property owners with a reliable system of laws and courts. The Administrative Litigation Law and economic courts operate under party guidance and are limited in mission. But conservatives argue that full legal protection for private property will doom the Communist system, not only economically but also politically. It will set up independent power centers hostile to the party on which the party must rely for economic results and hence legitimation. They fear the regime is making its survival hostage to antagonistic forces.

The reformers are up to more than providing a safety valve for social discontent, as Schell surmises, but less than Kristof implies when he says in one of the chapters he authored, that "even [some] senior party officials were against the party." The reformers' strategy is to weaken party control and install a market and even multiparty democracy, so the party can regain its legitimacy and survive. As a senior reformist told me, "Our current leaders are not legitimate in the eyes of the people, but they can become legitimate if they continue reform and develop a degree of democracy. We will support them in this. It's no good to negate the authority of the Chinese Communist Party because then China would dissolve." In effect, the reformers believe that the price of continuing Communist power is an end to communism as China has known it.

As Deng's illness deepened, the struggle between development and control intensified. While the provinces and enterprises fought for more credit, the central authorities led by Vice Premier Zhu Rongji tried to restrict it. Beijing ordered limits on markets in stocks, commodities, futures, and real estate; provincial officials circumvented them. Beijing tried to increase the share of taxes passed on to the central government by local tax collectors; regional authorities and local enterprises fought for rebates and postponements.

At the level of ideology, the conflict took the form of debates over property rights and privatization, the nature of socialism, and the degree to which the party's values should limit economic dynamics. In these polemics the conservatives' voices were loudest. They controlled the Central Committee Propaganda Department and through it the main Beijing print media, known as the "two newspapers and seven magazines." Their outlets argued that, in the words of Premier Li Peng, "No state industry, no Chinese-style socialism."

The conservatives' constituencies included state enterprise workers who had lost out in the reforms, farmers stuck on the land, retired people left adrift by the collapse of the communes and hollowing of state enterprises, some retired cadres and intellectuals who believe in the vision of the 1950s. Incredible though it seems to anyone who knows history, many Chinese—especially those too young to remember them—

think of the Mao years as a time of social fairness, order, equality, incorruptibility and government concern for the common man. They trace the abandonment of Maoist values in the 1980s to Western economic pressure and cultural subversion and not to the failure of the system itself.

The most important conservative power base remained the elders. They were seven or eight men, in or near their 90s, who poked their noses into everybody else's business. Their graceless calligraphy was all over Beijing, on highway overpasses, magazine titles, book covers, and office nameplates. Their lurching brushwork silently reminded the public that Big Brother was not dead yet. The atmosphere in Beijing was so tense that some reformers feared a possible Soviet-style conservative coup after Deng's death, though this fear was more a measure of reformist anxiety than conservative strength.

In the provinces, the debates in Beijing were irrelevant. "Since Comrade Deng Xiaoping went on his Southern tour," a local official told me, "our thought has been liberated. All that counts here is economic growth." Referring to the chief conservative ideologist in Beijing, this official continued, "Let Deng Liqun serve as a mayor and he would give all that up." In this respect, the Beijing focus of both books is a disadvantage. Neither makes clear that the provincial and lower-level bureaucracies are reformist-controlled, or that this is important for understanding the explosive response to Deng's Southern sayings.

When reformist leaders Hu Yaobang and Zhao Ziyang fell from power in 1987 and 1989 respectively, their followers below the central level stayed in place. All the local cadres one meets today were promoted by Hu and Zhao during the vast personnel turnovers they carried out in the party and state bureaucracies in the 1980s. The mayors and county chiefs around the country, who are now in their thirties and forties, come from industrial backgrounds, unlike their predecessors who were fifty or older and had agricultural backgrounds. The old cadres tried to meet Deng's goal of "doubling and redoubling GNP" by developing agriculture. The new men try to put factories in every mountain and valley. Even among the vast mass of CCP officials, only growth makes their own rule legitimate. Local officials will be sacked by superiors if they fail to meet demanding targets of local development.

The Chinese seem universally to believe that the sole bottleneck to economic growth is lack of capital for investment. Neither the country as a whole nor any administrative unit within it thinks it has enough local money to meet its growth targets. Many tacitly (and wrongly) attribute

China's growth to money from abroad, which (counting both loans and investment) totals roughly $90 billion since the start of the reforms, or about $5 per year per Chinese citizen. Local officials have become fund raisers as tireless as American university presidents. For a given city or county, outside capital can come from government banks (whose lending ceilings, however, are tied to local savings), the provincial or central governments (say, by way of a dam project), mainland Chinese enterprises in other provinces (which may want access to a local raw material, for example), or investors abroad, including Taiwan and Hong Kong (who invest for cheap labor or access to Chinese markets). In a manner reminiscent of the pledges of higher production targets during Mao's Great Leap Forward, local officials call meetings to stoke investment fever. Growth is not the most important thing, it is the only thing.

Toting Motorola cellular phones and riding in a hierarchy of cars— from joint venture-produced Jeeps and VW Santanas to imported Lexuses and Mercedes (stratified less by rank as in the past than by enterprise profitability)—local party members do whatever works. They set up private factories disguised as collective enterprises; establish false-front joint ventures with local capital laundered through Hong Kong; commandeer peasants' land without adequate compensation to build factories; import contract workers from poor villages nearby and poor provinces far away; ignore environmental regulations; and sell public land to foreign investors at low prices in the guise of land-use leases. Then they treat themselves to overseas inspection tours paid for by local entrepreneurs, especially to Thailand, where they can study both light manufacturing and the sex industry.

On a visit to a small Chinese provincial city I was honored at a banquet with a live fish that had been held briefly in boiling oil from the gills down and was served staring and gulping for air, lifting its head in a vain attempt to move the rest of its body. The Chinese Communist Party is like this fish: although the head in Beijing is alive, the apparatus in the provinces does not respond. Provincial officials know there are rules against all sorts of things that they do, but they have also learned that Beijing loves a fait accompli. As the saying goes in Guangdong, "Go on green, speed on yellow, go around on red."

Kristof calls the result of this activity "market Leninism." It is a catchy term, but not entirely correct. If a market is an exchange mechanism open to all participants on an equal basis, China does not have many markets. If Leninism is a system of centralized political control, China no longer has much Leninism. What governs China today is more like a network, a kind of Chinese six degrees of separation in which everyone who counts works through links to everybody else who counts. Buying and selling are done through friends and involve commissions. An enterprise may need the help of someone who knows someone to solve problems with land rights, roads, water, electricity, labor, pollution, or taxes. To prepare for this, managers sound out influential people socially to see if they are "the kind of person one can talk to." Any exchange of favors occurs as between friends. In these transactions it doesn't matter whether one is a reformer or a conservative. Nobody is against "human feelings."

"The collective is a great invention," one entrepreneur told me. (This is the term for enterprises that are neither state-owned nor openly private; their aggregate output value now approximately equals that of the state sector.) "It borrows from the bank, expands into a group company, spends money directly on its officers in the form of expense money, and keeps all profits after taxes. Yet it is registered with the state, and supervised by local government in a friendly, helpful way."

"Many organs are supposed to supervise us, but none does," said another manager. "I have no mothers-in-law [government organs meddling in my management of my business]. I don't have to pay assessments. But I voluntarily gave 450,000 yuan [about US$53,000] to a school. I paid 40,000 yuan for roads for two villages, and gave several thousand yuan to the peasants living in the mountains."

A rough kind of ward-boss democracy is developing out of the influence market of officials and entrepreneurs. In one village a farmer made 3 million yuan in private enterprise, then built a road and office building for the village and invested in a collective cement factory. He was selected village chief and party secretary. Such acts may be in the spirit of Mao's adage, "serve the people." But a Chinese friend pointed out, "Everyone would be coming to him for money anyway. Once they have this much money, they have enough to spend and they need political power so other people won't oppress them."

Ordinary people have to be just as deferential to the new entrepreneur-officials as they were to the old commissars. Whatever their benevolence toward clients and friends, the new men are no more subject to checks and balances than the old were. They often represent the interests of a dominant clan. In the worst cases, some of which Kristof and WuDunn report, they act like a "thugocracy."

Networks do not function just among the elite. Migrant workers from different provinces have their capos; gangs who kidnap and sell women as wives to poor villagers have their links across the country; underground publishers and book distributors have their systems of connections. As WuDunn shows in her description of kidnappers and Schell in his description of booksellers, the outlaw and underground networks are as liable to link themselves back to party members as are more respectable entrepreneurs. China doesn't have a Mafia like Russia because in China the Communist Party is the Mafia.

This doesn't mean the state is rotting, as Kristof says it is. In *Governing China*, Kenneth Lieberthal provides an insightful description of the structure and working of the Chinese government.[4] He shows that the apparatus is much changed from the rigidities of the Mao era, thanks to Hu Yaobang's and Zhao Ziyang's replacement of commissars with technocrats and to the decentralization of administrative power. The party-state has become flexible, adaptable, and effective.

But without a charismatic leader like Mao and a driving ideology, this complex, multifunctional bureaucracy—the largest in the world, with the widest-ranging duties—has become overloaded at the top and gridlocked below, a system Lieberthal calls "fragmented authoritarianism." This has given rise to decisionmaking by negotiation and consensus. Since the bureaucracy covers almost all of society and the economy, almost all of society and the economy participate in the negotiations. The process is slow. Efficiency comes by accelerating bureau-to-bureau, region-to-region, and government-to-society interactions through the use of informal mechanisms. Whatever their functional necessity, to many Chinese these interactions look, walk, and quack like corruption. A popular ditty goes, "A sharp new car, shiny and fine, the guy inside is on the take / Shoot him first and later try him, guaranteed there's no mistake."

If China has neither markets nor a Leninist bureaucracy, it also lacks a civil society, another concept both books try to employ. In the West, civil society grew from within the market, which operated apart from the state. The concepts of market, state, and society lack clear referents in the Chinese situation. In "the economy," the relationship between enterprises and the bureaucracies that either "own" or regulate them is so negotiable that the Chinese analogue to civil society exists within the ambit, and even inside the formal confines, of the bureaucracy. In "society," almost every ostensibly independent organization—institutes, foundations, consultancies—is linked into the party-state network through formal registration, informal patronage, or both. It is hard to say whether the state penetrates society or society penetrates the state.

The ambiguity of the boundaries between state and society may explain why the Chinese value their dissidents so much less than the West does. Wei Jingsheng, China's candidate for a Nobel Peace Prize, was released from fifteen years' imprisonment in September 1993, but insisted on speaking his mind with foreign reporters, including Kristof and WuDunn, and on sending prison manuscripts to Hong Kong journals. He was detained again in the spring of 1994. Han Dongfang, the labor leader who is the subject of a chapter in Schell's book, got early release from prison because of tuberculosis with which the jailers purposely infected him, came to the United States for medical treatment and has since been trying to return to resume his work as an organizer.

Most Chinese are unmoved by such heroism. They think the network provides the best way to do things. Just as in Chinese religion the gods are pleased by ritual conformity rather than by inner faith, so in political society the security ministry doesn't seem to care what people think or even what they say, as long as they don't say it in the wrong time and place. Tact is more important than substance in a network society. Virtually anything can be said in private, and radical ideas can even be published in academic journals, in appropriate language. The same sentiments become political crimes when voiced to foreign reporters. The dissidents court repression because they insist on their rights. It is hard for most Chinese to see why this is worth doing. That is why so few of them need to be repressed.

Repression looms large to foreign reporters because they are, along with the dissidents, its main targets. The government marks Western journalists who fail to play by Chinese rules as hostile. Even the sophisticated Ministry of Foreign Affairs seemed not to understand why people like Schell, Kristof, WuDunn and former *Washington Post* reporter Lena Sun refused to help their minders do their jobs. They went after them not with the gray routine of Smiley's war but with an authentic sense of outrage. (The stories are told well in both books.) Reporters treated this way see the negative side of the system in more detail than most Chinese. As Kristof observes, the regime "has the worst public relations sense of any major government in the world."

Many human rights promised in the Chinese constitution do not exist at all, such as the right to a free press, to assembly and demonstration, to a fair and public trial. Yet in other ways Chinese society is free. Says Schell, "A combination of freedom in the marketplace and response to foreign pressure made it possible for Chinese to buy what they wanted, enjoy private lives, speak more openly, and even to travel abroad more freely than ever before." Jobs and inflation, housing and traffic, noise and bad air worry most Chinese. They often greet Western human rights concerns with hostility. This is not a reason for the West to reduce its attention to human rights problems in China, but it suggests why the language of rights gets a limited response among the mass of those deprived of many of their rights.

Not that the public's complacency about rights makes the regime feel secure. There are "live volcanoes everywhere," a social scientist told me. Factory workers feel powerless within their enterprises. Farmers resist government orders on what to plant and how much to sell. Financially burdened local governments multiply assessments on villagers, who have started to resist. June 4 remains an unsettled issue, both inside and outside the party. The government was rumored to have spent 8 billion yuan (nearly $1 billion) in the spring of 1994 preparing to put down potential demonstrations on the anniversary of June 4. A reversal of the goverment's verdict that Tiananmen constituted "turmoil," rather than a patriotic action, is widely expected with Deng's death.

And yet the authors of these books did not discover anybody who was trying to overthrow the Chinese Communist Party. The dissidents remain peaceful and moderate. Many intellectuals are rethinking their role in 1989, in a trend called neoconservatism which supports the idea of authoritarian development. One researcher who predicted the disturbances of 1989 told me that another outbreak is not in the cards today. In 1987 his public opinion surveys showed parallel rising lines representing people's wants for the future and their expectations. In late 1988 the lines suddenly diverged. Wants were still rising, but the abortion of price reform and subsequent economic shakeout pushed hopes down. According to a formula as old as Machiavelli, desire minus anticipation equals trouble. It was the collapse of hope more than rising anger at inflation or corruption that led people into the streets in 1989. The lines returned to their parallel course after the crackdown, mainly because people reduced their hopes while the government managed to deliver more than they expected. Surveys then showed expectations rising again, but optimism for the future kept pace, at least while Deng still lived.

Some Chinese believe that economic backwardness dooms the country to dictatorship indefinitely. As a party official said, "Our people are not ready for democracy. They aren't interested. Their educational standard is too low, and they don't know anything about politics. They are too poor; their bellies are not yet full." But it is also true that many ordinary Chinese are more optimistic than their masters. A Beijing resident remarked to me, "Of course we mind our own business: the 1989 demonstrations showed that the people have no power. But change is inevitable. People say the Chinese people don't know enough to be voters, but that's because they put up some candidate nobody knows, they don't explain what he stands for, and you have to vote for him anyway. If there was an election campaign people would see what the candidates could do for them, and they would know how to vote."

So what is the Party afraid of? Projecting blame on foreigners for prostitution, corruption, dissent, bad art, the high cost of international capital, the Tibetan independence movement, and for China's poverty—whether traced to the Opium War, Bush's sanctions, or Washington's demand that China open its market as a precondition for joining the World Trade Organization (formerly GATT)—seems to hide the Party's bad conscience. As a Chinese friend remarked, "The CCP's problem is CCP."

Kristof and WuDunn consider a number of scenarios for China's future. Some are more blood-curdling than most China specialists are willing seriously to envision: the loss of Tibet and Xinjiang, Cantonese independence, and a national coalescence of worker and peasant uprisings to overthrow the regime. But they give greatest emphasis to the scenario suggested by their title, that the economic boom will continue, making China in the next century "the biggest player in the history of man," in the words of Singapore's Lee Kuan Yew. Kristof portrays a possible resurgent China of "blood and iron," armed with enough nuclear weapons and aircraft carriers and burning enough oil to destabilize the world's military balance, oil markets, and environment.

Meanwhile, many Chinese regard outsiders' fear of China as the instrument of malicious intent, designed to sow discord between China and its neighbors, spur a regional arms race, and obstruct China's development. If mutual fear is not alleviated by more openness on both sides, the two devil theories may cycle with one another until they produce a mutual paranoia.

"You thought you could strangle us with your sanctions," a factory manager bellowed at me between challenges to drain cups of maotai. (The misunderstanding is widespread in China that George Bush's post-Tiananmen sanctions restricted U.S. trade and investment; they didn't.) "China is the best country in the world. Neither you nor anybody else can stop our growth. America and China are different. One side will never understand the other. I don't care if 300 or 3,000 people were killed in Tiananmen. It's a small matter." On occasions like this, one glimpses the specter of a possible Chinese national socialism, a frightening mix of Confucian and Marxian anti-individualism, statism, irridentism, and xenophobia.

China today can be described accurately only by self-contradiction. Autonomous forces are inside the party-state; operation outside the network of power is permitted by linkages within it; insiders are the most successful outsiders. Such eluding of our categories of thinking is disturbing partly because we are anxious to reach a judgment. "We wish we could balance good against evil on a single scale and come up with a net positive or negative reading," writes Kristof. He knows that such a balance is impossible. Still, both books are testimony to the desire for it; they are like diaries of their authors' contradictory emotional responses to contradictory realities. Yet China's paradoxes may be more than a feature of transition. They may be constitutive of a system in which power is so all-encompassing yet decentralized that the trinity of state, society, and economy have become one. This may just be the way China works.

15

The Constitutionalist Option

Of the plausible scenarios for China's future, the possibility of a new constitutionalism has been taken seriously by only a few Western specialists.[1] Yet the constitutionalist scenario gains credibility from the improbability of the alternatives. Civil disorder is the worst fear of most Chinese, and few stand to gain from it. Local separatism would do more economic harm than good to the southeastern coastal provinces that are viewed as the most likely to secede, and would be opposed by the Chinese army. Some in Tibet and Xinjiang would like independence, but they lack the military power to seize it. Coup plotters would need broad support that would be difficult to marshal in the vast civil-military command apparatus. No one in the new generation of leaders seems to have strongman potential. And a factional stalemate would be only an interim stage in the search for a solution to the problem of political authority. So the worst one can say against the constitutionalist scenario is that it seems too sensible to be a genuine option.

Recent writings by Chinese scholars both within China and abroad suggest what the constitutionalist option might look like if it came to pass.[2] Since Deng Xiaoping's reforms began, the authorities have licensed three waves of discussion of constitutional issues. The first occurred during the drafting of the new Constitution that was promulgated in 1982.[3] The second took place during preparation for Zhao Ziyang's Political Report to the Thirteenth Party Congress in 1987. The third has consisted of a series of studies and conferences in academia and within the staff of the National People's Congress (NPC) since 1990, paralleled by work among members of the Chinese democracy movement now in exile.

The discussions are interesting as much for their diagnoses of what is wrong with the current system as for their proposals for reform. The diagnoses often carry implications too bold to be stated explicitly under today's political constraints. This essay details four sets of diagnoses and proposals on which the debate has focused, and which seem likely to be high on the agenda of post-Deng reformers whether the Chinese Communist Party (CCP) remains in power or not. The debates provide a script for reform efforts that are likely to be made in the coming years no matter who comes to power. For those interested in comparative constitutional design, the debates suggest how people living under a Soviet-style constitution see its possibilities for evolutionary reform.

Empowering the National People's Congress

The heart of most political-reform proposals is empowerment of the NPC.[4] Under the present Constitution the NPC is sovereign. There is no division of powers. The judicial and administrative branches report to the NPC. Either directly or through its Standing Committee, the NPC legislates; elects and recalls the top leaders of the other organs of state; supervises those officials' work, including the state budget and development plans; and interprets the Constitution and laws.

But the Constitution also acknowledges that the organs of the state operate under CCP leadership. In the NPC this leadership is exercised in a number of formal and informal ways. Party members make up from one-half to over three-fourths of the membership of the NPC, including the top layer of NPC officials and the majority of its Standing Committee, Secretariat, committee heads, and Presidium, as well as the bulk of its staff. Party cells guide the work of all these organs and staff. The central party organs instruct the NPC whom to elect to such posts as head of state, chair of the Military Affairs Commission, president of the Supreme People's Court, and procurator-general. The party center controls the NPC's budget, sets its long-term work plan, determines the agenda of its meetings, drafts much of the legislation that the NPC considers (although some drafting work is assigned by the party center to government agencies or NPC staff), and helps guide bills through committees to the final stage of passage by the NPC plenum.

The NPC's structure limits its ability to develop an autonomous ethos. It normally meets only once a year, usually in March, for twelve to twenty days; the Standing Committee (consisting of about 150 members) meets every two months for approximately one week. During NPC sessions, the huge membership of about three thousand convenes in full only to vote. Debate and discussion are limited to caucuses of provincial delegations. Nonetheless, the legislature has shown a growing measure of assertiveness. In 1986, the Standing Committee refused to clear a draft of the Bankruptcy Law for presentation to the NPC plenum; it had to be returned to the relevant government agency for redrafting. In 1989, a substantial number of delegates opposed a State Council-drafted bill relating to the delegation of certain legislative powers to the Shenzhen Special Economic Zone, so the bill was postponed and later replaced by one that answered the members' objections. In 1992, only two-thirds of the deputies voted in favor of a proposal to build a huge dam on the Yangtze River at the Three Gorges; approval was postponed. In 1994, 337 votes were cast against the Budget Law, with another 274 abstentions and invalid ballots. In 1995, NPC delegates cast a total of 1,006 abstentions, spoiled ballots, and votes against the nomination of Jiang Chunyun as vice premier, and many withheld support from the draft Central Bank and Education laws and from the work reports (reports of work performed over the past year and plans for future work) of the Supreme Procuratorate and the Supreme People's Court. In 1996, hundreds of delegates voted against or abstained from voting on the work reports of the procurator-general and the chief judge of the Supreme People's Court.

These events indicate that NPC members are taking their roles more seriously. The Congress passed 175 laws from 1982 to 1994 and is in the middle of a CCP-assigned five-year legislative plan to promulgate by the end of the century 152 additional laws deemed essential to China's economic and administrative modernization. NPC delegates and staffers have gained a greater sense of responsibility as their duties have expanded.

Freeing the NPC further from CCP control lies at the heart of the proposals for NPC reform, even though the proposals do not mention the problem explicitly. Proposals include the following:

Reducing the size of the NPC. Scholars argue that the large size of the NPC makes it unable to discuss proposals in plenary meetings, while discussion in small groups provides no efficient means of communication among members. Since the delegates' groups are divided mostly by territorial administrative unit, the discussion is dominated by high-ranking officials from the localities. To increase the ability to communicate and the efficiency of proceedings, scholars have proposed reducing the membership to between 700 and 2,000.

Lengthening sessions. Longer sessions would allow delegates to discuss proposed legislation more adequately.

Strengthening the committee and staff systems. The 1982 Constitution established a system of six committees for the NPC; two more were set up in 1988. The committees are supposed to help the Standing Committee with the study, review, and drafting of legislation and the supervision of other agencies of government. Scholars have proposed that the system be strengthened, though without suggesting specific methods of doing so. A related proposal is to establish (or strengthen, in the few cases where they exist) professional staff offices to help legislators at the national and provincial levels discharge their duties. The staff would consist of legal specialists working as full-time professionals.

Improving the qualifications of NPC members. Scholars have proposed that fewer officials and model workers be chosen for the NPC and that more professional politicians, legal specialists, and social activists be selected. Another proposal has been to establish a training school for NPC members.

Clarifying or improving the legislative process. Proposals include allowing NPC delegates to introduce legislation (they can do so in principle but never do in practice), ending CCP preview of legislation, allowing more time for NPC debate over legislative proposals, opening NPC sessions to the public and the press, and making a practice of voting on each part of a bill separately rather than on the bill as a whole. The idea behind these proposals is to center legislative action within rather than outside the NPC.

Increasing the NPC's role in rule-making. Scholars argue that the boundary between the legislative process and the process of framing administrative regulations is currently misplaced. Because the NPC meets so seldom, fewer rules are put through the legislative process than in most countries. Wide latitude is left for administrative agencies (the State Council, ministries and commissions, and others) to enact regulations that have the character of laws. This phenomenon is referred to as administrative legislation (*xingzheng lifa*). For example, the NPC has left the rule-making process pertaining to military affairs almost entirely to the Military Affairs Commission (nominally a state agency, but in actuality a party organ). Scholars have proposed a clarification of the division of rule-making powers between NPC and administrative organs in such a way as to give a larger role to the legislature.

Introducing two chambers. Some scholars argue that the NPC already has certain features of a two-chamber system and that these should be strengthened. Members of the Standing Committee are usually leaders of lower-level people's congresses or retired senior party, government, or military officials. Currently the Standing Committee exercises more power than the NPC itself because it meets more often and has more influential members. One proposal is to elect an upper chamber with three members from each province or provincial-level unit, with a lower chamber elected in proportion to population. The division of powers between the two houses is not generally specified.

Introducing the no-confidence vote. Scholars have proposed that if the work report of the government, Supreme People's Court, or Supreme Procuratorate is not approved by the NPC either initially or after one round of revision, the relevant official (premier, Supreme People's Court president, or procurator-general) should resign.

The common theme of these proposals is to increase the autonomy of the NPC and reduce the CCP's authority over it.

Invigorating Elections

Scholars have also put forward proposals to invigorate the process by which the NPC is elected. If implemented, they would also help make the legislature more autonomous.[5]

Of the four levels of people's congresses—national, provincial, county, and local—the two higher levels are indirectly elected, with NPC deputies elected by provincial congresses and provincial-congress deputies elected by county congresses. Local (village) people's congresses have been directly elected since the first elections in 1954. The Electoral Law of 1979 provided for direct election at the county level, as well as for multicandidate elections. With scattered exceptions in 1979–80, the county-level elections have not turned into competitive campaigns owing to tight party control through the local election committees.

The term "election" is a misnomer for the delegate-selection process, which is sometimes referred to more forthrightly as "production" (*chansheng*). At each level of people's congresses, the standing committee organizes the selection process for the level directly below. The standing committee supplies lists of persons who must be chosen in order to meet quotas of females, national minorities, "democratic personages," and other categories and to ensure that top party officials are included. It also supplies lists of other candidates from whom the remaining delegates must be selected. Few of the candidates are well known to the electors.

Reformers propose to free the elections from CCP control in several ways:

Improving the nomination process. Although ten citizens can join to nominate a candidate, this seldom happens. Even when it does, the final list of nominees is produced through a CCP-controlled consultative process. Rarely are there candidates not approved by the Party. (These details pertain to county-level people's-congress elections, but the same types of procedures are used in elections at all levels, including the indirect elections to the NPC Standing Committee.) Reformers propose changes not in the rules but in their implementation, to allow genuine nominations from below with less party control over the process.

Reducing malapportionment. The Chinese system intentionally gives urban districts four times as many delegates per voter as rural districts in the county-level congresses; the imbalance is even worse at higher levels. This practice is justified by the Marxist theory that the urban proletariat is more progressive than rural peasants. Many reformers are nervous about granting too much power to rural people, whom they view as backward and pro-authoritarian. Political leaders fear that a farmer-dominated legislature would not support longstanding CCP policies unfavorable to rural residents. At least one scholar, however, has proposed reducing the rural-urban disparity to two-to-one. I am not aware of any proposal to move to a "one person, one vote" system.

Shifting to single-seat districts. At the county level, each district elects from one to three representatives to the people's congress. (Taiwan also has a multiseat-district system for its Legislative Yuan, but I have been unable to discover whether these two Chinese systems have a common historical origin.) Some writers have suggested moving to a single-seat system as a way of tightening representatives' links with their constituencies. This reform would force the CCP to work harder to ensure representation of its own cadres and protected categories such as women and national minorities. I do not know whether Chinese scholars have begun to look seriously at other institutional choices in the design of an electoral system, such as balloting rules, which could ultimately affect the party system and the stability of governments.

Direct elections. Scholars have refuted the idea that China is too backward or too large for direct elections to the NPC. They argue that the idea of direct elections is found in the Marxist classics, and that Chinese citizens who have been educated in advanced socialist ideas for more than forty years must have as strong a democratic consciousness as did the citizens of capitalist systems when the direct election of parliaments began. As for constituency size as an obstacle to direct elections, they point out that each of the current NPC delegates represents a population of 360,000—fewer than the 510,000 represented by each U.S. congress-man.

Competitive campaigns. Direct election would not be meaningful without reform of campaign procedures. The direct elections for local people's congresses feature an often perfunctory process of official "introductions" of candidates to voters, either on paper or at meetings. Reformers have suggested that the job be done better, that those who nominate candidates be allowed to speak for them, and that more time be spent on the process. The new procedures could build on the experience of competitive village-committee elections that have been going on since 1987, an experiment that some senior leaders see as a first step in training rural residents for a more democratic system.

Multipartism. Scholars have also proposed new legislation on parties that would allow multiparty competition, arguing that a party claiming to represent the people's interests should submit to the test of competitive elections. The CCP has advantages over other parties and could benefit from such elections, they contend. They argue that competition is a natural law and a dynamic of social development, not a monopoly of the bourgeoisie. Multiparty elections would keep the CCP on the right track and prevent the emergence of another Cultural Revolution.

Against the concern that electoral competition would create an out-of-control NPC, reformers argue that a more strenuous election process would be good for the CCP. Because the Party faces no real competition and has most of the best potential candidates in its ranks, electoral reform would facilitate the advancement of the best CCP members as candidates. If campaigns are competitive, the CCP members closest to the people will win.

Constitutional Supervision

The Constitution gives the NPC the power to "supervise the enforcement of the Constitution" (Article 62) and empowers the NPC Standing Committee "to interpret the Constitution and supervise its enforcement" and "to interpret statutes" (Article 67).[6] These powers of supervision and interpretation are not equivalent to constitutional review in a system of divided powers. Since the NPC makes the laws, it could not very well declare one unconstitutional. Rather, supervising enforcement (*jiandu shishi*) means supervising the implementation or carrying out of the Constitution. Nominally, the NPC does this by hearing work reports from the other organs of government. It has seldom exercised its supervisory power in a more concrete way. A supervision law (*jiandu fa*), which would detail the means by which the NPC can exercise its supervisory power, exists in draft form, but its contents are not public.

Nor does the NPC Standing Committee often exercise its power of constitutional interpretation. It has responded occasionally to requests for interpretation from lower-level people's congresses. It has also issued a small number of "internal interpretations" (*neibu jieshi*) in response to requests from other government agencies. Such clarifications have the character of ad hoc problem solving, rather than formal constitutional interpretations.

Other agencies often substitute for the NPC Standing Committee in interpreting statutes. For example, the Supreme People's Court issued a brochure on how to understand the concept of marital breakdown under the 1980 Marriage Law. The Court has done similar work for the Civil Procedure Law of 1991, the Inheritance Law of 1985, and other laws. These activities seem to go beyond the constitutional authority of the Supreme People's Court to "supervise the administration of justice by the local people's courts" (Article 127); rather, the Court got involved because the NPC Standing Committee abdicated authority owing to a lack of time or expertise. The understaffed courts themselves often yield authority to administrative agencies, which have yet more personnel and expertise.

By making these diagnoses, scholars imply that the NPC's constitutional-supervision function should be strengthened. To this end, some have recommended the establishment of a specialized organ to exercise the powers of constitutional interpretation and supervision. Three proposals have been floated. The first is to establish a subsidiary committee under the Standing Committee to advise it in interpreting the Constitution.[7] The second is to establish a separate constitutional-supervision committee within the NPC, equal in rank to the Standing Committee and able to supervise all organs of state including the Standing Committee itself. The third is to establish a constitutional court with authority to reverse the actions even of the NPC, in effect creating a separation of powers and broadening the constitutional-supervision function to include constitutional review. Only the first of these proposals could be implemented without a constitutional amendment.

The discussion draws attention to the absence of a locus within the state apparatus where problems of jurisdiction and other intrastate issues can be solved. It also implicitly identifies the problem of CCP dominance as an obstacle to the lawlike functioning of the state. In addressing this issue, scholars have debated whether the CCP could be subjected to constitutional supervision. On the one hand, the Party might be considered not subject to the Constitution, since CCP leadership is listed as a principle of state power in the Constitution's Preamble. On the other hand, the academic consensus is that the Party is in principle subject to the Constitution, both because the Constitution lists political parties among the entities that it governs, and by virtue of the Party's charter, which calls for it to obey the Constitution. But scholars recognize that it is impractical to exercise constitutional supervision over the Party now. They envision a transitional stage during which the NPC might review selected CCP documents and notify the Party of any contradictions with the Constitution so that the Party can rectify them itself.

Judicial Independence

The Chinese Constitution states that people's courts "shall . . . exercise judicial power independently and are not subject to interference by administrative organs, public organizations or individuals" (Article 126).[8] This is not a provision for what those in the West understand by the term "judicial independence"—that is, the protection of each individual judge from interference in the lawful exercise of judicial authority. Literally, it holds that the courts should "independently carry out the judging power" (*duli xingshi shenpanquan*), meaning—as Chinese scholars interpret it—that the court as an organization should do its job exclusively, rather than having other organs share in the function, as occurred, for example, during the Cultural Revolution.

There is debate about the scope of the term "public organizations" (*shehui tuanti*, literally, "social groups") that appears in Article 126. The question is whether the CCP is included among these entities that constitutionally cannot interfere with the work of the courts. The dominant interpretation is that the category does not include the Party. Scholars note that the 1982 phrasing is different from that of 1954, which stated, "People's courts independently carry out judgment, following only the law" (Article 76). In listing the entities that are prohibited from interfering in judicial processes, the 1982 Constitution seems to make room for groups that are not listed—namely, the CCP and the NPC—to get involved. In light of this reasoning and the fact that the Constitution mentions the principle of "Party leadership" in its Preamble, involvement of the CCP in the work of the courts is not deemed interference, but rather constitutionally sanctioned leadership.

Party "leadership" takes three forms. One is collective decisionmaking. Under the "report and approval system," authority for court judgments is vested in a judicial committee of each court (*shenpan weiyuanhui*) that is led by the court president and vice-president, who are invariably also officials of that court's party group or cell. Thus judicial independence in China is not the independence of individual judges, but the independence of any given court as an organ. As one sitting judge told me, "If the [court] leaders want to change my decision, I have no power to interfere [*ganshe*]." In the Chinese judicial system, then, it is a judge's sticking to his own decision, rather than court authorities' changing it, that constitutes "interference."

The second form of CCP "leadership" is the "asking for instruction" system, by which lower courts are expected to bring important or complicated cases to higher courts to obtain instructions before handing down a judgment. Ostensibly aimed at avoiding the reversal of judgments, the process provides the opportunity for the party organs located in higher-level courts to decide the outcome of cases in lower courts.

Third, local CCP authorities (who are also administrative authorities) often issue directives to local courts on how to decide individual cases. The practice is of questionable constitutionality but is built into the system of party leadership. At each level of the administrative hierarchy (say, in a city), the local party committee has a subsidiary organ known as a political-legal committee (*zhengfa weiyuanhui*), which brings together the heads of the police, procuratorate, court, department of justice, state-security department, and civil-affairs department so that they can coordinate their work. As part of such coordination, the courts are required to seek the committee's guidance in deciding important or difficult cases (*zhongda fuza anjian*). If opinions are divided or the case is especially crucial, the political-legal committee may refer the issue to the full party committee at that level of the hierarchy.

The courts not only are led by the CCP but are constitutionally subordinate to the legislative branch. The Constitution says the courts are "responsible to" their respective people's congresses (Article 128). A people's congress cannot constitutionally interfere in a specific case, but it can require a report on a case, organize an investigation into the suspected mishandling of a case, or cashier and order the indictment of judicial officials who criminally mishandle a case. The frequency with which this happens is uncertain, but improper interference in court cases by people's congresses was sufficiently problematic that the NPC Standing Committee in 1989 issued a decision stressing the limits on such interference, presumably as a reminder to lower-level people's congresses.[9] Since local people's congresses are controlled by local CCP authorities, this seems to be a second channel for party control of the courts.

Judges and scholars have drawn attention to ways in which subordination to the CCP disrupts the courts' ability to perform their functions. Local courts often fail to enforce judgments in favor of out-of-town Chinese (or foreign) plaintiffs. Judges are reluctant to rule against local administrators in suits lodged by individual citizens under the Administrative Litigation Law of 1989 and the Compensation Law of 1994.

Proposals for improving the functioning of the courts are modest. Most involve improving the professional quality of judges and establishing better remuneration and more secure tenure. Judges in China, as in other civil-law jurisdictions, are civil servants. Their ranks are equivalent to those of various other bureaucrats across the system. Their incomes tend to be less than those of factory workers, educators, doctors, and government officials in many fields because of the lack of outside opportunities, bonuses, and supplements.

In 1995, the NPC adopted new legislation concerning judges.[10] The Judges Law mandates minimum qualifications for judges and specifies circumstances under which they can be removed from office. In these small ways it increases their independence. It states further that anyone who interferes with judges' exercise of their duties will be prosecuted according to law. But there is no law under which to prosecute such people, nor does the Judges Law define interference. The law does not solve the problem of inadequate remuneration; does not create a standard of judicial conduct; and supplies too many and too broadly stated causes for which judges can be dismissed. Some judicial reformers nonetheless see the Judges Law as the start of a trend toward independent individual judges who have job security, professional prestige, and adequate remuneration.

Other proposals relating to the judiciary include shifting more of the burden of evidence collection from judges to litigants, thus putting judges in a more neutral position; ending the system whereby judges get approval for their rulings from their administrative superiors; and reducing the practice of lower courts' seeking directives on specific cases from higher courts. A proposal has also been made to do away with the police power to sentence people under the "administrative punishment" system of labor reeducation. By moving many acts now deemed noncriminal into the criminal category, this would increase the number of cases that would have to be taken to court for judgment.

The central point of these reforms would be to strengthen the autonomy of individual judges in trying cases. More boldly, some Chinese legal workers view the arrangement by which people's congresses can intrude into judicial affairs as invasive, and have argued that the NPC's power over courts should be limited to reviewing their annual reports. This approaches advocacy of separation of powers.

Other Proposals

Aside from the proposals described so far, the constitutionalist debate has raised a number of other significant issues.[11]

The legal force of the Preamble to the Constitution. The debate over the legal force of the Preamble is in effect a debate over whether Deng Xiaoping's "four basic principles" (socialism, people's democratic dictatorship, Marxism-Leninism-Mao Zedong Thought, and Communist Party leadership), which are contained therein, are legally binding. Some scholars hold that the Preamble has legal force. A second view is that while the Preamble as a whole does not have legal power since parts of it are simply assertions of historical facts or goals, some stipulations in it have legal authority, including the four principles. A third view holds that the Preamble does not have legal authority because it is not written as a formal article. Rather, it is a statement of purposes and values, compliance with which is optional for law-abiding citizens who are not CCP members. Peking University professor Gong Xiangrui has gone so far as to argue, "The Constitution is, after all, not the Party's constitution. The spirit of the Preamble is in conflict with the principles of constitutionalism."[12]

Citizens' rights versus human rights.[13] Many scholars argue that the constitutional notion of citizens' rights should be changed to a notion of human rights as a way of symbolizing the importance of individual rights. Legal specialists have argued for years that certain laws—including the Public Demonstrations Law and the State Secrets Law, both passed in 1989—should be revised to protect such rights. The difficulty of finding the right balance between protecting and limiting rights has delayed the adoption of a press law that has been undergoing drafting on and off for more than a decade. A revision of the Criminal Procedure Law in March 1996 increased the impartiality of judges, improved defense lawyers' access to clients and evidence, limited detention without charge to one month, and improved other procedural safeguards for defendants, at least on paper. Proposals have also been made to expunge crimes of counterrevolution from the criminal code and to eliminate the power of the police to imprison people for up to three years without trial ("administrative detention").

Separation of powers. Since the top leadership has ruled this subject out of bounds, it is seldom discussed explicitly. But some scholars privately favor greater separation of powers. They view the Paris Commune model of single-branch government (the historic root of the current system) as an immature one that was adopted under conditions of civil war in a single city and lasted only a few weeks. When implemented in a large country over an extended period of time, it confuses the division of labor between the legislative and executive branches, allows an unhealthy growth of executive powers, and undermines the ability of the legislature to supervise the executive. Some scholars see a germ of separation of powers in the provision in the current NPC Organic Law that states that members of the NPC Standing Committee cannot hold full-time offices in state administrative organs. A similar provision governs members of standing committees of local people's congresses.

Subjecting the Military Affairs Commission to the authority of the NPC. The Military Affairs Commission is a CCP organ, although it has a second, nominal, identity in the Constitution as a state organ. It promulgates its own laws and regulations without the involvement of the NPC. Some scholars argue that this exercise of legislative power violates the Constitution; some have suggested amending the Constitution to state more strongly that the Military Affairs Commission is subordinate to the NPC.[14] This would be a move toward shifting the military from party to state control, a process referred to in Chinese as "statization" (*guojiahua*) of the military. However, civilian control of the military through the Military Affairs Commission is already weak, and some scholars worry that it would be even weaker under the NPC unless the NPC were much more vigorous than it is now.

Federalism. China is a unitary state but has some quasi-federalist traditions. The Constitution and the Regional Autonomy Law for Minority Nationalities (1984) provide for the nominal autonomy of minority-inhabited areas. Deng Xiaoping's idea of "one country, two systems" for Hong Kong and Taiwan is reflected in the inclusion in the 1982

Constitution of Article 31, which provides for the establishment of Special Administrative Regions. Under the reforms, provinces have developed substantial economic, fiscal, and policymaking powers. Some Chinese scholars think that making the system more explicitly federal would help clarify Han-minority relations and center-province relations. Abroad, Yan Jiaqi has argued this position most strongly.[15] Within China, scholars tend to avoid the term "federalism." Nevertheless, several have argued for new, clearer definitions of central and local powers, or for a "financial apportionment committee" under the State Council or the NPC Standing Committee to resolve issues of central-local revenue sharing and interprovincial financial transfers. Since the NPC is made up of local CCP elites, strengthening the role of the NPC would likely lead to increased articulation of provincial interests. In contrast to a national breakup, which would be inimical to constitutionalism, the lawful institutionalization of power-sharing between the center and the regions would be a move in the direction of a more constitutionalist regime.

Leninism and the Rule of Law

Although individually modest, the proposals reviewed here array themselves around the issue of the role of the CCP. The diagnoses of problems and proposals for change are cautious and technical, but they make clear that the authors see the Leninist one-party system as the main obstacle to the rule of law. In fifteen years of legal reform, the Leninist core has developed mechanisms to bargain with, consult, and persuade other actors in an increasingly complex society. But power is neither grounded in popular consent nor limited by laws. As Carol Hamrin and Suisheng Zhao argue, China under Deng is a form of "bureaucratic authoritarianism."[16]

Legal scholars themselves are not a powerful constituency. Yet they possess expertise that the leaders need in order to fix problems in the system. As marketization erodes the old techniques of control, the leaders have turned to law to direct lower-level officials and constrain independent economic actors. Lawyers, judges, law professors, and NPC staff are pointing out that legal institutions cannot perform the tasks they are charged with unless they are given more autonomy. As one Chinese scholar put it, "When conditions are ripe, we should move from conceiving of [our government] as a 'people's democratic dictatorship' and start calling it a 'people's democratic constitutionalism' or a 'socialist constitutionalism.' "[17] Reliable and predictable processes of rule-making, adjudication, and enforcement will constrain the party leaders as well as other actors.

There are also more directly political reasons why some CCP leaders have promoted the discussion of constitutionalism. Politicians associated with the NPC (formerly Peng Zhen and Wan Li, now Qiao Shi) want to enlarge the NPC's power in order to increase their own influence. The regime is also influenced by foreign pressure and example with respect to investment law, tax law, contract law, court procedures, intellectual property rights, human rights law, and so on.

Constitutionalism also has opponents. If one faction would benefit from an increase in the NPC's strength, others would benefit from a continuation of the status quo. While law in some ways improves the functioning of the economy, many entrepreneurs and local communities have learned to profit through evasion of laws and personal connections. The experience of postcommunist Russia is often cited as evidence that China cannot afford to democratize. In its transition "from utopia to development," to use Richard Lowenthal's phrase, the regime has not found a way to replace revolutionary legitimacy with legal-democratic legitimacy. Constitutionalization would serve the CCP's interests in legitimation and stability. If the reform proposals reviewed in this essay were implemented, China would still be a dominant one-party system with weak separation of powers and weak federalism. To be sure, the process of transition to constitutionalism has been turbulent almost everywhere, and China's earlier history of failed experiments is not encouraging. But constitutionalism—which is not necessarily democracy American-style or Russian-style—is one of the most conservative options for change in a situation where stasis seems impossible.

16

Human Rights and American China Policy

Accommodating a rising China has become one of the most difficult challenges for the foreign policies of the West and Japan. A consensus has formed in the United States that progress can be made on issues involving trade, intellectual property rights, arms proliferation, and Taiwan by taking clear stands in favor of core Western interests. But division over both ends and means has brought human rights policy to a state of crisis.

In the last few years, as outrage over the government's response to the 1989 Tiananmen Square uprising receded and U.S.-China economic ties grew, a clash emerged between perceived business and human rights interests in China. In 1994, at the urging of the business community, President Bill Clinton abandoned his attempt to link human rights progress to China's trade privileges and turned instead to "comprehensive engagement." China's rights performance then worsened, poisoning the atmosphere in which the administration pursued other policy issues.

The United States shifted in 1996 to a policy of "strategic dialogue." The new approach quickly ran into trouble as the Chinese government sentenced Wei Jingsheng to fourteen years in prison, sent Liu Xiaobo for three years' labor re-education without trial, and gave harsh sentences to other prominent dissidents.

On the eve of then-Secretary of State Warren Christopher's November 1996 visit, the Chinese government staged a show trial that sentenced Wang Dan to an eleven-year prison term on flagrantly flimsy grounds, thus signaling Beijing's refusal to consider human rights a serious part of the bilateral agenda. At the start of his second term, President Clinton found himself trying to negotiate the conditions for a summit meeting with Chinese leaders who exile, imprison, and torture the very dissidents whose names have topped the White House's and State Department's list of human rights concerns for years.

China human rights policy has been a failure not because China is intractable on the issue. Indeed, during the years when public consensus allowed the White House and Congress to push the issue vigorously, China responded by releasing some 881 Tiananmen prisoners; lifting martial law in Beijing; permitting Fang Lizhi to go abroad from his refuge in the U.S. Embassy; initiating a human rights dialogue with U.S. officials; and freeing such big-name prisoners as Han Dongfang and Wang Juntao (both of whom are now in exile), and Wei Jingsheng, Chen Ziming, and Wang Dan (who have since been re-imprisoned and, in Chen's case, re-released). China signed a memorandum of understanding with the United States to restrict export of prison labor products to the United States, provided information on political prisoners, and held talks on prison visits with the International Committee of the Red Cross (ICRC). Beijing dispatched two human rights delegations to the West in 1991–92 to talk with nongovernmental organizations and specialists and to gather information; the Chinese government later issued a series of White Papers on human rights to respond to international concerns. China's official statements moved further than before toward accepting human rights as a valid subject of international dialogue. Progress slowed (and on political rights, reversed) only when U.S. irresolution convinced the Chinese authorities that they no longer needed to take the issue seriously.

The United States today is divided over the importance of human rights, how hard to fight for the issue, and what a human rights policy toward China should be expected to achieve. In government and out, many believe that the United States can no longer afford to hold larger issues hostage to the fate of a few dissidents; that it should not overlook long-term favorable trends because of the regime's harshness toward the few who challenge it directly; and that it must not let petulance over violations of Western values blind Washington to the chance to improve the lives of large numbers of people and reduce the risks of war in Asia by developing closer relations with China's leaders.

These views now dominate U.S. policy. They dovetail with business fears that human rights pressure will spoil the environment for trade and investment. Human rights remains on the list of U.S. diplomatic concerns with China, but it has slipped to the bottom—after security on the Korean peninsula, arms proliferation to Pakistan and Iran, the trade deficit, and other issues. The United States defends its human rights concerns half-apologetically, as if attempting to leaven necessary *realpolitik* with a measure of fidelity to its parochial values.

China has become the hard case for U.S. human rights policy as a whole, and human rights has become the toughest issue for China policy. Without a credible position on human rights in China, U.S. rights policy in Asia and the rest of the world risks incoherence, and Washington may lose a historic post-Cold War opportunity to strengthen the international human rights regime that a succession of U.S. presidents since World War II has worked so hard to build. As Clinton's second term begins, the administration must think through fundamental U.S. interests in Chinese human rights and find ways to promote U.S. goals.

China policy in other areas has produced results by proceeding from the insight that China is a realist power with which one can reach accommodation through hard bargaining over real interests. U.S. human rights policy should be reconstructed on the same basis. It should concentrate on fundamental U.S. interests in China's responsible international behavior, domestic prosperity and stability, and participation in the international human rights regime. The United States should separate human rights from democratization, focus on abuses that are illegal under international law, and preempt the charge of cultural imperialism by framing the issue as one of compliance with international norms.

The State of Human Rights in China

The international law of human rights centers on the Universal Declaration of Human Rights, adopted by the United Nations General Assembly on December 10, 1948, and on the two covenants—one on civil and political rights, the other on economic, social, and cultural rights—adopted by the UN General Assembly in 1966. Like all nations, China is bound by the Declaration. Although it has not acceded to the two covenants, they represent appropriate standards against which to evaluate any country's behavior. China has acceded to and is bound by nine UN human rights conventions, including the one against torture, and a number of International Labor Organization conventions related to workers' rights.

The international human rights regime requires individual liberty, but it does not require any particular kind of political or economic system. As the product of negotiations among all nations, the regime is not a weapon in the clash of civilizations. In light of Chinese fears of Western subversion it is important to separate human rights from democratization and treat it as the international idea that it is, not as a code word for Westernization.

Under Mao Zedong, and even more rapidly since the beginning of Deng Xiaoping's reform, China made progress in supplying its citizens with economic and social rights. Living standards have increased, compulsory education has been extended to nine years, adult literacy stands at 79 percent according to official figures, and life expectancy at 69 exceeds that of many middle-income countries. Nevertheless, the record may not be as good as it is generally thought to be: A recent World Bank study finds that more than 350 million Chinese live in conditions of grinding poverty.[1] But pending more research, the focus of foreign concerns is appropriately on the deprivation of civil and political rights.

In this realm, pervasive and systematic violations occur, many of them carried out as matters of government policy.[2] The violations that should be of central international concern are those that are conducted by government agents, transgress China's international obligations, and are indefensible under even the most culturally relativist standards. The fact that such violations are sometimes carried out under the auspices of Chinese law should not mislead policymakers. Many abuses transgress the clear language of the Chinese Constitution, the law of criminal procedure, and other enactments. Governments apply their own laws, but when they stretch the law beyond all sense they abuse, not interpret, it. A good example is Wang Dan's illegal pre-trial detention and the four-hour show trial at which he was convicted.

Nor should the United States be dissuaded from recognizing rights violations by the fact that many Chinese citizens have gained new liberties of personal movement and of private political expression under Deng's reforms, or by the fact that the victims of rights abuses are a minority. As in U.S. history, rights are not rights when they are limited to actions the government chooses to tolerate, or to speech by persons with whom the government agrees.

The major categories of rights abuses are as follows.

- *Imprisonment, arbitrary detention, or forced exile* of people who have not used or advocated violence, but whose political beliefs counter those of the government.[3] The victims include democracy movement activists arrested for such acts as writing articles and petitioning the National People's Congress, Tibetans detained for verbally supporting independence, Mongols detained for a cultural revival movement, people detained for protesting about personal grievances, and people accused of divulging state secrets for circulating publicly available information.[4]

- *Religious repression*, including the arrests and beatings of adherents of the autonomous Catholic and Protestant movements; detention of Tibetans for religious practices; the house arrest of a six-year-old child who was designated by the Dalai Lama as the incarnation of the Panchen Lama.[5] Religious victims are often charged as counterrevolutionaries, yet in many instances they have carried out no political acts.

- *Violations related to criminal procedure*, including lack of procedural safeguards against police abuse, especially during the process of "shelter and investigation" (*shourong shencha*); insufficient safeguards against unlimited detention without trial; failure to provide fair trials (no publicity, insufficient provision for notice to family and preparation of a defense, lack of a presumption of innocence); lack of independence of the judiciary; and the widespread use of "re-education through labor" as a form of imprisonment at police initiative without benefit of trial (as in the recent case of Liu Xiaobo). The 1995 Judges Law and 1996 amendments to the 1979 Criminal Procedure Law addressed some of these issues, but they did not resolve them.

- *Torture and abuse of inmates of prisons and labor camps*, and imposition of forced labor on inmates. The Chinese government has signed the convention against torture, has intermittently campaigned against the use of torture by police and jailers, and reiterated the outlawing of torture in its 1994 Prison Law. But the practice remains prevalent. In the case of many political prisoners it is evidently condoned by the central authorities. Prominent political prisoners recently or currently mistreated in prison included Wei Jingsheng, Liu Gang, and Xu Wenli; those denied adequate medical care included Chen Ziming and Bao Tong.

- *Forced resettlement*, suppression of dissent, and violation of labor rights in connection with work on the Three Gorges project.[6]

- *Forced abortion and sterilization* as part of population planning practices. These acts violate declared central government policy, yet are carried out by local officials on what appears to be a widespread basis.

Other civil and political rights violations have been less noticed in the outside world but are also appropriate subjects of concern. These include denial of the right to strike, denial of the freedom of the Chinese and foreign press, mistreatment of homosexuals, eugenic practices, and state interference in the practice of Islam and Buddhism.

A number of issues that have drawn foreign attention are more debatable as rights violations. In dealing with them, Western policy should focus on the ways in which these actions clearly violate international law. Such issues include the following:

- *Capital punishment.* Its use is not against international or Chinese law. Yet China uses the penalty exceptionally widely and with grossly inadequate safeguards. Moreover, international law considers public execution, still widely practiced in China, to be a violation of human dignity.
- *Harvesting of organs from condemned prisoners for transplantation.* Organ transplant does not violate international law. But in China the need for organs reportedly leads to frequent violations of due process, and the authorities seldom obtain donor consent.[7]
- *Kidnapping, trafficking, and abuse of women and girls.* The government has campaigned against these practices, yet they continue on a widespread basis, and some analysts plausibly argue this is only possible with the cooperation of local officials.
- *Export of prison labor products to the United States.* This violates U.S. law but not international law. But when prison labor is compulsory, as appears to be the case in Chinese prisons and labor camps, it is prohibited by ILO conventions.

Human Rights as Realpolitik

It is often noted that human rights represent Western values, and that no China policy that ignores them can achieve stable public support. It is less widely realized that promotion of human rights serves Western interests. Humanitarian sympathy and moral outrage can drive human rights policy, but consistency of purpose and clarity of focus must come from thinking through human rights as realpolitik.

The United States has devoted increasing effort since the end of the Cold War to strengthening the international system of rules that benefit the West in such areas as arms proliferation, trade, and the environment. It should give equal attention to fortifying the international human rights regime, which was one of the earliest regimes the world started building after World War II. This regime provides the framework for countries to intercede peacefully against domestic abuses in other states that potentially have serious international consequences. It has growing utility in the post-Cold War world as part of an emerging new international order.

First, the theory of the "democratic peace" that goes back to Immanuel Kant remains a good guide to policy, even though it is not universally accepted by political scientists. The exercise of political rights by citizens is conducive both to reducing governmental misjudgments in foreign affairs and to creating a more peaceful, rational, and predictable foreign policy. Countries that respect the rights of their own citizens are less likely to start wars, export drugs, harbor terrorists, or generate refugees.

In China's case, respect for human rights is a precondition for peaceful resolution of the Taiwan issue and successful management of Hong Kong's transition to sovereignty by the People's Republic on July 1, 1997. The human rights gap is a source of Beijing's difficulties in both situations. Taiwanese president Lee Teng-hui cites human rights violations as a reason for his government's reluctance to accept unification. Hong Kong citizens protested the Wei Jingsheng and Wang Dan trials; they were similarly horrified when China's foreign minister responded that their freedom of speech after 1997 would exclude the right to criticize mainland policy on dissidents. A blowup in either situation will involve U.S. and other Western interests. Besides its economic stake in both places, the United States is committed to peaceful resolution of the Taiwan issue by the 1979 Taiwan Relations Act, and to supporting Hong Kong's freedom and prosperity by the McConnell Act of 1992. In promoting human rights in China, the United States helps prevent these situations from exploding in its face.

Second, China's stability and prosperity have been declared interests of the West since the early 1970s when Henry Kissinger was Secretary of State and Richard Nixon was the first president to travel to Communist China. A stable and prosperous China will anchor a stable Asia and contribute to global prosperity through trade. A corrupt, unstable, economically stagnant China will contribute to regional disorder, pollution, and refugee flows, and in the extreme case could heavily tax outside resources for relief. China's rapid development has created such a mobilized and sophisticated population that the government can no longer legitimize itself without allowing a measure of political freedom and participation, and without legitimacy its political stability is at risk. The latest repressions testify to the fragility of the regime, which sees a handful of peaceful dissenters as an intolerable threat to its survival.

This is not to say that China should be pushed to adopt a particular model of political system. But long-term stability will elude it until it honors the political freedoms so wisely recognized in all four of its own Constitutions since the founding of the People's Republic. This argument has been propounded within China by party reformers since the mid-1980s. It is now being promoted by officials who are experimenting with village-level elections aimed at consolidating, not undermining, Chinese Communist Party power.

Third, it is sometimes argued that human rights violations are a necessary, temporary tradeoff to achieve economic development. But few Chinese rights violations (for example, mistreatment of prisoners or violations of due process) have any plausible link to development. The few that have—such as deprivations of freedom of speech and political action, which may be considered necessary to keep political order—more often lead to developmental mistakes than to developmental achievements. Others, such as coercive population planning practices, are shortcuts to achieve targets that could be achieved equally well or better by legal methods, and probably with more secure results. Meanwhile, the violations in themselves worsen the quality of life and constitute a form of underdevelopment unmeasured in gross domestic product (GDP) and other statistics.[8]

The relationship between human rights and development is in fact the reverse. Systems that violate political rights tend to generate distorted communications and commit policy mistakes. Suppression of information contributed to a vast famine during the Great Leap Forward, devastation of forests, salinization of farmland, and a series of dam collapses in 1975.[9] Repression need not be widespread to send a signal to all Chinese that they should remain silent. Rights violations throttle the channels of discussion that China desperately needs to manage its problems in the midst of rapid economic and social change. Enforced silence worsens corruption, removes checks to environmental damage, and clears the field for potential megadisasters like the Three Gorges Dam, which specialists think may do extensive ecological damage. Nor can China compete successfully in world markets in the age of information when it filters Internet access, tries to control financial reporting, censors the domestic and foreign press, and otherwise interferes with the flow of ideas.

Fourth, human rights diplomacy is often erroneously presented as standing in conflict with Western business interests. In fact, even at the height of the Most-Favored-Nation (MFN) debates in the United States, U.S.-China trade boomed. In 1995, placing orders for European-made Airbus Industrie airplanes, Premier Li Peng indicated that the Chinese government was penalizing the competing U.S. supplier, Boeing, for U.S. human rights pressure. But most observers believe the Airbus decision was made for business reasons, with the human rights linkage tacked on later. I know of no other case in which the Chinese government discriminated against a U.S. company because of U.S. human rights activism. Continued U.S. division over human rights, however, may encourage the Chinese to start enforcing such linkages.

So far, maintaining the human rights issue on the bilateral agenda seems to have strengthened the U.S. hand in a number of trade and other negotiations. After Tiananmen, the anti-China atmosphere weakened Beijing's negotiating position in talks over intellectual property rights and market access. In both negotiations, faced with a threat of trade sanctions made credible by the general U.S. willingness to be tough on China, Beijing made concessions to Washington's demands. The fact that China was on the defensive on human rights weakened its ability to block U.S. and French arms transfers to Taiwan, probably helped explain the replacement of a conciliatory Hong Kong governor with one who confronted Beijing on the issue of Hong Kong democratization, and may have accelerated China's accession to the nuclear nonproliferation treaty (NPT). Western pressure on human rights did not prevent and may have facilitated progress over issues like arms proliferation, Korean denuclearization, and global environmental degradation, as China sought to improve its image and to escape international isolation.

Rule of law is essential to protect U.S. and other foreign interests (business and otherwise) in China. Today, those Chinese who make and enforce the laws (legislators, procurators, and judges) are chosen, promoted, and kept or fired at the pleasure of political authorities. They write, adopt, revise, and apply the laws under party supervision, with little independent input.

Enforcement of the laws is arbitrary and the courts have no autonomy. The lawlessness of the Chinese legal system is experienced as much by foreign business people as by Chinese dissidents. What happened to Wei Jingsheng has happened in different forms to the Australian businessman James Peng, International Monetary Fund official Hong Yang, Royal Dutch Shell employee Xiu Yichun, and others.[10]

If the law is a system of rules that are known in advance and enforceable by appeal to independent arbiters, then China's legal system will become a rule of law only when it incorporates respect for human rights. Expanding the legal code will not solve the human rights problem. Rather, making advances toward a true rule of law and guarantees of human rights will solve the problems with the legal code. A human rights-neutral improvement of the Chinese legal system is impossible.

The community of nations has a strategic interest in improving the human rights regime in all countries, not just in China. But China's demographic and geographic size, its strategic and economic importance, its status as a permanent member of the UN Security Council, and its position of leadership in the developing world make international interest in Chinese human rights practices greater than interest in many other nations' practices.

The difference between a China and a Vietnam, a Zaire, or a Saudi Arabia—or even an Indonesia or an India—is not the international standards applied to it, but the country's potential impact on Western and global interests. China should be held to the same standards as other countries, but its international importance justifies giving its rights violations more urgent and sustained attention than the world can afford to spend on every offending country.

The United States is not alone in its concern for human rights in China.[11] Strong NGOs focused on human rights can be found in Britain, France, Australia, and to a lesser extent in Japan and Germany. Paris and London have interceded intermittently on human rights issues; Bonn and Tokyo occasionally. The European Parliament has passed numerous resolutions and in 1996 awarded Wei Jingsheng the Sakharov Prize, an award that recognizes contributions to freedom. France, Britain, and Australia will no doubt take steps to defend human rights in China even if the United States does not, but their pressure can seldom be effective without U.S. involvement. Japan and Germany are less likely to act on their own, and even if they act in concert with the United States they will usually tailor their actions to be less conspicuous than U.S. actions. In this as in so many other areas, U.S. leadership is essential.

The outside world's interest in Chinese human rights presents no threat to Chinese interests, properly understood. The goals of the international human rights regime are consistent with China's announced internal goals of rule of law, prosperity, stability, and more open decisionmaking. As a weaker power, China stands to benefit from strengthening international regimes that impose limits on stronger powers and buttress the prerogatives of sovereign states as regime participants and makers. China benefits from the norms of proceduralism and multilateralism that are embedded in international regimes. Only through active participation can China take a hand in shaping regimes further to serve its needs. All these arguments apply as much to the international human rights regime as they do to regimes in such areas as trade and nonproliferation of arms.

To be sure, the Chinese government fears it will be criticized and even overthrown when citizens are able to exercise freedom of speech. But repressing criticism is not a long-term strategy for stabilizing power, as many in the ruling party know. An old Chinese proverb says, "You can dam a river forever, but not the mouths of the people."

Shaping Policy

If the goal is to change China's behavior, the best means is to enforce and strengthen the international human rights regime. By disentangling human rights from democratization and "Western values," such a policy can avoid stimulating reactive nationalism and regain the polemical initiative lost to proponents of "Asian values" in China and Southeast Asia. By multilateralizing the human rights issue, the United States can work more successfully with allies and can more readily enlist the cooperation of sympathetic policymakers within the Chinese bureaucracy. Multilateralism would make it harder for the Chinese government to divide its critics abroad. But fundamentally, multilateralism is important because a major goal of human rights policy is to strengthen multilateral institutions.

Representations on human rights issues should be accurate and within the ambit of international law. The stress should not be on U.S.-China or West-China value differences, but on Chinese compliance with international norms and Chinese cooperation with international human rights mechanisms. The human rights agenda is damaged when it is mixed with other goals, including opposition to communism, antagonism to population planning, or promotion of Tibetan independence. If promoting democracy is a goal of the West's China policy, it should be justified on its own grounds and pursued by separate agencies and actors.

Washington should take the lead in coordinating G-7 and other approaches to China on human rights. The United States should hold regular high-level consultations with individual European allies, the European Union (EU), and Japan, and it should provide energetic leadership to forge common policies toward common goals. The Clinton administration should employ more resources than it did in 1996 to sponsor and pass resolutions at meetings of the UN Human Rights Commission in Geneva condemning Chinese human rights violations.

The United States and its allies should seek China's enhanced participation in the institutions of the international human rights regime. It
should press China to ratify the two international human rights
covenants and encourage China to extend invitations to the UN "thematic mechanisms," such as the special rapporteurs on torture, freedom
of expression, independence of the judiciary, violence against women,
and religious intolerance. It should press China to meet its treaty obligation to honor the two UN human rights covenants in post-reversion
Hong Kong.

Grounding its China rights policy in the international regime will
bring pressure on the United States to enter more fully into compliance
with the regime itself. It should accede to the International Covenant on
Economic, Social and Cultural Rights (it has already joined the civil and
political convention), and remove the excessive reservations it lodged
against a number of UN conventions it signed. Joining the regime more
fully involves some sacrifice of U.S. sovereignty, but no more than did
accession to the Uruguay Round of the General Agreement on Tariffs
and Trade and the World Trade Organization, the Anti-Ballistic Missile
treaty, the Law of the Sea, the North American Free Trade Agreement,
and other international agreements. In each case, the United States has
to decide whether making other governments subject to these agreements is worth making itself subject to them as well. In most cases involving human rights, the answer should be yes, both because the United
States' own human rights record is generally good and because the end
in view is to build an international system of law and justice that will serve
Western interests.

Exposure and stigmatization of Chinese abuses is a valuable tactic and
should be used more effectively. President Clinton and Vice President Al
Gore should publicly condemn human rights violations and personally
intervene when necessary with Chinese President Jiang Zemin and other
top officials via letter or telephone. The Chinese are adept at distin-
guishing between pro-forma and real interventions. In certain circumstances private contact may be best; in other circumstances only public
interventions have credibility.

But Western policy also needs to have teeth. MFN conditionality is
dead, but World Bank and WTO-related conditions are worth considering—not to interfere with trade or development but to communicate
Washington's sense of the importance of human rights improvements to
its own interests and to China's development. At a time when China is ret-
rogressing in the area of political rights, the United States should use its

influence at the World Bank to suspend or to delay for consideration loans to Chinese government-sponsored development projects except for those serving basic human needs; Washington should also seek to condition China's WTO entry on specific, relevant human rights improvements.

Substantial human rights improvements should be a precondition for a U.S.-China summit. Summits are valuable to the West in pushing forward negotiations on a wide range of issues, but they are even more valuable to Chinese leaders for the face they give and the opportunity to seek U.S. concessions on long-standing issues. Negotiations for a summit therefore offer the West the opportunity to bargain for progress on matters it believes are important.

Moreover, the international human rights regime is a system of norms, and norms become established through symbolic communication. The diplomacy of human rights heavily depends on symbolically recognizing the legitimacy of government policies and leaders associated with progress, and the illegitimacy of those associated with retrogression. Symbols of regard and support, such as state visits and heads-of-state summits, should not be awarded without adequate human rights progress. Hard bargaining over a summit does not mean having no summit; it means getting what the administration needs out of a symbolic exchange that gives the other side something it wants.

The human rights agenda with China should include both immediate and longer-term issues. Certain goals deserve tactical priority not because they are intrinsically more important than other goals, but because of their human urgency; their importance at the center of the human rights idea; their conformity with development trends within Chinese reform; and their political, ideological, and cultural bases of support inside and outside China. Progress on these issues will open the way to progress on other topics. Priority issues include the following:

- *Release of political prisoners and international access to prisons.* Although progress on individual prisoner cases may seem to make for only superficial improvement in China's human rights situation, such cases (like that of Wei Jingsheng and Wang Dan) have crucial symbolic significance and must form a focus of Western human rights diplomacy if such diplomacy is to make sense to concerned publics in China and abroad. Because of their symbolic value, such cases should be viewed as involving more than the fate of individuals. Initiatives on individual cases should be pursued in concert with efforts to open the Chinese prison system to international humanitarian organizations such as the ICRC. This would help the central government in its goal of improving conditions of detention of all prisoners, political and otherwise.

- *Legal reform and institution-building.* The outside world can support and accelerate Chinese legal reform and the construction of Chinese legal institutions. The West should maintain a focus on key problems such as arbitrary detention, procedural safeguards in criminal trials, reform of provisions of the criminal code that violate international norms, and international access to trials. These issues touch on the basic nature of the Chinese legal system and reform in these areas already commands substantial support within China. Pressure from outside helps focus the minds of the leaders on proposals they are already receiving from internal sources.[12]
- *Ending religious repression.* This is an area of deep concern to many Western publics, and the repression is out of proportion to any realistic threat to the interests of the Chinese state.
- *Guaranteeing the continuity of civil and political rights in Hong Kong after its reversion to Chinese rule on July 1, 1997.*

Western policy should combine negative sanctions with constructive efforts such as educational and technical assistance, exchanges of specialists, and institution-building. Both government agencies and nongovernmental foundations, universities, and exchange organizations can contribute. Promising areas of institution-building include deepening Chinese involvement in the UN thematic mechanisms, building the court system, reforming legal codes, training the legal profession, upgrading prison administration, and improving social welfare systems. Businesses and other nongovernmental actors in the West (foundations and universities, among others) should maintain and enhance educational and exchange programs that assist Chinese agencies in fulfilling the Chinese government's declared human rights policies.

A policy of economic engagement is an adjunct to, not a substitute for, a human rights policy. Economic development and the opening to the West have helped raise living standards in China. But by themselves they will not solve China's human rights problems. On some fronts, economic development makes things worse (consider, for example, labor conditions in some foreign-invested and locally owned factories, abuse of migrant labor, eviction of farmers from land needed for development, and victimization of ordinary people by rising corruption).[13] In some areas, development helps improve human rights but it works slowly—too slowly, for example, to save prisoners now being mistreated in Chinese prisons—and on some human rights problems it has no effect; for example, lack of funds is not the cause of the high death rates in some Chinese orphanages.[14]

Economic development did not alone bring human rights improvements in South Korea or Taiwan—this required a long political and diplomatic struggle—and it has done little so far to improve human rights in Indonesia. The linkage between development and rights is too loose, the threshold too high, the time frame too long, and the results too uncertain to make economic engagement a substitute for direct policy intervention on human rights. A policy of economic engagement is neither an alternative to, nor a substitute for, a human rights policy. The West can walk and chew gum at the same time: Participate in China's economic development while at the same time working to improve China's compliance with the international human rights regime.

The Western business community cannot respond effectively to the human rights issue by wishing it would go away. Western businesses encounter not only practical difficulties but also public relations risks when they work in an environment that is abusive of fundamental human rights. The need to manage the issue more actively will be all the greater to the extent that the Chinese government begins to link business dealings and human rights. The business community should help the Chinese government respond constructively to Western human rights concerns, especially in areas in which business has an interest, responsibility, and experience like child labor, prison labor, women's rights, social welfare, independence of the judiciary, media freedom, and due process. Business approaches need not be confrontational. Working through technical assistance, personnel training, institution building, and grants, businesses can encourage Chinese reform to move in directions that are good for the business climate.

For its part, the human rights community should encourage consumers to take some responsibility for the conditions under which the goods they use are produced. Consumers should learn to look at labels and ask about labor rights, forced labor, and child labor in the factories that produce the goods they buy.

Human rights are not invariably the highest priority of China policy, but their importance is greater than the present administration gives them. Unless human rights are pursued consistently, Washington will lose a prime opportunity for change. When tradeoffs must be made to pursue other interests, the costs of failing to build a vital international human rights regime need to be weighed more accurately in the balance than they have been in the past.

Patience and persistence are crucial to a successful human rights policy, as they are to building any other international regime. The Chinese sometimes complain that Western human rights negotiators keep increasing their demands. In fact, the negotiation process regarding human rights should be no different from negotiating with China (or any other country) on issues related to other international regimes, such as arms control, intellectual property rights, or market access. Both sides should realize that the regime-building process is a long one; they should acknowledge long-term goals while pursuing urgent or achievable goals. The regime-building process has achieved much so far. Its further progress should not be sacrificed to a desire for smooth, conflict-free relations.

Conclusion

The Chinese government has succeeded in convincing many analysts that human rights pressure is counterproductive. Beijing has signaled that the subject cannot be part of normal diplomacy because of its need to save face, succession politics and the rise of the military, national pride in recovered sovereignty after a century of neocolonialism and exploitation, and the nationalistic "feelings of the Chinese people." Beijing has persuaded many that it cannot negotiate over human rights.

It is always useful for a government to convince its interlocutors that it is too rigid to bend on an issue. But in fact, in its human rights diplomacy as in other areas of foreign policy, China has behaved as a realist power, making those concessions it perceived as necessary to influence states with which it was interacting, and not making them when they were deemed unnecessary. Since the late 1970s, a Western human rights policy combining pressure and assistance has successfully supported an internal Chinese evolution toward improved human rights, achieving greater results when it was firm and lesser results when it was weak. The historical record suggests that the main obstacle to maintaining an effective human rights policy toward China is not Chinese intransigence but Western indecision.

China today understands the U.S. human rights policy as one of hostility, restriction, containment, and punishment. The policy should instead be articulated in a way that conveys that the United States accepts China's legitimate security and other needs but wants China to play by the international rules.[15] It should also stress that the desire to build an international human rights regime is not a code word for subverting the

Chinese system of government. At home, the Clinton administration needs to articulate its strategic rationale and thus build a domestic consensus for including human rights in its China policy.

Of all the international regimes with which the outside world wants a rising China to comply—the missile technology control regime, intellectual property rights, the WTO, and others—the international human rights regime is the oldest and the best established in international and domestic Chinese law. Less real conflict of interest exists between Chinese interests and the international regime in human rights than is the case with other areas of dispute. Moreover, the human rights regime is easily grasped by the relevant domestic publics—U.S., Chinese, European, Japanese, and others—and it can serve as a symbolic anchor for the otherwise somewhat elusive idea that the West wishes both to acknowledge China as a great power and to insist on China's obeying world rules as a great power should. In dealing with a realist power like China, the West will do better in building the human rights regime if it acts as a realist itself and maintains a consistent stand on behalf of its own interests.

Notes

Chapter 1. China Bites Back

1. "On Practice" (1937), in *Selected Works of Mao Tse-tung*, Vol. 1 (Peking: Foreign Languages Press, 1965), p. 300.

2. New York: Random House, 1994.

3. *YaMei shibao*, February 18, 1995, pp. 1–2.

4. *Dongxiang* (Hong Kong), August 1995, p. 47.

5. Lin Ke, Xu Tao, and Wu Xujun, *Lishi de zhenshi: Mao Zedong shenbian gongzuo renyuan de zhengyan* (The truth of history: the testimony of personnel who worked by Mao Zedong's side) (Hong Kong: Liwen chubanshe, 1995), pp. 110–114.

6. Song Qiang, Zhang Zangzang, and Qiao Bian, *Zhongguo keyi shuo bu: Lengzhanhou shidai de zhengzhi yu qinggan jueze* (China can say no: political and emotional choices in the post-Cold War era) (Beijing: Zhonghua gongshang lianhe chubanshe, 1996), pp. 146–147.

7. *Comrade Chiang Ch'ing* (Boston: Little, Brown, 1977).

8. Jasper Becker, *Hungry Ghosts: Mao's Secret Famine* (New York: Free Press, 1997).

9. Human Rights Watch/Asia, *Death By Default: A Policy of Fatal Neglect in China's State Orphanages* (New York: HRW/A, January 7, 1996).

10. *Hitler's Willing Executioners: Ordinary Germans and the Holocaust* (New York: Knopf, 1996), p. 414. Because I agree with this view, I regret that *The New Republic* inappositely titled my review essay "A Culture of Cruelty."

11. Daniel Chirot, *Modern Tyrants: The Power and Prevalence of Evil in Our Age* (New York: Free Press, 1994), p. 156.

12. A theoretical discussion of the relationship between culture and institutions is contained in Andrew J. Nathan and Kellee S. Tsai, "Factionalism: A New Institutionalist Restatement," *The China Journal* 34 (July 1995), pp. 157–192.

13. As I have done in *Peking Politics, 1918–1923: Factionalism and the*

Failure of Constitutionalism (Berkeley: University of California Press, 1976) and *Chinese Democracy* (New York: Knopf, 1985).

14. Forthcoming as *Political Participation in Beijing* (Cambridge: Harvard University Press, 1997).

15. New York: Columbia University Press, 1990.

16. Maurice Meisner, *The Deng Xiaoping Era: An Inquiry into the Fate of Chinese Socialism, 1978–1994* (New York: Hill and Wang, 1996), p. 343.

17. Hubert M. Blalock, Jr., *Basic Dilemmas in the Social Sciences* (Beverly Hills: Sage, 1984), pp. 90–95.

18. This lesson is often cited from Jonathan Spence, *To Change China: Western Advisers in China 1620–1960* (Boston: Little, Brown, 1969).

19. The full argument is contained in "Human Rights in Chinese Foreign Policy," *The China Quarterly* 139 (September 1994), pp. 622–643.

20. On China's foreign policy, see Andrew J. Nathan and Robert S. Ross, *The Great Wall and the Empty Fortress: China's Search for Security* (New York: Norton, 1997).

Chapter 2.   A History of Cruelty

1. Jonathan S. Spence, *The Search for Modern China* (New York: Norton, 1990).

2. Liu Binyan, *A Higher Kind of Loyalty*, Zhu Hong, trans. (New York: Pantheon, 1990).

3. Bette Bao Lord, *Legacies: A Chinese Mosaic* (New York: Knopf, 1990).

4. Jonathan N. Lipman and Stevan Harrell, eds., *Violence in China: Essays in Culture and Counterculture* (Albany: State University of New York Press, 1990), p. 1.

5. "Violence Against Women in Contemporary China," in Lipman and Harrell, eds., *Violence*, pp. 203–226.

6. *Escape from Predicament: Neo-Confucianism and China's Evolving Political Culture* (New York: Columbia University Press, 1977).

7. Liu Binyan with Ruan Ming and Xu Gang, *"Tell the World": What Happened in China and Why*, Henry L. Epstein, trans. (New York: Pantheon, 1989).

8. Norbert Elias, "Violence and Civilization: The State Monopoloy of Physical Violence and its Infringement," in John Keane, ed., *Civil Society and the State: New European Perspectives* (London: Verso, 1988), p. 197.

9. Thurston, "Urban Violence During the Cultural Revolution: Who Is to Blame?" in Lipman and Harrell, eds., *Violence*, pp. 149–174; Anne F. Thurston, *Enemies of the People* (New York: Knopf, 1987).

10. Lynn T. White III, *Policies of Chaos: The Organizational Causes of Violence in China's Cultural Revolution* (Princeton: Princeton University Press, 1989).

11. *Children of Mao: Personality Development and Political Activism in the Red Guard Generation* (Seattle: University of Washington Press, 1985).

Chapter 3.   Mao and His Court

1. This chapter consists of the following items, with footnotes added: "Foreword" in Dr. Li Zhisui with Anne F. Thurston, *The Private Life of*

Chairman Mao (New York: Random House, 1994), pp. vii-xiv; "The Road to Tiananmen Square," *The New Republic* (July 31, 1989), pp. 33–36; "The Enforcer," *The New Republic* (April 6, 1992), pp. 32–36.

2. Gaius Suetonius Tranquillus, *The Twelve Caesars*, trans. Robert Graves, revised with an introduction by Michael Grant (Harmondsworth: Penguin, 1979); Procopius, *Secret History*, trans. Richard Atwater (Ann Arbor: The University of Michigan Press, 1969); Albert Speer, *Inside the Third Reich*, trans. Richard and Clara Winston (N.Y.: Macmillan, 1970); *Svetlana Alliluyeva, Twenty Letters to a Friend*, trans Priscilla Johnson McMillan (New York: Harper and Row, 1967); Henri-Gratien Bertrand, *Napoleon at St. Helena: The Journals of General Bertrand from January to May of 1821, Deciphered and Annotated by Paul Fleuriot de Langle*, trans. Frances Hume (Garden City, N.Y.: Doubleday, 1952); David Irving, ed., *Adolf Hitler: The Medical Diaries, The Private Diaries of Dr Theo Morell* (London: Sidgwick and Jackson, 1983).

3. *Churchill, Taken from the Diaries of Lord Moran: The Struggle for Survival, 1940–1965,* (Boston: Houghton Mifflin, 1966); William H. Herndon, *Herndon's Lincoln: The True Story of A Great Life. The History and Personal Recollections of Abraham Lincoln*, 3 vols. (Chicago: Belford Clarke and Company, 1899).

4. Edited by Roderick MacFarquhar, Eugene Wu, and Timothy Cheek, with contributions by Merle Goldman and Benjamin Schwartz (Cambridge: Harvard Council on East Asian Studies, 1989).

5. Pants: Quan Yanchi, *Zouxia shentan de Mao Zedong* (Mao Zedong coming down off the altar) (Beijing: Zhongwai wenhua chuban gongsi, 1989), pp. 47–49; pork: Li Yinqiao as told to Quan Yanchi, *Zouxiang shentan de Mao Zedong* (Mao Zedong going toward the altar) (Beijing: Zhongwai wenhua chuban gongsi, 1989), p. 193.

6. *Huaqiao ribao,* June 14, 1989, p. 4.

7. Quan, *Zouxiang*, pp. 176, 192; *Zouxia*, pp. 62ff., 100, 117–18.

8. Quan, *Zouxiang*, p. 221.

9. Gong Yuzhi, Feng Xianzhi, and Shi Zhongquan, *Mao Zedong de dushu shenghuo* (Mao Zedong's reading life) (Beijing: Sanlian shudian, 1986), pp. 18–19.

10. John Byron and Robert Pack, *The Claws of the Dragon: Kang Sheng, the Evil Genius Behind Mao—and His Legacy of Terror in People's China* (New York: Simon and Schuster. 1992).

11. Boulder: Westview, 1992.

12. New York: Scribner's, 1991.

Chapter 4. Maoist Institutions and Post-Mao Reform

1. This chapter is abridged from "Totalitarianism, Authoritarianism, Democracy: The Case of China," in Myron L. Cohen, ed., *Columbia Project on Asia in the Core Curriculum: Case Studies in the Social Sciences, A Guide for Teaching* (Armonk, N.Y.: M.E. Sharpe, 1992), pp. 235–256.

2. Juan J. Linz, "Totalitarian and Authoritarian Regimes," in Fred I. Greenstein and Nelson W. Polsby, eds., *Handbook of Political Science*, Vol. 3 (Reading, MA: Addison-Wesley, 1975), pp. 175–411.

3. Andrew J. Nathan and Robert S. Ross, *The Great Wall and the Empty Fortress: China's Search for Security* (New York: Norton, 1997), ch. 1.

4. Lynn T. White, III, *Policies of Chaos: The Organizational Causes of Violence in China's Cultural Revolution* (Princeton: Princeton University Press, 1989).

5. Sulamith Heins Potter and Jack M. Potter, *China's Peasants: The Anthropology of a Revolution* (Cambridge: Cambridge University Press, 1990), Ch. 15.

6. Anita Chan, Richard Madsen, and Jonathan Unger, *Chen Village: The Recent History of a Peasant Community in Mao's China* (Berkeley: University of California Press, 1984); Andrew G. Walder, *Communist Neo-Traditionalism: Work and Authority in Chinese Industry* (Berkeley: University of California Press, 1986); Martin K. Whyte and William L. Parish, *Urban Life in Contemporary China* (Chicago: University of Chicago Press, 1984).

7. Richard Curt Kraus, *Class Conflict in Chinese Socialism* (New York: Columbia University Press, 1981).

8. Anita Chan, *Children of Mao: Personality Development and Political Activism in the Red Guard Generation* (Seattle: University of Washington Press, 1985).

9. Harry Harding, *China's Second Revolution: Reform After Mao* (Washington, D.C.: The Brookings Institution, 1987).

10. Chalmers Johnson, ed., *Change in Communist Systems* (Stanford: Stanford University Press, 1970).

Chapter 5. Chinese Democracy: The Lessons of Failure

1. Ernest P. Young, *The Presidency of Yuan Shih-k'ai: Liberalism and Dictatorship in Early Republican China* (Ann Arbor: University of Michigan Press, 1977), p. 221. The original version of this essay was presented at the Conference on the Shape of a Democratic China, American Enterprise Institute, May 1, 1991.

2. The definition follows Joseph A. Schumpeter, *Capitalism, Socialism and Democracy*, 3rd ed. (New York: Harper Torchbooks, 1962). The sense in which it is minimal has been discussed by Carole Pateman, *Participation and Democratic Theory* (Cambridge: Cambridge University Press, 1970).

3. On restrictions of political rights, see my contribution to R. Randle Edwards, Louis Henkin, and Andrew J. Nathan, *Human Rights in Contemporary China* (New York: Columbia University Press, 1986).

4. Lucian Pye, *The Dynamics of Chinese Politics* (Cambridge, MA: Oelgeschlager, Gunn and Hain, 1981).

5. See, e.g., William T. Rowe, *Hankow: Conflict and Community in a Chinese City, 1796–1895* (Stanford: Stanford University Press, 1989); David Strand, *Rickshaw Beijing: City People and Politics in the 1920s* (Berkeley: University of California Press, 1989).

6. E.g., see Susan Shirk, *Competitive Comrades* (Berkeley: University of California Press, 1982); Andrew G. Walder, *Communist Neo-Traditionalism: Work and Authority in Chinese Industry* (Berkeley: University of California Press, 1986.

7. Andrew J. Nathan and Tianjian Shi, "Cultural Requisites for Democracy in China: Findings from a Survey," *Daedalus* (Spring 1993), pp. 95–123 (chapter 11 in this volume).

8. R.J. Rummel, *China's Bloody Century: Genocide and Mass Murder Since 1900* (New Brunswick, N.J.: Transaction Publishers, 1991); *Indivisible Human Rights: The Relationship of Political and Civil Rights to Survival, Subsistence and Poverty* (New York: Human Rights Watch, 1992).

9. *Human Development Report 1990* (New York: Oxford University Press, 1990), p. 128.

10. Myron Cohen, "Cultural and Political Inventions in Modern China: The Case of the Chinese 'Peasant,'" *Daedalus* (Spring 1993), pp. 150–170.

11. James D. Seymour, "What the Agenda Has Been Missing," in Susan Whitfield, ed., *After the Event: Human Rights and Their Future in China* (London: Wellsweep, 1993), pp. 36–49.

12. Donald Share, "Transitions to Democracy and Transition through Transaction," *Comparative Political Studies* 19:4 (January 1987), pp. 525–548; Adam Przeworski, "Some Problems in the Study of the Transition to Democracy," in Guillermo O'Donnell, Philippe C. Schmitter, and Laurence Whitehead, eds., *Transitions from Authoritarian Rule: Comparative Perspectives* (Baltimore: The Johns Hopkins University Press, 1986), pp. 47–63.

Chapter 6. The Democratic Vision

1. Michel Oksenberg and Marc Lambert, eds., *Beijing Spring, 1989: Confrontation and Conflict, The Basic Documents* (Armonk, N.Y.: M.E. Sharpe, 1990); Tony Saich, ed., *The Chinese People's Movement: Perspectives on Spring 1989* (Armonk: M.E. Sharpe, 1990); Jonathan Unger, ed., *The Pro-Democracy Protests in China: Reports from the Provinces* (Armonk: M.E. Sharpe, 1991).

2. Fang Lizhi, *Bringing Down the Great Wall: Writings on Science, Culture, and Democracy in China*, ed. and trans. James Williams (New York: Knopf, 1991); Wang Ruowang, *Hunger Trilogy*, trans. Kyna Rubin with Ira Kasoff (Armonk: M.E. Sharpe, 1991); David Bachman and Dali L. Yang, ed. and trans., *Yan Jiaqi and China's Struggle for Democracy* (Armonk: M.E. Sharpe, 1991).

3. Han Minzhu and Hua Sheng, eds., *Cries for Democracy: Writings and Speeches from the 1989 Chinese Democracy Movement* (Princeton: Princeton University Press, 1990).

4. Berkeley: University of California Press, 1987.

5. Liu Xiaobo, "The Inspiration of New York: Meditations of an Iconoclast," trans. Geremie Barmé, *Problems of Communism* 40:1–2 (January–April 1991), p. 118.

Chapter 7. The Decision for Reform in Taiwan

This is a revised version of a paper presented at the Conference on Chiang Ching-kuo, University of Virginia, Charlottesville, Virginia, March 16–18, 1990. The authors would like to thank Columbia University's Taiwan

Area Studies Program for financial support; Szu-chien Hsu for research assistance; Hsu Lu for comments; and Edwin A. Winckler and other members of the Conference for criticisms and suggestions.

Abbreviations for Chapter 7 Notes

CCKHCYLC: *Chiang Tsung-t'ung Ching-kuo hsien-sheng hsien-cheng yen-lun chi* (Taipei: Kuo-min ta-hui mi-shu-ch'u, 1984).
CCKYLHP: *Chiang Tsung-t'ung Ching-kuo hsien-sheng yen-lun chu-shu hui-pien*, 15 volumes (Taipei: Li-ming wen-hua shih-yeh ku-fen you-hsien kung-ssu, 1981–1989).
CYJP: *Chung-yang jih-pao.*
HHW: *Hsin Hsin-wen.*

1. The characterization of the regime as soft authoritarian as of the mid-1980s is borrowed from Edwin A. Winckler, "Institutionalization and Participation on Taiwan: From Hard to Soft Authoritarianism?" *The China Quarterly* 99 (September 1984), pp. 481–499, although Winckler's argument is that the regime was just beginning to enter soft authoritarianism at the time he was writing. He characterizes the regime as still soft-authoritarian in "Taiwan Politics in the 1990s," in Harvey Feldman, Michael Y. M. Kau, and Ilpyong J. Kim, eds., *Taiwan in a Time of Transition* (New York: Paragon House, 1988), p. 234.

2. E.g., the essays by Whitehead, Przeworski, Stepan, and Cardoso in Guillermo O'Donnell, Philippe C. Schmitter, and Laurence Whitehead, eds., *Transitions from Authoritarian Rule: Comparative Perspectives* (Baltimore: The Johns Hopkins University Press, 1986).

3. Interview with James Soong, HHW, January 2–8, 1989, p. 17; also see interview with Ma Ying-jeou, ibid., p. 27.

4. Yangsun Chou and Andrew J. Nathan, "Democratizing Transition in Taiwan," *Asian Survey* 27:3 (March 1987), pp. 277–299; reprinted as Chapter 8 in Andrew J. Nathan, *China's Crisis: Dilemmas of Reform and Prospects for Democracy* (New York: Columbia University Press, 1990).

5. Taiwan academic, party, and legal circles had been involved for years in public discussions of some of the key issues pertinent to the future reform, including the legal status of the martial law decree and of the various martial law provisions adopted under it, ways of reforming the representative structures prior to retaking the mainland, and how to legalize the formation of new parties. It is plausible that these debates influenced CCK, but we have not been able to locate evidence of this influence. At a minimum it seems probable that when he made the decision to adopt reform policies, this discussion had prepared a broad consensus as to what the reform would have to minimally involve.

6. Tun-jen Cheng, "Taiwan in Democratic Transition," in James W. Morley, ed., *Driven by Growth: Political Change in the Asia-Pacific Region* (Armonk: M.E. Sharpe, 1993), pp. 211–212.

7. Julia Leung and Barry Wain, "Chatty Chiang Sheds No Light on

Motives Behind His Push for Democratic Reform," *Asian Wall Street Journal*, November 2, 1987, p. 16.

8. Interview with Ma Ying-jeou, HHW, January 2–8, 1989, pp. 28–29.

9. Tillman Durdin, "Chiang Ching-kuo and Taiwan: A Profile," *Orbis* 18:4 (Winter 1975), p. 1024.

10. "President Chiang Ching-kuo's Interview with an Editor of *Der Spiegel*, May 16, 1983," *Parliament Monthly* 14:6 (June 1983), pp. 3–4.

11. Interview with Wang Chia-hua, HHW, January 2–8, 1989, p. 21.

12. Ibid., p. 28.

13. CCKYLHP 12:423.

14. Hung-mao Tien, "Taiwan in Transition: Prospects for Socio-Political Change," *China Quarterly* 64 (December 1975), p. 617.

15. CCKYLHP 12:438.

16. On Deng's image in the West, see Nathan, *China's Crisis*, ch. 4.

17. Daniel Southerland, "Taiwan President to Propose End to Island's Martial Law," *Washington Post*, October 7, 1986, p. A18.

18. CCKHCYLC, p. 19.

19. CCKYLHP, 12:434.

20. CCKHCYLC, p. 84.

21. *Chung-yang jih-pao* 1986.10.13.1; English version in *Newsweek*, October 20, 1986, p. 31.

22. Ma interview, HHW, January 2–8, 1989, p. 28.

23. E.g., CCKYLHP 15:419–420.

24. The story through the 1983 election is recounted by Winckler, "Institutionalization and Participation," pp. 494–499. We have also drawn upon Li Hsiao-feng, *T'ai-wan min-chu yun-tung ssu-shih nien* (Taipei: Tzu-li wan-pao, 1987), and John F. Copper with George P. Chen, *Taiwan's Elections: Political Development and Democratization in the Republic of China*, Occasional Papers/Reprints Series in Contemporary Asian Studies, No. 5–1984 (64) (Baltimore: University of Maryland School of Law).

25. Jürgen Domes, "Political Differentiation in Taiwan: Group Formation within the Ruling Party and the Opposition Circles 1979–1980," *Asian Survey* 21:10 (October 1981), p. 1012.

26. John F. Copper, "Taiwan's Recent Election: Progress Toward a Democratic System," *Asian Survey* 21:10 (October 1981), pp. 1029–1039.

27. Li Hsiao-feng, *T'ai-wan min-chu yun-tung*, pp. 1029–1039.

28. Soong interview, HHW 89.1.2–8, p. 17.

29. *Chung-yang jih-pao* October 9, 1986, p. 2; English version in *Newsweek*, October 20, 1986, p. 31. Our thanks to Hsu Szu-chien for suggesting this analysis of Chiang's statement.

30. Analyzed in Chou and Nathan.

31. For example, Tun-jen Cheng, "Democratizing the Quasi-Leninist Regime in Taiwan," *World Politics* 61:4 (July 1989), pp. 471–499.

32. James C. Hsiung, "Taiwan in 1985: Scandals and Setbacks," *Asian Survey* 26:1 (January 1986), p. 93.

33. Tobari Haruo (Hu-chang Tung-fu), *Chiang Ching-kuo ti kai-ke* (Hong Kong: Kuang-chiao ching ch'u-pan she, 1988), pp. 77, 79.

34. Ma Ying-jeou interview, HHW, January 2–8, 1989, pp. 28–29.

35. *Chung-yang jih-pao*, October 16, 1986, p. 1. The significance of this meeting is explained in Chou and Nathan, p. 289.

36. Daniel Southerland, "Chiang Envisions Change for Taiwan," *Washington Post*, October 13, 1986, p. A18.

37. Ch'en P'ei-k'un, "T'ai-wan ti chieh-pan wei-chi," *Kuang-chiao ching* No. 157, October 16, 1985, p. 56; *Newsweek*, International Edition, October 20, 1986, pp. 28–29.

38. Ch'en P'ei-k'un, "T'ai-wan ti chieh-pan wei-chi," p. 56; Parris Chang, "Taiwan in 1982: Diplomatic Setback Abroad and Demands for Reforms at Home," *Asian Survey* 23:1 (January 1983), p. 42.

39. *Time*, September 16, 1985, p. 46. That this was Chiang's first comment on this issue is stated by Ch'en P'ei-k'un, "Taiwan ti chieh-pan wei-chi," p. 54.

40. CYJP, December 26, 1985, p. 1.

41. Daniel Southerland, "Taiwan President to Propose End to Island's Martial Law," *Washington Post*, October 8, 1986, p. A18.

42. E.g., at a meeting of the Central Standing Committee on October, 15 reported in CYJP, October 16, 1986, p. 1; and in a charge to the KMT members in the Executive Yuan involved in drafting certain reform bills, reported in CYJP, October 30, 1986, p. 1.

43. Soong interview in HHW, January 2–8, 1989, p. 17.

44. Interview with Ma Ying-jeou, HHW, January 2–8, 1989, p. 28.

45. Li Yi-an, "Taiwan ti yue-yang ta t'iao-chan," *Kuang-chiao ching* No. 165 (June 16, 1986), p. 56.

46. Edwin A. Winckler, "Elite Political Struggle 1945–1985," in Winckler and Susan Greenhalgh, eds., *Contending Approaches to the Political Economy of Taiwan* (Armonk: M. E. Sharpe, 1988), p. 157; Durdin, "Chiang and Taiwan," p. 1032.

47. CCKYLHP 10:53.

48. CCKHCYLC, p. 30.

49. Arthur J. Lerman, "National Elite and Local Politician in Taiwan," *American Political Science Review* 71:4 (December 1977), pp. 1408–1409. For the broader Chinese tradition of democracy into which this view fits, see Andrew J. Nathan, *Chinese Democracy* (Berkeley: University of California Press, 1986).

50. CCKYLHP 10:53.

51. CCKYLHP 10:537.

52. CCKYLHP 10:544.

53. CCKYLHP 10:537.

54. Przeworski in O'Donnell, et al., eds., *Transitions*, p. 47.

55. Stepan, "Paths Toward Redemocratization: Theoretical and Comparative Considerations," in O'Donnell et al., eds., *Transitions*, pp. 73–75.

56. As Andrew J. Nathan has argued in "The Effect of Taiwan's Political Reform on Mainland-Taiwan Relations," in *China's Crisis* (New York: Columbia University Press, 1990), Ch. 9.

Chapter 8. Electing Taiwan's Legislature

1. *Lien-he pao*, December 20, 1992, p. 1. Party totals include self-nominated candidates without party endorsements.

2. An account of the early stages of the transition is in Yangsun Chou and Andrew J. Nathan, "Democratizing Transition in Taiwan," *Asian Survey* 27:3 (March 1987), pp. 277–299; reprinted as chapter 8 in Andrew J. Nathan, *China's Crisis: Dilemmas of Reform and Prospects for Democracy* (New York: Columbia University Press, 1990).

3. Cf. David Butler, "Electoral Systems," in Butler et al., eds., *Democracy at the Polls: A Comparative Study of Competitive National Elections* (Washington, D.C.: American Enterprise Institute, 1981), pp. 11–19; Rein Taagepera and Matthew Soberg Shugart, *Seats and Votes: The Effects and Determinants of Electoral Systems* (New Haven: Yale University Press, 1989), p. 28. Secretary Hsu Kui-lin of the Central Election Commission told us that this system dates back to the 1947 elections on the mainland, and was modeled on the Japanese system.

4. Japan had 130 electoral districts electing 512 lower house representatives, compared to 27 ROC districts electing 119 delegates. See Gerald L. Curtis, *The Japanese Way of Politics* (New York: Columbia University Press, 1988), pp. 165–175. Japan later abandoned this system.

5. Territorial districts are those listed in table 8.1, which excludes the aboriginal, at-large, and overseas Chinese constituencies. Except as otherwise noted, the entire discussion below concerns these territorial constituencies.

6. This is leaving aside certain small districts such as P'eng-hu, Lien-chiang, and Chin-men counties where even smaller vote counts are sufficient to win because of small population size. Registered voter and turnout data are courtesy of the Central Election Commission.

7. The minimum electoral base needed to encourage a candidate to run depends on the size of the district, the number of seats to be filled, and the projected size of the vote for the top vote-getters.

8. *China Post*, December 21, 1992, p. 15. Deposits are lost when the candidate receives less than 10% of the quotient resulting from dividing the total number of eligible voters in the candidate's constituency by the total number of the officials to be elected therein. For example, if there are five candidates in a district, a candidate will lose his deposit if his vote falls below 2% of the total of registered voters. The more candidates, the smaller the percentage of the vote required to avoid forfeit.

9. Briefing at Institute for National Policy Research, December 14, 1992, later updated by Chen in personal communication. See Joseph Bosco, "Taiwan Factions: *Guanxi*, Patronage, and the State in Local Politics," *Ethnology*, 31:2 (1992), pp. 157–183.

10. *Chung-kuo shih-pao chou-k'an* (American edition), no. 52 (December 27, 1992–January 2, 1993), pp. 38–39.

11. A news magazine article claims that the Yi-kuan-tao, a religious sect, is also a KMT electoral base, casting its votes in an organized way for specific KMT candidates (ibid., pp. 40–41).

12. *China News*, December 15, 1992, p. 1. The New Taiwan dollar (NT) is exchanged at approximately 25 to US$1.

13. Ibid., December 21, 1992, p. 2.

14. The DPP's 50 legislators come from 14 identifiable factions, according to *The China News*, December 21, 1992, p. 3.

15. In this calculation (and for the KMT below) only candidates with official party nominations were counted.

16. *Chung-kuo shih-pao*, December 20, 1992, p. 6.

17. *Tzu-li wan-pao*, December 20, 1992., p. 6.

18. *Tzu-li wan-pao*, December 20, 1992, p. 2.

19. This number includes all the officially nominated DPP candidates, in territorial, aboriginal, at-large, and overseas constituencies (*Lien-he pao*, December 20, 1992, p. 2).

20. Kau Ying-mao in *Chung-kuo shih-pao*, December 21, 1992, p. 10.

21. *Chung-kuo shih-pao*, December 20, 1992, p. 7.

22. Thanks to Ming-tong Chen for this term.

23. These trends have been clear for some years, as argued by Andrew J. Nathan, "The Effect of Taiwan's Political Reform on Taiwan-Mainland Relations," in Tun-jen Cheng and Stephan Haggard, eds., *Political Change in Taiwan* (Boulder, CO: Lynne Reinner, 1992), pp. 207–219; reprinted as chapter 9 in Nathan, *China's Crisis*.

24. *Tzu-li tsao-pao*, December 20, 1992, p. 2.

25. I am grateful to Gerald L. Curtis for suggesting this point.

Chapter 9. The Struggle for Hong Kong's Future

1. Frank Welsh, *A Borrowed Place: The History of Hong Kong* (New York: Kodansha America, 1993).

2. T.L. Tsim and Bernard H. K. Luk, *The Other Hong Kong Report* (Hong Kong: Chinese University of Hong Kong Press, 1989), p. xxiv.

3. Quoted in Welsh, *Borrowed*, p. 507.

4. Christopher Patten, "Our Next Five Years: The Agenda for Hong Kong," Address at the opening of the 1992/93 Session of the Legislative Council, October 7, 1992, p. 1.

5. Cited in Zhiling Lin and Thomas W. Robinson, eds., *The Chinese and Their Future: Beijing, Taipei, Hong Kong* (Washington, D.C.: AEI Press, 1994), p. 301.

6. "Lu Ping Speech on Hong Kong's Future," from *South China Morning Post*, May 7, 1994, in Foreign Broadcast Information Service, *China: Daily Report*, May 9, 1994, p. 73.

7. Paul Chun-Kuen Kwong, *Hong Kong Trends, 1989–92: Index to the Other Hong Kong Report* (Hong Kong: Chinese University Press, 1992), p. 7.

8. "Xu Jiatun's Memoirs," from *Lien Ho Pao* May 4–13, 1993, in Foreign Broadcast Information Service, *China: Daily Report*, March 8, 1994, p. 26.

Chapter 10. Is Chinese Culture Distinctive?

This article is a contribution to the Forum on Universalism and Relativism in Asian Studies initiated in *Journal of Asian Studies* 50.1 (February 1991):

29–83. For comments, the author wishes to thank Roger Ames, Lili Armstrong, Myron L. Cohen, Michael Gasster, Charles W. Hayford, Daniel W.Y. Kwok, Margot Landman, Jeremy Paltiel, Randall P. Peerenboom, Andrew G. Walder, John R. Watt, and other participants in a seminar at the Univesity of Hawaii at Manoa on January 20, 1993, and in the Modern China Seminar, Columbia University, on May 13, 1993, as well as two anonymous reviewers for the *JAS*.

1. I am concerned with culture as a pattern of values, attitudes, beliefs, and affects, not as a pattern of behavior. The anthropologists' view of culture as including both values and behavior has its uses. But when one wants to use culture as an explanation for behavior, one must define culture as a pattern of mental attitudes separate from the pattern of behaviors that such attitudes are thought to explain.

2. "Clio's New Cultural Turn and the Rediscovery of Tradition in Asia," keynote address by Ying-Shih Yü at the Twelfth Conference of the International Association of Historians of Asia, University of Hong Kong, June 24–28, 1991, published as a pamphlet by that group. The distinction does not entirely correspond to that between humanistic and social scientific approaches, because many practicing social scientists use hermeneutic methods and there is occasional use of positivistic methods in humanistic research. Nor do the hermeneutic and positivistic approaches exhaust the list of approaches available in social sciences and humanities; Rabinow and Sullivan, for example, also refer to structuralist and neo-Marxist positions: Paul Rabinow and William M. Sullivan, "The Interpretive Turn: Emergence of an Approach," in Rabinow and Sullivan, eds., *Interpretive Social Science: A Reader* (Berkeley, Calif.: University of California Press, 1979), p. 1. The present discussion, however, has neither the need nor the space to complicate the problem.

3. Geertz, *The Interpretation of Cultures* (New York: Basic Books, 1973), p. 89; Benjamin I. Schwartz, *The World of Thought in Ancient China*, Cambridge: Harvard University Press, 1985, pp. 3, 413. Schwartz rightly points to important differences between his approach and Geertz's, but these are not relevant here.

4. Wang Gungwu, *The Chineseness of China: Selected Essays* (Hong Kong: Oxford University Press, 1991).

5. Tu Wei-ming, ed, "The Living Tree: The Changing Meaning of Being Chinese Today," special issue of *Daedalus*, Spring 1991; published under the same title by Stanford University Press, 1994.

6. Benjamin Schwartz, *China's Cultural Values*, Occasional Paper No. 18, Center for Asian Studies, Arizona State University (Tempe, Arizona: Center for Asian Studies, 1985). Schwartz developed some of the themes of his 1982 lectures in *The World of Thought in Ancient China*. I have chosen to review the shorter and earlier of the two books because it makes more explicit comparative statements, and because it has had influence among social scientists seeking concise statements about what makes Chinese culture distinctive. I do not criticize what Schwartz says, but attempt to point out how he can be misread.

7. Lucian W. Pye, *The Spirit of Chinese Politics*, New Edition (Cambridge: Harvard University Press, 1992).

8. *The Mandarin and the Cadre: China's Political Cultures* (Ann Arbor: Center for Chinese Studies, University of Michigan, 1988), p. 8.

9. Giovanni Sartori, ed. *Social Science Concepts: A Systematic Analysis* (Beverly Hills, CA: Sage Publications, 1984), pp. 44–46; Sartori, "Concept Misformation in Comparative Politics," *American Political Science Review* 64:4 (December 1970), pp. 1033–53.

10. "Among the wise," states Pye in *The Mandarin and the Cadre*, "it is unnecessary, indeed somewhat insulting, to clutter up analysis with the obvious qualification that such collectivities are not homogeneous entities" (p. 28).

11. See Arthur L. Stinchecombe, *Constructing Social Theories* (New York: Harcourt, Brace, 1968), pp. 101–129. Thanks to Andrew Walder for the citation.

12. Rodney L. Taylor, *The Religious Dimensions of Confucianism* (Albany: State University of New York Press, 1990), ch. 3.

13. Fei Xiaotong, *From the Soil: The Foundations of Chinese Society, A Translation of Fei Xiaotong's Xiangtu Zhongguo,*, trans. Gary G. Hamilton and Wang Zheng (Berkeley: University of California Press, 1992).

14. The comparison is limited to urban populations of the two societies. Ruan Danqing [elsewhere Danching], Lu Zhou, Peter M. Blau, and Andrew G. Walder, "A Preliminary Analysis of the Social Network of Residents in Tianjin with a Comparison to Social Networks in America," *Social Sciences in China* 11.3 (September 1990), pp. 68–89.

15. This point is developed in Ruan Danching, "Interpersonal Networks and Workplace Controls in Urban China," *Australian Journal of Chinese Studies* 29 (January 1993), pp. 89–105.

16. One finding of the research project described here is that "The similarity between the microstructures of interpersonal relations in the P.R.C. and the U.S. is impressive, considering the differences in culture and tradition." From Peter M. Blau, Danching Ruan, and Monika Ardelt, "Interpersonal Choice and Networks in China," *Social Forces* 69:4 (June 1991), p. 1049.

17. Lau Siu-kai and Kuan Hsin-chi, *The Ethos of the Hong Kong Chinese* (Hong Kong: The Chinese University Press, 1988), p. 101; Gabriel A. Almond and Sidney Verba, *The Civic Culture*, abridged ed. (Boston: Little, Brown, 1965), p. 148. Although Pye may not consider Hong Kong very Chinese culturally, Lau and Kuan make extensive use of Pye's arguments in interpreting their findings. In any case, the point here is to illustrate the types of findings that survey-based comparisons produce, and only secondarily to suggest a test for Pye's hypothesis.

18. Andrew J. Nathan and Tianjian Shi, "Cultural Requisites for Democracy in China: Findings From a Survey," *Daedalus* 122:2 (Spring 1993), pp. 95–123; reprinted here as chapter 11. The present essay elaborates points originally offered in the last few pages of the *Daedalus* article.

19. The ISSP is a continuing program of cross-national collaboration conducted in Australia, Germany, the United States, Great Britain, Austria, and Italy. See *International Social Survey Programme, Role of Government—1985 Codebook ZA-NO. 1490*, Ann Arbor: ICPSR, University of Michigan. The stimulus posed in the 1985 ISSP survey was, "There are some people whose views are considered extreme by the majority. Consider people who want to overthrow the government by revolution." It was followed by the same three questions.

20. See Frederick W. Frey, "Cross-Cultural Survey Research in Political Science," in Robert T. Holt and John E. Turner, *The Methodology of Comparative Research* (New York: Free Press, 1970), pp. 173–294; Sidney Verba, Norman H. Nie and Jae-on Kim, *Participation and Political Equality: A Seven Nation Comparison* (Cambridge: Cambridge University Press, 1978), pp. 32–40.

21. Nathan and Shi in *Daedalus*, pp. 108–110.

22. Richard W. Wilson, *Compliance Ideologies: Rethinking Political Culture* (Cambridge: Cambridge University Press, 1992).

23. R. David Arkush, *Fei Xiaotong and Sociology in Revolutionary China* (Cambridge, MA: Council on East Asian Studies, 1981), pp. 57–103. After 1949, the people living in the Fei team's Yunnan field site were classified as non-Han minority Bais; see David Yen-ho Wu in Tu, p. 169. This gives an ironic twist to the effort to use Fei's insights to prove the distinctiveness of Chinese culture. My thanks to Charles W. Hayford for suggesting this point.

24. Lucian W. Pye, with Mary W. Pye, *Asian Power and Politics: The Cultural Dimensions of Authority* (Cambridge: Harvard University Press, 1985), p. vii.

25. There is debate about how strong an explanation culture gives of any societal outcome. Pye's analogies of culture to music (in *Asian Power and Politics*, p. 20) or to grammar (in *Mandarin and Cadre*, p. 9) seem to me about right. And how much difference has a country's musical tradition or grammar made to its modernization or democratization? The alternative to a cultural explanation is usually an institutional or structural one. See, for example, David J. Elkins and Richard E. B. Simeon, "A Cause in Search of Its Effect, or What Does Political Culture Explain?" *Comparative Politics* 11 (January 1979), pp. 127–45; Bruce J. Dickson, "What Explains Chinese Political Behavior? The Debate Over Structure and Culture," *Comparative Politics* 25.1 (October 1992), pp. 103–18. Pye, however, considers this debate "pointless"; *Mandarin*, pp. 20–22.

26. Metzger, *Escape From Predicament* (New York: Columbia University Press, 1977).

27. *Mandarin and Cadre*, p. 30.

28. Arkush, *Fei*, p. 144.

29. Although the difference in the prevalence and functions of networks versus organizations in China and the West remains largely an empirical mystery, the two societies are demonstrably different in the self-image that each has about its respective reliance on networks and organizations. For this statement, the Fei and Hamilton essays themselves serve as evidence, because each embodies its own society's self-perception of the difference.

Although the difference in self-perception does not prove that there is a difference in social functioning, it reasonably generates the hypothesis that there is. But one cannot test this hypothesis by using separate conceptual categories for separate countries.

30. Schwartz persuasively rebuts such a claim in *The World of Thought*, pp. 3–7.

31. Ambrose King seems to place himself in the same contradiction when he argues both that *guanxi* is a uniquely Chinese phenomenon and that for this very reason the word should be incorporated into modern social science as an analytic term. King in Tu, ed., p. 68.

Chapter 11. Cultural Requisites for Democracy in China

The authors acknowledge the support of National Science Foundation grant INT-88–14199, a grant from the United Daily News Cultural Foundation, and the assistance of the Opinion Research Center of China, Social and Economic Research Institute of Beijing, under directors Chen Ziming and Wang Juntao.

1. See, for example, Lucian W. Pye with Mary W. Pye, *Asian Power and Politics: The Cultural Dimensions of Authority* (Cambridge: Harvard University Press, 1985); Lucian W. Pye, *The Mandarin and the Cadre: China's Political Cultures* (Ann Arbor: Center for Chinese Studies, 1988); Andrew J. Nathan, *Chinese Democracy* (New York: Knopf, 1985); and various articles in "The Living Tree: The Changing Meaning of Being Chinese Today," *Daedalus* 120:2 (Spring 1991).

2. Pye, *Mandarin and Cadre*, p. 8, uses this term.

3. Well-known examples of this kind of work dealing with China, besides those cited above, include Lucian W. Pye, *The Spirit of Chinese Politics* (Cambridge: MIT Press, 1967); Benjamin I. Schwartz, *China's Cultural Values* (Tempe, AZ: Center of Asian Studies, 1985); and Richard H. Solomon, *Mao's Revolution and the Chinese Political Culture* (Berkeley: University of California Press, 1971).

4. Outstanding examples of the use of this approach include Gabriel A. Almond and Sidney Verba, *The Civic Culture* (Princeton: Princeton University Press, 1963; abr. ed., Boston: Little, Brown, 1965; abr. ed. reprint, Newbury Park, Calif.: Sage Publications, 1989); Alex Inkeles and David H. Smith, *Becoming Modern: Individual Change in Six Developing Countries* (Cambridge: Harvard University Press, 1974); Samuel H. Barnes et al., *Political Action: Mass Participation in Five Western Democracies* (Beverly Hills, CA: Sage Publications, 1979); Ronald Inglehart, *Culture Shift in Advanced Industrial Societies* (Princeton: Princeton University Press, 1990); and Scott C. Flanagan et al., *The Japanese Voter* (New Haven: Yale University Press, 1991).

5. Gabriel A. Almond, "The Study of Political Culture," in A Discipline Divided (Newbury Park, CA: Sage Publications, 1990), p. 42.

6. According to Ibid., 143–44, political culture consists of the set of subjective orientations to politics in a national population or subset of a national population; has cognitive, affective, and evaluative components; is the result of childhood socialization, education, media exposure, and adult political

experiences; and reflects and affects political and governmental structure and performance.

7. A possible exception is a survey conducted by the State Statistical Bureau for Ronald Inglehart on materialism and postmaterialism. At the time of writing this paper, we do not know the details of this study. Statistical induction is the process of generalizing from the characteristics of a sample to the characteristics of the population from which it was selected.

8. See, for example, Paul J. Hiniker, *Revolutionary Ideology and Chinese Reality: Dissonance Under Mao* (Beverly Hills, CA: Sage Publications, 1977); Solomon, *Mao's Revolution*; Susan L. Shirk, *Competitive Comrades: Career Incentives and Student Strategies in China* (Berkeley: University of California Press, 1982); Nathan, *Chinese Democracy*; William L. Parish and Martin King Whyte, *Village and Family in Contemporary China* (Chicago: University of Chicago Press, 1978); and Martin King Whyte and William L. Parish, *Urban Life in Contemporary China* (Chicago: University of Chicago Press, 1984).

9. Dong Li, "Public Opinion Polls and Political Attitudes in China, 1979–89," (Ph.D. diss., Columbia University, 1993).

10. Min Qi, *Zhongguo zhengzhi wenhua* (Kunming: Yunnan renmin chubanshe, 1989). By national, we mean covering the entire Chinese mainland with the possible exception of certain remote and lightly populated areas.

11. Previous large-scale studies of mass behavior in communist societies were based on surveys of emigrants. The largest were reported in Alex Inkeles and Raymond A. Bauer, *The Soviet Citizen* (Cambridge: Harvard University Press, 1959) and James R. Millar, ed., *Politics, Work, and Daily Life in the USSR: A Survey of Former Soviet Citizens* (New York: Cambridge University Press, 1987). Since the fall of communism, the survey enterprise has accelerated in the postcommunist societies, but national level surveys remain rare. We are aware of surveys in progress by Arthur H. Miller (Russia, Ukraine, and Lithuania); James Gibson (Russia); Samuel Barnes and Peter McDonough (Eastern Europe); and Sidney Verba, Cynthia S. Kaplan, and Henry E. Brady (Russia and Estonia).

12. The ISSP is a continuing program of cross-national collaboration conducted in Australia, Germany, the United States, Great Britain, Austria, and Italy. It brings together preexisting national social science projects and coordinates research goals by adding a cross-national perspective to the individual national studies. See *International Social Survey Programme, Role of Government—1985 Codebook ZA-NO. 1490* (Ann Arbor: ICPSR, University of Michigan).

13. We define democracy as a system of authentically competitive elections for national and local offices. Authentic competition requires freedom of political organization, freedom of political speech, the right of citizens to run for office, and the secret ballot.

14. Almond and Verba, *Civic Culture*; J. Roland Pennock, *Democratic Political Theory* (Princeton: Princeton University Press, 1979), pp. 36–59; and Robert A. Dahl, *A Preface to Democratic Theory* (Chicago: The University of Chicago Press, 1956). Some works stress cultural prerequisites for democratization; some stress cultural requisites for the stability of democratic systems.

Although the two arguments are logically distinct, the attributes cited are generally the same.

15. James L. Gibson and Raymond M. Duch, "Emerging Democratic Values in Soviet Political Culture," in Arthur H. Miller, William M. Reisinger, and Vicki L. Hesli, eds., *Public Opinion and Regime Change: The New Politics of Post-Soviet Societies* (Boulder, CO: Westview, 1993), p. 1.

16. Almond and Verba, *Civic Culture*, pp. 9–88; abr. ed., pp. 6–52. Of course, the term "local government" refers to different objects in different countries; this partially explains different levels of awareness in different countries. In China, for example, people may think it is the "party" or "cadres" and not the "government" that affects their lives locally. But if one anticipates this and asks a different question in each country, the results cannot be considered comparable. Generally, the most equivalent stimulus is the one that uses the most similar language. After getting an initial measure of differences across countries based on an equivalent stimulus, one can ask additional questions to explore hypotheses that one thinks may explain cross-national differences.

17. Revisionist views have been presented by Vivienne Shue, *The Reach of the State* (Stanford: Stanford University Press, 1988), and Victor Nee, David Stark, and Mark Selden, eds., *Remaking the Economic Institutions of Socialism: China and Eastern Europe* (Stanford: Stanford University Press, 1989), among others.

18. Parish and Whyte, *Village and Family in Contemporary China*; Whyte and Parish, *Urban Life in Contemporary China*; and Jean C. Oi, *State and Peasant in Contemporary China: The Political Economy of Village Government* (Berkeley: University of California Press, 1989).

19. Samuel P. Huntington and Joan M. Nelson, *No Easy Choice* (Cambridge: Harvard University Press, 1976), pp. 3–45.

20. We distinguish rural and urban sectors by the respondent's type of household registration. The actual place of residence at the time of the survey may be different, but the household registration establishes an individual's legal permanent residence, and usually corresponds to the actual place of residence.

21. Almond and Verba, *Civic Culture*, p. 6; abr. ed., p. 2.

22. These figures accord closely with those for the population as a whole derived from census data, testifying to the accuracy of our sample.

23. Almond and Verba, *Civic Culture*, pp. 7–19; abr. ed., pp. 6–17.

24. See among others, Norman H. Nie, G. Bingham Powell, Jr., and Kenneth Prewitt, "Social Structure and Political Participation: Developmental Relationships," Parts I and II, *American Political Science Review* 63:2 (1961), pp. 361–78; and 63 (3) (1961), pp. 808–32; Lester Milbrath and M. L. Goel, *Political Participation: How and Why Do People Get Involved in Politics?*, 2d ed. (Chicago: Rand McNally, 1977), pp. 58–59; Russell J. Dalton, *Citizen Politics in Western Democracies* (Chatham, N.J.: Chatham House Publishers, 1988), p. 50; and M. Stephen Weatherford, "Measuring Political Legitimacy," *American Political Science Review* 86:1 (March 1992), pp. 149–66.

25. Angus Campbell, Gerald Gurin, and Warren E. Miller, *The Voter Decides* (Evanston, IL: Row, Peterson, 1954), p. 187.

26. Almond and Verba, *Civic Culture,* p. 14; abr. ed., pp. 168–69.

27. Campbell, Gurin, and Miller, *The Voter Decides.*

28. Stephen C. Craig, Richard G. Niemi, and Glenn E. Silver, "Political Efficacy and Trust: A Report on the NES Pilot Study Items," *Political Behavior* 12:3 (September 1990), p. 290.

29. To avoid response set, some questions are asked in a positive form, some in a negative form; for national-level political understanding, a "disagree" answer indicates efficacy.

30. For example, "People like me don't have any say about what the government does."

31. Milbrath and Goel, *Political Participation,* chap. 3 and 4.

32. Almond and Verba, *Civic Culture,* pp. 110–11; abr. ed., pp. 73–74.

33. They are explored in Tianjian Shi, "Political Participation in Beijing: a Survey Study," Ph.D. diss., Columbia University, 1992; published as *Political Participation in Beijing* (Cambridge: Harvard University Press, 1997).

34. Ibid.

35. See among others, Larry Diamond, Juan Linz, and Seymour Martin Lipset, eds., *Democracy in Developing Countries: Asia,* vol. 3 (Boulder, CO: Lynne Rienner, 1989), pp. 16–17; James L. Gibson, "The Political Consequences of Intolerance: Cultural Conformity and Political Freedom," *American Political Science Review* 86:2 (June 1992), pp. 338–56; and Gibson and Duch, "Emerging Democratic Values," p. 72.

36. Lucian W. Pye, *The Spirit of Chinese Politics,* new ed. (Cambridge: Harvard University Press, 1992), pp. 67–84.

37. *International Social Survey Programme, Role of Government—1985 Codebook.*

38. The Gang of Four is a very different stimulus from revolution, but we would have endangered our project if we had raised the question of overthrowing the government in China. The Gang of Four was the most equivalent feasible stimulus we could think of. Many of the population attribute their suffering during the Cultural Revolution to the Gang of Four. In the early 1980s, the regime carried out a purge of alleged sympathizers of the Gang, expelling many from the Party and giving prison terms to some.

39. These figures are net of "don't know" answers, which constituted 18.0 percent on speaking, 20.9 percent on teaching, and 21.2 percent on publishing. The high "don't know" percentages indicate that for many respondents the question was too controversial to answer.

40. Seymour Martin Lipset, *Political Man,* exp. and updated ed. (Baltimore: Johns Hopkins University Press, 1981), chap. 4; and Gibson, "Political Consequences," p. 346.

41. This is with the exception of the two cases from the American sample who had no formal education and were intolerant. We deleted them from the display because their tiny number makes the association between education and intolerance in their case statistically insignificant.

42. These findings are consistent with those of Evelyn Sakakida Rawski, *Education and Popular Literacy in Ch'ing China* (Ann Arbor: The University of Michigan Press, 1979).

43. We could recalculate the figures in terms of urban and rural places of birth instead of urban and rural places of current household registration, and correct for disproportionate deaths above the national average in each population segment in order to recover the population makeup of earlier time periods.

44. Our data show that tolerance levels in China decrease sharply with age.

45. Ted Robert Gurr, *Why Men Rebel* (Princeton: Princeton University Press, 1970).

46. Ambrose Yeo-chi King, "Guanxi and Network Building: A Sociological Interpretation," *Daedalus* 120:2 (Spring 1991), pp. 63–84.

Chapter 12.   Left and Right in Deng's China

The authors acknowledge the support of National Science Foundation grant INT-88–14199, a grant from the United Daily News Cultural Foundation, and the assistance of the Opinion Research Center of China, Social and Economic Research Institute of Beijing, under the directors Chen Ziming and Wang Juntao. An earlier version of the paper was presented at the Conference on Left, Right, and Center: Party and Ideology after the Cold War, sponsored by the Symposium on Science, Reason, and Modern Democracy, at Michigan State University, April 21–24, 1994. That paper is to be published in different form in a book edited by Arthur M. Melzer, Jerry Weinberger, and M. Richard Zinman. For comments we are grateful to conference participants and to Michael R. Chambers, Margot E. Landman, Dong Li, Kenneth Lieberthal, James D. Seymour, Robert Y. Shapiro, Lawrence R. Sullivan, Kellee S. Tsai, and Lynn T. White III.

1. Seymour Martin Lipset and Stein Rokkan, *Party Systems and Voter Alignments* (New York: Free Press, 1967).

2. Arend Lijphart, "Political Parties: Ideologies and Programs," in David Butler, Howard R. Penniman, and Austin Ranney, eds., *Democracy at the Polls: A Comparative Study of Competitive National Elections* (Washington, D.C.: American Enterprise Institute, 1981).

3. For example, see Russell J. Dalton, Scott C. Flanagan, and Paul Allen Beck, eds., *Electoral Change in Advanced Industrial Democracies: Realignment or Dealignment?* (Princeton: Princeton University Press, 1984); Arend Lijphart, "Religious vs. Linguistic vs. Class Voting," *American Political Science Review* 73 (June 1979); and Sidney Verba, Norman H. Nie, and Jae-on Kim, *Participation and Political Equality: A Seven Nation Comparison* (New York: Cambridge University Press, 1978).

4. Ronald Inglehart, *Culture Shift in Advanced Industrial Societies* (Princeton: Princeton University Press, 1990), pp. 73–78.

5. Pamela Johnston Conover and Stanley Feldman, "The Origins and Meaning of Liberal/Conservative Self-Identifications," *American Political Science Review* 25 (November 1981); and Stanley Feldman and John Zaller,

"The Political Culture of Ambivalence: Ideological Responses to the Welfare State," *American Journal of Political Science* 36 (February 1992).

6. Shawn Rosenberg, "The Structure of Political Thinking," *American Journal of Political Science* 32 (August 1988); and Paul M. Sniderman et al., *Reasoning and Choice: Explorations in Political Psychology* (Cambridge: Cambridge University Press, 1991).

7. John R. Zaller, *The Nature and Origins of Mass Opinion* (Cambridge: Cambridge University Press, 1992), p. 6.

8. Hans D. Klingemann, "Measuring Ideological Conceptualizations," in Samuel H. Barnes et al., *Political Action: Mass Participation in Five Western Democracies* (Beverly Hills, CA: Sage Publications, 1979), p. 29.

9. Ibid., 230.

10. Philip E. Converse, "The Nature of Belief Systems in Mass Publics," in David E. Apter, ed., *Ideology and Discontent* (New York: Free Press, 1964). But see Christopher H. Achen, "Mass Political Attitudes and the Survey Response," *American Political Science Review* 69 (December 1975); and Inglehart, *Culture Shift*, ch. 3.

11. Robert Axelrod, "Where the Votes Come From: An Analysis of Electoral Coalitions, 1952–1968," *American Political Science Review* 66 (March 1972); Douglas A. Hibbs Jr., "Political Parties and Macroeconomic Policy," *American Political Science Review* 71 (December 1977); Seymour Martin Lipset, *Political Man: The Social Bases of Politics*, rev. ed. (Baltimore: Johns Hopkins University Press, 1981), pp. 30–300; and Herbert McCloskey and Alida Brill, *Dimensions of Tolerance: What Americans Believe about Civil Liberties* (New York: Russell Sage Foundation, 1983), pp. 70–414.

12. Cognitive sophistication is also referred to as cognitive mobilization, cognitive ability, cognitive competence, and political sophistication, among other terms. Philip E. Converse, "Public Opinion and Voting Behavior," in Fred I. Greenstein and Nelson W. Polsby, eds., *Handbook of Political Science*, vol. 4 (Reading, MA: Addison-Wesley, 1975); Ronald Inglehart, "Cognitive Mobilization and European Identity," *Comparative Politics* 3 (October 1970); Robert C. Luskin, "Measuring Political Sophistication," *American Journal of Political Science* 31 (November 1987); Norman H. Nie, Sidney Verba, and John R. Petrocik, *The Changing American Voter*, rev. ed. (Cambridge: Harvard University Press, 1979), pp. 48–55; and Sniderman et al., *Reasoning and Choice*.

13. Benjamin I. Page and Robert Y. Shapiro, *The Rational Public: Fifty Years of Trends in Americans' Policy Preferences* (Chicago: University of Chicago Press, 1992), p. 15.

14. Angus Campbell et al., *The American Voter* (1960; reprint, New York: John Wiley, 1980), chaps. 9–10; Daniel Lerner, *The Passing of Traditional Society: Modernizing the Middle East* (New York: Free Press, 1958); Rosenberg, "Structure,"; Sniderman et al., *Reasoning and Choice*; and James A. Stimson, "Belief Systems: Constraint, Complexity, and the 1972 Election," *American Journal of Political Science* 19 (August 1975).

15. Campbell et al., *American Voter*, p. 204.

16. Richard Curt Kraus, *Class Conflict in Chinese Socialism* (New York: Columbia University Press, 1981).

17. See, for example, Mao Zedong, "Resolution on Certain Questions in the History of Our Party," in *Selected Works of Mao Tse-tung*, vol. 3 (Peking: Foreign Languages Press, 1965).

18. [Mao Zedong], *Selected Works of Mao Tse-tung* (Peking: Foreign Languages Press, 1977), 4:184.

19. Yan Jiaqi and Gao Gao, *Wenhua dageming shinianshi* (History of the ten-year cultural revolution), rev. ed., 2 vols. (Taipei: Yuanliu chuban shiye gufen youxian gongsi, 1990), pp. 90–108.

20. Ibid., pp. 646–48; cf. William A. Joseph, *The Critique of Ultra-Leftism in China, 1958–1981* (Stanford: Stanford University Press, 1984).

21. Ruan Ming, *Deng Xiaoping diguo* (The empire of Deng Xiaoping) (Taipei: Shibao wenhua chuban shiye youxian gongsi, 1992).

22. As seen in the book title, Lü Wen (pseud.), *Zhongguo "zuo" huo* (China's "left" disasters) (Beijing: Chaohua chubanshe, 1993).

23. Perry Link, *Evening Chats in Beijing: Probing China's Predicament* (New York: Norton, 1992); Ching-chang Hsiao and Mei-rong Yang, " 'Don't Force Us to Lie': The Case of the *World Economic Herald*," in Chin-Chuan Lee, ed., *Voices of China: The Interplay of Politics and Journalism* (New York: Guilford Press, 1990); and Judy Polumbaum, "The Tribulations of China's Journalists after a Decade of Reform," in Chin-Chuan Lee.

24. Dong Li, "Public Opinion Polls and Political Attitudes in China, 1979–89" (Ph.D. diss., Columbia University, 1993), chap. 3.

25. Cf. ibid., chap. 4.

26. Marlowe Hood, "Reflections on Civil Society, 'Black Society,' and Corruption in Contemporary China" (Paper presented at the annual meeting of the Association for Asian Studies, Boston, March 25–27, 1994); Mayfair Mei-hui Yang, *Gifts, Favors, and Banquets: The Art of Social Relationships in China* (Ithaca: Cornell University Press, 1994).

27. X. L. Ding, *The Decline of Communism in China: Legitimacy Crisis, 1977–1989* (Cambridge: Cambridge University Press, 1994); Merle Goldman, *Sowing the Seeds of Democracy in China: Political Reform in the Deng Xiaoping Era* (Cambridge: Harvard University Press, 1994); and Link, *Evening Chats.*

28. Andrew J. Nathan, *Chinese Democracy* (New York: Knopf, 1985).

29. "On Questions of Party History: Resolution on Certain Questions in the History of Our Party since the Founding of the People's Republic of China," *Beijing Review* 24, no. 27 (July 6, 1981), pp. 10–39.

30. Baogang He, "Three Models of Democracy: Intellectual and Moral Foundations of Liberal Democracy and Preconditions for Its Establishment in Contemporary China" (Ph.D. diss., Australian National University, 1993), p. 257.

31. Li, "Public Opinion Polls," ch. 6.

32. Because of our expectation that left-right concepts would not be meaningful to respondents, our 1990 survey did not include a measure of left-right self-placement. Our 1993 surveys in mainland China, Taiwan, and Hong Kong included not only the issue priority battery reported here, but also a Chinese-traditionalism battery; a left-right placement battery for self,

CCP, father, and KMT; and a number of other relevant questions (speed of reform and of social change, liberalism, civil liberties, democracy). We plan to use these questions to compare the dimensionality of Chinese political issues across the three Chinese political systems.

33. As with similar questions commonly used in surveys in the West (e.g., Nie, Verba, and Petrocik, *Changing American Voter;* Page and Shapiro, *Rational Public*), we asked about issues we knew were on the public's mind. A technique used by researchers at National Taiwan University is to derive the issues they ask about from the platforms of candidates in election campaigns; see, e.g., Fu Hu, "The Electoral Mechanism and Political Change in Taiwan," in Steve Tsang, ed., *In the Shadow of China: Political Developments in Taiwan since 1949* (London: Hurst, 1993), pp. 54–59. This reduces the risk that issues will be arbitrarily left off the list. Because of the lack of competitive elections in China, that option was not available to us. It should also be noted that this item was not designed to be used as we use it here, to test hypotheses about ideological dimensions. Nonetheless, it proved usable in this way.

34. Besides Beijing, there were demonstrations in at least thirty other cities, but few are known to have occurred outside cities.

35. Low expressed interest, in turn, may reflect an issue's lack of perceived salience to the respondent or the respondent's lack of information about the issue, or both. The difference between these two causes is not germane to the analysis here. Alternatively, one might hypothesize that "don't know" answers are given when an issue is politically too sensitive or dangerous to talk about honestly. In another article, however, one of us has demonstrated that this is not the case. "Don't know" responses are correlated with measures of respondents' cognitive deficiency rather than with measures of their political vulnerability. Tianjian Shi, "Survey Research in China," in Michael X. Delli Carpini, Leoni Huddy, and Robert Y. Shapiro, eds., *Research in Micropolitics, vol. 5, New Directions in Political Psychology* (Greenwich, CT: Jai Press, 1996).

36. Factor analysis is best used to confirm the existence of dimensions that were theorized in advance. Otherwise, the risk is that almost any factor structure can be given a forced interpretation. As noted earlier, we did not have a theory of issue dimensions in mind when we constructed the list of issue items. But since the individual items have the kinds of face relationships that are described in the text, we feel justified in proceeding to factor analysis. The validity of the factor analysis gains further credibility when the factor results prove to be meaningful with respect to other variables in the study, as in Table 12.3.

37. There is no reason to expect all the items to cluster tightly around a given number of factors, since the list of items presented to respondents was not drawn up to test a theory of issue dimensions.

38. The weak loading of "environment" and "consumer rights" on this factor may support Inglehart's suggestion that materialist and postmaterialist issues are distinct in the public mind. But a separate factor analysis of these six items alone produced loadings on only one factor, not two. Six items may be too few to reveal the materialist-postmaterialist cleavage.

39. Type of household registration is not a measure of actual place of residence. However, those registered in the cities tend to live in cities, while those registered in rural areas either live in rural areas or are in the cities temporarily, without access to the privileges accorded urban residents. Sulamith Heins Potter and Jack M. Potter, *China's Peasants: The Anthropology of a Revolution* (Cambridge: Cambridge University Press, 1990), chap. 15.

40. Table 12.4 is a better guide than Table 12.3 to the impact of age and sex on selection of agendas, because it shows their effects when other variables are controlled.

41. For similar arguments about the former USSR, see Ada W. Finifter and Ellen Mickiewicz, "Redefining the Political System of the USSR: Mass Support for Political Change," *American Political Science Review* 86 (December 1992); and Arthur H. Miller, Vicki L. Hesli, and William M. Reisinger, "Reassessing Mass Support for Political and Economic Change in the Former USSR," in *American Political Science Review* 88 (June 1994).

42. These sets of questions touch on what Flanagan calls the "authoritarian-liberal" dimension. Our questions are not the same as his because we designed the questionnaire to collect information on public attitudes to certain specific issues of concern to us. Our 1993 questionnaire includes a "traditionalism" battery that includes some of Flanagan's items and others analogous to his. Scott Flanagan, "Value Change in Industrial Societies," *American Political Science Review* 81 (December 1987).

43. The statements were
—If there are too many political parties in a country, it will lead to political chaos.
—If people's ideas are not united, there will be chaos in society.
—Broadening the scope of democracy in our country now would affect stability.
—It is now very necessary to broaden the scope of democracy in our country.
—The realization of democracy in our country depends upon the leadership of the party.
—Some people believe heads of cities (counties) should be elected by the people, others believe they should be appointed by the higher authorities. What do you think?

44. The questions were
—Do you care if you do not have a son?
—A couple has been married many years, but their feelings all along were incompatible, and the wife has fallen in love with another man. Some people think that under this type of situation, it should be permitted for the couple to divorce; some people think it should not be permitted for them to divorce. What is your opinion?
—If your unmarried son wanted to marry a divorced woman, would you approve?
—If your immediate supervisor were a woman, would you feel annoyed?

—The educational level of a wife should not be higher than her husband's.

—The salary of a wife should not be more than her husband's.

—Ruthless criminals should be punished immediately, without having to follow complicated legal procedures.

—When trying a major case, the judge should solicit the opinions of the local government.

45. Nathan, *Chinese Democracy*; this interpretation gains support from the fact that the same constituency supports pro-democratic attitudes and the Tiananmen Agenda, as we are about to show.

46. We acknowledge the possibility that respondents were afraid to withhold agreement from this proposition, since CCP leadership is one of Deng Xiaoping's "four basic principles," which every Chinese citizen is supposed to support. This analysis should not be taken to imply that Chinese political culture is inhospitable to democratization; cf. Andrew J. Nathan and Tianjian Shi, "Cultural Requisites for Democracy in China: Findings from a Survey," *Daedalus* 122 (Spring 1993) (chapter 11 in the present volume); and Andrew J. Nathan, "Is Chinese Culture Distinctive?" *Journal of Asian Studies* 52 (November 1993) (chapter 10 in the present volume).

47. For example, Elisabeth J. Croll, *Changing Identities of Chinese Women: Rhetoric, Experience, and Self-Perception in the Twentieth Century* (Hong Kong: Hong Kong University Press, 1995); Xiaoxian Gao, "China's Modernization and Changes in the Social Status of Rural Women," trans. S. Katherine Campbell, in Christina K. Gilmartin et al., eds., *Engendering China: Women, Culture, and the State* (Cambridge: Harvard University Press, 1994); and Margery Wolf, *Revolution Postponed: Women in Contemporary China* (Stanford, CA: Stanford University Press, 1985).

48. We asked more questions about gender attitudes in our 1993 survey, which will enable us to test this hypothesis.

49. McCloskey and Brill, *Dimensions of Tolerance*, ch. 4; James W. Prothro and Charles M. Grigg, "Fundamental Principles of Democracy: Bases of Agreement and Disagreement," *Journal of Politics* 22 (May 1960).

50. Nathan and Shi, "Cultural Requisites."

51. Factor analysis confirmed that the three sets of questions concern three different issue-areas, each of which emerged as a distinct factor. Thus, scaling is an appropriate technique here. The democracy and social liberalism scales ran from 1 to 6, and procedural liberalism from 1 to 2.

52. McCloskey and Brill, *Dimensions of Tolerance*; and Page and Shapiro, *Rational Public*.

53. We decided to exclude Tibet from this study for a number of reasons. Transportation there is difficult since there is no railroad and the highway system is not well developed. Many Tibetans do not speak Chinese. And it is difficult to find qualified interviewers to work there.

54. Guowuyuan renkou pucha bangongshi (State Council, Population Census Office), *Zhongguo 1990 nian renkou pucha 10% chouyang ziliao* (Ten percent sample data of China's 1990 census), electronic data edition, ed.

Guojia tongjiju renkou tongjisi (Beijing: State Statistical Bureau Office of Population Statistics, 1990).

55. Ministry of Public Security of the PRC, ed., *Quanguo fenxianshi renkou tongji ziliao, 1986* (Population statistics by city and county of the People's Republic of China, 1986) (Beijing: Ditu chubanshe, 1987).

Chapter 13. The Place of Values in Cross-Cultural Studies

For comments on earlier drafts of this paper I am grateful to Paul Cohen and Merle Goldman, who edited the volume in which it first appeared, to participants in the Modern China Seminar and the Comparative Politics Group at Columbia University, and to Lisa Anderson, Linda Gail Arrigo, Douglas A. Chalmers, Michael Gasster, James C. Hsiung, Peter Juviler, Anthony Kane, Terrill E. Lautz, Steven I. Levine, Thomas A. Metzger, Don K. Price, James D. Seymour, James N.C. Tu, Ned Walker, John R. Watt, C. Martin Wilbur, Roxane Witke, and Kenton Worcester.

1. See, among others, Giovanni Sartori, "Philosophy, Theory and Science of Politics," *Political Theory*, 2:2 (May 1974), pp. 133–162; Richard J. Bernstein, *The Restructuring of Social and Political Theory* (Philadelphia: University of Pennsylvania Press, 1978) and *Beyond Objectivism and Relativism: Science, Hermeneutics, and Praxis* (Philadelphia: University of Pennsylvania Press, 1983); Abraham Edel, *Science, Ideology, and Value* (New Brunswick, N.J.: Transaction Books, 1979), 1:276–332 and 2:339–363; Norma Haan, Robert N. Bellah, Paul Rabinow, and William M. Sullivan, eds., *Social Science as Moral Inquiry* (New York: Columbia University Press, 1983); Duncan MacRae, Jr., *The Social Function of Social Science* (New Haven: Yale University Press, 1976), Chs. 3–4; Frank Fischer, *Politics, Values, and Public Policy: The Problem of Methodology* (Boulder, CO: Westview Press, 1980).

2. I have in mind works like Thomas A. Metzger's *Escape from Predicament* (New York: Columbia University Press, 1977) and Wm. Theodore de Bary's *New-Confucian Orthodoxy and the Learning of the Mind-and-Heart* (New York: Columbia University Press, 1981). Authors who undertake such a project may have a passionate value agenda of their own, and it may be quite clear from their work, yet the works in question are essentially descriptive rather than advocatory or judgmental.

3. See David Bidney, "Culture: Cultural Relativism," in David L. Sills, ed., *International Encyclopedia of the Social Sciences* (New York: Macmillan, 1968), 3, pp. 543–547.

4. For example, Peter Winch, "Understanding a Primitive Society," in *Ethics and Action* (London: Routledge and Kegan Paul, 1972), pp. 8–49; Paul Rabinow and William M. Sullivan, eds., *Interpretive Social Science: A Reader* (Berkeley: University of California Press, 1979); Martin Hollis and Steven Lukes, eds., *Rationality and Relativism* (Oxford: Basil Blackwell, 1982); Gerald James Larson and Eliot Deutsch, eds., *Interpreting Across Boundaries: New Essays in Comparative Philosophy* (Princeton: Princeton University Press, 1988). An extreme position is that of Edward Said, *Orientalism* (New York: Pantheon, 1978), who argues that the difficulty of cross-cultural under-

standing is so great as to bring into question question "whether there can be true representations of anything" (p. 272).

5. See, among others, Charles Taylor, "Interpretation and the Sciences of Man," in Rabinow and Sullivan, *Interpretive Social Science*, pp. 25–71; Alisdair MacIntyre, "Is a Science of Comparative Politics Possible?" in his *Against the Self-Images of the Age: Essays on Ideology and Philosophy* (Notre Dame: University of Notre Dame Press, 1978), pp. 260–279. Howard J. Wiarda's "Is Latin America Democratic and Does It Want To Be?" in Wiarda, ed., *The Continuing Struggle for Democracy in Latin America* (Boulder, CO: Westview Press, 1980), pp. 3–24, illustrates the danger of confusing these two questions. discusses the conceptual distortions that arise when Western-based concepts are carelessly used in the *analysis* of Latin American politics, but then slides, in my view illogically, to the conclusion that Western values should not be used to *evaluate* Latin American politics.

6. See Paul Rabinow, "Humanism as Nihilism: The Bracketing of Truth and Seriousness in American Cultural Anthropology," in Haan, et al., eds., *Social Science as Moral Inquiry*, pp. 52–75.

7. John K. Fairbank, *China: The People's Middle Kingdom and the U.S.A.* (Cambridge: Harvard University Press, 1967), p. 142.

8. "Our Chances in China," *The Atlantic Monthly* (September 1946), reprinted in *China Perceived: Images and Policies in Chinese-American Relations* (New York: Knopf, 1974), pp. 7, 9.

9. *Chinabound: A Fifty-Year Memoir* (New York: Harper and Row, 1982), pp. 317–318.

10. Bruce Douglass and Ross Terrill, eds., *China and Ourselves: Explorations and Revisions by a New Generation* (Boston: Beacon Press, 1971), p. xv.

11. Ross Terrill, ed., *The China Difference: A Portrait of Life Today Inside the Country of One Billion* (New York: Harper and Row, 1979), pp. 7–9.

12. Paul Hollander, *Political Pilgrims* (New York: Oxford University Press, 1981), ch. 7. For debate over the relationship between China studies and politics, see Edward Friedman, "In Defense of China Studies," *Pacific Affairs* 55:2 (Summer 1982), pp. 353–366; Friedman, "Maoism and the Liberation of the Poor," *World Politics* 39:3 (April 1987), pp. 408–428; Harry Harding, "From China, With Disdain: New Trends in the Study of China," *Issues and Studies* 18:7 (July 1982), pp. 12–39; Sheila K. Johnson, "To China, With Love," *Commentary* 56:6 (June 1973), pp. 37–45; and Robert Marks, "The State of the China Field Or, The China Field and the State," *Modern China* 11:4 (October 1985), pp. 461–509.

13. The following paragraphs and some material elsewhere in the essay draw from my article, "Meiguo dui Zhongguo de taidu," (America's atttitudes toward China), *Zhishi fenzi (The Chinese Intellectual)* 1:3 (March, 1985), pp. 11–12.

14. See, for example, Richard Bernstein, *From the Center of the Earth* (Boston: Little, Brown, 1982) and Fox Butterfield, *Alive in the Bitter Sea* (New York: Times Books, 1982).

15. A good example was the scholarly discovery at about the time that it was beginning to disappear of the extremely important, pervasive, and unattractive, but hitherto unknown, *chengfen* (class-status) system. See Richard

Curt Kraus, *Class Conflict in Chinese Socialism* (New York: Columbia University Press, 1981.

16. *The New York Times*, February 24, 1987, p. A7.

17. An exception is Merle Goldman, "The Persecution of China's Intellectuals: Why Didn't Their Western Colleagues Speak Out?" *Radcliffe Quarterly* (September 1981), pp. 12–14.

18. Such articles in economics are too many to cite. In political science, they include Michel C. Oksenberg, "Evaluating the Chinese Political System," *Contemporary China* 3:2 (Summer 1979), pp. 102–111; Alan P. L. Liu, "How Can We Evaluate Communist China's Political System Performance?" *Issues and Studies* 23:2 (February 1987), pp. 82–121; and Stephen C. Thomas, "Social and Economic Rights Performance in Developing Countries: The People's Republic of China in Comparative Perspective," *Policy Studies Journal*, 15:1 (September 1986), pp. 84–96.

19. I have explored some of these differences in *Chinese Democracy* (New York: Knopf, 1985) and in my contribution to R. Randle Edwards, Louis Henkin, and Andrew J. Nathan, *Human Rights in Contemporary China* (New York: Columbia University Press, 1986).

20. See, for example, the remarks of Carole Pateman, *Participation and Democratic Theory* (Cambridge: Cambridge University Press, 1970), pp. 1–17.

21. See *Chinese Democracy*, chs. 3–6.

22. *Mao's China and After: A History of the People's Republic*, rev. and exp., paperback ed. (N.Y., Free Press, 1986).

23. Thomas A. Metzger, "Developmental Criteria and Indigenously Conceptualized Options: A Normative Approach to China's Modernization in Recent Times," *Issues and Studies* 23:2 (February 1987), pp. 19–81, quotation from p. 26.

24. Said, *Orientalism*, cited earlier. Although a 1980 *Journal of Asian Studies* symposium ([39:3], pp. 485–517) respectfully reviewed the application of this concept to East Asian studies, Said himself exempts post-1960s East Asian studies from his charges (p. 301).

25. An example of this process is found in Howard J. Wiarda, "The Struggle for Democracy and Human Rights in Latin America: Toward a New Conceptualization," in Wiarda, ed., *The Continuing Struggle*, pp. 231–254. Here he redefines human rights and democracy to fit the theories of Latin American military and authoritarian elites (whom he identifies with "Latin American culture"). This enables him to reach a far more favorable evaluation of Latin American democracy, but with the result that dialogue on important issues is evaded rather than advanced. For a similar exercise with respect to the concept of "development," see Wiarda, "Toward a Nonethnocentric Theory of Development: Alternative Conceptions from the Third World," in Wiarda, ed., *New Directions in Comparative Politics* (Boulder, CO: Westview Press, 1985), pp. 127–150.

26. Gerald James Larson, "Introduction: The Age-Old Distinction Between the Same and the Other," in Larson and Deutsch, eds., *Interpreting Across Boundaries*, p. 17.

27. Bernard Williams, "An Inconsistent Form of Relativism," reprinted from his *Morality: An Introduction to Ethics* (New York: Harper and Row, 1972), in Jack W. Meiland and Michael Krausz, ed., *Relativism: Cognitive and Moral* (Notre Dame: University of Notre Dame Press, 1982), pp. 171–174; and Geoffrey Harrison, "Relativism and Tolerance," in Meiland and Krausz, p. 239.

28. Although Hume argued that ethical standards are merely likes and dislikes, he went on to show that these likes and dislikes are far from arbitrary, and almost by definition no serious ethical philosopher denies that values can be reasoned about. For recent works, see, e.g., Frank Fischer, *Politics, Values, and Public Policy,* and Duncan MacRae, *The Social Function of Social Science,* and David B. Wong, *Moral Relativity* (Berkeley: University of California Press, 1984).

29. Paul W. Taylor, *Normative Discourse* (Englewood Cliffs, N.J.: Prentice-Hall, 1961).

30. A similar point is made by I.C. Jarvie, "Rationality and Relativism," *The British Journal of Sociology* 34:1 (March 1983), pp. 44–60.

31. Paperback ed., New York: Signet, 1967, p. 22; orig. published McGraw-Hill, 1966.

32. *Experience Without Precedent: Some Quaker Observations on China Today,* Report of an American Friends Service Committee Delegation's Visit to China, May 1972 (Philadelphia: AFSC, 1972), p. 7.

33. Williams, "An Inconsistent Form of Relativism," in Meiland and Krausz, ed., *Relativism,* p. 173.

34. Ken Ling, *The Revenge of Heaven* (New York: Putnam, 1972).

35. Richard M. Pfeffer, "Serving the People and Continuing the Revolution," *The China Quarterly* 52 (October/December 1972), p. 650.

36. Stephen Andors, *China's Industrial Revolution: Politics, Planning, and Management, 1949 to the Present* (New York: Pantheon, 1977), p. 242.

37. *Experience Without Precedent,* p. 52.

38. Cf. C. Martin Wilbur, "China and the Skeptical Eye," *Journal of Asian Studies* 31:4 (August 1972), pp. 761–768.

39. The Universal Declaration is systematically applied to China in James D. Seymour, *China Rights Annals, 1: Human Rights Developments in the People's Republic of China from October 1983 through September 1984* (Armonk: M.E. Sharpe, Inc., 1985).

40. Third ed., paperback (New York: Harper and Row, 1962.)

41. E.g., Carole Pateman, *Participation and Democratic Theory* (Cambridge: Cambridge University Press, 1970); Robert A. Dahl, *Dilemmas of Pluralist Democracy: Autonomy vs. Control* (New Haven: Yale University Press, 1982; Benjamin Barber, *Strong Democracy: Participatory Politics for a New Age* (Berkeley: University of California Press, 1984).

42. For useful recent surveys of this vast topic, see Graeme Duncan, ed., *Democratic Theory and Practice* (Cambridge: Cambridge University Press, 1983), and David Held, *Models of Democracy* (Stanford: Stanford University Press, 1987).

43. The case for this is too familiar to need repeating here. For classic

statements, see Robert A. Dahl, *A Preface to Democratic Theory* (Chicago: University of Chicago Press, 1963) and John Plamenatz, *Democracy and Illusion: An Examination of Certain Aspects of Modern Democratic Theory* (London: Longman, 1977).

44. Metzger, "A Normative Approach," p. 45, points out that these thinkers did not advocate full-scale "American democracy." But he would presumably concede that what they advocated encompassed the three minimal conditions of Schumpeterian pluralism.

45. See Benedict Stavis, *China's Political Reforms: An Interim Report* (New York: Praeger, 1987), pp. 129–145; and Andrew J. Nathan, "Reform at the Crossroads," in Anthony Kane, ed., *China Briefing, 1988* (Boulder: Westview, 1989), pp. 7–25.

46. Peng Zhen, "Zai bufen Yan'an shidai wenyi laozhanshi zuotanhuishang de jianghua," *Renmin ribao* (overseas ed.), May 16, 1987, p. 4.

47. AP report in N.Y. *Chung pao*, 1987.5.29.1.

48. Zhao Ziyang, "Advance Along the Road of Socialism with Chinese Characteristics," *Beijing Review*, North Amer. Ed., 30:45 (November 9–15, 1987), p. 37.

49. J. Roland Pennock, *Democratic Political Theory* (Princeton: Princeton University Press, 1979), pp. 239–253.

50. See, e.g., Wm. Theodore deBary, *The Liberal Tradition on China* (Hong Kong: Chinese University Press, 1983); Metzger, *Escape From Predicament*; Metzger, "A Normative Approach"; Hao Chang, *Liang Ch'i-ch'ao and Intellectual Transition in China, 1890–1907* (Cambridge: Harvard University Press, 1971); Benjamin A. Elman, *From Philosophy to Philology: Intellectual Aspects of Change in Late Imperial China* (Cambridge, MA: Council on East Asian Studies, 1984; Merle Goldman, "Human Rights in the People's Republic of China," *Daedalus* 112:4 (Fall 1983), pp. 111–138; Vitaly A. Rubin, *Individual and State in Ancient China: Essays on Four Chinese Philosophers*, trans. Steven I. Levine (New York: Columbia University Press, 1976); Edwards, Henkin, and Nathan, *Human Rights*.

51. "Di'erhzhong zhongcheng," originally published in *Kaituo*, no date given, reprinted in *Zhengming* 96 (October 1, 1985), pp. 48–61. Some other cases are described in *Chinese Democracy*, pp. 25–26.

52. Wei Jingsheng offered the former argument, but received little support for it even among the democratic activists. The latter argument was offered by Hu Ping, in a mimeographed essay that formed the basis of his 1980 people's congress campaign at Beijing University and which in July 1986 was published in *Qingnian luntan* (Wuhan). In the anti-bourgeois liberalization campaign of 1987, *Qingnian luntan* was closed.

53. Leszek Kolakowski, *Main Currents of Marxism*, P.S. Falla, trans., paperback ed., 3 vols. (Oxford: Oxford University Press, 1981) 2:49 and throughout.

54. *Chinese Democracy*, pp. 98–100. For Wang's unrepentant later views see *Wei rendaozhuyi bianhu* (Beijing: Sanlian shudian, 1986).

55. *Zhongguo zhi chun* No. 42 (December 1986), pp. 33–35, 45 (March 1987), pp. 11–33 and 46 (April 1987), pp. 61–74; partial translations in *China Spring Digest* 1:2 (March/April 1987), pp. 12–38.

56. Yangsun Chou and Andrew J. Nathan, "Democratizing Transition in Taiwan," *Asian Survey* 27:3 (March 1987), pp. 277–299.

57. Reprinted in *Political Man: The Social Bases of Politics*, expanded and updated ed., paperback (Baltimore: The Johns Hopkins University Press, 1981), pp. 27–63.

58. *Contemporary Democracies: Participation, Stability, and Violence*, paperback ed. (Cambridge: Harvard University Press, 1982), pp. 34–41.

59. See, for example, "Meiyou gaige jiu meiyou Zhongguo tese de shehuizhuyi," *Renmin ribao (haiwaiban)*, June 5, 1987, p. 2.

60. I am using the 1972 figures reproduced in Powell, *Contemporary Democracies*, p. 36, and also, for the purposes of illustration here, his list of what were at that time democratic regimes. And I am using the World Bank's evaluation of China's GNP per capita as standing at $300 in 1980 and aiming at $800 (in 1980 dollars) in 2000 in *China: Long-Term Development Issues and Options*, paperback ed. (Baltimore: The Johns Hopkins University Press, 1985), p. 21.

61. For the concept of civic culture, see Gabriel A. Almond and Sidney Verba, *The Civic Culture: Political Attitudes and Democracy in Five Nations*, abridged, paperback ed. (Boston: Little, Brown, 1965).

62. Karl Popper, "The Myth of the Framework," in Eugene Freeman, ed., *The Abdication of Philosophy: Philsophy and the Public Good* (LaSalle, Illinois: Open Court Publishing Company, 1976), p. 38.

63. K. R. Popper, *The Open Society and Its Enemies* (Princeton: Princeton University Press, 1963), vol 2., p. 375.

64. *The World of Thought in Ancient China* (Cambridge: Harvard University Press, 1985, p. 14.

Chapter 14. The Chinese Volcano

1. Orville Schell, *Mandate of Heaven: A New Generation of Entrepreneurs, Dissidents, Bohemians, and Technocrats Lays Claim to China's Future* (New York: Simon and Schuster, 1994), p. 325.

2. Nicholas D. Kristof and Sheryl WuDunn, *China Wakes: The Struggle for the Soul of a Rising Power* (New York: Times Books, 1994).

3. Adam Przeworski, *Democracy and the Market: Political and Economic Reforms in Eastern Europe and Latin America* (Cambridge: Cambridge University Press, 1991), ch. 2.

4. *Governing China: From Revolution Through Reform* (New York: Norton, 1995).

Chapter 15. The Constitutionalist Option

1. Besides some of my own writings, see Arthur Waldron, "China's Coming Constitutional Challenges," *Orbis* 39 (Winter 1995), p. 26. A longer and more fully referenced version of the present essay will appear in a book on consolidating the third-wave democracies edited by Larry Diamond, Marc F. Plattner, Yun-han Chu, and Hung-mao Tien (forthcoming in 1997 from Johns Hopkins University Press).

2. Much of the information presented here was gleaned from seminar meetings and papers from a three-year study project on "China and Constitutionalism" conducted at Columbia University from 1992 to 1995. The project was supported by the Henry Luce Foundation, the National Endowment for Democracy, and the United Daily News Foundation. A series of papers from the project is being published over the course of several years in the *Journal of Asian Law* (formerly *Journal of Chinese Law*), starting with the Spring 1995 issue.

3. Official English translation published in *Beijing Review*, 27 December 1982, 1–29.

4. This section draws chiefly on Cai Dingjian, *Zhongguo renda zhidu* (The Chinese people's congress system) (Beijing: Shehui kexue wenxian chubanshe, 1992); Cang Lin, "Zhongguo lifa gaige de jige wenti" (Several issues in the reform of China's legislation), working paper, China and Constitutionalism Project, Columbia University, Spring 1995; Cao Siyuan, *Siyuan wenxuan* (Selected works of [Cao] Siyuan) (Beijing: Jingji ribao chubanshe, 1995); and Kevin J. O'Brien, *Reform Without Liberalization: China's National People's Congress and the Politics of Institutional Change* (New York: Cambridge University Press, 1990), ch. 7.

5. This section is based chiefly on Li Lin, "Zhongguo xianfa yanjiu de xianzhuang yu zhanwang" (The situation and prospects of constitutional research in China), working paper, China and Constitutionalism Project, Columbia University, April 1994, pp. 12–16; Cang Lin, "Zhongguo lifa gaige," 21ff.; and Wang Liqun, "Zhongguo xuanju zhidu de juxian jiqi wanshan" (The limitations of China's electoral system and its improvement), *Renda yanjiu* (NPC studies) 11 (1992), pp. 8–12.

6. This section draws chiefly on Tao Ren, "Zhongguo de xianfa jiandu he xianfa jieshi" (Constitutional supervision and interpretation in China), working paper, China and Constitutionalism Project, Columbia University, Spring 1994. See also Susan Finder, "The Supreme People's Court of the People's Republic of China," *Journal of Chinese Law* 7 (Fall 1993), pp. 164–90; and Anthony R. Dicks, "Compartmentalized Law and Judicial Restraint: An Inductive View of Some Jurisdictional Barriers to Reform," *China Quarterly* 141 (March 1995), pp. 82–109.

7. In 1989, some NPC deputies submitted a proposal to establish such a committee to help the Standing Committee review constitutional issues; it was never listed on the agenda of the session. *Renmin ribao* (People's daily), overseas edition, October 30, 1989, p. 1.

8. This section is based chiefly on Qiang Zhou, "Judicial Independence in China," working paper, China and Constitutionalism Project, Columbia University, Spring 1995. See also Shao-chuan Leng and Hungdah Chiu, *Criminal Justice in Post-Mao China: Analysis and Documents* (Albany: State University of New York Press, 1985); Donald C. Clarke, "The Execution of Civil Judgments in China," *China Quarterly* 141 (March 1995), pp. 65–81; and Finder, "Supreme People's Court," 145–224.

9. Peng Chong, report on behalf of the NPC Standing Committee to the full NPC, March 28, 1989, in *Zhonghua renmin gongheguo quanguo renmin dai-*

biao dahui changwu weiyuanhui gongbao (Gazette of the Standing Committee of the PRC National People's Congress), May 5, 1989, p. 108.

10. The PRC Law on Judges, Foreign Broadcast Information Service (FBIS), *Daily Report: China*, March 21, 1995, pp. 32–37.

11. This section draws on interviews with participants in the Constitutionalism and China Project and on Li Lin, "Zhongguo xianfa yanjiu."

12. Gong Xiangrui, "Zhongguo xuyao shenme yang de xianfa lilun" (What kind of constitutional theory does China need?), *Faxue* (Law science monthly), April 10, 1989, p. 6.

13. Albert H.Y. Chen, "Developing Theories of Rights and Human Rights in China," in Raymond Wacks, ed., *Hong Kong, China and 1997: Essays in Legal Theory* (Hong Kong: Hong Kong University Press, 1993), pp. 123–49.

14. See Jeremy T. Paltiel, "Civil-Military Relations in China: An Obstacle to Constitutionalism?" *Journal of Chinese Law* 9 (Spring 1995). pp. 35–65.

15. Yan Jiaqi, *Lianbang Zhongguo gouxiang* (A conception for a federal China) (Hong Kong: Mingbao chuban she, 1992).

16. Carol Lee Hamrin and Suisheng Zhao, eds., *Decision-Making in Deng's China: Perspectives from Insiders* (Armonk, N.Y.: M.E. Sharpe, 1995), pp. xxix-lviii.

17. Du Gangjian, "Cong zhuanzheng dao xianzheng" (From dictatorship to constitutionalism), *Zhejiang xuekan* (Zhejiang journal) 3 (1992), p. 39.

Chapter 16. Human Rights and American China Policy

This essay is drawn from a longer version that was commissioned by the Council on Foreign Relations and will be published in a book edited by Michel C. Oksenberg and Elizabeth Economy. The views in this essay are those of the author alone, not those of any organization.

1. Patrick E. Tyler, "In China's Outlands, Poorest Grow Poorer," *New York Times*, October 26, 1996, p. A1.

2. Most documentation on this subject can be found in Andrew J. Nathan, "Human Rights in Chinese Foreign Policy," *China Quarterly* 139 (September 1994), pp. 622–643. In this article, I have provided references to material that has come out since the *China Quarterly* article was written.

3. On forced exile, see Human Rights Watch/Asia (HRW/A) and Human Rights in China, "China: Enforced Exile of Dissidents" (New York: HRW/A, January 1995).

4. For recent information on rights abuses of Tibetans, see Tibet Information Network and HRW/A, *Cutting Off the Serpent's Head: Tightening Control in Tibet, 1994–1995* (New York: HRW/A, 1996).

5. HRW/A, "China: Religious Persecution Persists" (New York: HRW/A, December 1995).

6. HRW/A, "The Three Gorges Dam in China: Forced Resettlement, Suppression of Dissent, and Labor Rights Concerns" (New York: HRW/A, February 1995).

7. HRW/A, "China: Organ Procurement and Judicial Execution in China" (New York: HRW/A, August 1994).

8. Amartya Sen has written extensively on these themes; for a synopsis of many of them see his "Human Rights and Economic Achievements" (paper presented at a conference on "The Growth of East Asia and Its Impact on Human Rights," Tokyo, June 23–25, 1995).

9. For a good description of communications pathologies generated by Chinese authoritarianism, see Kenneth Lieberthal, *Governing China: From Revolution Through Reform* (New York: Norton, 1995), pp. 174–179; for an example of the policy results see HRW/A, "The Three Gorges Dam in China," pp. 37–44; the story is also summarized in Audrey R. Topping, "Ecological Roulette: Damming the Yangtze," *Foreign Affairs* 74, no. 5 (September /October 1995), pp. 132–147.

10. HRW/A, "China: The Cost of Putting Business First" (New York: HRW/A, July 1996).

11. See, for example, Commission of the European Communities, "A Long Term Policy for China-Europe Relations" (1995), Part B.2, reprinted in David Shambaugh, *China and Europe: 1949–1995*, Research Notes and Studies no. 11 (London: Contemporary China Institute, School of Oriental and African Studies, University of London, 1996).

12. Andrew J. Nathan, "China's Constitutionalist Option," *Journal of Democracy* (October 1996), pp. 43–57 (chapter 15 of this volume).

13. Sidney Jones, "The Impact of Asian Economic Growth on Human Rights," *Council on Foreign Relations Asia Project Working Paper* (New York: Council on Foreign Relations, January 1995).

14. HRW/A, *Death By Default: A Policy of Fatal Neglect in China's State Orphanages* (New York: HRW/A, January 7, 1996).

15. Jianwei Wang, "Coping with China as a Rising Power," in James Shinn, ed., *Weaving the Net: Conditional Engagement with China* (New York: Council on Foreign Relations, 1996), pp. 133–174.

Index

Studies of the East Asian Institute

Selected Titles

The Origins of the Cultural Revolution: Vol. III, *The Coming of the Cataclysm, 1961–1966*, by Roderick MacFarquhar. New York: Columbia University Press, 1997

Honorable Merchants: Commerce and Self-Cultivation in Late Imperial China, by Richard Lufrano. Honolulu: University of Hawai'i Press, 1997

Print and Politics: 'Shibao' and the Culture of Reform in Late Qing China, by Joan Judge. Stanford: Stanford University Press, 1996

China in My Life: A Historian's Own History, by C. Martin Wilbur. Armonk, NY: M.E. Sharpe, 1996.

Landownership under Colonial Rule: Korea's Japan Experience, 1900–1935, by Edwin H. Gragert. Honolulu: University of Hawaii Press, 1994.

China's Transition from Socialism: Statist Legacies and Market Reforms, 1980–1990, by Dorothy Solinger. Armonk, NY: M.E. Sharpe, 1993.

Pollution, Politics and Foreign Investment in Taiwan: The Lukang Rebellion, by James Reardon-Anderson. Armonk, NY: M. E. Sharpe, 1993.

Driven by Growth: Political Change in the Asia-Pacific Region, edited by James W. Morley. Armonk, NY: M. E. Sharpe, 1993.

Schoolhouse Politicians: Locality and State during the Chinese Republic, by Helen Chauncey. Honolulu: University of Hawaii Press, 1992.

Constitutional Reform and the Future of the Republic of China, edited by Harvey J. Feldman. Armonk, NY: M.E. Sharpe, 1991.

Sowing the Seeds of Change: Chinese Students, Japanese Teachers, 1895–1905, by Paula S. Harrell. Stanford: Stanford University Press, 1992.

The Study of Change: Chemistry in China, 1840–1949, by James Reardon-Anderson. New York: Cambridge University Press, 1991.

Anarchism and Chinese Political Culture, by Peter Zarrow. New York: Columbia University Press, 1991.

China's Crisis: Dilemmas of Reform and Prospects for Democracy, by Andrew J. Nathan. New York: Columbia University Press, 1990.

Missionaries of the Revolution: Soviet Advisers and Chinese Nationalism, by C. Martin Wilbur and Julie Lien-ying How. Cambridge, MA: Harvard University Press, 1989.

Single Sparks: China's Rural Revolutions, edited by Kathleen Hartford and Steven M. Goldstein. Armonk, NY: M.E. Sharpe, 1989.

Contending Approaches to the Political Economy of Taiwan, edited by Edwin A. Winckler and Susan Greenhalgh. Armonk, NY: M.E. Sharpe, 1988.

Human Rights in Contemporary China, by R. Randle Edwards, Louis Henkin, and Andrew J. Nathan. New York: Columbia University Press, 1986.

Discovering History in China: American Historical Writing on the Recent Chinese Past, by Paul A. Cohen. New York: Columbia University Press, 1984.

The Origins of the Cultural Revolution: Vol. I, *Contradictions Among the People, 1956–1957*; Vol. II, *The Great Leap Forward, 1958–1960*, by Roderick MacFarquhar. New York: Columbia University Press, 1974, 1983 (Vol.III, *The Coming of the Cataclysm, 1961–1966*, 1997 ace to p. 295).

Education Under Mao: Class and Competition in Canton Schools, by Jonathan Unger. New York: Columbia University Press, 1982.

Class Conflict in Chinese Socialism, by Richard Curt Kraus. New York: Columbia University Press, 1981.

Uncertain Years: Chinese-American Relations, 1947–1950, edited by Dorothy Borg and Waldo Heinrichs. New York: Columbia University Press, 1980.

Unwelcome Muse: Chinese Literature in Shanghai and Peking, 1937–1945, by Edward M. Gunn, Jr. New York: Columbia University Press, 1980.

Yenan and the Great Powers: The Origins of Chinese Communist Foreign Policy, by James Reardon-Anderson. New York: Columbia University Press, 1980.

Perspectives on a Changing China, edited by Joshua A. Fogel and William T. Rowe. Boulder, CO: Westview Press, 1979.

The Memoirs of Li Tsung-jen, by T.K. Tong and Li Tsung-jen. Boulder, CO: Westview Press, 1979

The Medieval Chinese Oligarchy, by David Johnson. Boulder, CO: Westview Press, 1977.

China's Political Economy: The Quest for Development since 1949, by Carl Riskin. Oxford: Oxford University Press, 1987.

Anvil of Victory: The Communist Revolution in Manchuria, by Steven I. Levine. New York: Columbia University Press, 1987.

Sun Yat-sen: Frustrated Patriot, by C. Martin Wilbur. New York: Columbia University Press, 1976.

Escape from Predicament: Neo-Confucianism and China's Evolving Political Culture, by Thomas A. Metzger. New York: Columbia University Press, 1976.

Cadres, Commanders, and Commissars: The Training of the Chinese Communist Leadership, 1920–45, by Jane L. Price. Boulder, CO: Westview Press, 1976.

The District Magistrate in Late Imperial China, by John R. Watt. New York: Columbia University Press, 1972.

Money and Monetary Policy in Communist China, by Katharine Huang Hsiao. New York: Columbia University Press, 1971.

The Communists and Peasant Rebellions: A Study in the Rewriting of Chinese History, by James P. Harrison, Jr. New York: Atheneum, 1969.

Cadres, Bureaucracy, and Political Power in Communist China, by A. Doak Barnett. New York: Columbia University Press, 1968.

Reformer in Modern China: Chang Chien, 1853–1926, by Samuel Chu. New York: Columbia University Press, 1965.

The Ladder of Success in Imperial China, by Ping-ti Ho. New York: Columbia University Press, 1962.